The Kingdom of Sicily

The Kingdom of Sicily
1130-1860

Louis Mendola

Copyright © 2015 Louis A.M. Mendola. All rights reserved.
Published by Trinacria Editions, New York.

This book may not be reproduced by any means whatsoever, either traditionally or electronically (digitally), in whole or in part, including illustrations, photographs and maps, in any form beyond the fair-use copying permitted by the United States Copyright Law and except by reviewers for the public press (magazines, newspapers and their websites), without written permission from the copyright holder.

The right of Louis Mendola to be identified as the author of this work has been asserted by him in accordance with the Copyright, Design and Patents Act, 1988 (UK).

Some material contained herein, authored by Louis Mendola, was previously published in *The Peoples of Sicily: A Multicultural Legacy* © 2013 Louis A. M. Mendola, and in *Sicilian Genealogy and Heraldry* © 2013 Louis A.M. Mendola. Material from *Women of Sicily: Saints, Queens and Rebels* © 2014 Calogera Jacqueline Alio, and *Margaret, Queen of Sicily* © 2015 Calogera Jacqueline Alio, is used by permission.

Legal Deposit: Library of Congress, British Library (and Bodleian Libraries, Cambridge University Library, Trinity College Library), Italian National Libraries (Rome, Florence, Palermo).

The title of this book was assigned a Library of Congress Control Number on 13 March 2015, when the ISBN of the first edition was also registered. The first printing of this work was in September 2015.

Illustrations, photographs, maps, cover design and image editing (of historical imprints in the public domain) by the author.

Printed in the United States of America on acid-free paper.

10 9 8 7 6 5 4 3

ISBN 9780991588671 (print)
ISBN 9780991588695 (ebook)

Library of Congress Control Number 2015904129

A CIP catalogue record for this book is available from the British Library.

IN MEMORIAM

Douglas Elton Fairbanks, Jr.
Marquis Achille di Lorenzo
Jacques Paul, Cardinal Martin
Charles Edward Stourton, Baron Mowbray
Commander James Charles Risk
Prince Cyril Leo Heraclius Toumanoff

The world is much the lesser for their passing.

ABOUT THE AUTHOR

Louis Mendola is what used to be called a *polymath,* and he uses a multidisciplinary approach to decipher history.

His work has appeared in everything from books to academic journals to in-flight magazines. He co-authored *The Peoples of Sicily: A Multicultural Legacy* and he wrote a guide to historical research, *Sicilian Genealogy and Heraldry,* which established a new Dewey catalogue subject category in the British Library and in the New York Public Library.

Both scholar and popularizer, Louis Mendola, who has earned the nickname "Sicily's Historian," is today the most widely-published chronicler of Sicilian history. He stands out as one of just a few Sicilian historians whose work is known beyond Italian borders. Having researched in Italy, Britain, Germany, France, Spain and the Vatican, he has been consulted by the BBC, *The New York Times,* The History Channel and the *Almanach de Gotha,* and lectured at New York University. His online articles have been read by millions since 1999.

He has been decorated by the Royal House of Savoy, the Royal House of Bourbon of the Two Sicilies, the Sovereign Military Order of Malta and the Imperial House of Ethiopia.

PREFACE

"The farther backward you can look, the farther forward you are likely to see."

— Winston Churchill

It was never just an island in the sun. Never was a conquest of Sicily an exercise in the prosaic. *Sicilia* has always been a protagonist in events far greater than herself, events that changed the course of history. Sicily is the world's island. The Italians just happen to be her guardians.

Sicily's recorded yesterdays place its continuous history among the earliest of Europe. The Sicilians' ancestors built Europe's first megalithic temples on Malta some 5600 years ago, and in antiquity Sicily, the Mediterranean's largest island, became a key stepping stone for bold leaders seeking to build empires that would span continents.

History's protagonists are defined by the long shadows they cast — along streets, in squares and at remote sites in the hinterland. Sicily boasts impressive archeology, including a few of the best-preserved Greek temples and theatres, upon which some medieval castles were built. Palermo's Norman Palace has Punic foundations.

Set against such a backdrop, the story that unfolds in the following pages is recent history, but no less important for its juvenility.

At the height of its prosperity during the Middle Ages, the world's most conquered island was a crossroads of civilizations from Africa, Asia and Europe. The kingdom founded during this ephemeral golden age survived, in one form or another, until the reign of Queen Victoria and the presidency of Abraham Lincoln.

But this is not merely a story of kings and queens. It is the people who make any society what it is, and it is from a diversitude of cultures that the social fabric of Sicily was woven. Sewn into this tapestry is the story of the Greeks, Arabs, Jews, Germans, French, Spanish and, finally, the Italians. And the semi-forgotten Phoenicians, Romans, Vandals, Ostrogoths, Berbers, Fatimids, Normans and Lombards from whom the modern Sicilians are descended.

The Sikelians and Sicanians of the Bronze Age gave their name to the island, while the Elymians, Mycenaeans, Minoans and Ausonians forged what little of its early culture is known to us. Like other ancient Greeks, Sicily's Siceliots often warred among themselves, and to the Phoenicians and Carthaginians the western part of the island was variously a base for emporia and then military outposts. To the Romans, Sikelia was the fledgling Empire's first province, a flourishing cornerstone of expansionism. In the wake of mighty Rome's fall, the Vandals and Ostrogoths were little more than greedy guests. Brightly as their cultures shone, the medieval Greeks and Arabs seemed to regard Sicily as just one of many pieces in vast empires ruled from the eastern Mediterranean, with the Kalbids looking to the powerful Fatimid Caliphs of Cairo as their suzerains just as the Byzantine Greeks looked to Constantinople's Eastern Roman Emperors.

If, in this polychrome mosaic, we seek to distinguish the colors of a true Sicilian identity, its roots will be found tangled someplace in the multicultural milieu that gave birth to the *Regnum,* the Kingdom, for this is where the medieval Sicilian language, a true Sicilian state, and genuine Sicilian sovereignty originated. Not until this time was Sicily anything that most of us would describe as a country.

While the signal year of 1130, the date Sicily's ruler, Roger II, was crowned its first king, is a convenient place to begin, the polyglot *Regnum* was several centuries in the making before his birth. Its heritage finds expression in the multilingual tombstone, created during his reign, shown on this book's back cover.

Some interesting milestones are the fruit of Sicily's golden age. Divorce was legal and women could inherit property. Rape was not only outlawed but severely punished. Unfortunately, personal rights of this kind, guaranteed in the reign of Roger's grandson Frederick II, were eventually abandoned; divorce was not legalized again in Italy until 1970, and only in 1996 was rape made a felonious form of violent assault.

Yet in 1231 these principles were enshrined in a legal code that also protected the environment and defended the rights of religious minorities.

Every society's glory waxes and wanes over the long march of centuries. Today, historians generally concur that freedom, literacy and wealth declined in Sicily after 1300, certainly compared to what they had once been. By then, Sicilian society had forsaken its multicultural roots to embrace a Latin monoculture. This is not to suggest a causality, as if the island's socioeconomic decline resulted directly from the emergence of the monoculture, but the correlation cannot be ignored. It is clear that the island's Arabs, Byzantines and Jews placed a high value on literacy that was lacking by the time these cultures came to be assimilated, amalgamated or suppressed in Sicily.

In our times, it would be overzealous for any commentator to claim to discern in Sicily or Sicilians a specific, characteristic ethos or world view, but a certain commonality of attitudes, an obligatory mass conformity, was prevalent in the long centuries from 1500 to 1800, fostered in no small part by the dominant Roman Catholic culture.

Why are you reading these words? Why do we contemplate history?

Is it to learn? Is it to confirm our perceptions, or perhaps to correct them? Is it to appease our teachers? Do we read history simply to aggrandize our own egos, to claim a recondite knowledge superior to that of others, or do we turn its pages out of genuine curiosity, in our quest for intellectual edification — to know more tomorrow than we knew yesterday?

"Nescire autem quid ante quam natus sis acciderit, id est semper esse puerum," said Cicero, whose words are just as resonant in plain English: "One who is ignorant of what happened before his birth will always be a child."

History can be interesting, even entertaining, but its most essential duty is to teach, to enlighten, to inspire. We can learn from Sicily's trimillennial triumphs but also from her monumental failures.

Sicily teaches us that the irrepressible human spirit can take root in the most barren soil. She teaches us that, like ancient peoples, we can be at one with nature. Sicily teaches us that we abandon the weaker among us — the destitute, the illiterate, the inherently disadvantaged — only at the peril of society as a whole. Sicily tells us that a privileged elite must never exploit the lesser-privileged majority that constitutes the very essence of society. Sicily's experience teaches us that we must embrace everybody in our community — defying the seeming barriers imposed by differences in gender, beliefs or ethnicity — if we wish to endure or even survive. Sicily lights our path, teaching us that law without compassion is tyranny, admonishing us to never succumb to evils like the Inquisition or Fascism just because they seem opportune at the moment. Sicily's history teaches us that each place, each region, each people on this earth is deserving of its own identity.

We are all Sicilians.

The tortuous journey of the Kingdom of Sicily engenders interest among scholars and history aficionados alike, especially, it seems, in those places having historical, cultural and dynastic connections to it. That the study of Sicily under the Normans would provoke curiosity in England, Normandy and even Ireland is unsurprising. Germans and Austrians look to Sicily in relation to the Swabian kings who ruled the Holy Roman Empire from Palermo. In the Arab and Muslim worlds, the enlightened Fatimid influences in the *Regnum* are studied, along with Sicily's syncretic Norman-Arab architecture. Sicily's brief Angevin phase finds favor among the French, and the heart of Saint Louis rests in Monreale's cathedral. The Judaic heritage is not to be overlooked, and at Siracusa is preserved Europe's oldest mikveh. Spaniards, naturally, have an abiding affinity for Sicily, and in Palermo two churches are still the property of the King of Spain.

While it was often ruled from afar, especially after 1400, Sicily legally remained a sovereign kingdom, with its own government and laws, until 1816, when the heretofore distinct states of Naples and Sicily were officially conjoined to form the Kingdom of the Two Sicilies. This was ruled from Naples by the Bourbons until 1861, when it was annexed to the newly-formed Kingdom of Italy. The Two Sicilies was the largest, most populous, most prosperous, most technologically advanced, most industrialized of the states that constituted the unified Italy.

In this survey, the reader may expect accuracy and facts, not platitudes and clichés. The truth, but also the audacious spirit of endeavor that brought it to us.

History is a possession for eternity. So said Thucydides of his account of the Peloponnesian War, a conflict that touched Sicily.

Our trek through Sicily's eclectic history will serve us the bad with the good, but it will serve us well. Wherever it takes us, one thing is certain: We will know more at our journey's end than we did at its beginning.

Buon viaggio.

ACKNOWLEDGEMENTS

"If I have seen further, it is by standing on the shoulders of giants."

— Isaac Newton

No scholar, be his endeavor humanistic or scientific, stands on his own. Had any one of the six elder statesmen mentioned in the dedication been absent from my circle, the facts to be found in this book might have been presented differently, and far less trenchantly. As witnesses to great events that shaped recent history, these learned men provided me a wealth of information beyond what was written in the books I read from a young age. Indeed, these were the kind of men historians sought out when researching such books. It was an uncommon privilege to benefit from their knowledge and experience.

My research might find me poring over twelfth-century manuscripts signed by Sicily's Hauteville monarchs — the seal of Queen Constance attached to such a charter appears on this book's cover — or scaling rugged slopes to reach the fortresses of Cefalù, Enna and Sicignano. But my friends' everyday haunts, existing somewhere along my annual circuit from Rome to London to New York, were less dusty and altogether more urbane: Caccia, Scacchi, White's, the Cavalry and Guards, the Harvard Club, 21, the Sky Club. A shared passion for history was our *lingua franca.*

Douglas Fairbanks was a thespian, a confidant of kings who played his greatest role in military intelligence; he trained a specialized unit that saw action in Operation Husky, the Allied invasion of Sicily. **Achille di Lorenzo** was an anti-Fascist close to the surviving Bourbons of Naples; he was part of the rescue mission to save Umberto Nobile's last, ill-fated Arctic expedition. **Cardinal Martin** was Prefect of the Pontifical Household and assisted Pope John Paul II in exorcisms; he facilitated my unrestricted access to the Vatican Secret Archive. **Charles Mowbray** was premier baron of England and a war hero; his name seemed to open the door to every obscure archive in Britain. **James Risk** was an American naval officer present at the invasion of Sicily in 1943, serving in the Allied Military Government, and later a numismatist and sometime diplomat; he knew Queen Elizabeth II and the last King of Italy. **Cyril Toumanoff** was a native of Saint Petersburg, where he witnessed the Russian Revolution; he was a longtime history professor at Georgetown University, and in retirement High Historical Consultant of the Order of Malta.

An entire volume could be written about this impromptu pantheon.

Sir Steven Runciman, with whom I was less acquainted, wrote defining works on the Crusades, the Byzantine Empire and the Sicilian Vespers, unbiased histories presented from two or three perspectives rather than just one as was customary since Gibbon's time. He was a gentleman scholar in the best Oxbridge tradition. As a youngster, reading the original edition of his *Sicilian Vespers,* I was enthralled by its persuasive prose and fold-out pedigrees.

Invaluable context for certain details in the two final chapters was provided over the years by **Urraca de Bourbon of the Two Sicilies**, her cousin **Giovanni de Bourbon of the**

ACKNOWLEDGEMENTS

Two Sicilies, and others mentioned under Supplementary Sources.

Among the living, **Jacqueline Alio**, my co-author on The Peoples of Sicily, permitted me to use a few excerpts from her book Women of Sicily and two maps from her Margaret, Queen of Sicily. *Grazie*.

Thanks are due the staffs at archives and libraries in Italy, Britain, Spain and France, especially the British Library, the Archive of the Crown of Aragon in Barcelona, the state archives of Palermo and Naples, and the Vatican Secret Archive.

Less personally but no less importantly, a number of hardy, dedicated historians besides Steven Runciman have written about Sicily over the last fifty years, advancing our *corpus* of knowledge while fostering a revival of interest in our island. Prominent among this cosmopolitan community of scholars are Britons and Italians, with a few Germans and one or two Americans. Their praiseworthy work is mentioned elsewhere in this volume.

Any shortcomings which might present themselves in the pages that follow are, of course, solely my responsibility as *auctor et scriptor* of this work.

— L. Mendola

Montefranco, Sicily
Aprilis 2015 - Nisan 5775 - Jumada al-Thani 1436

CONTENTS

Preface	9
Acknowledgements	15
Introduction	21
Maps & Imprints	35
Prologue	55
1. Prelude: Ancient Sicily	59
2. The Golden Pillars	73
3. Overture: Monarchy	83
4. The Normans	103
5. The Swabians	139
6. Angevin Interlude	171
7. Aragon, Catalonia, Castile	181
8. Hapsburgs and Bourbons	205
9. The Two Sicilies	241
10. Postlude: Italian Sicily	287
Epilogue	307
Chronology	311

Appendix 1: Kings of Sicily 331

Appendix 2: Knightly Orders 339

Appendix 3: Sicilian Peerage 361

Appendix 4: Genetic Legacy 365

Appendix 5: Milestones 1735-1860 369

Appendix 6: Constitution of 1812 371

Appendix 7: Nobiliary Laws 1743-1861 375

Appendix 8: Pragmatic of 1759 379

Sources, Notes, Bibliography 385

Index 421

INTRODUCTION

"Any fool can know. The point is to understand."

— Albert Einstein

We can choose to dwell on history for its own sake, or we can seek to learn from it. This is a generalist's view of Sicilian history over the course of many eventful centuries. In striving for the pragmatic over the pedantic or semantic, it seeks to present the most neutral, unbiased view humanly possible, in the least ambiguous terms. Compared to some tomes, this account is distinguished by its brevity and, one hopes, its clarity.

No history is perfect. None ever has been. Deciding what to include or exclude from a historical overview of this kind presents a perpetual challenge to authors, and every solution is flawed. The historian need not entertain pretensions to plenitude.

Unlike some histories of Sicily published in English during the last thirty years, this one won't insult your intelligence.

History is not religion. History has knowledgeable experts but no immutable authorities. No historian has the right to impose his dogmatism on others. History is best approached with the same rigor as science. A work of this kind is not the place for "mysticism," self-interest, ethnocentrism or fanciful theories. History is based on what it actually is, not on what we'd like it to be.

In these pages, the author, while acknowledging the contributions of serious scholars, gives pride of place to contemporaneous records rather than "secondary" commentaries written long after the facts they describe.

The first serious general history of Sicily ever published, as opposed to medieval manuscripts read by only a few, was the post-incunable *De Rebus Siculis* by Tommaso Fazello, in 1560. He is considered "the father of modern Sicilian history." (The coat of arms shown in the frontispiece is from his book.) Two years later, Francesco Maurolico, a contemporary of Fazello known as a mathematician and astronomer, published an equally meticulous history, *Sicanicarum Rerum Compendium*. To the extent that either author was opinionated, Fazello advocated for Palermo while Maurolico favored Messina, there being a rivalry between the two cities.

It was during the same period that important manuscript histories of Sicily — primary sources — found their way into print. A notorious example was an account of the Norman reigns by the pseudonymous "Hugh Falcandus." A frontispiece engraving reproduced following this book's maps graced a 1725 compendium of texts transcribed from the manuscripts of several codices in Milan's *Biblioteca Ambrosiana,* most prominently the medieval chronicle of Romuald of Salerno.

Giovanni Di Blasi's *Storia del Regno di Sicilia* was published in 1844, itself preceded by Francesco Ferrara's *Storia Generale della Sicilia* in 1831. While such histories may have sung the praises of the reigning dynasty, they were tame compared to what came after 1860.

More recently, a number of fine histories have been published which focus on the Kingdom of Sicily during specific periods, such as the Norman or Swabian eras, or on particular areas, such as literature, the economy or Jewish society; some are mentioned at the end of this book. Given the presence of those works, there was no need for this author to "reinvent the wheel," and at all events a survey of this length cannot possibly present all the *minutiae* found in a verbose volume whose raison d'être is the story of a single king.

For slightly more expansive considerations of Sicily's civilizations and religions, *The Peoples of Sicily: A Multicultural Legacy* is complementary to this book, while Jacqueline Alio's *Women of Sicily: Saints, Queens and Rebels* offers insights into the role of women in Sicily during the period covered in this volume.

Historian Cyril Toumanoff was fond of the aperçu that "everything that built Western civilization emanated from the Mediterranean," and the Sicilian saga is best understood if we chart the course of our travels from east to west across this timeless Sea.

"If you wish to understand anything," said Aristotle, "observe its beginning and its development."

The typical general history assumes the form of an analytical chronicle. This one conforms to that traditional paradigm but for a solitary distinction, namely its occasional forays into social history, and this bears explanation. A prevailing school of thought posits that there are now two principal approaches to the study of history. The "political" deals with great events and famous figures while the "social" considers society at large and the everyday lives of the majority of the population, the "common folk." At work in these pages are elements of both. As a *caveat,* it must be observed that the line defining each approach is not always very finely drawn.

Here a ready example from modern European history is the First World War and Great Britain. A focus on major, public events, the economy and industry would constitute, arguably, "political" or "macro" historiography. The war's influence on the everyday lives of Britons, such as the widespread antipathy toward Germans (resulting in the regnant dynasty's change of name from *Saxe-Coburg and Gotha* to *Windsor* in 1917) and the dearth of marriageable men in the conflict's aftermath, might be considered "social" or in some cases perhaps even "micro" history.

In the Americas, the arrival of Christopher Columbus and the subsequent colonization by Europeans could be regarded as "political" history, while the plight of the indigenous peoples, as well as the slaves brought from Africa, might be considered a manifestation of "social" history. Each is equally important in our assessment of the past.

The diary of an individual whose involvement in major events was not decisive for the population at large is best characterized as "micro" history. Here a well-known example is Anne Frank. Conversely, the memoir of a personage such as Churchill or Stalin — so famous that they are instantly identifiable by their surnames — falls more solidly into the realm of "macro" history, witness Eisenhower's *Crusade in Europe*.

These imperfect terms may occasionally overlap, but they reflect what is being advocated in academia in our century and they provide us with a solid footing.

In connection with this, there are events of which we have but single surviving accounts, such as those of Diodorus Siculus and Falcandus, to inform us, with little or no corroboration from other writers. The author approaches such affirmations in a general way, without dwelling on every utterance of these early historians; exclusivity does not make one's words sacrosanct.

An attempt has been made to describe the perennial elements of Sicily's monarchy, namely feudalism, the baronage and knightage, the merchants and guilds, the ever-present Church and Crown. For ready consultation, some of this is presented in an introductory chapter. In our age of republics the functional institutions of monarchies, be they kingdoms, emirates or principalities, are largely overlooked in written histories which presume the reader's prior knowledge of the subject.

History aficionados know that there is a paucity of books written in English, or even in Italian, on the general history of Sicily. It might even be suggested, quite uncharitably, that precious few "general" histories of Sicily written in Italian in the original after 1860 have borne even the semblance of scholarly impartiality until the advent of some recent imprints.

In Italy, the approach to historiography has evolved, if laggardly, as the revisionistic apologia that sought to bolster a new nation, with its segue to the Fascist dictatorship, has been supplanted by a more critical, more scholarly exegesis based on fact rather than political expediency.

Thus have we witnessed Italians' changing historical views of Vittorio Emanuele II, Garibaldi, Cavour and other protagonists of the unification movement, with legitimate criticism gradually supplanting the unabashed hagiographies that permeated the writings of Italian historians until the country's liberation by the Allies during the Second World War, and even for a few decades thereafter. Hence the Italian government's feeble attempt to celebrate the sesquicentennial of unification in 2011 was met with sardonic, sometimes vehement, derision by a great many citizens, the cynicism affecting Piedmontese, Tuscans and Lombards as well as Apulians, Calabrians and Sicilians.

Following the war, it was foreign historians such as Evelyn Jamison, Steven Runciman and Harold Acton — all Britons — who led the vanguard of scholars advocating accuracy in the telling, or retelling, of Italian history. The first major international academic symposium on the Sicilian Normans to be held in Sicily was convened only in 1972, the year of Jamison's death.

True, Ferdinand Chalandon had already written a balanced treatment of Sicily's Normans, but Michele Amari's book about the Sicilian Vespers was colored by Risorgimentalist political views. Sadly, much of the propaganda perpetuated in Italy after 1860 remains part of Italian public consciousness. Italians are led to believe that Piedmont's *Statuto* of 1848 was Italy's first modern constitution, while Sicily's ephemeral, British-influenced Constitution of 1812 is ignored. The Kingdom of the Two Sicilies is depicted as a region of endemic illiteracy and abject poverty even though its literacy level circa 1860 (something under twenty percent as confirmed by vital statistics records requiring signatures or marks) was comparable to that of every other part of the unified Italy, and even though, until around 1870, Italy's greatest emigration was an exodus not from the South but from the comparatively poor North. Sicily is painted as an island of landless peasants, yet the *riveli,* tax rolls of the *donativi* dating from around 1500 to the early years of the nineteenth century, indicate that the typical Sicilian head of family living in the countryside owned his (or her) own home and at least a garden or a small plot of land.

History should not be written by politicians. Italy's failure to teach her children an *accurate* version of history has proven problematical because, as Abraham Lincoln observed, "the philosophy of the schoolroom in one generation is the philosophy of government in the next."

Published in London in 1838, *The Normans in Sicily,* by Henry Gally Knight, was the first modern "historical travelogue" in English dedicated to Norman Sicily. Speaking generally, the work of British, German and Arab scholars seems more soberly analytical than that of their Italian peers, largely because of the sophistication with which they compare Sicily to their own multicultural societies — nations or regions boasting their own Norman, Swabian or Fatimid patrimony.

The Kingdom of Sicily was multiethnic *a natura eius.* To study it even superficially one must perforce cast a glance toward various cultures. Sicily's historical connections to a dozen countries will take the serious scholar far and wide, certainly to Spain, Germany, England, France and Tunisia. However, there is no substitute for being based in Sicily, which affords the historian a familiarity with the place and its people beyond what is offered by the documentary record. In climbing the slopes crowned by impregnable Enna, the author grew to appreciate why that ancient city fell to the Normans only through treachery hatched within its walls. Meeting the late Princess Urraca of the Two Sicilies, who knew Queen Maria Sophia and donated the private papers of King Francesco II to Italy following the Second World War, provided a rare glimpse into the esoteric world of living links to a bygone kingdom.

This book addresses, first and foremost, the centuries until 1860, the year that culminated in Sicily's annexation to the neocratic Kingdom of Italy; the consideration of developments after that time provides a basis for comparison between (for example) life in the Kingdom of the Two Sicilies circa 1850 and in the unified Italy a half-century later. There the scope is not a lengthy comparative analysis so much as the presentation of a few facts for the sake of perspective. The jeremiad that is Italy's recent history, the last two hundred years, is blunt and gritty enough without any rhetoric being heaped upon it.

In these pages Sicily is not defined "dialectically" by the state that emerged after 1860, nor is that state generally relevant to Sicilian history before that time except for isolated developments like its foreshadowing by the unificationist movement, and of course the matter of historiography already mentioned. Here Sicily is not simply a "region" of the unified Italy, but a place that, like Bavaria, Catalonia and Scotland, boasts its own identity and heritage. Yet the views reflected in these pages are not secessionist. The author's only "agenda" is a presentation of factual history, be it palatable or not; his approach to history is methodical, not haphazard, with an emphasis on sound epistemology and an eye to the European and Mediterranean contexts in which Sicily has found herself from the earliest times. The point of view employed is neither Sicilianist or Italianist, nor is it specifically Eurocentric or Mediterraneanist. It is not nativist, conformist or revisionist. It is not specifically monarchist or republican.

The truth is not European, African, Asian or American. It is Human. Is that not what history should be?

Historicity reigns supreme. Many "primary" (contemporary) archival sources have been consulted in the author's researches over the last thirty years. Two examples: the charter of Queen Constance to which her seal (shown on this book's front cover) was attached pertains to the widespread introduction of serfdom in formerly Arab lands by 1200; the Harley Trilingual Psalter in the British Library collection suggests the mechanism of the conversions of Sicily's Muslim Arabs to Catholicism (implying the existence of multiethnic congregations) circa 1140.

Unlike most general histories based exclusively on "common knowledge" or previously published studies, this one reflects a few nuggets derived from the author's original (academic) research, some of which have appeared previously in his articles in academic journals. While such details are indicated in the Sources, they are worth listing *pro forma* here for the sake of transparency. Briefly, those most germane to this work are: the tardy inception of armorial heraldry in Sicily (probably after circa 1180) but the Anglo-Norman "Plantagenet" kings' probable inspiration for using the "English lion" as a symbol based on its earlier use in Sicily; the ready capitulation of certain isolated castles during the Vespers War in 1282 (which sheds light on the nature of Angevin administration); the presence of a man who was most likely Jewish holding feudal property in Sicily in the middle of the fifteenth century (a highly exceptional and perhaps unique case of European Jews as part of the feudal nobility at an early date); tentative confirmation of the traditional dating of the Assizes of Ariano to 1140 based on a reference found in an uncatalogued, near-contemporary manuscript; an approximative assessment of comparative literacy levels in Sicily over time based on extensive consultation of vital statistics records (indicating that the literacy level was most likely higher in 1130 than in 1860); conclusions drawn from the extensive consultation of the tax rolls as mentioned above.

Sicily's finest historians are independent scholars rather than academics, and their work is virtually unknown outside Italy. The *Archivio Storico Siciliano* (from which a number of articles are cited in the notes of this book), the nearest thing in Sicily to an academic journal in the broad field of Sicilian history, is not published by a university. Italy has no Oxbridge, no Ivy League, nor a single university ranked in the world's top hundred, and most of the best minds leave the country. *Una situazione davvero pessima.*

Until recently, a devil's advocate could make the case, albeit tenuously, that the exact extent of the presence of certain populations in medieval Sicily was "unproved" because, after all, there were no Muslims and Jews left to identify themselves by 1500, while certain medieval estimates were obviously inaccurate. We now look to Sicily's plethora of genetic haplotypes as a tangible sign of the past, just as biologists use similar means to ascertain the precise path of evolution. Thus are the signs bequeathed us by history complemented by our own genes. While it is not essential to the study of the Kingdom of Sicily *per se*, phylogeography is certainly pertinent to our study of its peoples, especially during the Middle Ages. In the case of Sicily, the genetic record confirms the exactitude of the historical record.

Sicilian history has its benchmarks. Sicily's Norman Conquest, beginning five years before England's and lasting longer, is one of these, and so is the War of the Vespers. These pivotal events altered the course of history not only of Sicily but of Europe and the central Mediterranean. The Peloponnesian War and the Second World War, to cite just two examples beyond the scope of this book but mentioned in its framing chapters, found the contested island involved in wider conflicts. Medieval developments such as the Assizes of Ariano and the Constitutions of Melfi are also important. The War of the Vespers, of course, was an event that changed history, but Sicily witnessed — and survived — a number of turning points.

The following pages presume little, if any, prior knowledge of Sicily on the part of the reader. It is hoped that the chronology, maps, pedigrees and appendices will suffice in providing additional information, and that the Prelude and Postlude, as "book ends," will afford the reader sufficient context along this journey. Because this is not a book of dynastic history *per se*, the extended families (and non-regnant heirs) of Sicily's sovereigns are not considered unless they are immediately relevant. Therefore, the travails of the Bourbon and Savoy dynasts after the loss of their thrones are of little concern.

While this book is intended for a general readership or as an introduction for university students, the Sources provide enough information for the more curious reader to plot a course for further study. This format was chosen over a separate reading list. If only for its use as a guide and syllabus, this is the kind of book the author truly wishes were available some forty years ago when he began his serious study of the Kingdom of Sicily.

Prefatory remarks regarding details are necessary in this kind of book.

The author has sought to avoid the pedantry endemic in this field. The Latin *Offamilias* probably refers to "familiaris," serving the royal Hautevilles, and not "the mill" as some previously thought; the Church of Saint John of the Hermits may stand on the site of a mosque, but it seems likely, based on archeological excavations, that an earlier Byzantine chapel stood there before the arrival of the Arabs; the Assizes of Ariano might not be dated precisely to 1140 but they were certainly in force by 1144. The War of the Vespers probably did not begin with a Sicilian woman being molested by obnoxious soldiers but was most likely instigated by outsiders.

Wanton iconoclasm is avoided; Roger II and his grandson Frederick II are given their due. Certain terms are more geographical than political, especially in their medieval context: Italy, Germany, Spain, Palestine.

Rebuttals to historical clichés were, for the most part, unnecessary. In *The Sicilian Vespers* Steven Runciman felt called upon to refute the crazed rantings of Michele Amari, and in *Frederick II* David Abulafia debunked the whimsy of Ernst Kantorowicz. "Corrective revisionism" of that kind is sometimes inevitable, and often valuable. It comes as no great revelation that historians like Ernst Kantorowicz and Benedetto Croce were highly politicized.

A leitmotif running through most general histories of modern Sicily is the Mafia. In the minds of many, unfortunately, the very word is a synecdoche for Sicily. However, as that form of criminality was not a major factor in Sicilian life before the nineteenth century, it is not considered at great length in this book.

A note on translations and orthography is in order. Except for famous literary passages that were previously published, most translations from Latin and Italian are the author's. Transliterations from Arabic are those in common use, hence their lack in uniformity. Spelling is based on Italian names for recent dynasts of the Two Sicilies and Italy, so *Carlo* instead of *Charles*. Proper nouns such as place names vary depending on general usage and historical context. *Hymera* is preferred over *Himera* or *Imera*. The Anglice *Syracuse* refers to the city in ancient and medieval times, the Italian *Siracusa* more recently. The Order of *Santiago* is preferred to *Saint James of the Sword*, but *Saint Januarius* (an early martyr) rather than *San Gennaro*. Most English spellings are American but — in consolation to my friends in the peerage — a few are British, so *acknowledge-*

ment and *behove*. Ethnonyms and demonyms are those most traditionally English, so *Messinian* rather than *Messinese*. The abbreviations BC and AD are used where necessary, with BCE and CE introduced once under each heading.

It may surprise some readers that certain medieval dates, even years, are approximate. There are several reasons for this, apart from the case of the Assizes of Ariano already mentioned. A chronicle may not indicate clear dates, or it might simply give seasons; Winter extends from one year into the next. The Hijri year, from Muharram to Duh al-Hijjah, is based on a lunar calendar, and it can likewise extend from one solar year into another. The Gregorian calendar itself reformed the Julian system in 1582. The Norman conquest of Palermo began late in 1071, ending early in 1072, which explains the occasional reporting of differing dates. During Sicily's long Spanish administration, a decree might be issued with effect several months hence, perhaps during the following year.

Following this Introduction are numerous maps charting some thirty centuries of history, placed together in one section for ready consultation; genealogical tables are included in the appendix listing Sicily's kings.

Sources and notes are grouped together by chapter in a simple, if slightly unconventional, format, and as these list books and academic articles there is no separate reading list or bibliography. There are end notes, rather than footnotes, to indicate sources, further reading, and many things which would have been cumbersome digressions if presented in the main text.

The chronology is an integral part of this work. Despite the temptation to extend it forward and backward, it is a slice of history from 1000 to 2000; a "complete" timeline would have been unwieldy.

An effort has been made to avoid excessive redundancy, but certain details are repeated in later chapters or appendices to refresh the memory of the reader, who in such a work is confronted by a cacophony of names and events, some of which are confusingly similar to each other. Moreover, some readers may be perusing this book in search of specific information, without reading the entire text, and such a task is easier in the ebook than the printed edition.

Impartiality is a holy grail of historical writing. Here the reader can expect dispassionate objectivity about the Bourbon and Savoy kings who ruled Sicily, this despite the author's longstanding acquaintanceship with a few of their heirs, *i signori Borbone e Savoia*.

In response to a question that sometimes arises, the author wishes to state that, in their conversations with him, Douglas Fairbanks, KBE, Achille di Lorenzo, LM, and James Risk, CVO never disclosed classified military information, but some of this has been revealed recently with declassification of certain wartime documents by the British and American governments.

The author does not represent, nor has he ever been employed by, the Italian government or any of the governments, universities, agencies, institutions, organizations or persons mentioned in this book. He has never been affiliated with any political party (or movement) in Italy.

Having established the path to our discovery, let us begin the telling of Sicily's story.

Buon proseguimento.

MAPS
&
IMPRINTS

THE KINGDOM OF SICILY

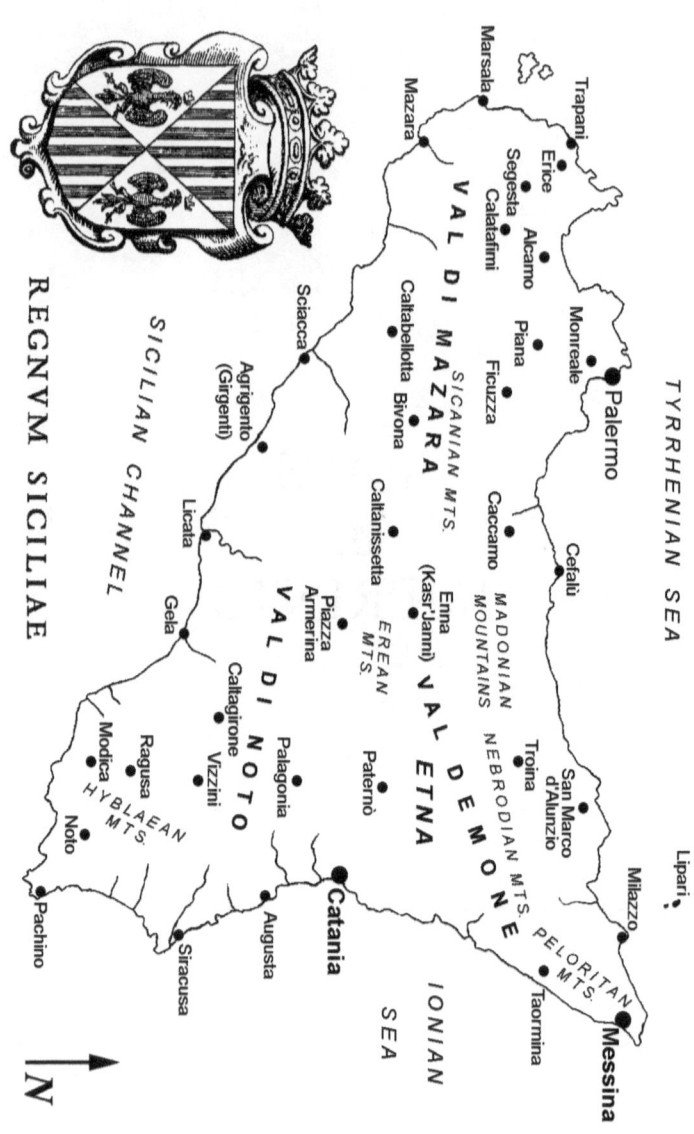

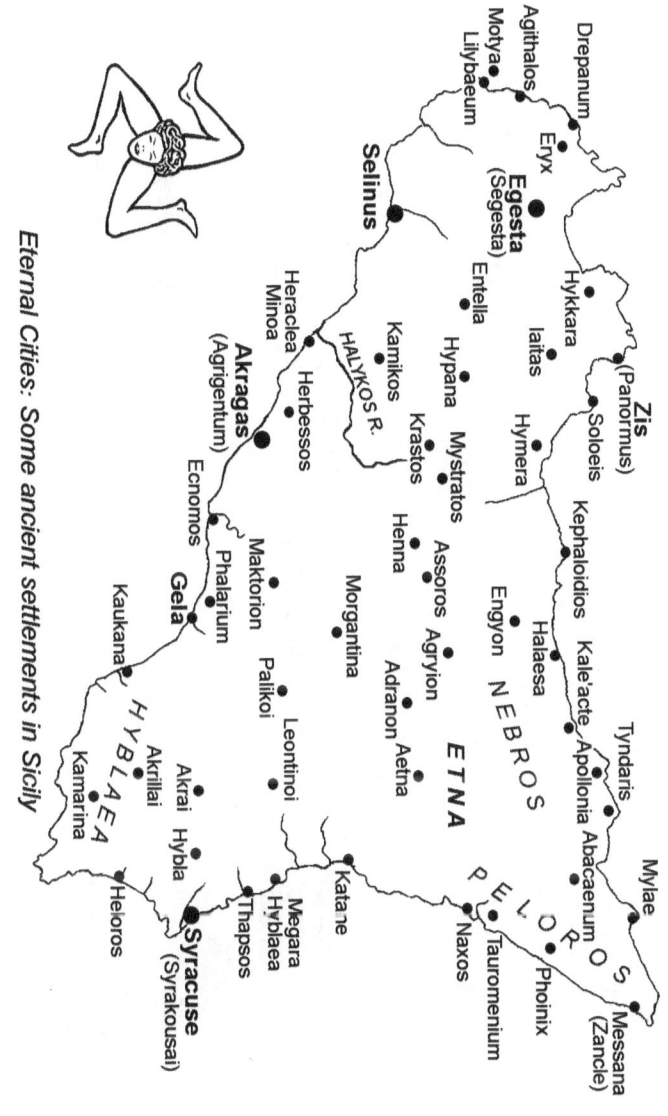

Eternal Cities: Some ancient settlements in Sicily

THE KINGDOM OF SICILY

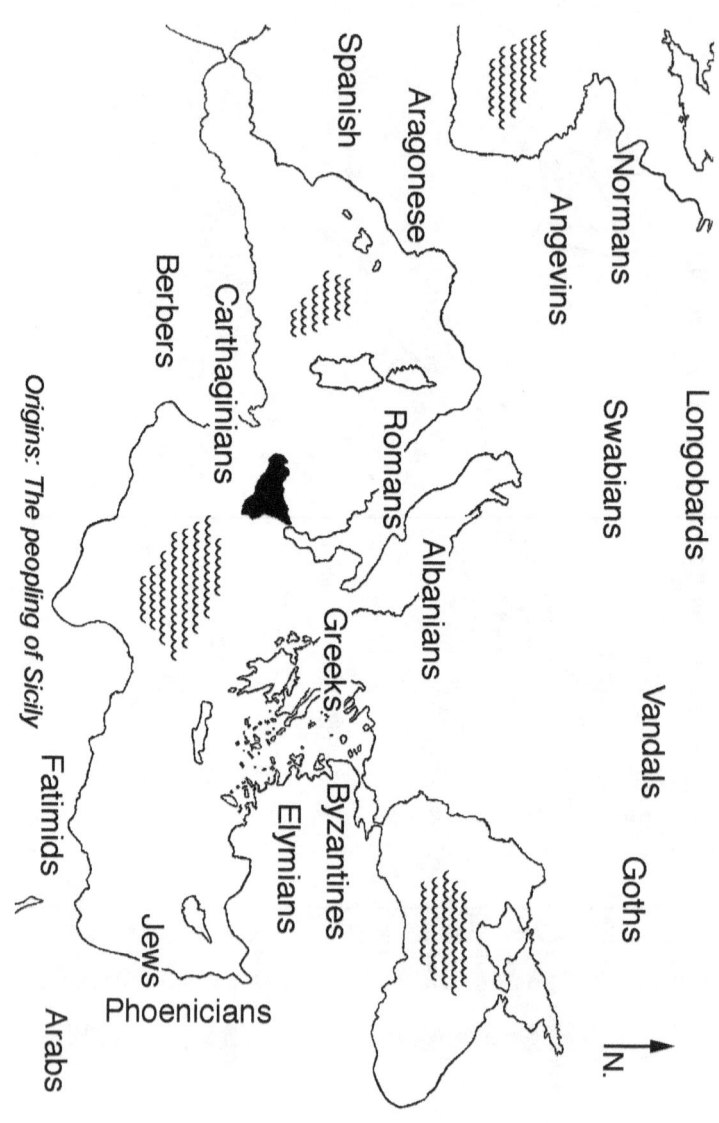

Origins: The peopling of Sicily

MAPS & IMPRINTS

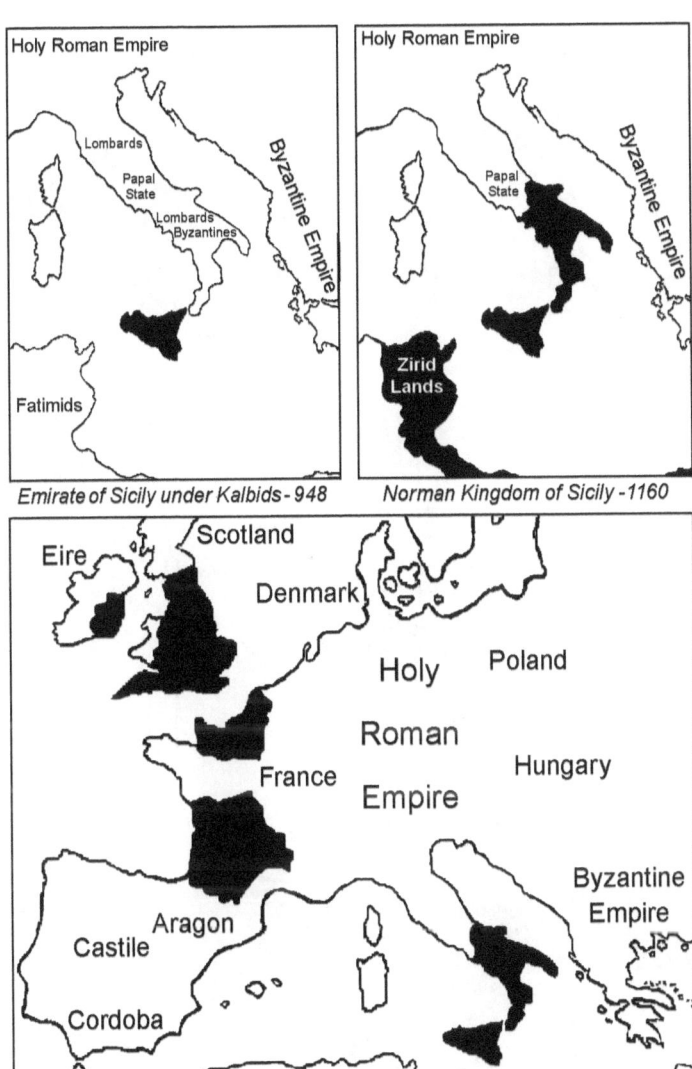

Emirate of Sicily under Kalbids - 948

Norman Kingdom of Sicily - 1160

Norman control in 1180: Normandy, Sicily, England, Ireland, Aquitaine, Malta

THE KINGDOM OF SICILY

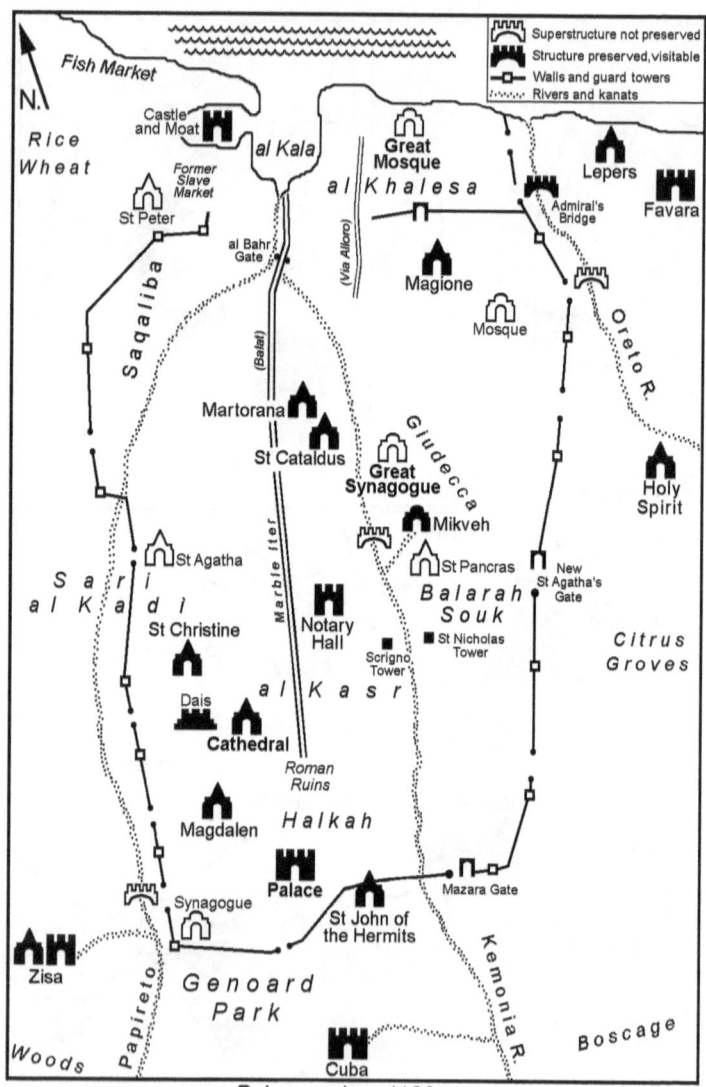

Palermo circa 1180

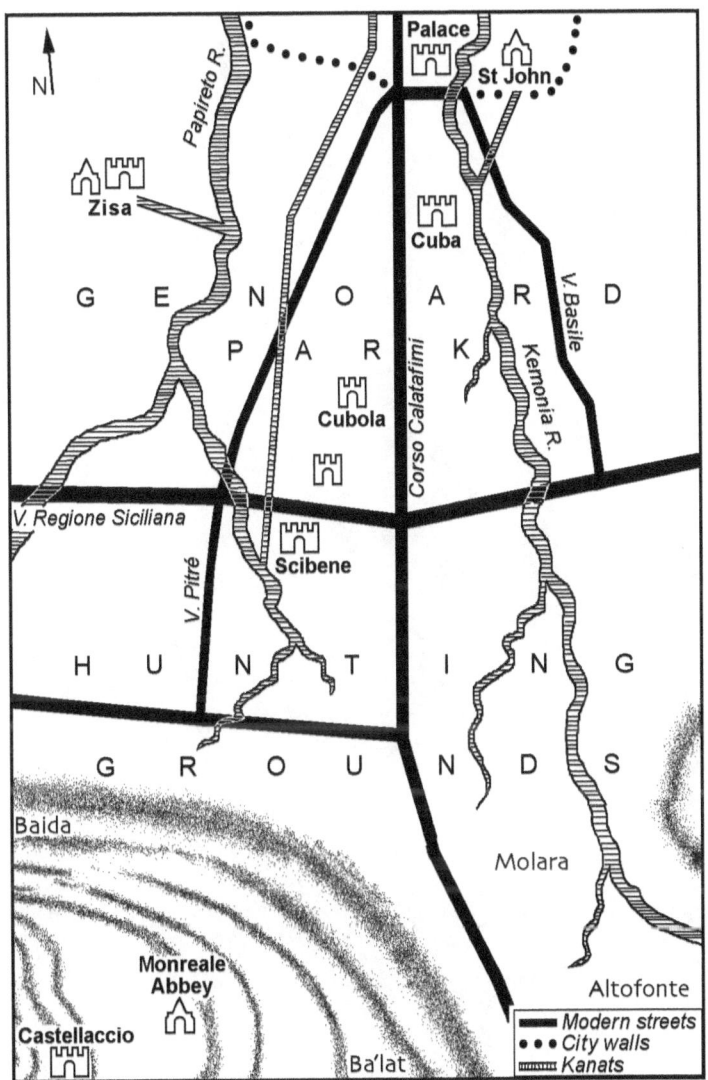
The Genoard Park circa 1180

THE KINGDOM OF SICILY

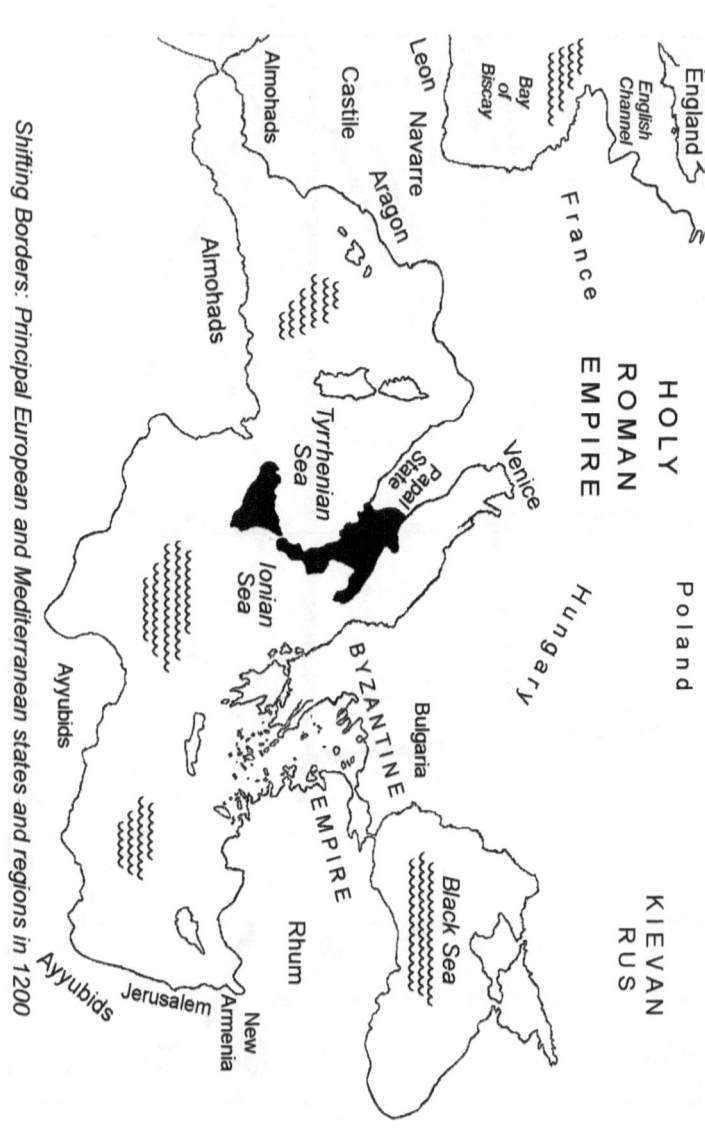

Shifting Borders: Principal European and Mediterranean states and regions in 1200

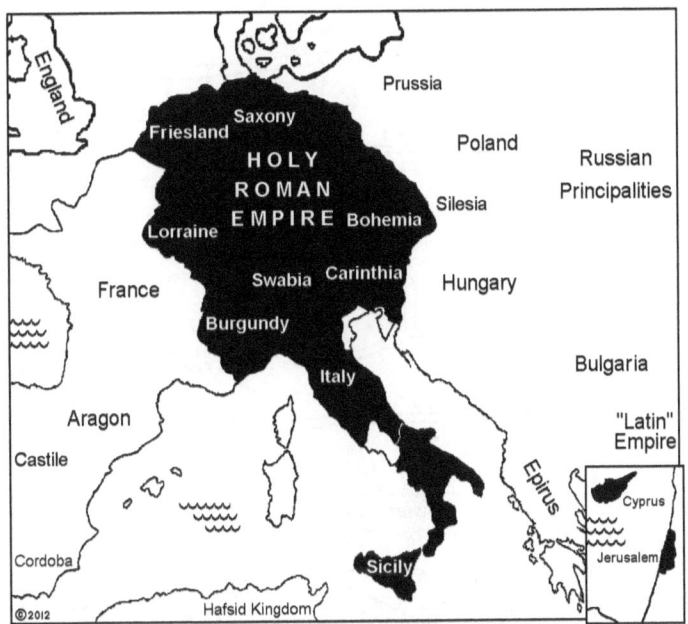
Greatest extent of Hohenstaufen dominion under Frederick II - 1230

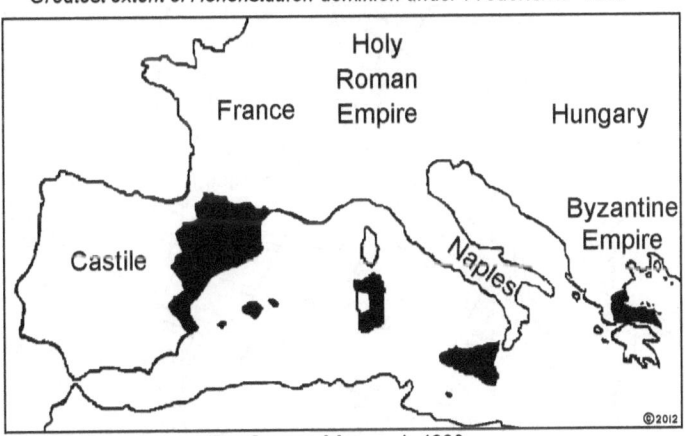
The Crown of Aragon in 1330

THE KINGDOM OF SICILY

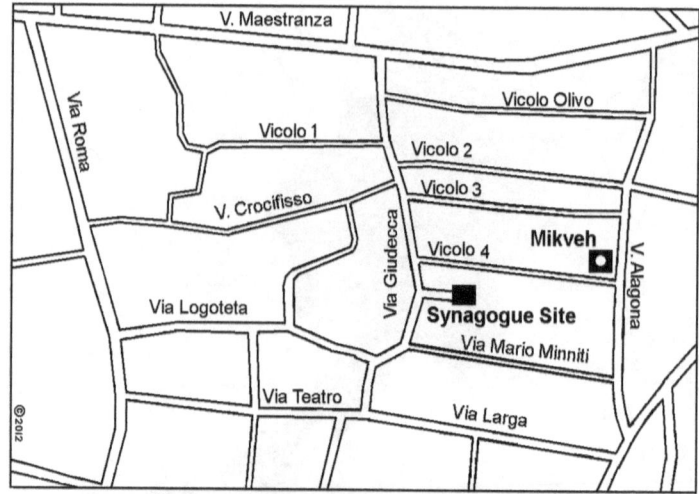

Giudecca (Jewish Quarter) in Ortygia, Siracusa
Great synagogue site is St John's Church. Mikveh at Via Alagona 52.

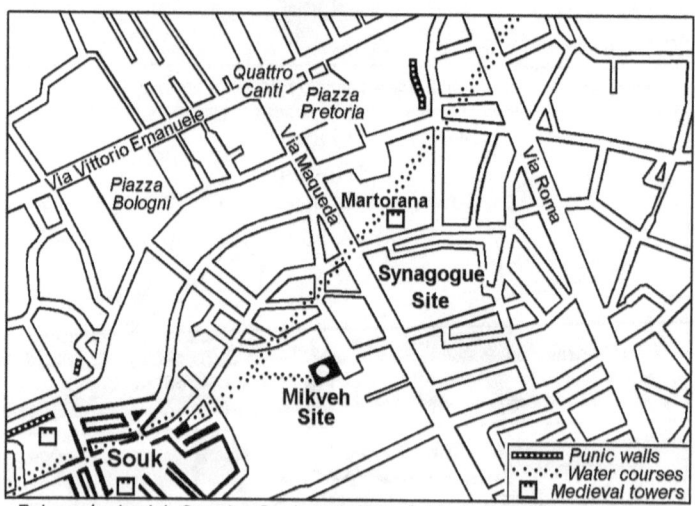

Palermo's Jewish Quarter, Souk (now Ballarò Market) and Kemonia Spring
Great synagogue site is San Nicolò da Tolentino Church. Mikveh in Palazzo Marchese.

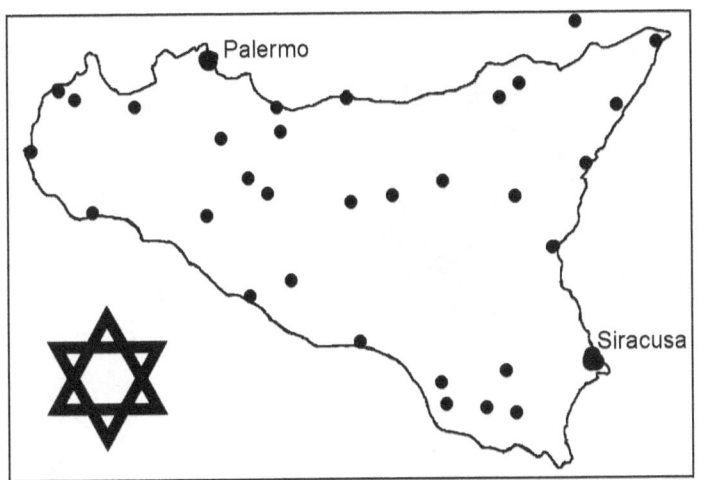
Jewish communities in 1490

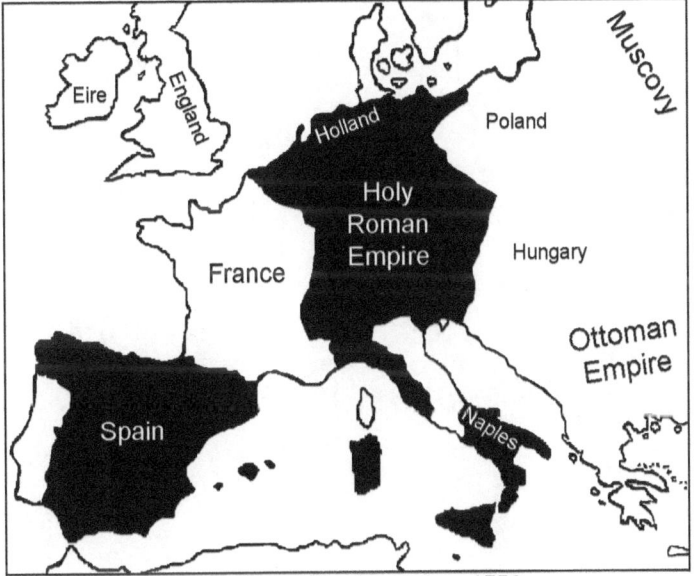
Domains of Charles V circa 1550

THE KINGDOM OF SICILY

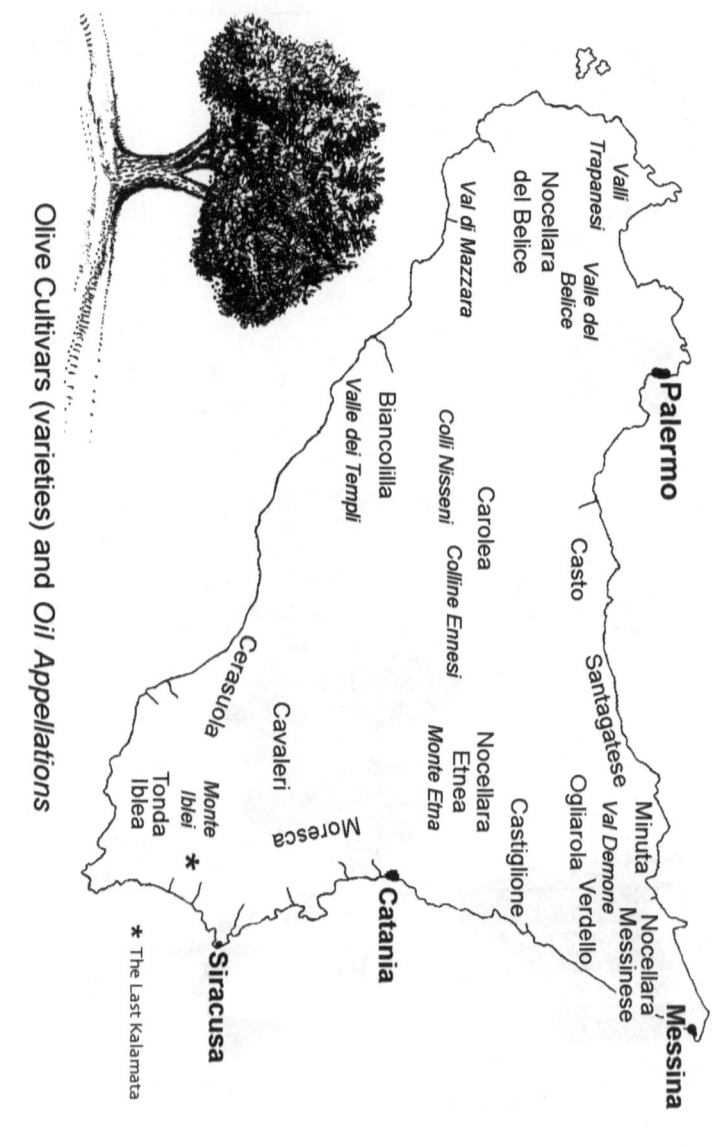

Olive Cultivars (varieties) and Oil Appellations

* The Last Kalamata

Palermo circa 1570 in engraved map showing city walls

THE KINGDOM OF SICILY

Kingdom of the Two Sicilies

Italy in 1859 prior to unification

CHRONICON
ROMUALDI II.
ARCHIEPISCOPI SALERNITANI.

In Christi nomine incipit Chronica.

DE ÆTATIBUS.

Prima mundi ætas est ab Adam usque ad diluvium, côtinens annos, juxta Hebraicam veritatem mille sexcentos quinquaginta sex, juxta septuaginta verò Interpretes duo millia ducentos quadraginta duos ; generationes verò juxta utramque editionem numero decem, quæ universali est deleta diluvio , sicut primam cujusque hominis oblivio demergere consuevit ætatem . Fuerunt Noë filii tres , ex quibus ita. sunt ortæ gentes . De Japhet quindecim . De Cham triginta . De Sem XXVII. Sem annos duos post diluvium genuit Salem : à quo Samaritæ & Indi . Sale genuit Heber : à quo Hebræi . Heber genuit Falech , cujus tempore turris ædificatur , & linguarum divisio fit . In solo Heber prisca remansit lingua, quia in ea conspiratione non fuit . Turris verò duo millia CLXXIV. dicitur passuum . Hanc Nembroth gigas construxit . Hac ætate Scitharum regnum oritur , ubi primus regnavit Ihannus . Tunc & regnum Ægyptiorum ubi primus regnavit Thoës . Dehinc regnum Assiriorum , ubi primus regnavit Belus , quem dicunt Saturnum quidam : deinde Ninus , qui condidit Ninivem . Hoc tempore Abraham nascitur : & post mortem Nini à Semiramide Regina reædificata est Babylonia, ubi regnavit annos quadraginta .

Secunda ætas à Noë usque ad Abraham generationes juxta Hebraicam veritatem complexa decem , annos autem ducentos nonaginta duos ; porrò juxta septuaginta Interpretes anni MLXXII. Generationes verò XI. hæc verò quasi pueritia fuit generationis populi Dei , & ideo in lingua inventa est Hebræa, à pueritia namque homo incipit noscere loqui, quæ idcirco appellata est , quòd fari non potest . Ab Adam itaque usque ad Abraham juxta Hebraicam veritatem computantur anni mille nongenti quadraginta octo , secundùm septuaginta Interpretes fiunt anni tria millia trecenti quatuordecim .

Tertia ab Abraham usque ad David generationes juxta utramque auctoritatem XIV. annos verò, secundùm Hebræorum auctoritatem nongentos quadraginta duos complectens; juxta septuaginta verò Interpretes anni tria millia CXXXVII. hæc velut quædam adolescentia fuit populi Dei , à qua ætate incipit homo posse generare , propterea Matthæus Evangelista generationum ab Abraham sumpsit exordium , qui etiam pater multarum gentium constitutus est , quando mutatum nomen accepit . Ab Adam verò juxta Hebræorum auctoritatem usque ad David fiunt anni duo millia octingenti nonaginta , secundùm septuaginta Interpretes anni tria millia CV. Cur autem annorum hæc diversitas sit , in sequentibus ostendetur .

Quarta à David usque ad transmigrationem

1725 edition of Romuald's chronicle of Norman Sicily

ITINERARIVM
BENIAMINI
TVDELENSIS;

IN QVO

RES MEMORABILES, QVAS
ANTE QVADRINGENTOS
annos totum ferè terrarum orbem notatis itineribus dimensus vel ipse vidit vel à fide dignis suæ ætatis hominibus accepit, breuiter atque dilucidè describuntur;

Ex Hebraico Latinum factum
BENED. ARIA MONTANO
INTERPRETE.

ANTVERPIÆ,
Ex officina Christophori Plantini,
Architypographi regij.
M. D. LXXV.

Early edition of the Itinerary of Benjamin of Tudela, from Navarre, who visited Norman Sicily and wrote about its Jewish communities.

PETRI DE VINEIS
JUDICIS AULICI ET CANCELLARII
FRIDERICI II. IMP.
EPISTOLARUM

Quibus
Res gestæ ejusdem Imperatoris aliaque
multa ad Historiam ac Jurisprudentiam
spectantia continentur

LIBRI VI.

Novam hanc Editionem adjectis
variis Lectionibus
curavit

JOH. RUDOLPHUS ISELIUS JC.

Accedit
Simonis Schardii Hypomnema de fide,
amicitia & observantia Pontificum Romanorum erga Imperatores
Germanicos.

Tom. I.

BASILEÆ,
Sumptibus JOH. CHRIST. MDCCXL.

Early printing of the Epistolarum (letters) of Pietro della Vigna, chancellor of Frederick II.

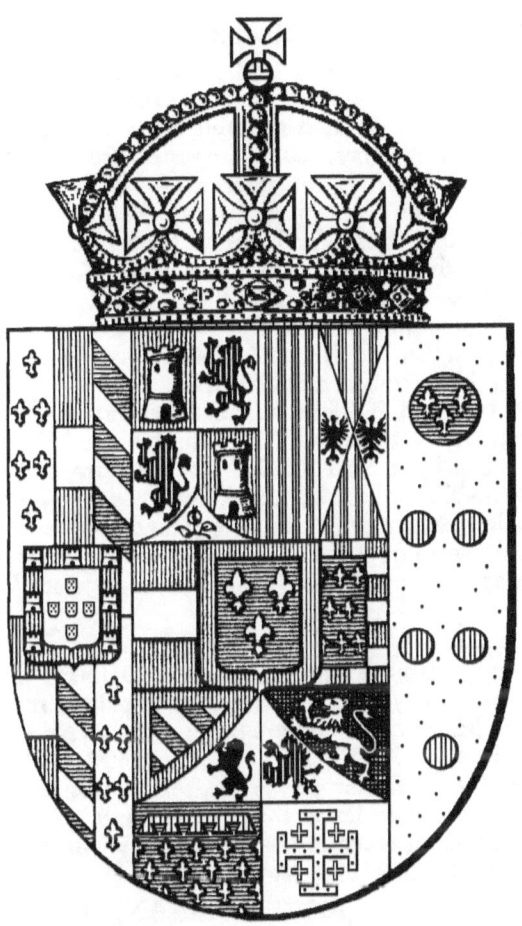

The coat of arms of Naples and Sicily beginning with the reign of Charles de Bourbon (later Charles III of Spain) in 1734. This was the coat of arms used in the Kingdom of the Two Sicilies until its demise in 1861.

ROYAL GIFT, AND THE KNIGHT OF MALTA, two valuable JACK ASSES,

WILL cover Mares and Jennies at MOUNT-VERNON, this Spring, for Five Guineas the Seaſon.

The firſt, is of the moſt valuable Race in the Kingdom of Spain.—The other, lately imported from Malta, by the Way of Paris, is not inferior.——ROYAL GIFT, (now 5 Years old) has increaſed remarkably in Size ſince he covered laſt Year—and not a Jenney, and ſcarcely a Mare to which he went, miſſ d.——THE KNIGHT OF MALTA will be 3 Years old this Spring—is near 14 Hands high—moſt beautifully formed for an Aſs—and extremely light, active and ſprightly.—Comparatively ſpeaking, he reſembles a fine Courſer.

Theſe two JACKS ſeem as if deſigned for different Purpoſes equally valuable.—The firſt, by his Weight and great Strength, to get Mules for the ſlow and heavy Draught.—The other, by his Activity and Sprightlineſs, for quicker Movements on the Road.—The Value of Mules, on account of their Longevity, Strength, Hardineſs and cheap keeping, is too well known to need Deſcription.

MAGNOLIO

Stands at the ſame Place, for FOUR POUNDS the Seaſon.—The Money, in every Caſe, is to be paid at the Stable, before the Mares or Jennies are taken away.----No Accounts will be kept.----Good Paſture, well encloſed, will be provided, at Half a Dollar per Week, for the Convenience of thoſe who incline to leave their Mares, and every reaſonable Care will be taken of them; but they will not be enſured againſt Theft or Accidents.

JOHN FAIRFAX, OVERSEER.

Mount-Vernon, March 12, 1787.

Advertisement for services of donkeys given to George Washington by King Charles III and by Emmanuel de Rohan-Polduc, Grand Master of the Order of Malta

PROLOGUE

"Where there is friendship, there is our natural soil."

— Voltaire

Late on a crisp, overcast Autumn afternoon, a sudden gust swirls a few leaves onto grayish stone steps worn by time. The top step, forming the platform, the stylobate, supports six graceful columns crowned by Ionic capitals.

Surrounded by the soaring skyscrapers of lower Manhattan, Saint Peter's Church is the heart of the first Roman Catholic parish in New York. Its founding patron was a former King of Sicily who as King Charles III of Spain became one of the first monarchs to recognize an inchoate republic founded by a few idealists.

Until 1785, the staid island of Manhattan had little in common with the triangular island in the middle of the Mediterranean. New York had recently extricated itself from the British, who ruled it as a colony for over a century. In their struggle for independence, the American revolutionaries rebuked the King of England while befriending the King of Spain, along with his French cousin Louis XVI. Britain's state of war with France, Spain and the United States formally ended with the Peace of Paris in 1783, which recognized the

Spanish control of Florida and the French possession of the vast Louisiana territory while ousting the British.

Rigorously Protestant since its settlement by the Dutch, the growing city on the Hudson lacked a Catholic parish, so Charles donated a thousand silver pieces to cover the initial cost of constructing a church, modelled loosely on Saint Paul's Chapel down the street, for Catholic Manhattanites. An early parishioner was kindly Elizabeth Ann Seton, the first saint born in what became the United States. Pierre Toussaint, a philanthropist and former slave, also worshipped here.

At first glance, Charles de Bourbon would seem to have little in common with the New Yorkers. After all, the words of Montesquieu, so revered in revolutionary America, were censored in Catholic Europe.

But the avuncular monarch was a complex figure. No theocrat, he had recently expelled the overzealous Jesuits from Spain and Sicily, as well as Mexico and California, and with this policy he began to curtail the Inquisition. It was rumored that he was contemplating the abolition of slavery in his American dominions.

The church erected with his support was replaced by the present structure following the Great Fire of 1835. The portico of this newer edifice, the city's second-oldest standing Catholic church — Old Saint Patrick's was erected in 1809 — was designed in the American "Greek Revival" style that faintly echoes the architecture of ancient temples like those standing in Sicily. The interior is unabashedly Baroque, like the churches built during the same period in Naples, Palermo and Madrid.

The most ambitious of sovereigns, Charles loved grandiose projects. His *Reggia di Caserta,* "the Italian Versailles," is the largest royal residence standing in Italy, while his *San Carlo* in Naples has been open longer than any other opera house in Europe. He would have marvelled at the World Trade Center towering over stately Saint Peter's.

PROLOGUE

Charles was King of Naples and Sicily for a quarter-century until 1759, when he left Italy to ascend the Spanish Throne, succeeding an elder brother. This meant renouncing his Italian dominions, leaving one of his younger sons to rule them.

Fond of George Washington, Charles sent him a pair of coveted Spanish donkeys for his estate, Mount Vernon in Virginia, where the general christened the surviving equine *Royal Gift*. Thus the enlightened despot extended his hand to a man of the Enlightenment.

But Saint Peter's was more than a token of fellowship. Here was a sign of faith and brotherhood, an enduring testament to the steadfast belief that amity could traverse oceans and perhaps even ideologies. Worlds and minds, old and young, might find a common path.

This singular gesture was a defiant declaration that differences in religion and language need not be obstacles to friendship.

We might not always worship together, but we could still walk together.

CHAPTER 1

Prelude: Ancient Sicily

"Our purpose in framing the state was not that our citizens should do whatever they like, but that they should serve the community for the common good."

— Plato

As the morning sunlight caresses the golden limestone columns of Segesta's ancient temple, the stately Doric monument speaks to us. It seems to have been built yesterday, or perhaps a few days before. Its condition belies its age, for it has witnessed much. When Persephone gathered flowers in the Vale of Enna, when Arethusa emerged as a spring in Ortygia, when Hephaestus and the Cyclops ruled the fiery summit of Etna, when Odysseus challenged Scylla and Charybdis, when the nymph Kyane swam in the river that bears her name, the Temple of Segesta stood guard over these hills.

The Sicilians no longer speak the language of the temple's builders, nor do they worship the deities of old, but timeless Segesta reminds us that we are all children of an unseen past, and that no society gives birth to itself.

The magnificent Greek temples of Sicily attest to more than an ancient people's passion; they represent the perfect union of Humanity and Nature. After thirty centuries of progress, it is a model of harmony still worth emulating, and one that we have largely abandoned.

It was a multicultural social milieu that gave rise to the Kingdom of Sicily. Its gift to us is the unspoken poetry of diversity. That was unplanned. Sicily's copious roots reach into the fertile soil of a distant past, long before medieval times, in the Mediterranean civilizations that flourished for millennia. It behoves us to cast a glance over this ancient continuum, if only laconically, if we dare to presume any familiarity with what came later.

In the Beginning

At 25,711 square kilometers (9,927 square miles), Sicily is the largest island in the Mediterranean and the largest of the Italian Republic's twenty political regions, slightly larger than Piedmont. For comparison, Wales covers 20,780 square kilometers and Massachusetts 27,340. In addition to the island of Sicily, the region includes a number of coastal and volcanic islands. For many centuries, Malta and Gozo were part of the Kingdom of Sicily.

The highest peak is Mount Etna, western Europe's largest active volcano, at a variable 3,329 meters (10,922 feet) above sea level, followed by rocky Pizzo Carbonara (1,979 meters) and several other summits in the Madonian range, and forested Mount Soro (1,847 meters) in the Nebrodian range. All of these peaks are covered with snow for at least two months of the year, Etna usually for three or four. The Hyblaean Mountains of the southeast are scenic but not nearly so high.

The mists of prehistory leave us with only imprecise dates, but cave drawings at Addaura, outside Palermo, and Levanzo, in Sicily's Aegadian Islands, have been dated to approximately 9000 BC (BCE), coeval with the monumental structures at Göbekli Tepe in Asia Minor.

The Proto Sicanians, Sicily's earliest indigenous civilization, constructed Europe's first megalithic temples on the islands of Malta and Gozo beginning around 3800 BC.[1]

The Sicily known to the ancients was an idyllic refuge of forests populated by deer, boar, hare, hedgehogs and striped cats. Sparkling streams full of fish meandered through lush meadows. Tempestuous Etna dominated the east, overlooking the scenic Nebrodian, Peloritan and Madonian ranges, where fir trees reached like spires toward the heavens. The Nebrodies take their very name from *nebros,* the Greek word for the deer that thrived there. Eagles and hawks soared above them, while grouse and pheasant populated the bush lands of the foothills.

Over time, rampant deforestation took its terrible toll. First, the rapacious Romans destroyed trees to make room for grain cultivation. Later, the Aragonese needed timber for ship building. In more recent centuries, overpopulation and mediocre land management have claimed many woodlands. There is less precipitation than there was in the Middle Ages, and the average annual mean temperature is higher.

The inception of Sicily's Bronze Age can be dated to around 2500 BC, preceded by the Copper Age a few centuries earlier.

Sicania

By around 2000 BC (BCE), Mycenaean and Late Minoan — Cretan and Aegean — cultures were present in isolated eastern localities of Sicily, especially near the Ionian coast, and by this time Malta's last temple builders, identified with the Tarxien Culture, had left Malta, with some perhaps settling in southeastern Sicily, in effect returning to the land of their ancestors. The Ausonians, an Italic people, traded with the Aeolian islanders and other peoples in the northeast, around Messina.

At some point before 1200 BC the indigenous Sicanians

were joined by the Italic Sikels in the east, and the Elymians, of Anatolian origin, in the northwest. These three societies seem to have coexisted peacefully, though our knowledge about them is sketchy at best. Sicily's name comes to us from the ethnonyms for two of these early civilizations, hence *Sicania* and *Sikelia*. By this time, the Iron Age had already begun in the Greek world.

Sikelia

The seafaring Phoenicians, who are identified with the Biblical Canaanites, founded Carthage in northern Africa around 840 BC (BCE). Within a few decades, the Phoenicians and Greeks began to colonize Sicily as part of their burgeoning empires. Of course, there were Phoenician influences long before this, their alphabet being perhaps the most obvious example, forming the basis of the Greek, Etruscan and Latin systems; some of the art they left in Sicily bears Egyptian motifs.

The Phoenicians established emporia in the island's west, especially at Motya (Mozia), Zis (now Palermo) and Solunto.

The Greeks founded colonies at Naxos (near Taormina), Agrigento, Catania, Selinunte, Messina, Gela and, most importantly, Syracuse (Siracusa).

The Elymians, whose major cities were Egesta (Segesta) and Eryx (Erice), readily assimilated with the Greeks.

The Sicanians had less affinity with Greek culture but seem not to have resisted colonization to a great degree. Except for excavations and necropoli, the tangible vestiges of their civilization are few, but the remains of a Sicanian temple rest atop the mountain overlooking Cefalù.

The Sikels, on the other hand, fought a long series of battles against the Greeks, and the last isolated pockets of Sikelian resistance, led by the man to whom Greeks ascribed the name

PRELUDE: ANCIENT SICILY

Duketios (Ducetius), were defeated only around 440 BC.

It wasn't long before the prolific Greeks colonized most of Sicily and most of the Apennine Peninsula south of Rome, a territory roughly contiguous to the Norman Kingdom of Sicily and the Bourbons' Kingdom of the Two Sicilies, but these colonies in *Megara Hellas,* or "Greater Greece," eventually emerged as sovereign, independent cities. United by language and culture, they were often divided by politics.

The *Siceliots* (as the Sicilian Greeks were known collectively) were frequently at odds with each other, and this sometimes led to war. Most often, these rivalries pitted cities like Selinunte and Agrigento against Syracuse, which was Sicily's largest, wealthiest metropolis throughout antiquity.

It is generally believed that the Greeks brought viticulture and oleoculture to Sicily, but wild grapes and oleasters thrived on the island since time immemorial, and a few native varieties are cultivated today. However, it is beyond doubt that the Greeks greatly augmented what agriculture they found.

A case in point is the Kalamata olive. An exemplar in the Hyblaean Mountains is genetically identical to Greek cultivars, descended from stock originating in the Peloponnese and introduced in Sicily nearly three thousand years ago. (One of this book's maps is dedicated to traditional Sicilian olive cultivars.)

Selinus (Selinunte) took its name from *selinon,* the wild celery that grew there. Artichokes, their English and Italian names deriving from the Arabic *kharshùff* rather than the Greek *cynara,* are indigenous; pistachios were brought from Asia.

It was not only their agriculture that the Greeks introduced in Sicily, but their philosophy and mythology. Representing triangular Sicily's three geographic extremities, the three-legged triskelion, or *trinacria* (shown at the beginning of this chapter), bearing the head of Medusa in the middle, is a Greek symbol; it may have inspired a similar emblem that came to identify the

Isle of Man.

The center of the Greek city, and the focus of local activity, was the *agora,* which survives today in the *piazza* or town square. Even the architecture of Sicilian cemeteries, tight rows of tombs outside town, reflects ancient Greek and Punic tradition. The Greeks have left some impressive temples, particularly those at Segesta and Agrigento, and two particularly large theatres at Taormina and Segesta.

The word *democracy* comes to us from the Greeks, but so does the word *tyrant.* The government of Greek cities varied from time to time. Administration, and the very philosophy of governing, might change at the whim of a single ruler or a few oligarchs; not all were very enlightened. Yes, life in a Greek community could be unpredictable.

Yet Greek culture has given us Sophocles, Aristotle, Plato, Aesop, Thucydides, and (in Sicily) Archimedes, Empedocles, Theocritus, Philistus, Stesichorus, Timaeus, Aeschylus, Diodorus Siculus, Epicharmus, Charondas and Gorgias.

When Phoenicia fell to the Chaldean Empire in 612, Carthage became the Phoenicians' major city. With the emergence of Punic Carthage as perhaps the wealthiest and most powerful metropolis in the Mediterranean, the Siceliots turned their attention to this new adversary. What followed was a complex series of wars over several centuries involving a tangled web of alliances with participants as far away as Persia.

In 480 the Carthaginians — exhorted to fight the Greeks by Xerxes of Persia who had won victories in Greece — were defeated by Gelon of Syracuse at the first Battle of Hymera. The Persians, meanwhile, were defeated at the Battle of Salamis.

These campaigns did not succeed in expelling the vanquished from the island. In the wake of their crushing defeat at Hymera, the Carthaginians enlarged a few cities in the western third of Sicily inherited from their Phoenician ancestors. Lying near the Tyrrhenian coast between two rivers that ran through a valley protected by a ring of rocky mountains, the most important of these seems to have been called *Zis*. It is known to us as Palermo. Set upon a mountain, impregnable Eryx was also enlarged. This Elymian city became a major Punic bulwark.

The constant menace of war was a Sword of Damocles — to quote a fitting Syracusan expression — hanging over the Siceliots' heads. Peace was rare; the list of battles between Punics and Greeks would make for a lengthy catalogue.

The Carthaginians weren't the only nuisance. A few years later, in 474, the Syracusans won a decisive naval victory over the Etruscans at Cumae, but the Etruscans' Latin successors, the Romans, would one day pose a far greater threat to Greek hegemony. Visiting Syracuse some eight decades later, Plato suggested Sicily as a potential model for his utopian society, an idea that must have flattered the proud Siceliots.

Raging from 431 to 404, the Peloponnesian War was particularly bitter, leading to the Athenians' invasion of eastern Sicily where, fortunately, the Syracusans defeated them in 413.

Another Carthaginian war broke out in Sicily, lasting from 346 to 341. Following an ephemeral peace, there was a Carthaginian incursion into a few Greek areas in 311. Not without reason, the Siceliots were tiring of incessant problems with their contentious western neighbors.

In 310, the Greeks under Agathocles invaded some Carthaginian territories of the African coast. A treaty signed in 306 established the Halycos (Platani) River as the Greco-Punic boundary in Sicily. Such matters were inevitably complex; in earlier times the Siceliot city of Akragas, lying near this boundary, traded with Carthage, exporting olives and wines to the African city.

The remaining Greek territories in the peninsular part of *Magna Graecia,* their *Megara Hellas,* fell to the Romans following the Pyrrhic War. Our phrase "Pyrrhic victory" originated in

Plutarch's description of some of the battles the intrepid Pyrrhus of Epirus won, so numerous were the lives sacrificed.

In 278, during this conflict, the Carthaginians — briefly, and anomalously, allied with Rome — laid siege to Syracuse until it was relieved by Pyrrhus, whose formidable forces then managed to occupy a few Punic cities in western Sicily for a short time.

By the time he departed their island, Pyrrhus was despised by the Greeks. The war's end a few years later marked Rome's emergence as a true power. The loss of the Italian peninsula dealt the Greeks a blow from which they would never recover. Their empire, such as it was, found itself deprived of the greater part of its western frontier.

Provincia Siciliae

Rome now coveted Sicily from across the Strait of Messina, where her Scylla faced the Greeks' Charybdis.

On the pretext of containing Punic influence in northeastern Sicily, where the Carthaginians maintained a garrison to keep an eye on the disgruntled Mamertines, the ambitious Romans invaded in 264 BC (BCE). The Punic Wars, which would continue for more than a century, were essentially a territorial power struggle rather than an ideological conflict, but the enmity was genuine and whoever controlled strategic Sicily would most likely emerge victorious. At stake was the entire Mediterranean, "the sea at the middle of the world."

In the southeast, in what was left of Greek Sicily, an effort was made to forestall annexation to either empire, Carthaginian or Roman. The Syracusans made a truce with Rome at the beginning of the invasion in 263, thus avoiding direct involvement in the First Punic War.

Akragas, instead, became the object of an interminable series of battles and sieges between Romans and Carthaginians.

PRELUDE: ANCIENT SICILY

It was soon Punic in all but name.

The end of this war in 241 saw *Sicilia* become Rome's first foreign province, although a few years passed before this status was defined precisely in law.

The Syracusans' truce with Rome ensured peace and the guise of independence for half a century, but their subsequent support of the defiant Carthaginian leader Hannibal during the Second Punic War, which began in 218, brought an angry Roman army to their gates in 212. While characteristically deep in thought, Archimedes, the most brilliant mathematician and engineer of his age, was killed by a Roman soldier. Much of Sicily's Greek culture died with him.

Contested Akragas was soon restored to Roman control. It was renamed *Agrigentum*.

The Romans appreciated Greek culture to the point of imitating its architecture and even adopting its deities under Latin names, but certain Greek advancements in the realms of science and technology were now stymied as Rome conquered the Greek regions. This has led to the modern belief that scientific knowledge might have developed more rapidly, and with fewer hindrances, had it not been for the growth of the Roman Empire and then the spread of Christianity.

Greek remained the island's chief vernacular language. Latin seems to have been spoken by a minority of Sicilians, but many were bilingual. Indeed, Greek became the second language of the Empire's intellectual and leadership classes.

Hannibal's defeat in 201 cleared the way for the ambitious Romans, who began to consolidate their influence in the central and western Mediterranean. The Second Punic War was over, but a third would follow, almost as an afterthought.

"Carthago delenda est," famously railed Cato the Elder. "Carthage must be destroyed!" His wish came true at the conclusion of the brief Third Punic War in 146.

Although the Romans imposed heavy taxes, Sicily flourished. The long Roman period was a prosperous one for Sicily. Indeed, the island emerged as an important crossroads in the sprawling Empire. Yet historians' references to it as "the bread basket of the Roman Empire" may manifest a slightly exaggerated perception, even though (as mentioned above) the Romans deforested many areas to make room for wheat cultivation.

The peace was punctuated by occasional unrest, such as slave revolts, the "Servile Wars." Eunus, a slave of Syrian birth, led a revolt in the Sicilian heartland beginning in 139, joined by another slave leader named Cleon. It took a Roman legion to subdue them. A second revolt, this time under Salvius, broke out in 104 in the western region around Segesta.

Under Rome, Sicily was to experience an unprecedented level of exploitation by a ruling class rife with greed and corruption. In 70, Cicero prosecuted Verres, the province's corrupt governor, who fled following the great orator's opening argument.

The first Jews of Sicily were present in Greek times; archeological evidence suggests that a community of the Samaritan sect flourished in Syracuse. More Jews arrived in Italy following Pompey's sack of Jerusalem in 63 BC. It has been suggested that the infamous Crassus, famous for defeating the slave army led by Spartacus, deported a number of Jews to Sicily, where they were enslaved, but evidence of this is sketchy.

There was unrest under the occupation of the island by Sextus, Pompey's son, in 44 BC, during the civil war that followed the assassination of Julius Caesar. After the defeat of Sextus in 36 BC, Octavian — who five years later found himself ruling the entire Empire — levied heavy taxes on Sicily.

Lasting from 27 BC until AD (CE) 180, the *Pax Romana* was a welcome interlude, yet it saw Jesus put to death in a localized disturbance around AD 33.

They have earned justified opprobrium for their brutal executions and their gladiatorial entertainment, but the Romans achieved much even as their imperfect society fostered countless contradictions. The evil of slavery existed, yet the blight of bigotry was largely banished. Peoples from around the vast Empire could become Roman citizens and many did. Rome brought writing to places lacking it. United by a common language, the inhabitants of disparate regions preserved many of their own local customs. Over time, there were emperors from Iberia, Africa and Asia Minor. The Romans' accommodation of this multiethnic panoply is something many modern nations would envy.

In some places the benefits of Roman rule were far greater than in others. Clearly, the Greeks had no need of Latin to achieve literacy, and neither did the Judeans, but written history in most of western Europe — including what are now Germany, England, France and Spain — arrived with the Romans. Here the *Germania* of Tacitus comes to mind; whatever its shortcomings, it filled a void in early historiography.

The Romans built roads and aqueducts. Concrete was one of their many innovations. They erected oval amphitheatres in Sicily while emulating the semicircular Greek theatre elsewhere in the expanding Empire. With its extensive mosaic pavements, the patrician villa outside Piazza Armerina is an abiding testament to Roman art.

Paul of Tarsus preached in Syracuse *en route* to Rome around AD 59. By then there was probably a small Jewish community there, and perhaps even a few Christians. At this early date, however, the Romans generally viewed Christianity as little more than an eccentric sect of Judaism.

The greatest influx of Jews arrived in Sicily during the decades immediately after 135, in the wake of the Romans' complete expulsion of the Jews from Jerusalem after Bar Kokhba's Revolt (which began in 132) during the rule of the Emperor Hadrian. This led to the *Diaspora,* from the Greek word for a "scattering" or dispersion.

Before long, Christianity came to be viewed as something more troublesome than Judaism, at least from what was then the prevailing Roman point of view. Christians were regarded with raw contempt. Saint Agatha was martyred in 251 and Saint Lucy suffered the same fate some fifty years later during the rule of the infamous Diocletian, who excelled at persecuting Christians.

Lucy's death in 304 came at the end of a long and wicked era. Emperor Constantine, whose rule began in 306, brought about a more tolerant treatment of Christians. His Edict of Milan of 313 legalized the open practice of the new religion. In 325 the Council of Nicea established a uniformity in its fundamental precepts, and it was the Empire's official faith by 380. Before long, even some foreign peoples beyond the Empire's frontiers began to adopt Christianity. This included various Germanic tribes.

In Syracuse, the temple dedicated to Athena was converted into a church. Although this trend continued throughout the Empire, Syracuse Cathedral, dedicated to the *Theotokos,* epitomizes it better than most. Some theologians posit that it represents a simple transition among the Syracusans from the worship of a virgin goddess to the veneration of the virgin Mother of God.

In 395, following the death of Theodosius I, the Roman Empire definitively split into Western ("Latin") and Eastern ("Byzantine") administrations. Sicily began in the West but would vacillate between the two. Seven years later, the capital of the Western Empire was transferred from Rome to Ravenna. Eastern administration was based at Constantinople, the former Byzantium.

Myriad influences combined to eviscerate the mighty Empire, whose decline cannot be attributed to just one or two factors within or without. In the event, Sicily was one of the last provinces to fall to external forces.

PRELUDE: ANCIENT SICILY

The Vandals and Ostrogoths

In 378, a Roman army was defeated at the Battle of Adrianople, now Edirne in European Turkey, by the ravenous Goths, a Germanic people forced into Roman territory by the migrating Huns. Clearly, circumstances were changing, even if bureaucrats in Constantinople and Rome were initially reluctant to acknowledge the political implications of the debacle that took place at this outpost.

The Romans should have known better, for the new adversaries did not come from nowhere; they had been familiarizing themselves with Rome's culture for centuries. Some of the greatest Germanic military leaders were trained by the Romans, who permitted people on the fringe of the Empire to obtain citizenship. In an earlier time, such a man was Arminius, or Hermann, who won a decisive battle against the Romans in the Teutoburg Forest in AD 9 using what today would be called guerilla tactics. By the fourth century, the Germanic ranks were full of Hermanns.

When the Vandals, Sueves, Burgundians and other tribes crossed the Rhine in 406, the "Great Invasion" had well and truly begun. Alaric's Visigoths, or "Western Goths," sacked Rome four years later.

In 429 the Vandals occupied the Roman province of Africa, within striking distance of Sicily. Their arrival in his city the next year was one of the last things witnessed by a dying Augustine of Hippo, who would not have approved of the invaders' Arianism.

An invasion of Sicily in 440 was followed by a series of mass raids, but the sporadic Vandalic incursions were halted by the Byzantines over the next few years.

What followed was a series of migrations and invasions throughout the moribund Empire. Attila's wandering Huns invaded northern Italy in 452. They never ventured as far south as Sicily.

Following the pattern established by the Visigoths, the Vandals sacked Rome in 455, returning to Sicily in a long series of raids in 461. By 468 they were masters of the island. Compared to much of their African domain, Sicily was a verdant jewel, a precious emerald in a sapphire sea. Syracuse was the wealthiest city under their direct rule.

The Vandals left most of the existing administration in place but — true to their eponym — they vandalized the synagogue of Syracuse, leaving it little more than a pile of rubble.

Odoacer deposed the last Western Roman Emperor in 476, and the beginning of the Middle Ages is usually dated from this time. The Vandal king Genseric, meanwhile, concluded a "perpetual" peace with Constantinople.

In 491 the Ostrogoths, or "Eastern Goths," achieved complete control of Sicily, ousting the Vandals, who retreated to their kingdom in Tunisia. The Goths made Ravenna their capital.

Like the Punic peoples before them, the Vandals and Goths suffered the fate of having their history written for them, in Latin, in a disparaging tone, by detractors. This has colored modern perceptions of these civilizations which are only now being corrected by historians.

While most of the peoples who conquered ancient and medieval Sicily left something of value behind, the legacy of the Vandals and Ostrogoths is more difficult to quantify, apart from some genes for blondish hair and blue eyes. Elsewhere, the Germanic languages are their legacy. Their rule defined a brief entr'acte, bridging the gap between what are now identified as the ancient and medieval epochs, but nobody living in the year 500 made such a distinction.

For now, their success seemed assured, but Sicily was a coveted gem. Only with the greatest effort might the Vandals and Ostrogoths keep the precious possession in their grip.

The Ostrogoth leader Theodoric the Great managed to keep his people unified against the Byzantines. His death in 526 brought an end to decades of peace.

CHAPTER 2

The Golden Pillars

"Disseminating sound knowledge is one of the most virtuous acts of righteousness."

— Malik ibn Anas

The phrase "Dark Ages" reflects a modern bias, but it seems an apt moniker for what was widespread across Europe in the immediate aftermath of the fall of the Western Roman Empire. A few vestiges of the grandeur that was Rome survived in the eastern Mediterranean, where Greek was more widely spoken than Latin, in what has come to be known as the "Byzantine Empire."

Byzantine Greek culture was a stalwart pillar supporting the prosperous, literate society the northern Europeans found in Sicily in the eleventh century; Arab culture, which we shall meet shortly, was the other.

Ascending the Byzantine throne as "Roman" Emperor in 527, Justinian already had his eye on Italy. Nobody in Constantinople seemed willing to assent to a jewel — and a territory of strategic importance to commercial shipping — like Sicily remaining in Ostrogoth hands.

In 534 the Byzantine general Belisarius defeated the Vandals at Carthage and the following year he expelled the Ostrogoths from Sicily. The island was now officially part of the Byzantine Greeks' Mediterranean empire.

But the tenacious Goths did not succumb easily. The Ostrogoth leader Totila raided Sicily in 550 in an attempt to reclaim it for his people. This occupation — if it could be called that — was short-lived, really little more than a lengthy incursion. Totila's defeat by Byzantine forces at the Battle of Taginae two years later signalled the end of Ostrogothic influence in Italy.

The next wave of northern invaders, the Longobards, who became Italy's Lombards, stayed longer.

The Byzantine Frontier

The Byzantines eventually gained control over much of Calabria, Basilicata and Apulia, where Bari was their principal city. Their main sphere of influence was Italy's Adriatic coast. Ravenna and Venice were briefly in Byzantine hands, an influence reflected in the splendid mosaics of their cathedrals.

The Longobards invaded Italy *en masse* in 568 following Byzantine victories over the Ostrogoths in the bloody Gothic War. They handily confiscated rural areas, where they introduced something vaguely resembling rudimentary feudalism. The Byzantines, for their part, were generally content to rule the more important centers, leaving the rest for the Lombards, but over the next few centuries there were occasional conflicts.

However, the decisive factor in Byzantine military strategy at this time had little to do with politics. For a generation or two, the problem was raising troops. An epidemic of bubonic plague in 541 decimated the population of the Byzantine Empire, rendering a reconquest of Italy from the Goths — and then the Longobards — all but impossible.

Significantly, the bishops in the Byzantine territories, and even in many of the Lombard ones, were under the ecclesial jurisdiction of the Patriarch of Constantinople, not the Pope of Rome. Equally important, the Byzantine cities implemented a variance of the Code of Justinian while in the Longobardic lands, at least initially, a form of Germanic law was enforced.

The Lombards never conquered Sicily, although a few arrived with the Normans. While the Italian regions under Lombardic control underwent the shift toward feudalism, Byzantine territories like Sicily retained a social and economic order more akin to the Roman model, at least for a time. Compared to the intellectual darkness that enveloped most of Europe, Constantinople was a beacon of learning and prosperity.

In 652 a small Arab force landed in Sicily but soon departed. Other raids followed. Mohammed had died in 632, and the Muslims' greatest assault on the island was yet to come. For now, the few Muslims in Sicily were traders.

The Emperor Constans transferred his capital to Syracuse for a few years beginning in 660. His main motive for the move was to establish a base for a Byzantine reconquest of peninsular Italy from the Lombards, but the fact that he considered the Sicilian city sufficiently important to substitute for Constantinople says much for its cultural and economic wealth.

Today we associate mosaics and other art with the Byzantines, but their society was much more than this, preserving a great deal of Roman and Greek learning in a changing world.

One thinks of scribes as monks, but the clergy, the "clerks," were not the only ones to perform this role. A number of manuscripts recording the work of great thinkers were preserved (in Greek) in the Byzantine Empire. Some were later translated into Arabic. Euclid's *Division of Figures* is an oft-cited example. In a few cases, the Arabic editions were the sources of later (Latin) translations when the Greek copies were lost or destroyed.

Venerated in East and West, Saint Agatho was one of the few Sicilian Popes (Bishops of Rome). It has been suggested that he began his religious vocation as a monk at one of the earliest Benedictine monasteries in Palermo, something which implies that in his time pockets of Western monasticism flourished in that part of Sicily amidst the Eastern majority. His pontificate lasted from 678 to 681. Agatho convened the Sixth Ecumenical Council at Constantinople in 680 to suppress the Monothelite heresy.

Although we have no reliable figures, such evidence as can be garnered suggests that general literacy in Sicily under the Byzantine Greeks was higher than in most of western Europe and that it increased further under the Arabs.

The Golden Emirate

Islam was the impetus for the spread of Arab power from east to west across northern Africa. The most popular modern definition of the demonym "Arab," which places any native speaker of Arabic in the same vague ethnic category, rings slightly simplistic to the ears of the medievalist. But Arabic is the language of the Koran, and in its nascent years Islam was inextricably linked to Arab culture. It was also a case of the Arabs having a written language, while some of the peoples they conquered did not.

Around 670 the Arabs founded Kairouan (Qayrawan), considered the first Muslim city of northern Africa, and by 700 the place we now call Tunisia was almost entirely under Muslim Arab influence. Before long, the great majority of Tunisians had converted to Islam and Arabic was the language that united them, but they were the descendants of Berbers, Carthaginians, Romans and even Vandals. For this reason, identifying the medieval Tunisians, or even the Moroccans, generically as "Arabs" is something of a simplification. Whatever one chooses to call them, there is no doubt that these peoples flourished as part of a larger Muslim society. Their influence eventually extended from Portugal to Pakistan.

The Muslims invaded Spain in 711, and Charles Martel stopped them at Tours in 732. Some years would pass before an invasion of Sicily was seriously contemplated.

In 827 Asad ibn al-Furat sailed from Tunisia with over ten thousand Arab and Berber troops, landing at Mazara in the western part of the island. Impressive as it was, this campaign was the result of Byzantine machinations and treachery as much as Arab ambitions. Euphemius, a Byzantine admiral and resident Governor of Sicily, found himself at odds with his Emperor, Michael II, and was exiled, so he offered the governorship of the island to Ziyadat Allah, the Aghlabid Emir of Kairouan, in exchange for his support. Euphemius was soon killed — reportedly by Byzantine soldiers in Sicily — and Sicily's Arab period began.

The Arabs met less resistance in the western part of the island than they would encounter in the east. In 831 Bal'harm (Palermo) was occupied by the Aghlabids, who came to refer to the city informally as *medina* and made it their seat of power in Sicily. This reflected a number of changes from the *status quo ante*. For over a thousand years Syracuse had been the island's most important city. Henceforth that distinction was to be reserved for Palermo.

There were several reasons for the preference of Palermo as the island's capital. It was closer than Syracuse to the Aghlabids' Tunisian capital, and farther away from the potentially troublesome Byzantines. Coming from the east, a Byzantine attack on the Syracuse region would leave time to notify Palermo of an attempted invasion.

In this magnificent city one of the largest souks became what is today the Ballarò street market (shown on the map of Palermo's Jewish Quarter). Its Sicilian name is thought to derive from the Arabic *Suk al Balari*. This may refer to much of the produce coming from *Bahlara*, a farming village near Monreale, or to *Ba'lat*, the name of Palermo's principal stone street.

By 903 the Arabs controlled all of Sicily, and Islam was the official religion. They tolerated Christianity and Judaism in Sicily, without encouraging either. In Sicily, the Arabs were rulers rather than colonizers, masters rather than leaders. Because Islamic law could be harsh to non-believers, many Christians converted, though precise numbers are not known and in the northeastern part of the island there were Byzantine monasteries throughout the thirteenth century. However, it must be said that Arab society and culture were advanced; under the Arabs Palermo emerged as one of Europe's richest cities.

In Islam, collections of *hadiths* containing *sunnahs,* or "laws," are very important. The Aghlabids advocated Maliki law, whose roots are to be found in the Sunni tradition. This says much about the legal system they brought to Sicily.

There were occasional conflicts between the predominantly Arab populations of Palermo, Marsala and Trapani, who controlled the island, and the Berbers who had settled in Agrigento and Sciacca to the south. To a great extent, these violent Berber revolts mirrored the situation in Tunisia, and worsened with the arrival of Fatimid rule after 909. They were, in effect, anti-Fatimid riots tantamount to a localized civil war that ended only following a siege at Agrigento, the Arabs' *Kerkent,* in 938.

Even though the Fatimids and their successors were Shiites they retained many laws established by the Aghlabids.

The Arabs introduced mulberries (for silk making), cotton, oranges, rice and sugar cane. The Fatimids are thought to have introduced the markhor, from which the Girgentan goat, with its distinctive corkscrewing horns, is descended.

The process of distillation, important in chemistry and in the making of spirits, was developed by the Arabs. They built water passages, *kanats,* under Palermo. Chess was played. Although some of these developments originated in India and

China, it was the Arabs who brought them to Europe and the Mediterranean. Europe's first paper was made in Sicily, where Europe's oldest surviving paper document is preserved, and in Spain. Hindi-Arabic numerals were introduced.

Advances in mathematics were facilitated by the use of the new numerals, which trace their origin to Brahmi and Sanskrit. In Baghdad, the ninth-century Persian mathematician Abdallah Mohammed al Khwarizmi made use of this numeration system to simplify Diophantus' algebra, whose modern name comes to us from the Arabic *al-jabr wa'l muqabalah*. Hindi-Arabic numerals are not merely a simpler writing system than Roman numerals; they more clearly isolate concepts such as fractions and *zero*, whose Medieval Latin form, *zephirum*, derives from the Arabic *sifr*, "cipher," from a Sanskrit word. Khwarizmi's studies also encompassed trigonometry, astronomy and geography.

Schools were established for girls as well as boys, and literacy became the norm. Paper made it that much easier for the young students to master writing.

The Fatimids migrated their center of power to Egypt in 948, delegating the administration of Sicily to the local Kalbids. Before long, Madiyah (in Tunisia) was eclipsed by Bal'harm.

There were isolated pockets of resistance from time to time. The Battle of Rometta, a town on high ground to the west of Messina, may have begun as little more than a rare Byzantine revolt, but the arrival of thousands of troops from Constantinople in 964 suggests, instead, that this was the last city in Sicily to fall to the Arabs. Its very name means "fortress," from the Greek *erymata*. Emir Hassan al-Kalbi was killed during the fighting, but the Kalbids prevailed.

Three years later, Cairo, destined to become one of the most important Muslim-Arab cities, was founded by a Sicilian, Jawhar al-Siqilli, in the name of the Fatimids. By now, Palermo was a metropolis whose opulence was said by one visitor to rival that of Baghdad.[2]

In 982, another Sicilian emir, Abu al-Qasim, was killed by Europeans at the Battle of Crotone, in Calabria, where the Byzantines joined the Arabs to defeat an invading army of the Holy Roman Emperor, Otto II.

The Arabs were prolific. They founded or resettled numerous fortified towns around Sicily. Most obviously, places whose names begin with *cal* or *calta* bear the mark of Arabic: Caltagirone, Caltabellotta, Caltanissetta, Calascibetta, Calamonaci, Caltavuturo, Calatafimi. Also in this category are places whose names begin with derivatives of *gebal* (Gibilmanna, Gibellina) and *recal* (Regalbuto, Racalmuto). This expansion, and the fact that wealthier Muslims could take more than one wife, explains how Sicily's population doubled or trebled during the few centuries of Arab rule. There were also many conversions to Islam, especially of young Byzantine women marrying comparatively affluent Muslim men. These facile conversions reflect the fact that in the Mediterranean many of the social differences between Muslims, Christians and Jews were fairly subtle well into the Middle Ages. Visitors such as Abdullah al Idrisi and bin Jubayr observed that the vast majority of Sicilian women dressed in a similar style which both chroniclers described as the "Muslim" fashion; in fact some kind of veil or scarf was traditional among Sicily's Jews and Christians as well as its Arabs.

By the middle of the eleventh century the island's populace was divided about equally between Muslims and Christians, with Jews constituting the remaining population, less than a tenth of the total.

Kalbite society had its strictures for non-Muslims. As *dhimmi,* Christians and Jews were taxed more heavily than Muslims, and there were restrictions on the number of new churches and synagogues that could be built (Palermo's cathedral and some other churches were converted to mosques). Church bells could not be rung, and Christians could not read aloud from the scriptures within earshot of Muslims or display large crosses in public. Christians and Jews could not drink wine in public, though Muslims sometimes did so in private. Jews and Christians had to stand when Muslims entered a room and make way for them in the souks, streets and other public places. In Arab Sicily there was harmony and tolerance if not absolute equality.

Constantinople still lusted after Sicily, and it now seemed opportune to exploit a growing factionalization among the island's population. In 1038 George Maniakes, at the head of an army of Byzantines, augmented by Norse, Norman and Lombard soldiers of fortune, invaded the island from the southeast. The elite Varangian Guard was led by no less than Harald "Hardrada" Sigurdsson, a future King of Norway.[3]

The Normans were commanded by William of Hauteville. Nicknamed "Iron Arm," he reputedly killed the Emir of Syracuse with a sword in single combat.

This expedition might have been successful had Maniakes not been abandoned by his foreign knights. When he was recalled to Constantinople in 1042, Syracuse once again fell to Arab control. The Norsemen and Lombards seemed to have had no special interest in Sicily, but the appetites of the land-hungry Normans had been whetted by the rich island.

Few purely Arab monuments survive, most Siculo-Fatimid art being part of the later Norman-Arab movement that flowered around 1100. (The painted ceiling of the Palatine Chapel and the Islamic geometry decorating the exteriors of the apses of the cathedrals of Palermo and Monreale are typical of this syncretic style.) Among the exceptions are the baths at Cefalà Diana. Constructed during the tenth century, this is the largest purely Arab structure still extant in Sicily. Similarly, Taormina's Palazzo Corvaja was erected during the Arab period, although parts of it have been altered over time. Some *muquarnas* are preserved in a tiny section of the ceiling in the vestry of Palermo's cathedral, once used as a mosque.

Besides the kanats, feats of engineering left to us by the Arabs include some well-constructed bridges outside Corleone, Adrano and Roccamena.

In 1044, Hasan as-Samsam (Samsam ad-Dawla) was deposed but not killed, and it seems that he retained some local power. At this time, if not earlier, the Emirate of Sicily was divided into four *qadits* but there were rivalries among the *qaids,* the local governors. Had the *qaids* of the four *qadits* been united, Maniakes would not have run amok, virtually unchecked, for so long.

Sicily was tenuously united so long as the Kalbids ruled. Following the death of Hasan as-Samsam, the last of his dynasty, in 1053, three warring emirs divided control of Sicily. Ibn al Hawas ruled northeastern Sicily (Val Demone) from Kasr' Janni (Enna), Ibn at Timnah ruled southeastern Sicily (Val di Noto) from Syracuse and Catania, and Abdullah ibn Hawqal ruled western Sicily (Val di Mazara), a region which included opulent Bal'harm, from Trapani and Mazara. The word *val* did not refer to a valley, as is often presumed today, but to a *district*.

During this period of political chaos and localised power struggles the title of *emir* came to be abused, occasionally usurped by the *qaids,* who were actually leaders of large towns rather than entire districts, hence there was a nominal "Emir of Bal'harm" resident in the Favara palace in what is now Palermo's Brancaccio district.

What awaited Sicily was a society very different from what she knew under the Arabs.

CHAPTER 3

Overture: Monarchy

"For your life and that of your heirs, we shall not appoint any bishops or abbots against your will in the lands you rule."

— Pope Urban II granting Legatine power to Roger I

Kings, bishops, knights. Medieval European society kept every man in his place on what some have compared to a chessboard. Except for queens and a few abbesses, most women found themselves on the edge of this orderly quadrangle of squares. It was a man's world.

No discussion of the Kingdom of Sicily can claim anything like completeness without addressing the topic of feudalism and other monarchical institutions.

As we saw in the last chapter, from the time it was seized from the Germanic "Barbarians" Sicily never descended into the chaos that enveloped much of Europe during the so-called Dark Ages. The Byzantines and Arabs were benevolent rulers motivated to cultivate and defend Sicily's riches. This they did until, in each case, internecine feuds made them vulnerable to outside forces.

Until the Normans arrived, Sicily and a few isolated parts of southern peninsular Italy existed in something most western Europeans might have viewed as an anachronistic cocoon.

The Byzantines and — in Sicily — the Arabs governed regions under their control based on a kind of collective land administration where smallholders were the foundation of agrarian life. There were rather few large estates in private hands, with most common resources, such as forests and rivers, held directly by the rulers. In practice, rule was usually hereditary, but it changed frequently enough, with various families vying for power.

Religion was an impetus of this form of government, as it was to earlier ones, but Sicily under the Byzantines and Arabs could not be said to be a theocracy in the truest sense of that term, nor was the Kingdom of Sicily a theocratic state. Indeed, its Norman and Swabian kings were often at odds with the Papacy.

Manorialism

Absent from Fatimid Sicily was *manorialism,* a system that emerged in Europe based on Frankish practices that could be traced to the days of Charlemagne, if not before. The Lombards had introduced rudimentary feudalism in much of Italy, but parts of the Byzantine south, such as territories in Apulia and Calabria, defied the trend, while Sicily was excluded altogether. This, of course, changed with the arrival of the Normans.

Nulle terre sans seigneur. "No land without a lord."

At its simplest, feudalism was a kingdom-wide system based on a hierarchy consistent with the general principles of monarchy and even Christianity as these existed in western Europe. In essence, feudalism was a social structure in which leading fighting men loyal to a king held land, the basic unit being the manor, or "fief," in return for their fidelity and military service. (Various forms of feudalism also emerged in other places, such as Japan, where they were consistent with local ideas regarding religion and families.)

This manorial arrangement is what most of us think of when we hear the modern word *feudalism*. (In modern usage, *feudalism* often refers to the entire monarchical society of Europe's Middle Ages, *manorialism* specifically to the relationship between fief holders and their tenants.) Manors were usually held by men who came to be referred to generically as "nobles" through *vassalage,* but religious orders such as the Benedictines also held manors.

The feudal system defined the relationship of all who controlled or worked the land, which was the greatest source and measure of wealth. Feudalism dictated that the rights of a bishop or nobleman were greater than those of the "common" people comprising the great majority.

The typical manor was a patchwork of numerous farms rented to tenants or, in modern times, owned outright ("freehold") by many farmers taxed by a feudatory. A manor might be divided in a process known as *subinfeudation.*

In this seemingly complex hierarchy, one wonders what, precisely, were the perquisites of nobles on their manors? Be the noble a baron, enfeoffed knight or simple manorial lord, a *seigneur,* he exercised virtually limitless control over his feudal property.

The tenant farmer could not dig a well, mine minerals or quarry marble on the manor without the baron's permission. He could not hold a fair or breed large livestock like horses without the lord's license. A smallholder might own part of a forest, but the right to hunt the deer, boar and wild cats that dwelled there belonged exclusively to the lord or even the king; even cutting down a very large oak or plane tree might be permitted only with the lord's consent. The baron might forbid the destruction of olive, chestnut and almond trees of a certain size, though citrus trees were considered less valuable. He controlled pasturage on "common" lands in his manor. The smallholder might raise certain crops, but only the lord could issue

THE KINGDOM OF SICILY

Roger II, depicted as a Byzantine basileus, crowned by Christ in engraving based on mosaic in Palermo's Martorana church

him a permit to sell these locally. Milling rights, olive pressing rights and local fishing rights could only be granted by the lord. Some barons controlled tiny lakes, but rivers were usually part of the royal demesne.

Within reason, the local lord could mete out justice, though in capital cases a justiciar, sometimes a circuit judge, would act on behalf of the Crown. Under most circumstances, only the Crown could establish and endow monasteries, which enjoyed a special status in the feudal system, but barons could donate to them.

Whereas the Byzantines and Fatimids had standing professional armies, the eleventh century found most European monarchs supported principally by their networks of vassals, each baron or enfeoffed knight providing a certain number of archers or other soldiers in time of war. It is for this reason that we often read about this or that king "raising an army." Indeed, the value of larger manors was based on how many knights each fief was to provide the king, anything from two to twenty; for this our knowledge comes from the *Catalogus Baronum,* a roll of vassals of the Kingdom of Sicily compiled in the middle of the twelfth century, the nearest thing to a *Domesday Book* preserved in southern Italy.

Sicily's Norman rulers augmented the enfeoffed knightage with a regular army almost from the beginning. The reasons for this were pragmatic as well as economic; the Arabs were usually more loyal than the avaricious Sicilian barons. At all events, the use of a professional fighting force inherited from the Fatimids was but one example of how Sicily's was a mixed or "bastard" feudalism.

As part of this bastardization, serfdom, a peasant being tied to the manorial land, was never applied universally in Sicily. This was partly a result of the way the Fatimid system of landholding made the transition to feudalism, but it went beyond that. For their part, Sicily's early kings were reluctant to risk

From emirate to kingdom: Census of serfs in a feudal manor in 1141, recorded in Arabic and signed in Greek by King Roger II of Sicily

leaving too much power in the hands of the baronage, so they decreed strategic towns *demesnial*. These were "free" or "royal" towns (and their rural districts) belonging directly to the royal demesne, administered on behalf of the king by local councils of *jurats* ("aldermen"), as opposed to the *feudal* towns under the direct control of barons. (This terminology varies somewhat from country to country.)

Likewise, a few "allodial" estates might be said to be outside the manorial system because the holder of an *allod* was not obligated to pay feudal fees to the Crown.

In addition to major cities — Palermo, Messina, Catania, Siracusa — places such as Castrogiovanni (Enna), Calascibetta, Vizzini, Cefalù, Trapani, Marsala, Girgenti (Agrigento), Monte San Giuliano (Erice), Mazara, Taormina, Noto, Corleone, Ragusa, Piazza Armerina and others were, at one time or another, demesnial territories administered by jurats. Their feudal lord was the king himself.

Monasteries were endowed with lands which did not in every instance entail serfdom, although the abbots were as greedy as any baron when it came to taxing those who leased their farms. Often, payment of taxes was made "in kind."

The knightly (crusading) orders also held fiefs from the Crown. The largest Sicilian estate of this kind consisted of the islands of Malta and Gozo, which the Hospitallers obtained in the sixteenth century.

In an effort to curtail baronial power, Sicilian kings were known to restrict the construction, or at least the size, of rural castles, but a number of fortresses built by the Fatimids, such as those of Mistretta, Caccamo and Mussomeli, were inherited and expanded by Norman knights.

Some mountaintop monasteries, such as that of Sutera, were fortified as if they were castles, complete with battlements. Monreale Abbey's massive defensive towers form part of the church, and the entire monastic complex was surrounded by walls and towers, of which several still stand. Some Sicilian castles, such as those of Erice and Cefalù, were built upon ancient structures already standing when the Arabs arrived. The seaside fortresses at Syracuse, Catania and Palermo had moats.

As early as 1140, King Roger's Assizes of Ariano protected the rights of peasants and serfs while distinguishing between the feudal prerogatives of "greater" and "lesser" barons. The greater barons were those holding large manors, by then coming to be known as *baronies,* and answerable directly to the Crown; the lesser barons held smaller estates, typically as sub-vassals of the greater barons. A large barony might comprise several manors, and a large manor could be divided into smaller units called *moieties*.

Not until the fourteenth century were counties introduced outside the royal family. An early exception was the vast County of Modica, which was one of the island's first such territories, erected formally by decree in 1296. Compiled around 1335, the *Descriptio Feudorum sub Rege Friderico* lists fief holders in Latin as *comes, baronis* or *miles* (counts, barons, knights). In theory, a county was presumed to consist of several baronies. This was rare in practice. In later times, more exalted titles (duke, marquis) were not necessarily correlated directly to the size of an estate. This reflects the fact that feudalism evolved over time, in Sicily as elsewhere.

Initially, fiefs were held *ad personam* for the life of the enfeoffed knight, but they soon became hereditary. For some years there existed in Sicily two means of inheritance. In the Frankish system favored by the Normans and Swabians male primogeniture was the rule. This differed from the Longobardic system preferred by a few Lombards, such as those who settled in the Nebrodian Mountains; here a manor was divided into equal parts for every son, with the obvious result that after three or four generations little remained of the original manor but a series of small farms.

In the classic scenario, a postulant to knighthood would acquire his military training as the esquire of an enfeoffed knight, perhaps living for a few years at the castle of a neighbouring lord or performing service at court.

By the middle of the thirteenth century, the effects of Frederick's Constitutions of Melfi were being felt. A daughter might inherit an estate if her father were a baron who had no sons or nephews to succeed him, while the institution of knighthood was reserved to men whose fathers had been knights unless, of course, the Crown assented to the elevation of a man of humble birth. There seem to have been few women inheriting estates, but there were many men of humble birth being knighted.

In view of succession by primogeniture, what fate awaited a baron's younger sons? The Norman Hauteville family that conquered Sicily is a good example of such men seeking adventures as soldiers of fortune in places unknown. Eventually, there were the Crusades and with them the crusading, or military-religious, orders. Present in Sicily by 1200, these institutions were full of *cadets,* the younger sons of barons.[4]

Certain nobles, and even senior feudal knights, could dub knights on their own manorial authority. In the days when the Normans arrived in Italy, a young esquire might be dubbed a knight with the light slap of a gauntlet across the face, this to ensure that the memory of the stinging pain would make him remember his commitment.

In time such simplicity was supplanted by the more punctilious rite of investiture, a tap of the sword on each shoulder during a religious ceremony overseen by a bishop, a royal prince or, when possible, by the king himself. This *accolade* more formally recognized fealty and homage as part and parcel of the status of knighthood.

The principle of military service rendered in exchange for the privilege of feudal tenure lasted only until it became convenient to substitute this obligation with the tax called *scutage,* a widespread practice by the fifteenth century. In 1458 feudal investiture, as a ceremony, was substituted by a simple declaration before a notary; henceforth it was a purely bureaucratic procedure. The professional (and non-knightly) cavalry was no longer the exception but the rule.

One of the trappings of nobility and knighthood was heraldry. Coats of arms became especially popular with the tournament. It seems that this colorful art was not introduced in Sicily until around 1190, decades after its emergence in France and England.[5] The right to a coat of arms was inherited in the same fashion as a barony, from father to son.

In Sicily there was never anything quite like the *Magna Carta* to guarantee baronial privileges, although the Aragonese era saw efforts made in that direction.

Until the nineteenth century, the king or viceroy "summoned a parliament" every so often. Sicilianists like to cite Roger's *Curiae Generales* of 1130 as the island's first "parliament," thus claiming antiquity over the English parliament established during the next century. In reality, these early "great councils" of Sicilian nobles bore little resemblance to true parliaments. However, the passing of time saw the evolution of a parliament consisting of three bodies or "chambers," namely the feudal (the barons), the demesnial (the jurats of royal towns) and the ecclesiastical (the bishops).

This should not be confused with the vague term "three estates," which usually refers to the tripartite segmentation of society into the clergy, the nobility and the commoners.

The term *pari* (peer) is a modern one denoting those few nobleman entitled to seats in parliament by virtue of their estates rendering a certain taxable income until the manorial system came to an end; in Sicily the peerage was recognized most recently with the parliament of 1848.[6]

King and Country

Before there were nations there were fundamental bonds of loyalty. In the distant past these were tribal or familial and usually pragmatic, undertaken for mutual protection.

In Roman times, the loyalty of the centurion and legionary was first and foremost to his commander. Later, Charlemagne's network of feudal vassals was loyal to the emperor only through a series of links reaching him as their sovereign. Feudalism, as we have seen, served to solidify the social order to a great degree, even if it was far from a panacea.

Hereditary monarchy seemed natural. It had existed since the days of the Egyptian pharaohs. It was an extension of the family. Monarchy's hereditary dictum is vulnerable to criticism in a democratic age, yet in our times fathers and mothers still leave estates to their sons and daughters, a principle enshrined in the property inheritance and probate laws of most nations. The scions of some plutocrats inherit commercial empires whose earnings exceed those of small countries.

The precise nature of kingship evolved over time and is much debated, especially in Sicily with its multifarious influences, but a few generalities hold true. Among these is the religious nature of most medieval monarchies, for human effort alone was rarely sufficient to keep a crown on a king's head for very long.

Kings rule by nothing if not the grace of God. For its part, the Church encouraged the stability offered by monarchy and the feudal system, which were complementary to its objectives, both spiritual and temporal. In doing so, it gave its *imprimatur* to institutions that reflected principles thought to be consistent with Catholicism, such as the axiom that kings reigned by Divine Right or the notion that nobility emanated from God, whose will was not to be challenged by those of humble birth, or indeed by anybody.

The Roman Catholic Church itself was a monarchy whose likening of Heaven to a "Kingdom of God" made temporal monarchies seem perfectly natural to all and sundry. Such beliefs formed the warp and woof of society. Woe betide the doubter who questioned this social order.

Islam embraced rather similar precepts regarding the rights of hereditary rulers such as Sicily's Kalbid emirs.

When Roger de Hauteville was crowned Sicily's first king in Palermo's cathedral, he was anointed by several bishops, although one would have sufficed. It was a universal constant that medieval monarchs, be they Catholic or — in the Byzantine Empire — Orthodox, were crowned during public coronations in cathedrals. The more public the event, the less likely was it to be credibly contested by naysayers in years to come. A coronation is a religious rite which confirms the ascendant monarch's right, authority and ability to rule. This usually presumes the material power to reign (over territory), approval by the Church at the time of the coronation (the bishop's role), and assent of "the people" (in practice the feudal nobility). To avoid possible contestations to succession, the Norman kings of Sicily and England sometimes nominated their eldest sons successors during their own lifetimes, and coronations were held to confirm each as *Rex Filius*.

Though a widowed queen might serve as regent for her young son before his majority, Salic Law meant that, strictly speaking, the king's wife was a queen-consort and not a queen in her own right. An early exception was Constance of Hauteville, daughter of Roger II and mother of Frederick II, who as Queen Regnant of Sicily issued decrees under her own name and seal.

When a monarchy already exists, succession is actually automatic if an heir apparent has been designated and is living. Hence the phrase: "The king is dead, long live the king!"

This was more a question of theology than prestige. Sicilian royal authority was thought to emanate from God Himself, an idea enshrined in the contemporary mosaic in Palermo's Martorana Church showing Roger II being crowned by Christ, and this influenced government and ecclesiastical policy in Sicily until the death of the oft-excommunicated Frederick II in 1250.

While it is true that certain battles, such as Hastings in 1066, were fought between armies led by reigning monarchs, the idea of a king single-handedly duelling a challenger to retain his crown owes more to legend than to fact. The duel planned between Peter of Aragon and Charles of Anjou at Bordeaux in 1283 (under the auspices of King Edward of England) for the Sicilian Crown never took place, and as early as 1231 the Sicilian nobles were finally setting aside the idea, inherited from their Norman forebears, of "trial by battle," duels between knights to adjudicate legal claims.

Although kingship and the institution of monarchy evolved over the centuries, in narrative historians tend to refer to a king and his advisors, council or cabinet generically, even collectively, as if they were one and the same. Apart from actual regency during the childhood of a king crowned at a very young age, it is clear that a monarch who reigns at the age of fifteen or sixteen is not acting entirely on his own. He benefits from the experience of trusted courtiers or aides-de-camp who are older than himself. This was as true in modern times as it was during the medieval era. Some kings, being chronically ill, delegated a great deal of their duties to ministers. Those ruling more than one kingdom appointed viceroys to act for them in their "secondary" realms, and this situation led to viceroyalty in Sicily in modern times. A young queen consort was advised by ladies-in-waiting.

The Church

In the wake of the Great Schism of 1054, the Christians the Normans found in Sicily were what would now be called

Greek Orthodox who practiced their faith under the ecclesial jurisdiction of Constantinople. Their liturgical language was Greek, and this segment of the population still spoke a medieval form of the Greek tongue. A few Orthodox monasteries survived in the Nebrodian Mountains into the thirteenth century, but the monarchy supported Papal authority even though the first two Sicilian dynasties were often at odds with the Papacy.

The abolition of Arab and Byzantine practices coincided with the conversion of Muslims and Orthodox to Catholicism, though for the latter this was a simple matter of gradual, subtle changes in liturgy and clergy over several generations.

Whether it was anointing kings, permitting knightly investitures in its chapels, illuminating precious manuscripts in its monasteries or dispensing alms to the poor, the Church exercised its influence over ever facet of life.

Though largely abandoned in our times, the concept of *legitimacy of birth* was essentially a theological one. Under most circumstances, it simply expressed the fact of a child being born to parents who were married at the time of his birth. This was of obvious importance in royal succession and in the transmission of manors held by barons, but even the inheritance of a tiny plot of land owned by a humble farmer was based on his heirs being born within marriage. In juridical vernacular there were "legitimate" children and "natural" (or "illegitimate") ones. It was possible for a child born outside wedlock to be "legitimized" by the Pope or, in some instances, by the Crown. The mere fact of a man "recognizing" a child (born outside marriage) as his own did not, in itself, legitimize that child; for that either the Church or the Crown had to render a formal pronouncement, but such a concession was a rarity outside the ranks of the aristocracy.

Latin monasticism arrived in Sicily with the Benedictines. Bishops appointed in the *Regnum* were Roman Catholic. The

Pax Dei (Peace of God), the *Treuga Dei* (Truce of God), interdicts, excommunications and anathemas all reflected the power of the Church in feudal society. The most zealous Popes even arrogated to themselves the authority to depose kings.

However, Sicily's first years of monarchy saw some interesting anomalies. Until the reign of Frederick II, the kings enjoyed the unique status of Apostolic (Papal) Legate which permitted them to appoint bishops and abbots, a privilege normally reserved to the Pontiff himself. This was prompted by Roger I arresting the Bishop of Troina and Messina who held the legateship until 1098. It was no mere concession by a weak Pontiff; Urban II, who granted this special prerogative, was the same Pope who preached the First Crusade.

Field and Forge

Opulent as medieval Palermo was, the greater number of people lived outside the few largest cities. Agriculture, of course, was the foundation of daily life. Unlike the Norman and Saxon towns of the English countryside, villages in Norman Sicily consisted of rows of connected stone houses along winding streets; there were few homes outside the towns. Not all cities and towns were walled, but a village set atop a mountain or hill might be built around a castle standing at the highest point. Vicari, Cammarata and Caccamo are typical examples. Farm houses set among fields were rare. Each day, farmers would hike out to the fields and orchards, returning at sunset.

Not all of Sicily's Fatimid agriculture survives today, when rice and sugar cane are no longer cultivated. Citrus fruits remain but mulberry trees are few and no longer used in silk manufacture. Idrisi described the making of spaghetti in Trabia during the reign of Roger II (although Marco Polo may indeed have seen a similar food in China). In Roger's time the stately

Nebrodian fir was still abundant.

The San Fratello horse was an Arab breed while the black Nebrodian swine is thought to be part boar; wild boar were hunted in Sicily and so were deer.

Guilds, which Italians called *maestranze,* developed rather late in the Sicilian kingdom, but the artisan class was a large one, and certain crafts, such as goldsmithing, were especially distinguished in Sicily.

By 1300, most of the best goldsmiths were Jews, and by 1400 most of Sicily's physicians were Jews.

Merchants and Bankers

In Italy's High Middle Ages the mercantile powers were the northern comunes. Maritime cities even had their own small but efficient navies to protect their shipping. The Pisans and Genoans, in particular, were represented in Sicily. At times the Amalfitans were part of the *Regnum*. Trade depended on this network.

By 1230, after most (formerly-Muslim) Arabs were integrated into Sicilian Christian society via conversion to Catholicism, local banking became the province of the Jews, but the chief focus of their transactions seems to have been extending small loans to local merchants. Until the death of Frederick II, the Kingdom of Sicily was wealthy enough to have little need of financing from outside sources.

There were plenty of taxes to be paid in Sicily. In the Middle Ages the *collecta* and other occasional taxes the Crown imposed on the general population existed alongside the scutage paid by feudal nobles, supplemented by various duties. Early in the modern era the *collecta* was abolished in favor of the infamous *donativo,* and in the seventeenth century a head tax was also imposed. The *rivelo* was a declaration of property taxes that were levied quite regularly every few decades beginning early in the sixteenth century to pay the various *donativi*.

Within Sicily, Hindi-Arabic numerals simplified accounting and commerce. Paper, introduced by the Arabs, was more commonly used than parchment or vellum for recording transactions. Into the Swabian period, its use also fostered high literacy.

Coinage

Frequent as barter was, coins were necessary and gold was always precious. As any numismatist knows, the largest silver coins were usually larger and heavier than the more valuable gold ones. Copper was not usually regarded as a precious metal. Because the value of gold and silver was essentially universal, the spending power of these metals formed the basic measure of economic wealth, making the "face value," the scale, of coinage less important than its value determined by weight and metallurgical purity. The authority to mint coins was the exclusive perquisite of the Crown. Coin clipping — trimming the edges off coins — was a serious crime.

As coinage and denominations changed fairly frequently, an exhaustive examination would not prove very beneficial here (and the following generalities regarding scale and value are not intended for use in monetary calculations). A variety of coins were minted contemporaneously at Palermo, Messina, Bari and Naples, while Fatimid and Byzantine coins were also in circulation for many years. Some coins were known by colloquial names, not unlike an American five-cent piece being called a "nickel."

Weighing about a gram, the Arabs' gold *tarì* was the basic unit initially. Indeed, the term "tarì" was used generically for certain small coins well into modern times. The *tarì* offered the advantage of international circulation around the Mediterranean, with other coins measured against it; values did not fluctuate wildly from year to year. The Arab *dinar* was worth four *tarì*, while the Byzantine *solidus* was worth six.

The *tarì* was worth twenty *grani*, or "grains." Initially, thirty *tarì* were equal to an *oncia*.

Roger II minted the silver *ducalis*, the first coin to become commonly known as a *ducat*. Ten of these were worth a *solidus*.

Frederick II minted the gold *augustalis*, equal to five *tarì*. Six *augustales* were equivalent in value to an *oncia*.

By 1500, the Sicilian gold *trionfo* was being struck in imitation of the size and weight of the widely-circulated Tuscan *florin* and Venetian *ducat*, its value thus linked to those currencies as it contained the same amount of gold.

In the Two Sicilies the principal coins circulated were the gold *ducat* and *onza*, and the silver *piastra* and *tarì*. The *tornesi* and *grana* were copper.

Peasants

Introduced in Sicily by the Arabs, chess makes for a convenient metaphor; indeed, the pieces of the game were adapted by European aristocrats to reflect the military machinations of the monarchical society they knew, full of bishops, castles and knights, the pawns representing foot soldiers. Beyond this chessboard dwelled the peasantry.

The term *peasant* broadly refers to farmers and laborers. The Italian *villico* or *villano* might denote either a peasant or a serf. As we have seen, a serf was a peasant tied to the land, as opposed to a free peasant. In Latin records there is occasional ambiguity due to the usage of terms such as *servi* for either serfs or slaves.

A more modern term used by historians is *commoner*, referring generically to anybody outside the titled nobility or higher clergy; this word was more suitable to the post-medieval Kingdom of England than to the Kingdom of Sicily. In modern parlance the Italian phrase *gente comune,* literally "common people," is sometimes offered as a translation, but it fails to capture the sense of the English word.

Slavery was largely but not completely abolished in Sicily by the end of Swabian rule. What we find after that time were, for the most part, men taken as prisoners of war pressed into servitude.

To the Black Death is attributed the end of serfdom in most of western Europe as it depleted the rural workforce and thereby attenuated the power of the landed nobility; by that time serfdom was all but unknown in Sicily.

Social mobility existed, but rare was the family that advanced its status from the peasantry to the nobility in just three or four generations. The origins of the oldest lineages of extant families are rooted in the High Middle Ages.

The surnames of medieval aristocrats were based on toponyms, the names of their manors, so we find names such as *de Hauteville* and *de Moac*. A peasant might be known by a patronym, thus *Giovanni di Pietro,* but a medieval surname of that type survived only one generation. Only in the fifteenth century did the majority of Sicilians assume hereditary surnames. These might be based on anything from familial professions to personal characteristics.[7]

Although the value of fruits, vegetables, grains and fish was to a great extent established by the market and might vary somewhat by locality, the Crown regulated the wholesale price of commodities; in Sicily this was chiefly durum wheat. The farmer had little say in the pricing of the produce of the land he cultivated, the fisherman very little more in the fruits of the sea that found their way into his net.

Wheat was always a staple, but Sicily's economic reliance on grain grew greater after the Middle Ages.

Who brought this elaborate social chessboard to Sicily? It was a family of bold adventurers from a faraway place.

CHAPTER 4

The Normans

"When acquiring lands in a place where there are differences in language, customs and laws, great luck and effort are needed to hold them."

— Niccolò Machiavelli

The conflict among Sicily's jealous emirs prompted one of them on the eastern side of the island into contact with a band of Europeans set on the conquest of Sicily. The Normans had been in Italy for decades, often serving as mercenaries fighting battles for Lombard or Papal patrons. Sometimes, as we have seen, they fought for Byzantine Greek generals like Maniakes. These martial arrangements occasionally pitted Norman against Norman. Yet by 1043 the knights errant from the Cotentin Peninsula managed to establish for themselves a capital of sorts at Melfi.

In light of the Great Schism in 1054, Pope Nicholas II, a Frenchman who enjoyed a good rapport with the Normans in Italy, made it understood that he wanted Sicily in Latin hands rather than Byzantine ones. This was not the only political consequence of the Schism, but it was the one most immediately shaped by it. Of course, Nicholas also wanted the Muslims ousted, or at least converted to Catholicism, and he made it known that the Normans could have as much of the island as they could wrest from its Arab masters, on condition that they pledge the Church in Sicily to Rome instead of Constantinople.

Only a conniving Pope could think of men-at-arms as men of God. The offer of Pope Nicholas meant that the knights from Normandy could have their own sovereign dominion, and to win it they need only seize power from a few Muslims — and along with them perhaps a few stubborn Eastern Christians like Bishop Nicodemus of Palermo. It sounded simple. In fact, the conquests of the world's most contested island had never been too easy for any invader, and the Normans' experience would prove no different. Nevertheless, the temptation was too great to resist, and any questionable commitments to the Papacy could always be negotiated anew once the conquest was complete.

Papal motives were clear enough. For their part, the knights were earnest in their ambitions, as hungry for Sicilian territory as the Papacy was covetous of Sicilian souls. Both would triumph in the end, firmly planting their banners in Sicilian soil.

On a clear Spring night in 1061, an audacious Norman lord named Robert de Hauteville, accompanied by several of his brothers, most notably the intrepid Roger, led an army of a few hundred knights across the Strait of Messina with their horses and weapons on specially-designed ships reminiscent of those of their Viking forebears. The Arab soldiers should have foreseen the invasion, for the Normans had attempted such a landing the previous year. In the event, the local garrison was taken by surprise and, with strategic Messina as a foothold, the conquest of Sicily was under way.

Significantly, the victory at Messina against Arab foes would serve as the blueprint for the Battle of Hastings against the Saxons a few years later, and it seems that several knights actually fought at both battles. But while Saxon lords paid fealty to William "the Conqueror" of England almost immediately, it took Roger and his knights years to achieve their objectives. The conquest of Sicily was a cumbersome enterprise not unlike the campaigns prosecuted by the Arabs during the ninth century and the Romans' Punic Wars in antiquity.

Supported by a force of numerous Normans and Lombards, the Hauteville brothers Robert and Roger made their way into Sicily with incursions into the rugged, forested Nebrodian Mountains. Conquering towns populated by Arabs and Byzantine Greeks, they encountered resistance from both; the former resented the invading infidels, the latter were offended by their Western Christianity.

The Normans' experience at the town of Troina stands out. It perfectly exemplifies what the piecemeal advance entailed, and the hardships that knights' wives endured, more out of duty than choice.

Troina

August 1062 found Roger and his wife, Judith of Evreux, at Troina, which a garrison had abandoned following a brief occupation. Here his force of several hundred spent a few weeks building fortifications. Then Roger left Judith in charge while he went off to campaign in the region with the larger part of his mounted contingent.

Troina's population, like those of many towns, was about evenly divided between Arabs and Greeks. The latter took particular offense to the ways of some young knights with the local women. That, of course, did not mean that the Greeks themselves were particularly chivalrous.

Emboldened, they sought to abduct Judith, attempting to make her their hostage, but failed when some Norman knights came to her aid. What ensued was more than a skirmish.

A few messengers managed to escape the mêlée to reach

Roger at Nicosia. By the time he returned, the situation had worsened; a number of Arabs from the surrounding country had joined the Greeks, forcing the Normans into a corner of the town.

The Normans retreated to some streets near the castle, where they quickly erected makeshift barricades. Caught unawares and under armed, they found themselves trapped, yet their besiegers lacked the capacity to overpower them. The dogged siege was to last for four long months.

Troina is over a thousand meters above sea level, and in the eleventh century it was surrounded by dense forests of conifers — stone pines and the Nebrodian fir. The climate was cooler then, and the town was blanketed by snow for several months of the year. Lacking provisions and warm clothing, Roger and his hardy knights were to endure one of the coldest Winters in Sicilian memory.

The weeks dragged on, the Normans butchering their horses for food. Judith and Roger shared a flimsy blanket of wool. By January, the coldest month of the season, food was running short.

One particularly cold night, the Normans noticed that the Arab sentinels were consuming a great deal of wine, probably in the hope of staying warm. The drunken guards were soon sound asleep and the Normans attacked.

The deep snow muffled the knights' footsteps as they took back the town. By morning, Troina was again theirs. The leaders of the uprising were hanged and a feast followed.

Troina became a Norman stronghold. Indeed, Judith governed the town in her husband's absence for long periods over the next several years.

This, however, was not the only town fortified by the Normans during this period. They erected their first Sicilian castle at Aluntium, now San Marco d'Alunzio, which would be a rural refuge of the Norman kings for a century.

Palermo

Even after the occupation of northeastern Sicily was assured, Palermo was far away. The Arabs' *medina* was captured in January 1072 following an epic battle by land and sea. When the fighting was over, Sicily was again part of Europe. Yet Kasr' Janni (Enna) fell only fifteen years later, and then only because ibn Hammud, the local emir, agreed to a negotiated surrender.

A few cities, like Catania and Syracuse, wavered back and forth between Arab and Norman control; the renegade local emir Bernavert (Bin al Wardi) of Syracuse was typical of those leading this resistance. Butera and Noto held out until 1091.

In the wake of this European conquest, most Arabs remained, for Sicily was the only home they had ever known. It was theirs. A few, like the poet ibn Hamdis, who was born in southeastern Sicily and probably supported Bernavert, chose to emigrate rather than be ruled by Christians. "Oh blond tribe," he wrote in his *Siqilliyyat,* "my blood is on your hands."

Many shared his concerns, unable to see how this polyglot place could be governed. In 1083, Roger appointed a Latin as Palermo's bishop. The Gallican Rite was introduced, if it were not already in use.

At the time, anybody who might have suggested that an unruly band of brigands from Normandy could establish Europe's first truly multicultural society would have been dismissed as insane. It was the beginning of medieval Europe's greatest — if unplanned — social experiment.

Styled "Count of Sicily," Roger brought to this new domain the complex, versatile feudal system we met in the last chapter. His rule also brought with it increased religious freedom and a sovereign government.

Anybody visiting Sicily would have encountered mosques, synagogues and plenty of churches, English bishops and Saracen imams. Most Sicilians who didn't speak Greek or Arabic spoke Norman French, the Jews spoke a peculiar Judeo-Arabic dialect, and court decrees were issued in several languages, including Latin. Soon a new language, Sicilian, would emerge from this eclectic mix.

Benedictine monks worked alongside Muslim scribes. The Normans accepted certain Byzantine, Jewish and Muslim legal practices; Islamic law as it then existed in Sicily was highly sophisticated for its time. For the first few decades, each Sicilian would be judged by his own religious law.

It was a rarified, magical moment, but no moment lasts forever.

The County of Sicily

Efficiency was the rule. Initially, as the Normans were few in number, they left most existing organs of government undisturbed. The precise extent to which Roger's administration was Byzantine or Arab is not known; clearly, it was a combination of both, with only traces of feudalism. The manorial system was introduced, but slowly, one estate at a time. Roger's standing army and royal Saracen bodyguard obviated the need for more than an elite cadre of knights, at least for now.

The Kalbids' "treasury," the *diwan,* was preserved. Its name survives in the French *douane* and Italian *dogana,* referring simply to a customs duty, but in Sicily the *diwan* was a key institution organized along Fatimid lines. Like other essential agencies, it was maintained in Palermo's *Khalesa,* which had been Bal'harm's administrative center. The *diwan* oversaw the wealth of the emirate and then the kingdom, its responsibilities ranging from the accounting of monies to landed estates to serfs. The *diwan* may have been more sophisticated than analogous financial institutions such as England's exchequer, but Sicily's exceptional wealth meant there was more to manage. That, however, did not diminish the need for foreign trade.

A trade treaty was negotiated with the Zirids of Tunisia in 1075, an agreement as advantageous to the sultan Temim as it was to Roger. Eventually, the Sicilians imported cotton cloth and beeswax, as well as gold sent by camel caravan across the Sahara to Kairouan and Mahdia, while exporting hard wheat and dried meats.

Roger's beloved Judith died young the following year, having given birth to four daughters but — as far as we know — no sons. She was the very embodiment of the stalwart woman of the Middle Ages. Oddly enough for the times, her betrothal to Roger does not seem to have been arranged very formally; the two had known each other in Normandy and they wed when he was still an impecunious knight errant. The next year, Roger married Eremburga of Mortain, who bore eight daughters. He wed his third wife, Adelaide del Vasto of Savona, in 1087.

The same year, Emir ibn Hamud surrendered the city of Kasr' Janni to the Normans. Broadly speaking, the Sicilian population was divided a bit unevenly, with more Arabs in the central and western regions and more Greeks in the northeast, but by 1090 there was a steady influx of immigrants and visitors from Italy and Normandy. Odo of Bayeux, half-brother of William the Conqueror, visited Roger *en route* to the First Crusade; he died in Sicily in 1097 and is buried in the crypt of Palermo Cathedral.

The Apostolic Legateship came in 1098, permitting the Norman appointment of bishops and abbots.

Consistent with their traditions, the Byzantines and Arabs of Sicily seem to have accorded Count Roger far more obeisance and authority than that to which the typical European Christian ruler was accustomed.

He spent much of his time traveling, but he and his large family of daughters and sons occasionally resided in a castle hastily erected on high ground in the *Halkah* section of Palermo's *Kasr* district at the site of an Arab fortress. The original royal chapel, a quaint structure below the present palatine chapel, can still be seen there.

The castle at San Marco d'Alunzio was maintained as a safe haven for Roger's children, and that seems to be where they were raised, speaking several languages. The dominions under his direct control were Sicily and a few pieces of peninsular Italy. At his death in 1101, he was buried at Mileto in Calabria. He is known to posterity as Roger I.

A number of Hautevilles went on the First Crusade, with Bohemond, a son of Robert Guiscard, founding a monarchy at Antioch. They are described in some detail by Anna Comnena, though rarely in flattering terms.[8]

How many Normans settled in Sicily? We don't know, but most were men, and most married Sicilian-born women. The best estimate of the Norman migration places it at fewer than eight thousand persons arriving between 1061 and 1161, but even this is highly speculative. It was not a mass immigration comparable to those of the Arabs or the ancient Greeks, but a constant influx.

Roger II

Count Roger was survived by a widow, the mother of his children, Adelaide del Vasto, who for over a decade exercised the function of *de facto* regent, a role that necessitated her suppression of a series of baronial revolts, especially on the mainland.

Roger's immediate heir was his elder son, Simon, who died in childhood. The knighting of his younger son, also Roger, in 1112, heralded the arrival of this boy's majority. Young, cosmopolitan, multilingual Count Roger II was well on his way to becoming an able ruler of Sicily. He was not yet a king, but his powers were formidable and, encouraged by his advisors, he was not afraid to use them.

Roger's first official acts were bold enough. In 1114, acting on the authority vested in him as Papal Legate, he deposed the Archbishop of Cosenza.

The widowed Adelaide crossed the Mediterranean to marry King Baldwin of Jerusalem, who was desperately in need of Norman funds and soldiers. As she was around thirty-six and might still bear another child, she stipulated that a hypothetical son should inherit the Hierosolymitan Crown. Unbeknownst to Adelaide, the wily Baldwin was already married to an estranged spouse he had confined to a convent. This bigamy resulted in an annulment of his union with Adelaide, but not the restitution of her entire dowry, of which Baldwin kept the gold. The queen dowager returned to Sicily humiliated if not broken-hearted. She died too young in 1118, but not before her son's marriage to Elvira, daughter of King Alfonso I of Castile. Adelaide was buried at the cathedral of Patti, where she rests.

Deposing an archbishop was easy enough. Roger's next task would test his mettle in a wider environment.

There was dissension among the Tunisians with whom the Sicilians had a trade treaty. This was rooted in a Zirid rivalry. The incumbent governor of Gabés was not kindly disposed to the trading monopoly the Normans had long ago conceded to the emir. Following a series of machinations, the Sicilians were banished from this lucrative market in 1118. Four years later, an Arab pirate fleet raided Nicotera on the Calabrian coast, killing, raping and enslaving the residents. These raiders were Almoravids from Morocco who, it seemed, had been encouraged by the Zirids, their allies in Tunisia, to harass the Normans. In 1123, Roger sent a fleet commanded by his best Byzantine admirals to Mahdia, occupying part of the coast and protecting trade. The island of Pantelleria, a useful outpost, became a permanent territory of Sicily where Siculo Arabic, similar to Maltese, was spoken until the eighteenth century.

At home, most of southern Italy was controlled by several

of Roger's Hauteville cousins. Like him, these were grandsons of Robert Guiscard. Prominent among these kin was William, Duke of Apulia and Calabria, with whom Roger had made peace in 1121. William's realm included most of Italy south of Rome. When William died without sons in 1127, Roger stepped forth as his legal heir. At Benevento, which remained a Papal city until 1861, Pope Honorius II assented to Roger's claims; a truculent faction of the Norman baronage was rather more reluctant but consented for lack of choice.

For the first time since the fall of the Roman Empire, almost half the Apennine Peninsula was united to Sicily, with Roger as the largest single landholder. There was more than enough land to carve out a new state.

By now, Elvira had given birth to three children: Roger in 1118, Tancred in 1119, Alfonso in 1121.

Rex Siciliae

The contentious Papal conclave of 1130 resulted in rival claimants to the See of Saint Peter, with Roger supporting Anacletus II over Innocent II. Anacletus conceded to Roger the one thing the Norman ruler did not yet possess: a crown.

Following baronial councils held at Salerno and Palermo for acclamation, Roger was crowned in the cathedral of Sicily's largest city on Christmas. The coronation of the first King of Sicily alongside Elvira, the realm's first Queen, was a lavish spectacle. By most accounts, and given Palermo's cultures and riches, its festivities may have been the most magnificent of medieval Europe until that time. Certain it is that they were different from others.

That day, on a feast celebrating the birth of Christ, the glory of Sicily was born, for the very word *regnum* connoted an idea that no aristocrat, no theocrat, no plutocrat could challenge. That day the islanders became Sicilians. The identity of a people was assured. New coinage reflected Roger's royal status, but also Sicily's new rank among European kingdoms. Not with indifference did rulers far and near gaze toward Sicily. Truly this was the birth of a nation.

Influenced by ancient monarchs and Byzantine imagery, Roger assumed as his royal symbol the gold lion *passant guardant*. Embroidered on his cloak, this motif later embellished the walls of the palatine chapel and the new cathedral, and it was adopted by England's Norman kings in the early days of heraldry.

Over the next few years, Elvira bore three more children. Adelaide and Henry died in infancy, William lived into adulthood.

Not everybody was impressed by Roger's elevation. Among the malcontents were a rival Pontiff, a Holy Roman Emperor and a score of disgruntled vassals.

Pope Innocent gained the support of Emperor Lothair III, who was preparing to march against Anacletus. Roger sent troops to defend his Papal ally, but for the moment he had to quell uprisings at Amalfi and in Apulia. Revolts of this kind followed for several years.

In early 1135, both Roger and Elvira fell ill. Elvira did not survive. Roger went into reclusion out of profound mourning, for so long that rumors spread that he was dead.

Roger didn't immediately remarry. Apart from the remorse he felt for Elvira, he had more immediate concerns.

Later in the year, Roger sent a naval expedition to Africa to occupy the strategic coastal island of Djerba, and by 1142 Mahdia was a protectorate of the Kingdom of Sicily.

In Spring 1137, Lothair finally entered southern Italy with his army and, with the help of some of Roger's disloyal vassals, made his way to Bari, occupying much territory along the way. But the German knights, having satisfied their feudal obligations, decided not to fight in the malarial Summer heat, so the expedition was called off. Lothair died crossing the Alps *en route* to his German lands in December, leaving his allies in Italy to combat Roger's troops; his death signalled the effective decline of his line of the Welf dynasty as Holy Roman Emperors, leaving the door open to the ambitious Hohenstaufens of Swabia.

The Papacy also underwent a change in rule when Anacletus died early in 1138. The next year, Innocent, now the uncontested Pontiff, invaded Roger's realm but was defeated and captured near Cassino, where, with the Treaty of Mignano, he recognized the rights and status of the King of Sicily. Except for a few isolated pockets of resistance, this ended the dissension. By the end of 1140, Roger's intrepid sons, Roger of Apulia and Alfonso of Capua, had annexed the Abruzzo region to the Kingdom of Sicily. King Louis VII of France now recognized Roger as sovereign of this extensive realm.

Only the irrational souls among us relish war. Enforcing the submission of insubordinate vassals and fending off intruders was a dirty business, albeit an intrinsic part of royal rule. Roger delegated as much of it as he could to his sons and to trusted courtiers like Robert of Selby. Naval expeditions were led by able admirals like Christodoulos, until around 1127, and then by the highly distinguished George of Antioch.

Law and Order

It was time to standardize the complex legal codes that governed life in the Kingdom of Sicily, from Salerno to Bari to Messina to Palermo.

Until now, the legal system, such as it was, reflected a hotchpotch of disparate codes, ranging from the feudal to the religious. Canon law, Maliki law, Halakha law. There was Justinian's *Codex Juris Civilis* but also the Lombards' *Codex Legum Longobardorum*. What was needed was a legal code that could be applied universally without undue complexity, in the process bolstering centralized government. For everybody.

Such were Roger's Assizes of Ariano, traditionally identified with the town of that name and thought to have been promulgated in 1140 or shortly afterward.[9] These statutes asserted royal power in a formal way, affirming the monarch's role as lawgiver. All subjects were equal in the eyes of the law, save for some exceptional feudal rights reserved to nobles. Various crimes were addressed, particularly violent ones. Arming a mob, thereby inciting riots, was a grave act. Bishops, like nobles, were accorded certain privileges. Among Christians, apostates and heretics lost their rights of citizenship.

Rape was explicitly outlawed, treason was made a capital offense, Jews were forbidden the holding of Christian serfs, jesters were prohibited from blaspheming, simony was made illegal, fugitives were permitted asylum in churches. Sentences for crimes against public officials were to be taken seriously, taking into account that these acts were, in effect, offenses to the Crown itself.

The forgery and theft of documents were unequivocally capital crimes. Counterfeiting or clipping coins was outlawed. The code required that knights, judges and notaries be descended from the nobility. Infringement of demesnial lands (royal estates) was outlawed. Marriage is required as the basis for legitimacy of heirs. Adultery and prostitution were addressed, ditto kidnapping and robbery. Licensing of physicians is established. Judges who accepted bribes could be executed.

Many of these principles were already known, some from the time of Justinian, but Roger made them the law of the land.

We know not the extent to which the new legal code was copied and distributed; no manuscripts are known to be preserved from the time of Roger's reign. Were the Assizes a contemporary document, or were they a later compendium based on decisions Roger is known to have made? We do not know.

In 1145, for example, Roger decreed that capital crimes such as murder were to be punished only on royal authority, never by a bishop or abbot. To permit otherwise, apart from any question of the king's prerogatives being infringed, would have meant clerics shedding blood. Nevertheless, it is clear that lesser officials occasionally meted out punishment, sometimes acting on the advice of justices, and so did barons.

Roger's justiciars were circuit judges responsible for specific regions or provinces where they would travel from town to town to hear cases.

It was at Ariano that Roger decreed the issuance of his *ducalis,* or *ducat,* the coin's name based on his *duchy* of Apulia.

Whenever they were formulated, the Assizes, and decrees adhering to their principles, clearly reflected a Latin theological orientation in the law. But Roger himself was amenable to hearing contrarian views, even those casting aspersions on Papal primacy. Around 1143, Nilos Doxopatrios, a *quondam* deacon of Saint Sophia in Constantinople who spent part of his later life in Sicily, authored a theological treatise supporting the Greek Church over the inexorable influences of the Roman Church: *The History of the Five Patriarchs.* Significantly, he made the case that Sicily belonged, by law and nature, in the Patriarchate of Constantinople. Did Roger perhaps plan to use this treatise as a tool in the event of a break with the Roman Pontiffs who so annoyed him? We shall never know.

Building a Kingdom

Not only was Roger building a kingdom, he was building castles and cathedrals. In Sicily there developed a distinctive style of syncretic Norman and Fatimid influences that has come to be called *Norman-Arab.* The style itself varied, and it often was embellished with Byzantine mosaic work. The cathedral at Cefalù, based on Caen's Saint Etienne, was very different from Monreale's abbey. Palermo's Greek Orthodox Martorana differed from Roman Catholic San Cataldo next to it. The palaces known as the Zisa and the Cuba were part of this trend; so was the Norman Palace. Sicily is dotted with churches and palaces built in this style.

This ambitious building program took money. It was said that the tax revenue of Palermo exceeded that of the entire Kingdom of England. This was no small boast considering England's prosperity during the twelfth century.

Another impressive sight was the vast park to the south of the palace, praised by visitors who had seen many wonders of the Arab world. *Gennàt al-àrd,* pronounced *Genoard* by the Normans, meant "Paradise on Earth" in Arabic. This was the name of the extensive park and hunting ground that Roger had Arab architects create for him. Extending across the capital's vast fluvial valley and beyond Monreale, Baida, Molara and Altofonte to the rugged mountains encircling the city, it was a marvel of Europe. Although its lakes and rivers are gone, along with most of its woods, a few of its palaces and pavilions survive amidst Palermo's modern urban sprawl.

To trace a path through what was a broad, central swathe of the Genoard and the royal hunting grounds beyond, one need only follow what is now Corso Calatafimi from Piazza Indipendenza toward Monreale. The park extended to an area near what is now the Viale Regione Siciliana motorway. This is where the hunting grounds began. (The map at the beginning of this book shows the park, kanats and former courses of the rivers; modern streets are indicated for reference.)

Long before the park existed, the countryside in the Valley of Palermo, surrounded by its natural amphitheatre made up of hills and mountains, was a miracle of flora and fauna, thanks to its fertile soil, rivers and springs. Beginning in the ninth century, long before the Norman conquest, the Arabs introduced new irrigational and agricultural techniques here, where they planted citrus groves, earning the valley its nickname *Conca d'Oro,* meaning "Golden Conch."

Indigo and henna were cultivated.

With its canals and *norias* (water wheels), the valley was so well irrigated that it was even possible to grow rice. Though rice has not been cultivated in Sicily for many centuries, this culinary tradition survives in *arancini,* or rice balls.

There were both common and exotic plants, bushes, and trees such as palms, plane trees (sycamores), citrus (oranges, lemons, citrons), almond, pistachio, chestnuts and walnuts, wild olive and fig trees, medlar trees, myrtle and laurel. There was also papyrus and sugarcane growing along the streams and the two rivers — the *Kemonia* and the suitably-named *Papyrus* or *Papireto.* The scent of jasmine and orange blossoms was everywhere.

While the precise extent of the Genoard park is unknown today, we do know that it embraced a series of streams and *kanats* (canals) linked to the palaces built in the valley for both emirs and kings, extending from the base of the mountain crowned by Monreale. It should be remembered that Monreale during the twelfth and thirteenth centuries was little more than a small hamlet built around an abbey.

Though the oldest of the Fatimid palaces was several miles east of the Genoard, it is worth mentioning because it was the inspiration for palaces constructed later. The *Favara,* also known as *Maredolce* in what is now the unsightly Brancaccio district of Palermo, was built by Ja'far, the Emir of Bal'harm, at the end of the tenth century. Its name derives from the two freshwater springs, *fawwàra* in Arabic, that supplied water to the area, flowing down from nearby Mount Grifone into the Oreto River. These natural springs permitted the emir's guests to luxuriate in a verdant park and bathe in a small lake.

Apart from a few Punic necropoli in the area, the oldest structure in the Genoard proper was the *Scibene* palace, probably contemporary to the *Favara* and predating the arrival of the Normans in Sicily.

Many descriptions of Roger's Sicilian paradise come to us from Abu Abd Allah Abdullah Mohammed ibn Mohammed ibn Ash Sharif al Idrisi (or Edrisi), who was living in Sicily by 1145 and became the court geographer. Descended through a long line of distinguished and aristocratic personages from the Prophet Mohammed, Idrisi seems to have spent his youth in Sabtah, now Ceuta (in Morocco), but he may have been born in Sicily, where his family had commercial interests. Regardless of his birthplace, Idrisi was not insignificant in the story of Norman Sicily.

His famous planisphere, a large global map made of precious metal (mostly silver), did not survive the twelfth century, but it is known to have been a noteworthy work of geography — probably the most accurate map of Europe, north Africa and western Asia created during the Middle Ages. An atlas produced during this period survived, and has been published in Germany and Iraq. A multilingual *Book of Simple Drugs* is also known to us.

Idrisi's greatest surviving work is, without doubt, his "Pleasure Excursion of One Eager to Traverse the World's Regions," better known as the *Book of Roger*. The book provides much information about Sicily's economy. In a casual observation, Idrisi mentions the making of spaghetti in Trabia. Some of the book's statements were unorthodox for their time, things like "the earth is round like a sphere." Today, the *Book of Roger* is considered one of the most important scientific works of the High Middle Ages.

Idrisi wasn't the only scholar accommodated at Roger's court. Many scientists, philosophers, mathematicians and geographers, particularly from Arab lands, arrived at Palermo. Roger could converse with them in Latin, Greek, Arabic or Norman French. What made this environment unique was that the scholars present were treated as peers, not as exotic visitors. Ptolemy's *Almagest* was translated at the Sicilian court.

Most Europeans who arrived in the *Regnum* during the twelfth century, at least those whose names are known to us, seem to have been clerics like John of Lincoln, Richard of Hereford, Herbert of Middlesex and William of Poitou. There were many from Italy.

Politics

It is said that England's sovereign reigns but does not rule. In the twelfth century, the constitutions that spawned such a reality could barely be imagined. The day-to-day duties of kings like Roger involved all manner of activities, some abhorrently unpleasant. Whoever suggested that the life of a king was a life of leisure must not have had medieval monarchs in mind.

Pope Innocent II died in 1143. His successor, Celestine II, who had long resented the Normans' power, refused to ratify the Treaty of Mignano by which Innocent had recognized Roger as King of Sicily four years earlier. Roger dispatched his English-born chancellor Robert of Selby, effectively his viceroy in peninsular Italy, to handle the matter. Selby did so by attacking Benevento, a Papal enclave surrounded by royal territory. Celestine was brought to heel, and anyway he died in March of the following year, but his successor, Lucius II, was not much more *simpatico,* and conflict continued.

"In peace sons bury their fathers but in war fathers bury their sons," said Herodotus. Roger's son, Alfonso, Prince of Capua, was killed in October 1144 during a skirmish connected with an incursion into Papal territory. This must have been a terrible blow to the king, and to Selby, who had been something of a mentor to the young Hauteville princes.

Robert of Selby was not the only Englishman in royal service in Sicily. One of his young charges was Thomas le Brun, or Brown, who became master of the royal *diwan* during Roger's reign. To the Arabs he was *Qaid* Brun.

Emperor Lothair's failed invasion of southern Italy had never been forgotten by his successors or by the Byzantines who had supported the German expedition. In a typically political matrimonial match, Manuel Comnenus of Constantinople wed Bertha (later Irene), sister-in-law of Conrad III Hohenstaufen of Germany. Conrad was never crowned Holy Roman Emperor, but with Manuel he contemplated an invasion of southern Italy.

Roger's forces captured Tripoli in 1146 and occupied Corfu the next year. The former conquest assured his control of the central Mediterranean, effectively dividing the Sea into east and west; the latter was essentially a strategic move to protect the eastern flanks of the Sicilian kingdom. A combined German, Byzantine and Venetian fleet repulsed the Sicilians in 1148 and Manuel repossessed Corfu the following year.

Manuel did not abandon his designs on Italy, but they would have to wait. A raid of Constantinople by the Sicilian fleet commanded by George of Antioch served to warn the Byzantines of Roger's naval power. The Sicilians even stole some fruit from the imperial gardens.

That Roger did not send troops on the Second Crusade in 1147 may be explained by several simple realities. Personally, he may not have been very kindly disposed toward the Kingdom of Jerusalem since the matrimonial fiasco involving his mother, Adelaide. Politically, in view of so many of his subjects being Muslims, he was reluctant to wage a "religious" war against the proponents of Islam. If Roger did not speak openly against the Crusade, it was only because this adventure occupied German troops that otherwise might attack his *Regnum*.

At home, the Sicilian Muslims were now being encouraged to convert to Christianity, and their numbers were slowly but steadily dwindling. At the same time, many lands on which the newly Christianized Arabs found themselves became manorial, controlled by Norman or Lombard barons, and serfdom sometimes resulted.

The times were changing. By now, most of the churches and monasteries in Sicily were Catholic rather than Orthodox. As the liturgical language, and the language of learning among the Catholics, who were now clearly in the majority, was Latin, this influenced the ever-evolving vernacular. Medieval Sicilian was a Romance tongue based on Latin, but it bore the marks of Arabic, Greek and French, among other influences; it was more musical, and altogether more pleasing to the ear, than the quasi-Catalan, guttural Modern Sicilian that emerged from this polyglot potpourri a few centuries later.

The death of Roger's eldest son, Roger of Apulia, in 1148, left the king with only one lawful male heir, William. In 1149, Roger took as his second wife Sybil of Burgundy, but this happy event could not diminish the magnitude of the challenges he faced.

Returning from their expedition, Roger's fleet attacked some Byzantine vessels, and a few French ships returning from the Crusade became embroiled in the battle. King Louis VII was traveling on one of these ships, and the Sicilians escorted him to Calabria. The two kings met at Potenza for a few days.

The next year, Roger, the consummate politician, met with Pope Eugenius III in an effort at negotiating a number of issues. He had supported the Pontiff against a popular movement among the Romans to make the city into a commune like those in northern Italy. Nevertheless, relations with the Pope, who cultivated a rapport with Roger's adversary Conrad III, left much to be desired.

After Sybil died giving birth, Roger wed Beatrice of Rethel. William married Margaret, daughter of Garcia IV Ramirez, King of Navarre.

In 1151, Roger crowned William as *Rex Filius,* thus leaving no doubts about the succession.

Conrad III died early the following year amidst plans to

march on the Kingdom of Sicily with Byzantine and Venetian support. Conrad's successor, his nephew Frederick "Barbarossa," assented to Pope Eugenius' request to make peace with the southern kingdom only with Papal approval. This was to prove troublesome. Pope Eugenius died in 1152.

By then, the remarkable admiral George of Antioch was also dead. Among his visible testaments are the splendid Martorana church he built for the Greek community of Palermo and the arched "Admiral's Bridge" in the same city. Christians still worship at the church, water no longer flows under the bridge.

Sicily's social fabric grew ever more complex, which is to say intolerant, and it seems that Antioch's successor, a certain Philip of Mahdia, secretly converted to Islam and was executed for this apostasy. The episode, if true, speaks poorly of the sunny kingdom.

Occupying a chunk of northern Africa was certainly advantageous to Sicily's economy. Instead of trade agreements with the Zirids, there was now direct control over Tunisian commerce.

In the Middle Ages, war was not a choice but a way of life. Roger sought to avoid it when he could, so long as doing so would not be construed by his adversaries as a sign of weakness. There is no evidence that Roger knew of Sun Tzu, but he seems to have believed in his dictum that "the supreme art of war is to subdue the enemy without fighting."

When Roger died in 1154, his wife, Beatrice, was with child. A daughter, Constance, was born a few months later.

Much has been written about Roger's reign, most of it good. He found a county, and founded a country.

King William I

William, who succeeded Roger, inherited a throne and a crown and some of his father's intellect. Into early adulthood, he did not expect to rule, but his three elder brothers predeceased him.

Thomas le Brun was removed from his position as master (administrator) of the *diwan,* probably at the urging of William's new admiral, Maio of Bari. Brun returned to his native England, where he became almoner to King Henry II and sought to popularize the acceptance of Hindi-Arabic numerals. It is has been suggested that he may have introduced some Maliki principles into English common law.[10]

Greatly esteemed by William, Maio had been appointed chancellor following the death of Robert of Selby two years earlier. He worked to centralize the function of government, something which sometimes involved curtailing feudal privileges. These efforts did not earn him the unstinting amity of the baronage.

Though raised in a Byzantine Greek family, Maio was a great advocate of Catholicism, erecting the austere church of San Cataldo next to the Martorana built by George of Antioch. He also encouraged immigration from Norman Europe; this brought Englishman Richard Palmer to Sicily as Bishop of Syracuse.

In 1154 another Englishman, Nicholas Breakspear, was elected Pope as Adrian IV, succeeding Anastasius IV who died just seventeen months into his pontificate. Adrian may have been born the subject of a Norman King of England, but he was to continue the established Papal policy toward the Normans of Sicily. First, he sought to quell the continuing revolts in Rome by a populace that was clamoring for independence of government; his uninspired solution was to place the entire Eternal City under interdict.

The same year, Frederick Barbarossa marched to Rome with a German army, suppressing the revolt. He was crowned Holy Roman Emperor in June 1155, and the riots resumed. The heat of Summer was oppressive. Abandoning his plans for a march southward to attack Salerno, Barbarossa returned to Germany, although he did not forget about the Kingdom of Sicily. This forced Adrian to make a truce with William.

Envious, underhanded Robert of Bassonville — a first cousin of William as the son of Roger's sister Judith — was less willing to do so. Here the Italian saying *parenti serpenti*, "kin are snakes," seems to have rung true. In late Summer, Robert joined up with Michael Palaeologus, a general in the service of Manuel Comnenus, and laid siege to Bari, one of the wealthiest cities in the kingdom and a hotbed of discontent with rule from Palermo. The two managed to occupy a number of smaller localities as well.

Michael was joined in this invasion by, of all people, Pope Adrian, who seemed willing to support the "schismatic" Byzantines when it suited him. Simultaneous risings in Sicily, where William was ill, further complicated the situation. Things looked dire indeed.

In the Spring of 1156, William led an army onto the mainland, shadowed by a formidable fleet. Hearing of William's advance, Robert fled; his ally Michael was already dead. Neither was present to see the annihilation of their troops remaining in Apulia. Bari was ruthlessly attacked and, after the Bariots were given time to evacuate, the city was essentially destroyed save for its chief churches. William then marched to Benevento where he met Adrian. Short and slight, history's only English Pope signed a formal treaty fully recognizing the King of Sicily. Present was Matthew of Aiello, who was being groomed to succeed Maio of Bari.

On the economic front, the Genoans were given special tax advantages in a trade agreement covering such products as wheat, cotton and skins.

Adrian died in 1159, succeeded by two rival claimants, one supporting Frederick Hohenstaufen, Holy Roman Emperor, and the other supporting William Hauteville, King of Sicily

— neither very enthusiastically. In view of recent events in Apulia, Barbarossa, however grudgingly, was beginning to respect his Sicilian counterpart.

By this time, William's interest in the affairs of the kingdom was desultory. These matters he left largely to Maio. Margaret, his wife, is described as a woman of great beauty, but William, like his father, kept a "harem" of concubines — officially these may have been silk weavers — in the palace. Nevertheless, the queen had a strong personality she inherited from her ancestor, *El Cid,* and on several occasions she was the motivating force behind William finally taking action in important matters, as he was too often slow and passive in taking decisions.

The next year, northern Africa was lost following a long series of revolts rooted, it must be said, in William's failure to respond adequately. Certain barons despised Maio more than ever, perhaps more for his domestic policy regarding Sicily's Muslims than for the loss of Tunisia.

Close to the capital, the greatest detractor was Matthew Bonellus, lord of Caccamo, who began to foment a conspiracy and who, it so happened, had asked for the hand of Maio's daughter.

In November 1160, the hated Maio was killed by Matthew Bonellus in Palermo. At first, considering Bonellus' popularity among the nobility, William was compelled to grant him a pardon. But the sovereign became irritated with Matthew's arrogance, and he eventually moved against the insolent baron just in time, for Matthew had fallen under the pressure of other conspirators to plan killing the king.

In this attempted regicide, Bonellus conspired with two close relatives of the king himself: his half-brother Simon (an illegitimate son of Roger II), who had been divested by William of the lucrative princedom of Taranto, and his nephew, Tancred of Lecce (illegitimate son of William's deceased brother Roger of Apulia), who had been thrown into the palace dungeons after an earlier revolt against the Crown.

Following much planning, Matthew and his wily accomplices bribed their way into the Norman Palace for a *coup d'état*. This seemed easy enough with the support of Simon and Tancred, who knew the palace well. Margaret and two of her sons were made prisoners in her private apartments, while the rebels started plundering the palace and killing helpless servants, including the king's concubines, who were violated and slaughtered in the palace harem.

Idrisi's planisphere was stolen during the looting and probably melted for its metal. The carnage spilled out into the streets; it led to the killing of many innocent people, but especially Muslim-Arab merchants, coin-minters and silk-weavers, and this brought on an angry response among the citizens of Palermo who sided with the king.

Within a few days, the king and his men were able to put an end to the rebellion, which had borne the ugly mark of bigotry directed at the city's Muslims, but not before William lost his son and heir, little nine year-old Roger, who had been struck by a stray arrow. A few months later, Bonellus was arrested, mutilated and cast into the dungeons where he died soon afterward. Politics begets metamorphosis, and the pompous baron spent his last days as a moribund pariah.

Now William put his kingdom into the hands of three men who formed a kind of triumvirate: Richard Palmer, who would later become Bishop of Syracuse, a certain *Qaid* Peter, a Christian Arab who became palatine chamberlain, and Matthew Aiello, who had been groomed as Maio's successor.

In 1166, William died of dysentery at the age of forty-six. Modern historians, perhaps overzealously, took to calling him *William the Bad*, sparing no effort to enumerate his supposed shortcomings. He is not remembered as a good king, for he often lacked confidence in his own power and capabilities to rule the kingdom he inherited.

Queen Margaret

It must have come as a surprise to the Sicilians when, as regent, Margaret began making decisions immediately after the king's death, despite the triumvirate's doubts about a woman effectively ruling in place of her twelve year-old son, the future William II.

The first thing Margaret did, right after her young son was crowned, was to declare a general amnesty and to abolish the collection of "redemption money" which was supposed to have been paid by the more obstreperous towns of the Kingdom of Sicily. She harbored serious doubts about the ruling triumvirate, and she felt it important that she and her son not be too closely associated with them in the public mind as they represented the previous rule of her husband.

She took under her protection some members of Thomas Becket's family who made their way to the Sicilian court during the exile of this Archbishop of Canterbury. This humanitarian gesture did not imply an overt endorsement of Becket's views. The stance of Henry II regarding Papal authority in England was not very unlike that of Roger II and the late William in Sicily. The Apostolic Legateship gave the Hautevilles more ecclesiastical power than the Papacy ever conceded to Henry.

In the beginning, Margaret gave full power to but a single member of the triumvirate, *Qaid* Peter, who of the three was the one furthest from the local aristocracy. At first, it seemed like a good choice, but soon the kingdom started to fall out of control, and Peter fled to Tunisia where he was said to have converted back to the Islam of his youth. Out in the streets, people spoke against Margaret.

After such a blow, the Queen had an even more difficult choice to make, but in the end she replaced the triumvirate, not with the most likely candidates chosen from the Sicilian nobility, nor from men of the Church who hovered around the court, and not with her half-brother Rodrigo who had recently arrived in Palermo, or her cousin Gilbert who she could not trust, but with a young cousin of hers, Stephen du Perche.

Upon arriving in Palermo, Stephen did not seem to harbor any ambitions of running the kingdom. He had just finished preparing to leave for the Holy Land and had with him a retinue of thirty-seven French soldiers. Before leaving on Crusade, together with his men he decided to come visit Margaret.

The queen persuaded him to stay, and she appointed him chancellor in November 1166. This decision did not fare well with the local nobility. It seemed to them that the court was becoming more and more foreign, especially because, besides his original French entourage, a number of Frenchmen were invited by Stephen to move to Sicily and they were granted manors on the island.

At least in the beginning, Margaret probably believed she had made a wise choice with the new chancellor. Stephen revealed himself as something of a reformer. But there were external problems. Sensing a lack of strong leadership, Frederick Barbarossa invaded the kingdom's northern marches, stopped only by a plague that hit his army during the hot month of August 1167. Summer always seemed to spell the undoing of German armies.

Margaret chose Stephen as the new Archbishop of Palermo and had him anointed just a few days after he had been ordained. Now even Matthew Aiello made no secret of despising him, and Stephen suspected everybody except his French entourage of continuously plotting against him.

He eventually unmasked and arrested some of the conspirators, but such extreme violence erupted in the streets of Palermo that Stephen was constrained to leave.

Before long, a council was constituted without Margaret's assent. It included nobles such as Richard of Molise, clerics like Richard Palmer, and Walter "Offamilias," who was soon to take the place of Stephen as Archbishop of Palermo. Matthew Aiello, who had briefly been imprisoned for his part in the conspiracy against Stephen, returned to a post in government.

Stephen was gone, but Margaret's Navarrese countryman, Benjamin of Tudela, paid a call at court toward the end of a long voyage. His description of Palermo is detailed and picturesque. A Jew, Tudela provides an informal "census" of Sicily's Jewish population, mentioning, for example, that there were only around two hundred Jewish families in Messina when he visited. His account is the primary historical and statistical record of the Jews of the Mediterranean in the twelfth century.

Estimates vary widely, but Palermo may have had as many as 120,000 residents when Tudela visited.

King William II

In 1171, William came of age and was finally able to rule. He was fluent in several languages, including Arabic. We know little about the king's youth. Bin Jubayr, who we shall meet shortly, recounted the story of the boy responding to an earthquake in 1169, consoling his subjects each to pray to his own God. Even if apocryphal, this story indicates William's kind disposition to Muslims and Jews as well as Christians in the lands he ruled.

The earthquake was extremely destructive. Falcandus reports that "at the prosperous city of Catania not a single house in the town center was left standing," *Cathaniensium opulentissima civitas usque adeo subversa est, ut ne una quidem domus in urbe superstes remanserit*. Fifteen thousand were killed in that city alone. The castle of Lentini collapsed, along with many around Syracuse and Catania, so great was the force. Observers in Taormina said they could see the summit of Mount Etna sink noticeably.

William's rapport with episcopal power was rather complex; for example, in a charter of 1172 he conceded to the Archbishop of Palermo the right to try adulterers, at least to the extent that these trials and penalties were not at variance with civil law.[11]

The young king's first major international act was a response, in 1174, to Amalric, King of Jerusalem, to send a large naval expedition to Alexandria in support of some rebels expected to rise against the city's leaders. The expedition was led by none other than William's cousin Tancred of Lecce, who had conspired with Bonellus years earlier. Its principal objective was to factionalize the Muslims threatening Jerusalem. Unfortunately, the revolt in Alexandria never occurred, the rebels' conspiracy having been discovered, and Amalric died two weeks before the Sicilian contingent arrived, so there were no troops from Jerusalem to reinforce them. William's fleet prudently withdrew, but many knights were taken prisoner by the valiant Saladin, whose Ayyubids had recently seized power from the ruling Fatimids.

Domestically, the young king's initial step was to demonstrate his independence while challenging the growing influence of Walter Offamilias. This he hoped to achieve with construction of hilltop Monreale Abbey, where a mosaic shows him accepting his crown directly from Christ (in imitation of the mosaic icon of his grandfather in the Martorana), and where a mosaic icon of Thomas Becket, murdered in 1170, is the earliest public holy image of the English saint. Erection of this great cathedral and monastery, and establishment of its diocese just a few miles from Palermo, was more than a gesture. It was meant to signal to the world that the young man was now a sovereign willing to exercise his authority.

Who would William marry? Frederick Barbarossa offered the hand of one of his daughters, but the Papacy refused to countenance a dynastic marriage that could potentially unite two powerful kingdoms, one to its north and the other to the immediate south. In 1177, William married the young Joan (or Joanna) of England, daughter of King Henry II. She may have given birth to a son, Bohemond, around 1182. Margaret, William's mother, died in 1183.

The death of the Pope who refused to permit William to marry Barbarossa's daughter cleared the way for another union. So it was that a marriage was arranged between Barbarossa's son, Henry Hohenstaufen, and Constance Hauteville, the posthumous daughter of Roger II. This seems to have been opposed on political grounds by Matthew Aiello, who feared for the royal succession, but after some delay the wedding took place in Milan early in 1186. Unfortunately, Constance's mother, Beatrice, the widow of Roger II, did not live to see it.

With her lavish dowry, Constance was the wealthiest bride of her era, but she was also exceptionally intelligent and politically savvy. Now in her early thirties, she was a decade older than her husband.

There was plenty of activity in Sicily to keep William busy.

In December 1184, the Muslim traveler bin Jubayr was shipwrecked near Messina. He was given hospitality by William and has left us an impressive description of northern Sicily, from Messina to Trapani. Said Jubayr of Palermo: "It is a wonderful place, built in the Cordoba style, entirely from cut limestone. A river divides the town, and four springs gush in its suburbs. The Christian women of this city follow the fashion of Muslim women, are fluent of speech, wrap their cloaks about them, and are veiled."

He also described the Martorana church, and specifically its bell tower, which was then higher than it is now. He observed that Messina was predominantly Greek Orthodox, with a dwindling Muslim community. Some of his comments are cryptic. He mentions a tax on Muslims, without making clear whether this tax was also levied upon Christians and Jews.

It is clear from his writings that Jubayr was devout in his Sunni faith, even something of a dogmatist. But the winds of religious intolerance were gathering force, and perhaps that is what he inferred from what he saw in Sicily, where he might have hoped to see more Muslims. His narrative is a link in a chain; Mohammed ibn Hawqal, a merchant from Baghdad with a penchant for geography, described an Arab-Byzantine Sicily in the time long before Idrisi and Jubayr, and a capital just as prosperous.

As Jubayr was leaving Sicily, a military fleet was preparing to embark. Alexius Comnenus, a claimant to the Byzantine throne (a nephew of Manuel Comnenus who had died in 1180) had gone to Sicily to ask William for assistance in conquering Constantinople. The offer was too tempting to resist.

Consisting of over two hundred vessels carrying tens of thousands of men, the fleet sailed in the middle of June 1185 from Messina to the Adriatic port of Durres (Durazzo), a western outpost of the Byzantine Empire in what is now Albania. This expedition, like the one in 1174, was led by Tancred of Lecce, this time accompanied by a general named Baldwin, of which little is known. It was not the first Norman attack on the Byzantine city. Robert Guiscard had been there a century earlier.

Two weeks after William's fleet set sail, Durres surrendered. In early August, having marched across the Balkan lands, the Sicilians laid siege to Thessalonika in an attack by land and sea. What followed was utter destruction and the killing of some five thousand civilians. The atrocities were legion. The Sicilian army then made it as far as Mosynopolis, within striking distance of Constantinople.

Isaac II Angelus, who had very recently ascended the Byzantine Throne, stopped the Sicilian advance and took Baldwin prisoner. Many knights made their way back to Durres.

They lived to fight another day. Having reached Constantinople, Tancred's fleet did not attempt a serious attack of the city and returned to Sicily. Eventually, Isaac Angelus agreed to a treaty but a certain bitterness remained in his soul; in view of Ayyubid threats in the eastern Mediterranean, it seemed absurd that a Christian ruler would embroil himself in a war of aggression resulting in the deaths of so many Greeks.

The Kingdom of Sicily never lacked for fine admirals, and Margaritus of Brindisi, who would prove a staunch ally of Tancred, soon occupied Cyprus, but in late 1187 he was recalled to Sicily for a more important mission.

Saladin's forces had successfully attacked the heart of the Kingdom of Jerusalem, leaving most of it under Ayyubid control. Consisting of sixty vessels and some two hundred knights, the Sicilian fleet commanded by the intrepid Margaritus set sail as soon as it could. At first, it patrolled the coasts, impeding Saladin's occupation of vital ports. In July of the following year, the arrival of the Sicilian fleet at Levantine Tripoli, its knights ready for an eastward incursion, induced Saladin to lift his siege of the fortress of the Hospitallers, Krak des Chevaliers. It is not with hyperbole that one states that Margaritus was the only serious opposition to Saladin in the aftermath of Jerusalem's fall.

William's untimely death in November 1189 brought an end to it. Remembered as *William the Good,* he left the world no surviving, legitimate male heirs. Indeed, there were very few Hautevilles left.

Inheritance

As a male, Tancred of Lecce might have seemed the obvious choice to succeed the young king. Though born outside marriage, Tancred was a Hauteville and, despite his obvious moral lapse in having chosen, decades earlier, to conspire with Bonellus, he had proven himself a competent leader, perhaps even a loyal one. Pope Celestine III immediately recognized him as King of Sicily, even though the available evidence suggests that William himself had designated Constance, his aunt, the posthumous but undoubtedly legitimate daughter of Roger II, as his successor.

Another figure frequently mentioned in this *mélange* is Roger of Andria, an official of rank on the mainland; whether he bore Hauteville blood is uncertain, but he stirred up some dissension on the peninsula by enlisting German military support. Politically, these incursions were little more than a nuisance, and the king's forces soon captured and executed Roger.

Tancred had problems of his own nearer to home. The first was a Muslim insurrection involving tens of thousands of disgruntled subjects in western Sicily. Dragging on for months, the suppression of this uprising led to countless deaths.

The death of her father-in-law, Frederick Barbarossa, in June 1190 during the Third Crusade, left Constance's husband, Henry, as the ruler of a large chunk of central Europe extending into northern Italy. In Rome the next year, he was crowned Holy Roman Emperor as Henry VI by Celestine, who probably hoped that the question of the Sicilian succession was thereby resolved.

It was not.

If Henry and Constance wanted the Kingdom of Sicily, they would have to launch a full-scale invasion. Their immediate problem was money.

Queens and Kings

One of Constance's most vocal supporters in Sicily was Joan of England, now queen dowager as the widow of William II. Fearing her influence among the nobility, Tancred placed Joan under house arrest to restrict her movements. He also purloined her feudal revenue from the County of Mount

Sant'Angelo she had received at marriage.

These facts did not set well with Joan's brother, Richard "Lionheart," at thirty-three now King of England and making his way to the Levant for the Third Crusade. From Salerno, Richard made it known that he wanted his sister freed and her revenues restored immediately. Furthermore, he wanted her to be provided with the golden throne which he believed to be her right as a Norman queen. Most importantly, he wanted the funds promised by the late William II for this Crusade. His threats were not idle ones; his army probably could have defeated Tancred's, and Lionheart may have had his own designs on Sicily. Richard indicated that he would not leave Tancred's territory until his demands were met. Arriving at Messina in September 1190 to rendezvous with his fellow crusader King Philip II "Augustus" of France, he ordered his troops to construct a fort of timbers on a hill overlooking the city where he would be staying for several months.

Tancred soon released Joan and compensated her for her losses. Richard took his sister to a monastery in Calabria for safety. However, Tancred did not immediately accede to Richard's other demands. Weeks passed. Messina became an occupied city, in fact if not in name.

At length, the Messinians grew annoyed at things like the English knights' overtly lustful treatment of the local women and their seizure of church property. A popular revolt ensued. In response, the English looted and vandalized the city. Tancred, in nearby Catania, could do nothing to stop the violent riots, although Richard finally restored order.

Meeting *en famille* at Catania, Tancred and Richard made peace, while Joan was paid for Mount Sant'Angelo. Before leaving Messina, Richard and Philip had recognized Tancred as King of Sicily. This agreement was opportune. Tancred's dynastic position was nothing if not tenuous, and a good rapport with the English and French kings might prove effective in curbing the ambitions of Constance and her German husband, keenly watching Sicilian events from afar.

In April, Eleanor of Aquitaine, mother of Joan and Richard, arrived at Messina with Berengaria of Navarre, Richard's betrothed. Eleanor had last called on Roger II at Palermo forty-four years earlier while returning from a pilgrimage (actually a crusade) to the Holy Land. Now sixty-nine, she visited Sicily briefly before returning to England. Joan left with Berengaria to visit Palestine, followed by Richard.

In Summer 1192, Tancred crowned his eighteen year-old son *Rex Filius* as Roger III. Unfortunately, Roger predeceased his father.

In Palestine, meanwhile, Richard proposed that his sister marry Saladin's brother, an idea which was soon cast aside. In December 1192, returning from the Levant, Joan and Berengaria — now Queen of England — visited Palermo to be received *en fête* with a properly royal reception from Tancred and his wife, Sibylla. Past acrimonies, if indeed they were ever very serious, had been set aside. The two young queens then set off to France and England. Joan preferred France, where she wed Raymond VI, Count of Toulouse.

His support of Tancred did not endear Richard to Henry, who would not forget this affront. Indeed, Lionheart's arrogance frequently earned him the antipathy of fellow monarchs. One such incident would come back to haunt him upon his return from the Holy Land, with the unintended consequence of sealing the fate of Sicily.

Leopold of Austria, a friend of Henry, was insulted by Richard during the Crusade and harbored a grudge. Travelling through Leopold's lands during his tortuous return to England, Lionheart was captured and imprisoned. Indeed, it seemed that God had delivered Richard into Leopold's hands.

Henry, meanwhile, had been trying to raise money and a powerful army so that he could conquer southern Italy and

Sicily and take the kingdom that he believed his by right of his wife.

A stroke of fortune fell upon Henry when Leopold consigned him his royal prisoner. No friend of Richard, Henry kept the English monarch in Trifels Castle from the end of 1193 until early February of 1194 when — ignoring excommunication by Pope Celestine for imprisoning a crusader — he managed to exact a ransom of 150,000 silver marks, an enormous sum for that era. The money was remitted to Henry personally by Eleanor of Aquitaine.

With this treasure, Henry raised the army needed for his southern conquest. Tancred's death in February 1194 paved the way for the Holy Roman Emperor to enforce his claim on the principle of *jure uxoris,* by right of his wife, to the Kingdom of Sicily. The only contestation came from an old man in Rome.

Events made this dynastic segue to Hohenstaufen rule more facile than it otherwise might have been. As Tancred's elder son, usually referred to as "Roger III," predeceased his father, there was no rallying point for the nobility except, in theory, his younger son, *William III,* still a boy. All but absent from the annals of history, this young William was probably assassinated by 1198. Whatever his fate, the two last Hautevilles are little more than a *coda* to their dynasty's history, lost among the mediocre afterthoughts that wallow in the looming shadow of greatness.

Only Roger II stands out among the men of the Hauteville dynasty who ruled the Kingdom of Sicily.

Destiny smiled upon him, and so did the chronicles of history.

CHAPTER 5

The Swabians

"Our purpose is to present the facts as we find them."

— Frederick II, *De Arte Venandi cum Avibus*

Henry Hohenstaufen was crowned King of Sicily in Palermo Cathedral on Christmas in 1194. The following day, in Jesi, outside Ancona, the previously childless Constance gave birth, at forty-one, to a red-haired son christened Frederick Roger. Although Henry could not be present, numerous witnesses were, making Constance's delivery one of the most crowded in history. Considering her age, the witnesses were deemed necessary to ensure that the heir was actually her child.

The couple was reunited on Easter in Bari where Constance was crowned Queen Regnant of Sicily, a position which was to be unique in the island's history. This coronation was no banal formality, for it confirmed Henry's right to rule the *Regnum*. It made his young son the heir to nearly half of western Europe.

The Emperor now found himself the ruler of most of the regions from Saxony to Sicily. The only part of Italy beyond his control was the Papal State.

The Pope and other sovereigns found the new situation disturbing — indeed overtly threatening.

Like Sicily's first Germanic occupiers, the Vandals and Goths, the Swabians initially left the existing social infrastructure undisturbed. Unlike them, they considered themselves part of the society they found, for their Empress was born a Sicilian princess and raised in Sicily.

There were significant differences in government between Sicily and the Imperial lands to the north, where factionalism was rife and the Emperor's power was often contested. In northern Italy's communes, for example, a bitter rivalry emerged between two parties. The *Guelphs* ("Welfs") supported the Pope, and later the Angevins as well. The *Ghibellines,* whose Italianized name was taken from that of the Hohenstaufen fortress of Waiblingen, supported the Emperor and the House of Hohenstaufen. This undercurrent shaped Imperial politics in northern Italy for decades, and one day it would decide the destiny of Sicily. In the event, Sicily's Swabian era was not to be a long one, but it left a great legacy of law and literature.[12]

Sicily never became part of the Holy Roman Empire, or indeed part of any other state (through annexation), until the nineteenth century. The simplest way to express this is that Henry bore the Crown of Sicily, as well as others, much as somebody might own two different houses in different cities, or keep two fine steeds in separate pastures. In our times, a similar situation exists in Canada, Australia and New Zealand, where the British monarch is the hereditary head of state while also reigning as sovereign of the United Kingdom.

Henry VI

His wife may have been the daughter of a Sicilian king, but the Sicilian barons did not welcome Henry and his suite of German knights and retainers very warmly; the typical Sicilian vassal's opinion of his new monarch was ambivalent at best.

Seldom indulgent of potential foes, Henry installed several

commanderies of the nascent Teutonic Order of knights in Sicily, appropriating for them Palermo's Magione church and constructing for them the Church of Saint Mary of the Germans in Messina, the latter being the earliest Sicilian example of Romanesque Gothic ecclesiastical architecture. The military support of these German knights could be relied upon in the event of challenges to Hohenstaufen authority by the restless Norman baronage.

When she arrived in Palermo in June 1195, Constance found that her husband had depleted the royal treasury. While Henry was away in Germany addressing a series of internal disputes and seeking to consolidate his son's position, Constance tried diligently to restore the kind of financial order that her subjects had been accustomed to when her father ruled. Unfortunately, she found this an impossible task to accomplish as Henry was of inherently different views regarding fiscal policy, at least where Sicily's wealth was concerned.

He was, however, astute politically, obtaining the Germans' early approval of his young son as successor to the German title *King of the Romans,* thereby qualifying Frederick to be elected Holy Roman Emperor.[13]

Henry sought to solidify his relations with the "other" emperor, in Constantinople. In May 1197, Irene Angelina, daughter of the Eastern Emperor Isaac II, wed Henry's younger brother, Philip. Irene Angelina was the young widow of Roger III, son of King Tancred of Sicily (who we met in the last chapter).

Henry VI died of dysentery in Messina in September of 1197, aged only thirty-two, while preparing for the Fourth Crusade. Had he lived longer, Henry might have led this expedition directly to the Levant as it was intended. Instead, the Crusaders sacked Constantinople in an episode that — indelibly if not uniquely — stains the pages of history with the blood of the innocent.[14]

THE KINGDOM OF SICILY

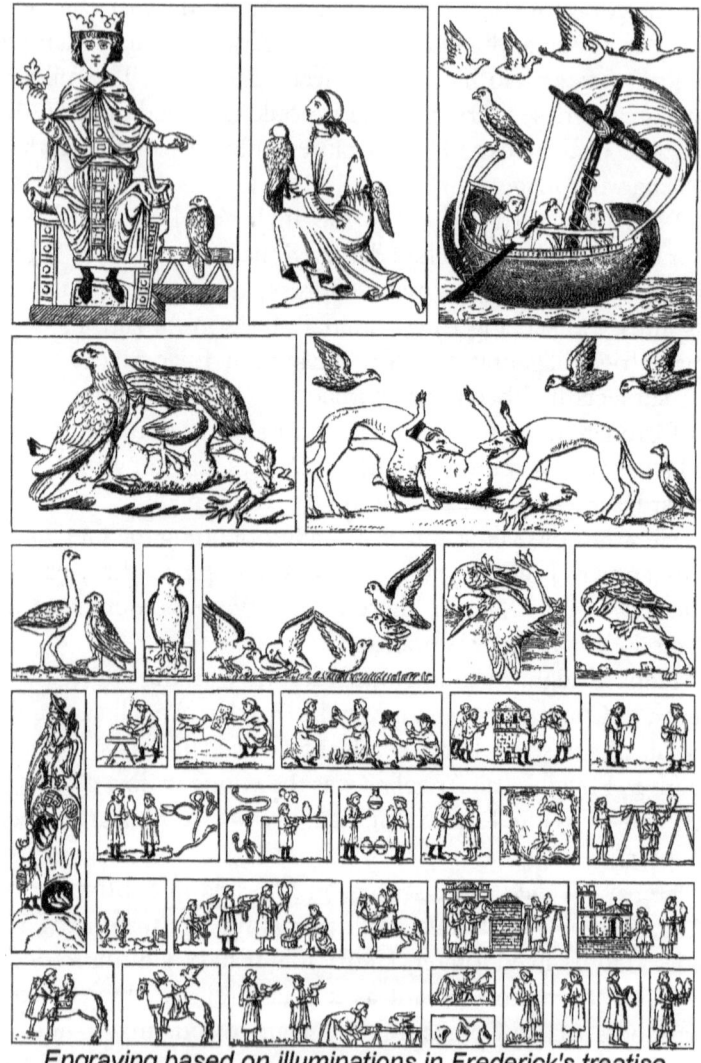

Engraving based on illuminations in Frederick's treatise on falconry (Frederick is shown at top left)

The death of Henry VI also had significant ramifications in his own dominions. Almost immediately, his brother Philip and his adversary Otto IV, heir of the rival Welf dynasty, both claimed the same right to be crowned Holy Roman Emperor. Nobody stepped forward to enforce the rights of *der junge König Friedrich,* whose claim would have to wait for another day. For now, support of the German elector princes was divided between Philip and Otto. Pope Innocent III initially supported Otto because having a Welf in power seemed like the simplest way to break the Hohenstaufen hold on the lands surrounding Papal territory.

Despite these machinations in faraway Germany, the widowed Constance raised her young son in Sicily in an era of peace, only to confront a series of challenges from unruly Sicilian barons eager to renege on their feudal obligations. As it happened, some of the Germans were equally troublesome.

One of these was Markward of Anweiler, the Imperial Seneschal, who Henry had appointed Margrave of Ancona and Count of Abruzzo, strategic regions bordering Papal lands. Like the Emperor he had once served, Markward eventually found himself excommunicated, though probably for political reasons, as the Papacy was trying to encroach on the lands he controlled.

Markward eventually came to support Philip, Henry's brother, as the late Emperor's successor. One can imagine Constance's reaction to the intrigues unfolding across the Alps, brought about by a subversive brother-in-law. Before long, she expelled the bothersome Markward from the kingdom and tried to prevent future German interference in Sicily.

Constance was the only Sicilian queen who ever reigned based on a legal status tantamount to *suo jure,* ruling in her own right. Her charters were issued under her own name and seal (one is shown on the cover of this book).

Sadly, Constance died in November 1198, but not before

CONSTITUTIONUM
REGNI SICILIARUM
LIBRI III.

Cum Commentariis Veterum Jurisconsultorum

ACCEDIT NUNC PRIMUM

DOMINICI ALFENI VARII J. C.
COMMENTARIUS

AD

FRIDERICI II.
IMPERATORIS ET REGIS CONSTITUTIONEM

De Rebus non alienandis Ecclesiis.

EDITIO ABSOLUTISSIMA.

NEAPOLI MDCCLXXIII.
SUMPTIBUS ANTONII CERVONII.

Constitutions of Melfi printed in Naples in 1773

ensuring young three year-old Frederick's patrimony in southern Italy by having him crowned King of Sicily six months earlier on Pentecost in May of that year. He was not *Rex Filius* but the unequivocal *Rex Siciliae*.

Constance named Pope Innocent acting Regent of Sicily and her son's official guardian. This "privilege" did not come without a devastating compromise; the Queen of Sicily had to give up her Norman dynasty's perquisite of Apostolic Legateship, the Hautevilles' political supremacy over the Church in Sicily.

Although Constance's formal submission to the Pope has been seen by some scholars as a betrayal of her ancestral dynasty's rights, it reflected a sincere effort to secure her son's future and ensure his position with Rome, however tenuously. Later Sicilian monarchs reasserted these Legatine powers.[15]

In 1201, Markward of Anweiler returned to Sicily, where he landed with an armed force, becoming *de facto* regent, with Pope Innocent as Frederick's official guardian. Following Markward's death in 1202, he was replaced by others in a complex power struggle that plagued Sicilian administration for the next few years. Frederick was declared of age in 1208.

Arts and Sciences

Stories of Frederick's childhood in Palermo — still an opulent city despite his father's construction of buildings on the fringe of the Genoard — are tinged with hyperbole, leading some to imagine that the boy wandered the souks unaccompanied, yet the intellectual environment was indeed exceptional, especially for a young prince. Frederick proved to be at least as intellectually curious as his grandfather, Roger II, and very much like him.[16]

Certain it is that Frederick learned a respect for the island's peoples and religions, acquiring a working knowledge of

Greek, Latin, German, French, Arabic and a new vernacular, Sicilian, influenced by all these languages. He was probably the first Sicilian ruler to speak Sicilian, and there exist a few verses of Sicilian poetry attributed to him.

More mellifluous and less guttural than its modern successor, Medieval Sicilian was heavily influenced by Latin; Modern Sicilian sounds a great deal like the Catalan introduced in Sicily after Frederick's time.[17]

Ciullo, or "Cielo," of Alcamo was one of the best known poets of the "Sicilian School" that found the epitome of its expression at the court of Frederick II. Here the sonnet was born, probably created by Giacomo of Lentini. It is quite possible that, had Frederick's dynasty — and Sicily's political importance — survived the thirteenth century, the modern Italian language we know today might be based on Sicilian rather than Tuscan. (Francis of Assisi wrote his *Canticle* during the same period.)

Ciullo's only complete surviving work is the *Dialogue*, variously known as *Rosa Fresca Aulentissima*, for its first phrase, or *Il Contrasto*. This poetry reflects the romantic Age of Chivalry in Sicily.

It has been suggested that the authors of the Sicilian School were notaries or scribes rather than full-time court poets. Differing from the majority of Sicily's chroniclers, most of whom were clerics or courtiers, they took their inspiration from the itinerant troubadours.

Ciullo and his poem are commended by Dante in his *De Vulgari Eloquentia* ("On Eloquence in the Vernacular") written early in the fourteenth century. By then, the prominence of the Sicilian language had vanished along with the polyglot kingdom that gave birth to it.

What some philologists regard as the most important work in Sicilian was a near-contemporary chronicle of the War of the Vespers and a primary source for that period. *The Rebellion of Sicily against King Charles* was written by a monk near Catania around 1290. Its Sicilian title is *Cronica di lu Rebellamentu di Sichilia contra Re Carlu.*

While linguists debate precise etymologies, at least a few seem solid.

A number of Sicilian words derive from Norman French: *buatta* (jar, from *boîte*), *custureri* (tailor, from *coustrier*), *largasia* (largesse), *racìna* (grape), *vuccèri* (butcher, from *boucher*), *accattari* (to buy, from *acater,* modern *acheter*).

And from Medieval Greek: *carusu* (boy, from *kouros*), *cona* (icon, from *eikona*), *crastu* (ram, from *krastos*), *pistiari* (to eat, from *apestiein*), *naca* (cradle, from *nake*), *bucali* (pitcher, from *baukalion*), *grasta* (a terracotta vase, from the classical *gastra*).

Among words from Middle High German we find: *arbitrari* (to work, from *arbeit*), *vardari* (to wait or watch, from *warten*), *sparagnari* (to save money, from *sparen*), *guastari* and *vastari* (to waste, from *wastjan*).

Provençal has made a few contributions, notably: *lascu* (thin or sparse, from *lasc*), *addumari* (to light, from *allumar*), *aggrifari* (to kidnap, from *grifar*).

Some words come directly from Arabic: *babbaluci* (also the Greek *boubalàkion*) for *lumache* (snails), *fatùk* and *fastùk* for pistachio, *saia* (from *saqiya*) for "canal," *gébbia* for "reservoir" and *azzizata* ("beautified") from *aziz.* Other words rooted in Arabic: *favara* (a well), *mischinu* (an unfortunate person), *zagara* (orange blossom), *zammù* (anise), *balata* (stone), *cafìsu* (a liquid measure, from *qafiz*), *tarì* (the coin).

Latin was an early influence, Catalan a later one, and Sicilian has inherited words from both.

In Palermo, Frederick heard from sailors and merchants of foreign lands and customs. He absorbed much knowledge from scholars, philosophers, historians, artisans, chroniclers and sundry scientists. The names of a few are known to us. Michael Scot, the court astronomer, mathematician and science advisor, translated *On the Sphere* by the Arab astronomer Al-Bitruji, or Alpetragius, who died circa 1204. He also translated Aristotle's *De Animalibus* from the existing Arabic translation of ibn Sina (Avicenna). Scot was a mentor to the young Leonardo Pisano Bigollo, or Fibonacci, the mathematician who introduced Hindi-Arabic numerals in northern Italy and other parts of Christian Europe. (These were already used in Sicily, while Spain's *Codex Vigilanus,* compiled in 881, features such numerals.)

Sicily's culinary culture owes much to this era, although few specific recipes have been recorded. It seems that Frederick enjoyed a type of lasagne, as well as a fish stew, *scapace,* made with wine and saffron. The sweet ricotta cheese filling used in cannoli may date from this period. An early form of the aubergine (eggplant) and caper salad known as *caponata* may have been consumed, likewise fried rice balls (arancini) and chick pea fritters (panelle).

Royal Authority

In 1209, as the result of the usual machinations by Pope Innocent III, Frederick wed Constance of Aragon, an older woman who could almost have been his mother. A widow, she had been married to the King of Hungary, by whom she had a child, now deceased.

Constance was raised in an exceptionally affluent atmosphere distinguished by a high level of culture. Governed from the Catalonian city of Barcelona, the Aragonese realm was an ethnically diverse region roughly contiguous to the area once ruled by the Visigoths, from whom its oldest nobility claimed descent, with several languages and its own tiny empire. The new queen would often serve as Frederick's regent, a kind of "viceroy," during his frequent absences from Sicily. In his early years as king, she was his anchor.

Frederick's marriage to the royal widow was an opportune one for another reason. Faithful knights were in short supply; the young monarch retained competent Muslim-Arab troops for precisely this reason while maintaining his father's rapport with the loyal Teutonic Knights of Messina and Palermo. Fortuitously, Constance brought with her some much-needed knights from Aragon. Most of this chivalric retinue eventually returned to Spain, but their presence in Sicily, so long as it lasted, bolstered Frederick's image and authority.

Like his predecessor William II, Frederick found himself in need of asserting himself. As it was natural that young kings would have advisors and tutors to counsel them, it is reasonable to believe that Frederick's initial policies reflected such advice, perhaps more so than his own ideas, but that would change.

The Sicilian baronage was the least of Frederick's problems. In northern and central Italy there were continuing conflicts between the Papal and Imperial camps, the Guelphs and the Ghibellines. In Germany, Philip, Frederick's uncle, had been assassinated. Otto, the Welf contender, was now claiming the Kingdom of Sicily. In late 1210 he marched into the *Regnum,* reaching Apulia the next year.

The Pope, obviously enough, was not happy about this development, for a Welf ruling two-thirds of Italy was no more desirable than a Hohenstaufen controlling the same territory. In other quarters, King Philip II of France was equally opposed to the expansionist Welf designs, as he was attempting to form an alliance with the Swabians to counterbalance Otto's support of England in the decade-long Anglo-French War. In practice, this meant thwarting the ambitions of King John of England, who claimed territories in France.

Revolts in northern Italy diverted Otto away from southern Italy. He took his army with him, and any fickle barons in the south were left without support against Frederick. The

Swabian faction in Germany now elected Frederick King of the Romans. This was good news.

Frederick crowned his newborn son, Henry, King of Sicily, and departed for Germany.

The Pisans had supported Otto, offering their naval power in his contemplated invasion of Sicily, so it was simple enough for Frederick to play this card in appealing to the rival Genoans, spending over two months in their city. This gave his supporters in northern Italy a chance to meet him. He then made his way northward across the Alps, plotting his route through towns known to be sympathetic to his dynasty.

He convinced the town of Constance to support him against the approaching Otto, who did not attack. Then Frederick worked his way northward, convincing town after town to join him, backing Otto away from the heart of the Holy Roman Empire. This groundswell of support paid off. In early December 1212, Frederick was formally elected King of the Romans at Frankfurt and then at Mainz. He now had an official "mandate" to be crowned Emperor.

A pitched battle against Otto seemed imminent, but it was not to be, at least not for Frederick, much as he might have savored the thought of beating the arrogant Welf into the ground.

At this point Providence smiled upon the young king.

In July 1214, Otto's forces, along with King John's army, were defeated by Philip II in a major battle at Bouvines, in Flanders, ending this Anglo-French War.

John made his way back to England with his tail between his legs. A side-effect of his defeat was the *Magna Carta,* as the English barons balked at being taxed for a costly, unsuccessful campaign far beyond the borders of their own country.

His dreams of Empire dashed, Otto IV never recuperated from his defeat at Bouvines. He abdicated the following year and died in 1218. Now most of Germany submitted to Frederick except for a few remote holdouts and some towns in the

Welfs' home region of Saxony. A coronation in Aachen, where Charlemagne was buried and where the Kings of the Romans were traditionally crowned, completed Frederick's immediate objective. He vowed to go on Crusade, but that dream would have to wait.

Before he could leave his German lands, Frederick had to address a number of fiscal matters. In some cases, this meant devolving more rights to the Imperial ("free") cities and to the bishops controlling ecclesiastical towns. Of equal importance was the delegation of local authority to loyal vassals; there was no telling when, or even if, Frederick would return to Germany to enforce the law himself.

In 1216, Frederick promised Pope Innocent that the Kingdom of Sicily would not be annexed to the Holy Roman Empire. Indeed, such a union appears never to have been very seriously contemplated. It seemed more than sufficient that both crowns would henceforth be balanced on the same red head. The loose confederation that was the Holy Roman Empire, famously said by Voltaire to be neither holy, nor Roman, nor an empire, was not very much like Sicily, with its comparatively centralized government, and there was nothing to compel anybody trying to make one fit the mold of the other. But Innocent III was soon gone.

Frederick crossed the Alps into Italian territory in 1220. He was crowned Holy Roman Emperor at Saint Peter's in Rome by Pope Honorius III on 22 November. By then, the Fifth Crusade led by Andrew II of Hungary and Leopold VI of Austria was being undertaken in Egypt, and it was on its way to becoming a military and strategic debacle for the Crusaders.

While relinquishing royal power in Germany, Frederick was augmenting it in Italy. Working his way southward, in December he issued a series of decrees known as the "Assizes of Capua." These were, in essence, a reiteration of the Assizes of Ariano promulgated by his grandfather.[18]

This was not his only legislation during this period. At Messina in 1221, he held a baronial meeting and issued some decrees regarding commerce and gambling, as well as the attire of Jews, this last based on dictates established at the Fourth Lateran Council a few years earlier. The chronicler Richard of San Germano also mentions a decree forbidding prostitutes entering public baths "with honest women," *cum honestis mulieribus*.

Back on the mainland early the next year, Frederick met Pope Honorius, and the Pontiff brought up the question of sending relief to the Crusaders in the Levant, but Frederick was not yet ready to lead a force there himself. In September, following the suppression of some wayward barons, a comet appeared. Taking this as an auspicious sign, Frederick issued some additional decrees regarding coinage minted in Apulia.

Constance died in June and Frederick married his second wife, young Yolanda (Isabella) of Brienne, in 1225. She was the daughter of John of Brienne, the exiled King of Jerusalem.

Following the execution of the Muslim rebel leader Morabit, in 1222, thousands of Muslims from the Iato area revolted with their leader Ibn Abbad, or Benaveth. Frederick deported them to Lucera in Apulia. Most Muslims had already accepted baptism and were integrated into Sicilian society as Arab Catholics, some for two or three generations. It seems that there remained a few Muslims in the west of the island, particularly at Mazara and Erice, and there may still have been a few mosques in Palermo, but this mass transfer to Apulia marks the effective end of the widespread practice of Islam in Sicily. As many as twenty thousand Muslims were resettled in Lucera.

This was not Frederick's only move against Muslims. He sent a fleet against Jerba, whose pirates were supporting the forces fighting against the Crusaders to the east.

Frederick founded the *Studium*, the University of Naples, in 1224. Generally acknowledged as the first European university established by charter, it may have been inspired by the Arabs' *dar al-hikma,* or "house of wisdom," in principle a secular place of learning. Thomas Aquinas was one of the first students. What made the *Studium* different was that, while it counted clergy among its teachers, it was not a school operated by a monastery. Moreover, in keeping with Frederick's own ideas, it placed a great emphasis on science. A rival medical school existed at Salerno, which until this era was a more important city than Naples. Students outside the aristocracy were sometimes admitted to the *Studium,* although these were the children of merchants and bankers rather than peasants.

In 1226, Frederick II summoned an Imperial Diet at Cremona. Arguably, this exercise in Imperial hegemony did not involve Sicily except perhaps by influencing its complex commercial and diplomatic rapport with the German princes and Italian communes. However, the next Crusade, the one to be led by Frederick, was outlined. This could no longer be postponed, but Frederick, who was usually more astute than his fellow crusading monarchs, had diplomatic ties to al Kamil, nephew of Saladin and now the Ayyubid Sultan of Egypt.

The Sixth Crusade

Ostensibly launched to obtain access to Jerusalem and perhaps conquer it, the Sixth Crusade, as it developed, was more personal than religious. Through his young wife Frederick claimed the Crown of Jerusalem *jure uxoris.*

In 1226, Frederick's "Golden Bull of Rimini" granted the Teutonic Knights the right to exercise effective sovereignty over any lands they occupied in Prussia or the adjoining territories to the east. This reinforced their loyalty to Frederick, something that would serve him well on the Crusade. (Sanctioned by the Papacy, this policy had the effect of encouraging the infamous "Baltic Crusades.")

The new Pope, Gregory IX, strongly advocated a crusade but not Frederick's ambitions. Indeed, this Pontiff would become a political adversary, a chronically annoying thorn in Frederick's side. In 1227, using the delay of the Crusade as a pretext, the petulant Pontiff excommunicated Frederick.

Yolanda, Frederick's wife, died the following year giving birth to a son, Conrad. In the eyes of some, the death of the sixteen year-old heiress complicated Frederick's claim to Jerusalem. Frederick, of course, saw no legal or dynastic complications in his wife's untimely death.

He embarked in 1228, arriving in Cyprus in the hot days of July. Here he claimed to be the feudal suzerain. The *de facto* ruler, John of Ibelin, regent of young King Henry of Lusignan, conceded this under duress, but two years later the Cypriots reclaimed their island. In the end, this unpleasant episode served only to set the powerful Ibelin baronial faction against Frederick, something which was to prove detrimental to his plans. The Ayyubids still controlled Jerusalem.

Frederick entered the Holy City in early 1229. In principle, he was regent for his young son, Conrad, the heir — through the late Yolanda — to the Hierosolymitan Crown. The Patriarch of Jerusalem did not anoint Frederick; there seems to have been no formal coronation. It would happen that the new King of Jerusalem was treated more kindly by certain Muslims than by some Christians.

Frederick was able to reach an accommodation with al Kamil without bloodshed. A truce negotiated with the sultan's representatives recognized Frederick's rights in Jerusalem, or at least most of the city. The Ayyubids also ceded control of Nazareth and Bethlehem. This freed al Kamil to address a series of internecine revolts in the region without having to worry about the "Franks," as European Crusaders were called, further encroaching upon Ayyubid lands. The agreement gave credibility to Frederick while placating some of the Christians.

Gifts were exchanged, including exotic African animals for Frederick's zoo, and the Treaty of Jaffa of 1229 was signed and sealed. This peace would last for ten years, the maximum term Muslims permitted such truces with Infidels.

On the wider stage, neither Muslims nor Christians were content, and the Knights Templar made their dissatisfaction known, along with the Christian barons allied with the Ibelins. Supported by the antagonistic Templars, Gerold of Lausanne, the Patriarch of Jerusalem, placed his own city under interdict. Back in Italy, the Pope was trying to seize Frederick's lands.

Upon his landing at Brindisi in June 1229, Frederick asserted himself with force. Much of his opposition began to fall away immediately.

Yet resistance remained, led in part by John of Brienne, who challenged his son-in-law's claim on Jerusalem. Though little more than a side show in the annals of history, this duel says as much about Frederick's determination as it does about John's pretensions. Under normal circumstances, a man might think better than to marry a girl whose father can muster an army against him, but Frederick was unimpressed by this clumsy attempt at victory by one of the military leaders of the failed Fifth Crusade.

Over the next few months, Frederick pushed John and his Papal allies westward across the peninsula. By Winter, some battles around Cassino had resolved the conflict in Frederick's favor. In September of the following year, Pope Gregory made peace with him.

A bone of contention remained with the Templars. Their commanderies and estates in Sicily proper were confiscated, assigned to the more amenable Hospitallers. Some years earlier, Frederick had ordered the destruction of several non-authorized feudal castles in Sicily. Over the next decade, construction would begin on a number of royal castles — Ursino Castle in Catania, Castel del Monte in Apulia and others.

Frederick was now at the zenith of his power, ruling expansive realms extending, like his father's, over most of what are now Germany, Austria and Italy (see the map section), while also controlling wealthy outposts in the eastern Mediterranean. He was the most powerful ruler in Europe.

It was time for the Emperor-King to address domestic matters. From the royal fortress at Melfi, he promulgated what is now regarded as the most important secular legal code seen in Italy during the Middle Ages.

The Constitutions of Melfi

The Constitutions of Melfi, also called the *Liber Augustalis* for Frederick's Imperial title, were intended as a general legal code in the tradition of the Assizes of Ariano of Roger II (see the previous chapter), and Frederick's own Assizes of Capua. Truth be told, these legal codes were not very different from many issued in England and elsewhere during the same period.

Frederick's laws clearly had to take into account the cultural diversity of the southern Italian realm he inherited, which even in 1231 still had sizeable Muslim, Jewish and Greek Orthodox populations. The Constitutions also considered certain lingering differences between Frankish and Longobardic law, important factors in feudal matters such as land inheritance and the designation of heirs.

Not only did the new legal code reinforce royal authority over the nobility and the use of natural resources, its references to heresy and to Roman canon law effectively formed the groundwork for Sicily's evolution into an overwhelmingly Roman Catholic island, or perhaps they merely reflected its existing status. Indeed, most Muslims and Greek Orthodox had already converted to Catholicism. The last holdouts were the Jews.

A few statutes (articles) stand out.

Like England's *Magna Carta,* the Constitutions of Melfi made a speedy judgment the right of civil litigants and even criminal defendants.

Juridical procedures are clearly established, while practices such as trial by combat (knights duelling to win a legal dispute) are essentially abolished.

The notion that justiciars (district judges) could not hear cases in lands where they held feudal estates was a prescient idea, similar to modern statutes proscribing conflicts of interest which might require a judge's recusal from a case.

Jews, but not Christians, could practice usury, though Judaic law formally discourages this.

A man could divorce his wife if adultery were proven; the same practice already existed among Muslims and may have been an influence here.

The law on divorce, though clearly weighted in favor of the husband, was innovative for its era. In fact, divorce had existed, in one form or another, among Christians since the faith's earliest days. It was only later that the Catholic hierarchy attempted to suppress the practice.

The sale of poisonous foods and potions was outlawed, and the burning or disposal of certain toxic substances was prohibited — flax and hemp couldn't be soaked in water near towns and yew (which can emit toxins) could not be disposed of in rivers.

Theft, trade and even the comportment of physicians are considered at length. So is cattle rustling, coin clipping and the forgery of documents, for which the punishment is severe.

Extensive legislation is devoted to women's rights, and to those of children. The statute defining penalties for mothers who prostitute their daughters implies that this occurred, but there are equally severe penalties for rape, and violence against prostitutes.

In a precedent which paralleled developments elsewhere, daughters were allowed to succeed to feudal property and titles of nobility in the absence of male heirs — a practice which survived into the nineteenth century. This is the origin of the so-called "Sicilian Succession."

A few laws seem less enlightened. Adultery itself is a crime, but a husband might not be punished if he kills his adulterous wife and her lover immediately upon catching them in the sexual act *in flagrante delicto*. A peasant who strikes a knight or noble might have the offending hand chopped off unless he can prove that he acted in self defense.

Capital punishment existed and is mentioned, but some scholars contend that the term as used in the Constitutions sometimes refers to loss of citizenship rather than loss of one's life. Translation of several Latin words is nuanced; for *servus* the term *serf* may be more accurate than *slave* in certain statutes.

Frederick upholds Roger's principle that only the son of a knight or noble may become a knight unless, in the case of a man of common birth, royal assent is granted. In practice, such assent was probably obtained quite often, yet the law is a clear attempt to restrict entry into the aristocratic class.

A curious section (to the modern mind) is the proscription on the use of paper for legal documents, with requirement of the use of parchment or vellum for this purpose. Parchment was, of course, more durable, less susceptible than paper to damage from moisture, folding or even ink. Sicily was ahead of most of Europe in the use of paper, introduced by the Arabs during the ninth century.

There are also attempts to regulate local government and the construction of towers and castles; as we have seen, the Crown sometimes ordered the destruction of fortifications built by barons without royal consent. This policy discouraged baronial power as well as the hypothetical development of communes similar to the northern Italian cities that continuously challenged Frederick.

Throughout the Constitutions it is abundantly clear that Frederick exercised an absolute authority in the Kingdom of Sicily that he did not enjoy in the German and northern Italian regions under his control.

No legal code is perfect, but Frederick's was significantly evolved for its era. Much analyzed and interpreted over time, the Constitutions speak eloquently enough for themselves.

Contrary to common belief, they were not entirely forgotten in later centuries; most widely disseminated was the 1773 printing in the Kingdom of Naples. What were abandoned were their principles, considered debatable in the eighteenth century. Divorce, for example, fell into abeyance as a civil right, to be legalized again in Italy only in 1970. The Italian Republic finally made rape a felonious form of assault in 1996.

Government

Relations with Venice improved when Frederick granted its merchants favorable trade conditions in Sicily, but some of his business was far less palatable. At the Diet of Aquileia in 1232, the Emperor was forced to reprimand his son, Henry, who was representing him north of the Kingdom of Sicily.

Essentially, the problem was that Henry was not enforcing the Emperor's authority adequately. As well as the German princes, the northern Italian communes, especially those in Lombardy, were ever malcontent when it came to central rule, accustomed as they were to governing themselves semi-independently. This was nothing new; the Lombard League was established in 1167 to challenge the attempts of Frederick's grandfather, Barbarossa, to assert Imperial authority over this region.

In this era we find the earliest roots of a phenomenon which in some ways plagues Italy to this day, and to some extent it explains certain lingering differences between the collective mentalities of northerners, on the one hand, and southerners on the other. While the northern communes, with their *seggi* (governing councils of local patricians), encouraged a true sense of citizenship and civic consciousness, the largest cities in the *Regnum* failed to maintain such an environment over time. These nascent differences may not have been obvious in 1232, but they were quite pronounced by 1400. To a Milanese or Pavian, the city streets are his own, and merit cleanliness; to a Neapolitan or Palermitan, everything outside the door of his own house belongs to the *padrone,* the "master," and its condition is of no real concern. In the end, these mentalities extended to smaller cities, hence Bergamo and Brescia exist in a state of government and conservation far superior to what one encounters in Cosenza and Caltanissetta. This gave rise to the perception that northerners were citizens while southerners were slaves, and while such stereotypes are unflattering they do reflect differing perceptions of community and even nationhood.[19]

Henry's behavior soon led to open conflict with his father.

Conrad of Marburg was a bishop who had prosecuted the Cathars, something Frederick officially condoned. In 1227, Pope Gregory empowered this sadistic cleric to eradicate heresy in Germany. Henry saw this as overzealous, considering that most of the "heresies" seemed to exist only in Conrad's fertile imagination. Acting against Conrad was moral but not very politic, as it cast a pall over Frederick's simultaneous attempts to garner Papal support against the Lombard League. (Bishop Conrad was eventually murdered.)

Frederick impetuously outlawed Henry, who had been crowned King of Sicily, as *Rex Filius,* and King of the Romans. Before long, Henry was in league with the League against his father. He was forced to submit to Frederick in 1235, when he was tried, dethroned and imprisoned. Conrad, his younger brother, then succeeded him.

We may question Frederick's wisdom in meting out such a severe punishment to his senior heir, but his sagacity shone in other matters. When thirty-four Jews were killed in Fulda, in Hesse, allegedly for having murdered several Christian boys, Frederick instituted an investigative commission composed of Jews and former Jews. The people who had been lynched were exonerated and measures were taken to protect the Jewish communities in the future.

In 1235 Frederick wed Elizabeth, daughter of King John of England (and sister of Henry III).

The next few years occupied Frederick with suppressing a series of revolts by the cities of the Lombard League. By 1239, Pope Gregory was again stirring up dissension. It seemed to be an obsession. He again excommunicated Frederick. The pious Louis IX of France rose to Frederick's defense, refusing Gregory's request that he fight a war against the King of Sicily.

At the Pope's instigation, some religious orders preached against Frederick. Gregory particularly favored the newly-founded Franciscans, who Frederick promptly suppressed in Sicily, effectively banishing them and prohibiting the foundation of new monasteries.

Frederick's military expenses necessitated the ever more frequent levying of the infamous *collecta,* a tax collected occasionally since Norman times. In 1238 this revenue totalled over a hundred thousand gold onze. A potential cost in both money and men would have been the defense of the Holy Roman Empire against Batu Khan's formidable Mongol-Tatar army, which made its way westward in 1241 after having sacked Kiev. This contemplated invasion of Frederick's dominions by the emergent "Golden Horde" was called off despite some early battles in the regions bordering the Empire's eastern reaches.

Pope Gregory's death in August brought a breath of fresh air, if only for a moment. In December, Frederick's wife Elizabeth died and was buried next to Yolanda in Andria Cathedral in Apulia, not far from Frederick's favorite fortress, the distinctive Castel del Monte. Each of these women was around twenty years younger than Frederick, who kept them largely secluded from public life. Like many kings of his era, he had a coterie of concubines, but his was similar to a harem.

In 1242 Henry was called to court. Perhaps Frederick was prepared to grant amnesty to his wayward son. This we shall never know, for Henry died in Calabria *en route* to the meeting with his father. He was survived by a wife, Margaret of Austria, and a son, Frederick.

Innocent IV, elected the next year, was an exceptionally intellectual Pope who initiated a series of political intrigues during his decade-long pontificate, even sending emissaries to solicit the religious conversions of Mongol khans. Nearer the Vatican, being excommunicated seems not to have bothered the King of Sicily.

The battlefield death of Frederick of Babenberg, Duke of Austria, while fighting Hungarian forces at the Leitha River in 1246, facilitated a new claim that might have extended Imperial territory. The fallen duke left no surviving heirs, but Margaret, his sister, was none other than the widow of Henry, Frederick's dispossessed son who had died four years earlier.

Nature and the Environment

Among his recreational interests, Frederick cultivated a passion for falconry, about which he wrote an illustrated guide completed by 1248. In Europe at this time falconry was the sport of kings and aristocrats. Dictated to scribes, his treatise is one of the rare examples of a book authored by a medieval king. Indeed, it is the longest thing written by a European monarch during the Middle Ages. The typical kings of this period left us little more than charters and correspondence, even if Frederick's could be exceptionally ebullient; in reply to Batu

Khan's written threat to dethrone him, the Emperor suggested that he might submit if he could be the Khan's falconer.

Significantly, *De Arte Venandi cum Avibus* (literally "The Art of Hunting with Birds") is considered the first zoological treatise based on what are now regarded as modern scientific principles. This cannot be overstated, for it distinguished Frederick's intellect in an age of superstition and witchcraft.

Some commentators have characterized Frederick as what today might be called a "freethinker." Whatever the case, ornithology was a clear reflection of his interest in nature. *Environmentalist* is a modern term whose use here might be anachronistic, but it seems suitable for a monarch who (as we have seen) decreed that flax, hemp and yew, which can emit toxins, could not be dumped in rivers.

Frederick's zoo included camels, elephants, panthers and what was probably the first giraffe ever brought to Europe — all gifts of the Sultan of Egypt, al Kamil. He paraded these animals, to public amazement, during a visit to Ravenna in 1231.

Stupor Mundi

Perhaps the years of ceaseless conflict, frenetic activity and constant travels had taken their toll. Frederick was struck down by fever in December 1250 in Apulia. He died just before his fifty-sixth birthday and was interred in the cathedral of his favorite city, Palermo, where he rests next to his most beloved wife.

It was with simple eloquence that Matthew Paris recorded: "Frederick, peerless wonder of the world, died in Apulia on Saint Lucy's Day." *Obiit insuper stupor mundi Frethericus, die Sanctae Luciae, in Apulia.* It is here, immediately after his death, that Frederick was attributed the enduring appellation *Stupor Mundi*.

Composing a profile of Frederick's personal character has

proven elusive. He rarely displayed hubris. On the other hand, he fathered numerous children outside his marriages, and his treatment of his later wives left much to be desired, even by the standards of the times. His personal religious beliefs were ambiguous at best. He was not especially devout, yet he zealously enforced Catholic law.

The fiercest modern criticisms of Frederick's personality reflect a conventional view of him as taciturn, obstinate, even sardonic. Such inferences are drawn from just a few contemporary accounts, yet they led the medievalist Morris Bishop to comment that Frederick was "enlightened, but he was not really a very nice man."

Frederick's death signalled the end of Sicily's great multicultural experiment, a decline that before long would culminate in a Sicilian "monoculture."

The Last Hohenstaufens

Who would rule the Kingdom of Sicily? Frederick was succeeded by Conrad, his son by Yolanda of Brienne, but he had several other sons, legitimate and otherwise. Most prominent among them was Manfred, who we shall meet shortly.

It was hoped that Frederick's grandson, his namesake Frederick (son of Henry and Margaret), might become Duke of Austria, but he died around 1252, little more than a footnote to history.

In 1246 Conrad had married Elizabeth Wittelsbach of Bavaria, who in 1252 bore him a son, also Conrad ("Conradin"), who was to figure in the history of the *Regnum*. In the event, although Conrad's reign was not a long one, he seems to have been willing to exercise more latitude than his father in domestic affairs. The Franciscans were permitted to return; their greatest church in Sicily is Saint Francis of Assisi in Palermo.

Amidst Papal intrigues and challenges to his royal authority in Germany, Conrad died of malaria in Basilicata in 1254, having been excommunicated the same year. He was succeeded by his young son, the Bavarian-born Conradin, whose regent was Conrad's half-brother Manfred, Frederick's natural son born in 1232 of Bianca Lancia, a noblewoman the Emperor was said to have wed when she was on her deathbed. Certain it is that Frederick cultivated an affinity for Manfred at least equal to that of his other sons, having bestowed upon him the lucrative principality of Taranto. That Conrad found Manfred overly ambitious was now a moot point with the former dead. Conrad's death had wide implications, as it brought about an interregnum in Germany that ended only two decades later.

One thing was clear: Rome did not want a Hohenstaufen on the throne.

Pope Innocent IV offered Sicily, which he viewed as a fief in his gift, to young Edmund "Crouchback," second son of King Henry III of England. His successor, Pope Alexander IV, confirmed this. Henry's taxation of his barons to defray the cost of ousting Manfred rekindled English memories of the fiscal policies of his father, King John, whose unbridled military spending added to the baronial indignation that led to the *Magna Carta*. This "Sicilian business" became a contributing factor, if only a peripheral one, in the Second Barons' War.

Manfred had himself crowned at Palermo in 1258 based on unfounded rumors that young Conradin (dynastically Conrad II) was dead.

When Pope Alexander IV died in 1261, he was succeeded by a Frenchman who took the name Urban IV. This coincided with the loss of Constantinople by the "Latin" kings who had ruled it since the shameful Fourth Crusade. The Byzantine Empire was thus restored to Greek control. One of Urban's first acts as Pontiff was an unsuccessful attempt to initiate a crusade to reclaim Constantinople.

The Pope was the common thread running through too many events. Faith, expressed through the Church, was a *sine qua non* of everyday life, but the Papacy was the most unsettling, conniving, debilitating political force in Europe during the High Middle Ages, its tendrils reaching into the Baltics, the Balkans and the Byzantine lands. It was a state within every state.

Most Popes were obsessed with power; that was part of the job. Rare was the humble man who was elected to the See of Saint Peter. Pity the king who found himself targeted by the Vicar of Christ. Pity still more the Waldensians and Cathars, and the Jews. Even the Orthodox Christians of the east were not safe from the clutches of Rome. Rarely was Papal politics rooted in true Christianity; most of the time Christianity had nothing to do with it. The medieval Papacy made it possible for bad Christians to be good Catholics. The worthy work of Francis of Assisi was condoned by the Papacy; that is because it posed no obvious risk to the Church as an institution. *Res Publica Christiana,* a phrase sometimes attributed to Frederick II, attempted to express the concept, vaguely similar to "Christendom," of one Europe under one Church. That wasn't enough. The Papacy wanted the world — this one and the next.

Whatever one thought of Manfred, he enjoyed a certain amount of support, even esteem, among the Sicilian baronage. Never lacking in self-confidence, he betrothed his daughter, Constance, to Peter III of Aragon in 1262.

Meanwhile, as English support for the "Sicilian business" evaporated, other candidates were sought. Surely, if *Pontifex Maximus* could decide who was to be crowned king, he might just as easily cast aside one designee in favor of another. Urban formally annulled the offer of the Kingdom of Sicily that had been tendered to Edmund of England. His new candidate was a fellow Frenchman, Charles of Anjou, younger brother of the ever-crusading King Louis IX.

Louis himself was initially unconvinced. Having supported Conrad as Frederick's legitimate heir, he subsequently endorsed the Papal choice of Edmund. Now, despite his antipathy for Manfred, he saw no immediate justification for an Angevin to be crowned King of Sicily. Yet he eventually consented to it in spite of these reservations.

In 1263, the ambitious Charles accepted a Papal offer weighed down by cumbersome conditions. Papal control of his Italian realm would be burdensome indeed. Legatine powers were to be abolished, and armies were to be provided the Pope whenever requested. A substantial annual tribute was to be paid to Rome. Naturally, there were to be no claims made by Charles on the Holy Roman Empire or any of its territories.

Here Urban was the quintessential Pontiff as Kingmaker. No wonder some historians have come to regard Charles as a Papal puppet.

The Crown itself was a more than sufficient incentive, but Charles may have accepted these outrageous terms partly due to his wife's endless prodding. Behind every ambitious man there is a woman, and Beatrice of Provence was nothing if not ambitious. Her sisters were already the queen consorts of England, France and Germany, and it irked her to be accorded lesser precedence than them.[20]

As Manfred's army made its way up the peninsula in 1264, Pope Urban IV, in flight from the Hohenstaufen, died in Perugia. The next Pope, Clement IV, also a Frenchman, was elected the following year. He had once been an advisor to the Angevins and strongly supported Charles.

As Charles made his way across Savoy and Piedmont into northern Italy, he negotiated cooperation from most of the cities and sovereigns in the region, Ghibelline as well as Guelph. He reached Rome in May 1265 and the next month he was proclaimed King of Sicily by the Pope. Charles was crowned on the Epiphany, 6 January 1266. Beatrice was finally a queen. Now a direct confrontation between Manfred and Charles was inevitable. The wait would not be a long one.

In late January there were some skirmishes around Capua, where Charles occupied several castles. San Germano (Cassino) was captured in early February. The adversaries knew where to find each other.

On the morning of 26 February, Manfred's army attacked Charles' forces outside the Papal city of Benevento. What followed was one of the major battles of the thirteenth century. Here, along rapid streams and rugged hills, two large armies of some three thousand knights each met head-on. Manfred's Saracen archers, recruited from the Muslim community at Lucera, also participated.

The battle was noteworthy for its technology. Some of the Swabian knights were outfitted with the newest innovation, plate armor, which seemed impenetrable until some of the Angevin knights realized that in raising their arms to strike, Manfred's knights exposed their armpits, a vulnerable area to stab.

Most battles have their tactical "turning points." Here it seems to have been a bottleneck formed by Manfred's cavalry while trying to cross a bridge over the Calore River in a charge against the Angevins. To his credit, Manfred was leading the attack that led to his demise.

By the end of the day, Manfred was dead and Charles was victorious. The Hohenstaufens were at an end, almost.

They still had their supporters. In September 1267, a fleet led by Frederick of Castile landed at Sciacca to support a rebellion that had been fomented in Sicily against the Angevins. This Frederick, a brother of King Alfonso X of Castile, had fought alongside Manfred at Benevento. Another brother, Henry, supported Charles but had grown disillusioned with him for not being repaid a loan. While they initially found themselves on opposite sides in the dispute between Charles and Manfred, Frederick and Henry shared a mutual hatred of their older brother, King Alfonso, who had deprived them of their estates in Spain, thereby forcing them to seek their fortunes abroad. In the tangled web of dynastic genealogies, the brothers were related to both Charles and Manfred.[21]

Frederick of Castile was based at Tunis, where he held a position in the service of Sultan al Mustansir. Although Palermo and Messina refused to join him, the rebellion spread to Calabria and Apulia. Undeterred by excommunication, he won a naval victory over a flotilla launched by Charles.

While Charles attempted to consolidate his power in the *Regnum*, the enmities between Guelphs and Ghibellines simmered to the surface, as they were wont to do every so often. So long as a Hohenstaufen heir lived, the Ghibellines would have a rallying point. Young Conradin responded to their pleas, leaving his Duchy of Swabia to reach Verona, a Ghibelline city, in October 1267. In July 1268, he was received by the crowds of Rome with unbridled enthusiasm.

Meanwhile Charles was laying siege to Lucera, trying to convince the Muslims to surrender to his authority. Learning of Conradin's approach, he lifted the siege and made his way up the peninsula.

On 23 August, the two armies did battle near Tagliacozzo in western Abruzzi. This time, Henry of Castile fought against Charles. Like Manfred, Conradin had the support of Muslim troops from Lucera, infantry as well as archers. Here too the battle was decided by factors fortuitous to Charles, who was all but defeated until one of his corps, having hidden itself, ambushed Conradin, who in the event managed to escape.

Conradin and his faithful supporter Frederick of Baden tried to make their way to Genoa, perhaps with the intention of sailing to Sicily; had they achieved this they might well have changed the course of history. Unfortunately, they were captured and tried. The trial itself was ridiculous, branding them as "traitors" and "murderers," but it suited Charles' purpose. Along with several military companions, they were beheaded in October 1268 in Naples, which by then Charles had made into his official capital. Conradin was sixteen.

The Hohenstaufen kings were gone. They would not be forgotten.

CHAPTER 6

Angevin Interlude

"Justice belongs to the subjects who are ruled as well as the kings who rule them."

— Thomas Aquinas

For now, Charles I Anjou "of Naples," King of Sicily, was free of dynastic challenges to his position. His socially ambitious wife was an uncontested queen. Charles had several children, including a son, also Charles, said to be exceptionally intelligent.

But his realm was not free of problems. Lucera, which for its Muslim Arab community was referred to in charters as *Lucaera Saracenorum*, revolted against his authority, and so did much of Sicily. In August 1269, walled Lucera surrendered following a long siege. Most of the Muslims were dispersed around the region and forced to convert; the Christian rebels were executed. Indeed, execution was becoming Charles' *modus operandi* in dealing with opponents.

From Palermo to Naples

Further afield, he tried to court the Guelphic element in Lombardy while containing, even eliminating, the Ghibellines. This met with mixed results.

At home, Charles increased taxation around the *Regnum,* from Abruzzo to Malta. He divested a number of vassals by means of legalistic logic, his habitual facade. Here he simply demanded proof that barons had held their lands before Frederick's excommunication and "deposition," reasoning that after that time Frederick and his heirs, not being "legitimate" kings recognized by the Pope, lacked the royal sovereignty to enfeoff anybody. Even many vassals who could meet this standard could not produce the required documentation and risked feudal divestiture, the loss of their lands. Charles gave many of these estates to Frenchmen.

If one seeks to find the origin of the crippling bureaucracy, contorted legal system and generally mediocre government that infect Italy to this day, the rule of Charles of Anjou offers as good an explanation as any. Under his Hohenstaufen predecessors, there was, after a fashion, a method to the madness. Taxation was kept in check and the justiciars meted out some semblance of equal justice. However, to be fair, it must be said that Charles was an able administrator, or at least an efficient one.

Now Charles and the Papacy colluded to impose their will throughout Italy, but achieving such objectives could take years.

More immediately, the transfer of royal power to Naples effectively toppled Palermo from its privileged perch as the capital of the Kingdom of Sicily, at least during the Angevin period. It educed the Sicilians' perception of their island's rule by "foreigners." While it was often misplaced — for Sicily occasionally boasted rule during successive periods by kings resident on the island — this idea became something of a cliché and also a convenient "crutch," a ready excuse to explain or justify every social ill, even (incredibly) the Mafia, a form of criminality that actually emerged many centuries later.[22]

Charles sent numerous French administrators to Sicily, but it was their actions, not their ethnicity, that fostered resentment initially. The ethnic bigotry, if it was ever even so widespread as some modern historians would have us believe, was an outgrowth of this.

In Naples, Charles erected grandiose castles and churches. Whereas this city, until now, had been surpassed in size and splendor by Salerno and Bari, Angevin rule saw it blossom into a magnificent metropolis.

The Catholic Kingdom

In 1270, Charles made one of his rare trips through Sicily *en route* to join his brother, Louis IX of France, in Tunis for the Eighth (or "Tunisian") Crusade. Here his motives transcended religious piety, as Sultan al Mustansir, obligated by longstanding treaty to pay tribute to the King of Sicily, had ceased his remittances. Charles reached Tunisia in late August, only to find that Louis had fallen ill and died. In the event, he negotiated a treaty before departing.

The first church funeral for Louis, who was almost immediately venerated, was held in Sicily. His remains, which are thought to have been preserved according to the *Mos Teutonicus,* were brought in a procession from the harbor of Palermo to Monreale Abbey along what is now Corso Calatafimi. Here his heart rests in an urn.[23]

This may have been a way for Charles to placate the restless Sicilians with a lasting gesture that clearly reflected his dynasty's goodness. An Angevin heart in the same church as the tomb of King William I conveyed the subtle message that a French monarch could be as much a part of Sicilian religious culture and dynastic continuity as a Norman. Here Monreale seemed a more suitable choice than Palermo's cathedral, where a Hohenstaufen tomb or two was located. Present at the funeral was the son of Louis, succeeding him as King Philip III of France, who was beginning to fall under the spell of his uncle Charles.

It is difficult to discern in Charles' policy a specific philosophy, yet his was an age of philosophies. Thomas Aquinas (Tommaso d'Aquino), a Dominican or "Black Friar," was a leading proponent of Natural Theology, which brought science and classical philosophy to Catholicism. Composed in the decade immediately prior to his death in 1274, the *Summa Theologica* advanced a reasoned basis for many Catholic beliefs. In retrospect, the writings of Thomas Aquinas, providential as they were, drove yet another wedge between the Christians of East and West, separated since the Great Schism in 1054.[24]

Constantinople, which had been occupied by Catholic "Franks" during the infamous Fourth Crusade but reclaimed by Byzantine Greeks from Baldwin II of Courtenay in 1261, was a jewel the Papacy wanted in its ecclesiastical crown. (See note 14.) Charles lusted after its political and economic value, much as a thief covets an antique pearl necklace for its monetary price "on the street" rather than its intrinsic artistic quality. Indeed, he had been plotting a "crusade" against the "schismatic" Greek Orthodox of the re-established Byzantine Empire for years before the Tunisian Crusade sidetracked him.

To justify his claims, the ever-legalistic Charles betrothed his daughter, Beatrice, to Philip, Baldwin's son, who was titular "Latin" Emperor of Constantinople. Beatrice died at Naples shortly after the wedding in late 1275, but not before bearing a daughter, Catherine. If needs be, Charles could use his young granddaughter as his "anchor" to claim the Byzantine Throne.

In an effort to establish alliances in the regions that extended toward the western frontier of the Byzantine Empire, Charles had already married a son and daughter to children of the King of Hungary.[25]

Constantinople maintained close links with the Italian mercantile cities, and particularly the Genoans. Emperor Michael VIII Palaeologus was funding the Ghibellines of northern Italy against Charles, and he was in contact with King Alfonso of Castile. His interests were also theological. At the Second

Council of Lyon, the Papacy made serious efforts to heal the rift of the Schism. Had its principles been implemented over the long term, they probably would have required the submission of the Patriarch of Constantinople to the authority of Rome; the conditions of the Council, though never accepted by most Orthodox Christians, were later repudiated by Michael's successor.

One of the Ghibelline proponents was a wealthy nobleman, John of Procida, at one time a leading professor at Salerno's medical school and a close counselor of Frederick II. He became Manfred's tutor. After the Hohenstaufen defeat at Tagliacozzo, his estates confiscated by the Angevins, he fled to Venice. He was friendly with newly-elected Pope Nicholas III, a member of the Orsini family lacking trust in King Charles and his motives. John of Procida maintained contact with Michael VIII as well as King Peter III of Aragon, who was married to Manfred Hohenstaufen's daughter, Constance.

Rare was the native baron who didn't have an axe to grind with King Charles. Around 1280, John or one of his sons surreptitiously visited Sicily, meeting with some of the island's malcontent nobles, bringing to them the message of Pope Nicholas that they should trust in Peter of Aragon to free them from the Angevin yoke.

Charles, meanwhile, was preparing a full-scale invasion of Constantinople despite the Papacy's peaceful overtures to Emperor Michael. The greater part of the fleet was being assembled at Messina. It was difficult to keep this activity secret. The local barons knew about it and, in all likelihood, so did Michael and John. Even if they were not privy to the details, it wasn't difficult for them to surmise Charles' intentions.

For his part, Charles seemed unconcerned with the news that John of Procida was convincing ever more Ghibellines to ally themselves with the King of Aragon. His faithful nephew, Philip III of France, advised him that a large

Aragonese fleet was being readied for a military expedition to Africa. Charles' own fleet was scheduled to depart Messina for the eastern Mediterranean in early April 1282.

What, exactly, was being planned by John, Michael and Peter?

The War of the Sicilian Vespers

There are events that stir the cauldron of the emotions for centuries. The War of the Sicilian Vespers is one of them.

It began with a riot in Palermo, and perhaps with an offense to a Sicilian woman's honor. Like many key events, this uprising has been romanticized almost to the point of fantasy, and sometimes manipulated by politicians.

In its traditional telling, the revolt was initiated on Easter Monday, 30 March 1282, near the Holy Spirit Church outside Palermo's city walls when an Angevin soldier harassed a local woman. Her husband and some other men present attacked the soldier and his companions, who may have been drunk. Chaos quickly enveloped the city.

Whatever spark ignited it, the uprising was immediately exploited by an embittered, vindictive baronage full of Swabian sympathizers. Swords and long knives appeared as if by magic. Every peasant seemed to be armed. Mass fighting spilled into the labyrinth of streets and squares between the Norman Palace and the shore. If only for its sheer scale, the rioting was astonishing, and it knew no distinction between social classes or even, in many instances, genders.

Never in the Middle Ages had urban street-fighting occurred in anything like these numbers. Such French as could regroup put up a valiant fight involving dozens of men-at-arms around the justiciar's residence near what is now Saint Ann's Convent. Here the combatants were knights and esquires trained in the best martial tradition. These were elite warriors, men who lived by the sword and were proud to die by it. Ferocity was their stock in trade. In evidence were plenty of swords and a few shields, but there was no time to don armor.

For centuries, since time out of mind, the code of chivalry had proscribed the killing of knight by knight in this type of fighting after the word of surrender was given. This was not a day for chivalry, nor was it a day for surrender. No prisoners were taken. The Angevin defenders were felled, down to the last man — knights and esquires and heralds and clerks. But they were not the only French in Italy's largest city.

United by a singular fury, the frenzied Palermitan populace killed French men and women wherever they could be found. Even monasteries were not immune to this communal rage, and French monks and nuns were murdered in cold blood. There was at least one case of a Sicilian woman pregnant by her French husband being cut open because her unborn child was French.

It was necessary to unmask the French, so the revolutionaries quickly devised a simple linguistic test. Those suspected of being French were ordered to pronounce the Sicilian word *ciciri,* for chickpea. Any Frenchman unable to pronounce it with an acceptably Sicilian accent instantly sealed his fate, and perhaps that of his wife and children.

By nightfall, *vendetta,* that much overused word, had earned its place in the Italian vernacular, its legacy written in blood.

Before long, most of the royal garrisons around the island had surrendered: Trapani, Sciacca, Marsala, Girgenti (Agrigento), Milazzo, Castrogiovanni (Enna), Taormina, Catania. Some offered only token resistance. At the large fortress of Caltanissetta, the castellan capitulated to a small group of armed men. The Angevins' under-manning of some garrisons may go a long way to explain how they fell so quickly.

At remote Sperlinga, which initially defied the rebellion by supporting the Angevins, the French garrison was permitted to depart for Messina which, defended by the Angevin fleet, held out for a time. By then, the death toll had soared into the thousands.

Unlike many of his compatriots, the justiciar for western Sicily, John of Saint Rémy, was known for his integrity. He took refuge in the mountains and was killed at the castle of Vicari during negotiations when an overzealous archer fired an arrow upward into a loophole and hit him. Saint Rémy otherwise would have been allowed safe conduct off the island. The vice-justiciar for western Sicily, the benevolent William of Porcelet, like Saint Rémy a Provençal, was escorted with his family from Calatafimi to the port of Palermo and permitted to leave.

Charles was incredulous. Pope Martin IV, a Frenchman of Angevin sympathies, was equally stupefied. The reports arriving from Sicily were shocking, inexplicable. Clearly, the invasion of Constantinople would have to wait. Instead, Charles had to divert ground troops to Sicily.

The urgency of the crisis was obvious. Here alacrity spelled survival. Yet, not expecting to engage forces other than those presently in Sicily, Charles took his time and planned a major strike.

By August, he had blockaded Messina and attempted landings there and at Milazzo, but without success. Prophetically, a few Aragonese barons were already in Messina, having left Peter's army in Africa to aid the Sicilians. Undeterred, Charles attempted a major assault of the strategic port city in the middle of September but the attackers were repulsed; to his everlasting credit, Alaimo of Lentini, the friend of John of Procida leading besieged Messina's defense, refused to be bribed by Charles into surrendering the city in exchange for reparations and a few estates.

King Peter of Aragon was already in Palermo, where the barons proclaimed him King of Sicily on 4 September. Now the civil war between rebels and their estranged monarch became a duel between kings.

In a series of battles at sea and skirmishes on land, the Angevin forces were defeated by Aragonese-Sicilian ones. Some of the fighting took place on the peninsula.

In April 1283, Queen Constance arrived at Messina with her children and John of Procida, who Peter named chancellor.

In one of the war's memorable episodes, Charles and Peter were to meet for a duel to decide the fate of Sicily, each accompanied by a hundred fighting knights. This was to take place in June at Bordeaux, capital of the neutral French territories of Edward, King of England. Each warring king agreed to appear with his suite but it was tacitly understood that each would arrive at a different time. Then each sovereign claimed that the other was a coward. Most of the military engagements were more serious than this charade.

In a significant incident, King Charles' son and heir, Charles "the Lame," was taken prisoner by Roger of Lauria during a naval battle near Naples in June 1284 and held in the citadel of Cefalù.[26]

By the time King Charles died early the next year, Angevin power in Sicily had all but vanished. The new king of Naples, his son (now Charles II), was still a prisoner, and the Papacy was at first reluctant to recognize him as the late monarch's heir. In the event, Pope Martin himself died a few months after King Charles.

In a gesture of alliance with his Angevin cousins, Philip III of France attacked Aragon, but his army was quickly defeated — as much by malaria as by force of arms.

In fact, all the key players were dead by the end of 1285: Charles of Naples, Philip of France, Peter of Aragon, Pope Martin (born Simon de Brion).

The conditions of Peter's will dictated that his eldest son, Alfonso, would succeed him as King of Aragon, with James as King of Sicily. According to these terms, neither son was to ever rule both realms at the same time.

Although the fighting was finished for the time being, the end of the political conflict was nowhere in sight. The very name of the kingdom was disputed. As there were now rival claimants to the *Regnum,* there were two "Sicilies," the island ruled from Palermo by the Aragonese and the mainland ruled from Naples by the Angevins.

The war's bloodshed was real. Yet destiny, be it expressed through public will or Papal resolve, had shown itself to be a palimpsest to be rewritten. It was politics that delivered Sicily into the hands of the Angevins, and it was politics that took it away.

Considering its effects on Mediterranean history, the resonance of the Vespers is more than justified. The revolt was certainly atypical of its era, yet very unlike the modern revolutions to which it is sometimes compared.

Was it part of a grand conspiracy to divert Charles' invasion away from Constantinople, or was that merely an unintended consequence? Here certainty lies beyond our grasp, but the known facts suggest a plot as a distinct possibility, with John of Procida sowing the seeds of dissent and the Genoans, occasional allies of the Byzantines, as covert supporters and obvious beneficiaries.

Paradoxically, the Vespers would serve as the impetus for centuries of rule from abroad, which was one of the things that the Sicilians ostensibly resented about the ousted French. Thus began Sicily's long "Spanish" period, even if Spain itself would not be unified for another two centuries.

On a wider stage, the swiftness, efficiency and ruthlessness of the Vespers quickly became known to monarchs across Europe, but its clarion call went unheeded, for what was its overt message except that common people in large cities could take up arms? Owing to its wide political impact, spanning the Mediterranean and a chunk of Europe, the conflict is referred to by a few modern historians as "the world war of the thirteenth century."

The Angevin presence in Sicily is a phase noted but rarely celebrated.

CHAPTER 7

Aragon, Catalonia, Castile

"Instead of noblemen, let us have noble villages of men."

— Henry David Thoreau

James, the second son of Peter of Aragon, was crowned King of Sicily in 1286 at the age of nineteen. With coronation came excommunication. No matter. He was acclaimed by the Sicilian nobility.

It was impossible to denigrate the position of King James on purely dynastic or juridical grounds. His mother, as a Hohenstaufen, was the last heiress of her house. His father's line had been Kings of Aragon for centuries. His elder brother had recently succeeded to the "Crown of Aragon," a burgeoning mini-empire, as Alfonso III. His young sister was married to the King of Portugal. Last but not least was the undeniable fact that James actually ruled Sicily.

What is more, the peninsular kingdom ruled by Charles II was for the moment in disarray, its *de jure*, if uncrowned, monarch now languishing in a Catalonian citadel, where he was detained to avoid any possibility of his liberation in Sicily by Angevin forces.

Apart from the excommunication of James, the new Pontiff sought to put affairs in order. His predecessor had placed

Sicily under interdict. Pope Honorius IV, conversely, wished to address the underlying problems that led to the war. In 1285, before the contested coronation, he had issued his *Constitutio Super Ordinatione Regni Siciliae,* a set of principles sympathetic to the Sicilians, which were to take effect in the event of an Angevin restoration in Sicily.

Pope Nicholas IV, who succeeded him three years later, was less amenable to reason. He ordered an attack on Sicily, which failed.

It was King Edward I of England, not the Pope, who mediated a tenuous peace in 1288. Charles was released on condition that he renounce his claim to the island of Sicily. When the freed monarch reached Italy, Pope Nicholas absolved him of his vow to abide by the conditions he had agreed in Catalonia. In short, the treaty Charles had negotiated with the Aragonese was annulled.

The following year, after recognizing the Pope as his feudal suzerain, Charles was crowned "King of Sicily."

Gazing upon the record of the next few decades, we see the Aragonese of Sicily and Spain pitted against the Angevins of Italy and France, with one Pope after another acting as judge, jury and excommunicator. An endless series of pacts were formulated, a few agreed to, and all broken. Several attempts were made to invade Sicily. All failed miserably.

In early 1291, Alfonso III signed a peace treaty with Charles II of Naples and with Philip IV of France. Pope Nicholas was dead by the end of the next year.

In Sicily, James and his government were displeased with a treaty that left them excluded and politically isolated, unable to call upon Aragon for assistance in the case of an Angevin attack on the island.

Two years later, Pope Boniface VIII forced upon King James the infamous Treaty of Anagni. According to its terms, James wed, as his second wife, Bianca, the daughter of Charles II. He was required to rule Sardinia and Corsica and cede Sicily to Angevin control. Instead, the following year James succeeded his elder brother, Alfonso, as King of Aragon. His younger brother, Frederick, became his regent, or "viceroy," in Sicily, which James — acting against the provisions of his father's will — refused to relinquish.

Sicily was becoming an Aragonese colony in everything but name. Catalan merchants supplanted many northern Italians in commerce, while Catalan nobles were given estates. (In Sicilian historiography, the ethnonym *Aragonese* refers generically to the society of Catalonia as well as Aragon.)

The baronage preferred their monarch to rule from their island, not from Aragon. Here their concerns were more financial than sentimental, as direct rule from faraway Barcelona meant higher taxes to defray the cost of Aragon's military power. To this end, in late 1295, they elected Frederick King of Sicily. This sparked a war with James which the Angevins exploited.

As a condition of his election, Frederick conceded to the barons a charter of liberties. According to this, he was not to leave Sicily or declare war without their consent. It was not the *Magna Carta,* but it might have led to similar developments in Sicily as occurred in England. Unfortunately, that was not to be the case.

A series of intrigues and battles continued until 1302, ending with a treaty known as the "Peace of Caltabellotta" (for the town where it was signed) and the marriage of King Frederick of Sicily to Eleanor, another daughter of Charles II. As a condition of this accord, Frederick was to be known officially as "King of Trinacria" while Charles in Naples would continue to be styled "King of Sicily."

Pope Boniface died the next year following a protracted feud with Philip IV of France. Dante put Boniface in Hell. More importantly, the poet's treatise *De Monarchia* was a riposte to the zealous Pontiff's claims to political supremacy.

Domestically, Frederick sought to regularize the law in the

peaceful years that followed. After Charles' death in 1309, King Robert, his son and successor, seemed willing to abide by the Peace of Caltabellotta, but Frederick's support of an invasion of Italy by the Holy Roman Emperor sparked another war with Naples in 1312. Although a truce was reached four years later, Frederick's appropriation of some Church revenues earned him excommunication. An interdict imposed on Sicily in 1321 lasted until 1335. Frederick died in 1337, succeeded by his son Peter II of Sicily, who had actually been crowned some years earlier.

Climate and weather could be as vindictive as any Pontiff. Europe was struck by a "Little Ice Age" that began around 1306. Then, beginning in 1315, incessant Spring snows and rains led to the Great Famine across Europe. Sicily may have been spared the worst wrath of these natural calamities, but their effects were still felt.

The political climate was equally complex. Tiring of the incessant wars, some Sicilian barons were proving reluctant to fulfill their military obligations.

The belated acceptance of reality was beginning to be reflected in occasional references to the mainland realm of the Angevins as the "Kingdom of Naples."

Sicily's close dynastic, diplomatic and commercial ties to Aragon were not severed. Indeed, King Peter's daughter, Eleanor, wed her cousin, Peter IV of Aragon, in 1349. A declared condition of this union was the renunciation of any claims to the Throne of Sicily by the King of Aragon. But such promises seemed made to be broken.

Denouement

The monoculture was taking root. The multicultural society that thrived under the Normans and, to a lesser degree, the Swabians had vanished. Here we see the first Catalan influences on the Sicilian language. On the peninsula, Dante Alighieri's *Inferno* was the first major work written in an Italian vernacular, following in the tradition established by the *Canticle* of Francis of Assisi and the *Dialogue* of Ciullo of Alcamo.

Islam was little more than a faint memory, and the Jews, an ever diminishing minority, were becoming more marginalized than ever. The Church was Latin and so was its language. To the intellectual class, such as it was, Arabic and Greek were indecipherable.

Jewish communities had schools for their own children. Among Christians, schools were the province of the monastic orders: Benedictines, Dominicans, Franciscans. Almost all the students were boys, although there existed schools for girls operated by nuns. Outside the aristocracy, it could no longer be presumed that a significant number of children of either gender would ever learn to read and write. Literacy levels declined across the island, perhaps more in rural areas than in the cities.

It would be convenient to claim the emergence of the Latin monoculture as the sole cause of widespread illiteracy and the decline in learning generally. That, however, would be a fragile hypothesis, for there is nothing intrinsic in predominantly Roman Catholic societies that prevents children learning to read. Yet it is a simple fact that the Muslims, and to a great extent the Byzantine Greeks, advocated fundamental reading and writing skills beyond the privileged ranks of the religious and aristocratic classes. What we see during the fourteenth century is a monarchical and ecclesiastical establishment that failed to perceive mass illiteracy as a potentially serious social problem. This, unfortunately, was the case throughout Italy and in much of Europe, not only in Sicily.

The island itself suffered. Deforestation became a serious problem, endangering species such as the Nebrodian fir, whose wood was used to build ships. Despite this, the much-coveted island was still reasonably prosperous, even if its image was tarnished by the writings of Dante, ever the Guelphic apologist. That the *Inferno,* a literary work (not a historical chronicle) written decades after the events it describes, was unkind to figures like Frederick II and his court physician Michael Scot cannot attenuate their achievements, but here, perhaps, were sown the first seeds of an overt disdain of Sicilians on the part of Tuscans and Lombards.

The *collecta* was imposed ever more frequently, and Sicily became more Catalonian, or even "Spanish," while the mainland, despite its political disunity, became more and more "Italian."

Sicily also had internal problems, some instigated by native elements that resented the Catalan influences in the economy.

Civil War

Peter II, the son of King Frederick of Sicily and Eleanor Anjou of Naples, was a good king surrounded by bad nobles. Born of envy, a certain factionalism emerged among Sicily's more important families, its lines drawn between local "Latin" families and the "Catalans" transplanted from Spain. This was contained so long as Peter lived, but it exploded following his untimely death in the royal town of Calascibetta in 1342.

Louis, his son and heir, was still a child. His appointed regent was a kinsman, John of Randazzo. John died a few years later, having nominated Blasco of Alagona, a Catalan serving as grand justiciar, as the boy's regent. At this point, however, Peter's widow, Elizabeth, took control of her young son's regency. King Louis was by now around ten years old.

The underlying problem in the emerging political fracas was that the Angevins in Naples still wanted Sicily, so they offered their support to the nativist "Latin" faction opposing the immigrant "Catalans," or perhaps it was the Latins who solicited the help of the Neapolitan Angevins. Here the Latins were merely heeding an old truism: My enemy's enemy is my friend.

The arrival of the Black Death at Messina in 1347 only made matters worse. The resulting pandemic decimated the European population. This, combined with the civil strife, left much farmland uncultivated, with obvious results for the economy.

Leading the Latin faction were the Chiaramonte and Ventimiglia families. The Catalans were led by the Alagona, Peralta and Sclafani families. In its essence, the conflict was motivated by simple opportunism, the desire for territory and wealth. While the political identification with either natives or settlers was more than a pretext, it certainly was not the only factor in the destructive wars. Some of these families had feuded for a generation or more. At this point they were simply exploiting the lack of a strong, adult monarch to settle their private scores while appropriating as much land as possible. The Chiaramonte, in particular, erected numerous castles, including the impressive Steri in Palermo, rivalled in that city by the Sclafani palace.

So vast was Manfred Chiaramonte's County of Modica that it was referred to as "a kingdom within the Kingdom." He was also Count of Malta. His fortress at Lentini is said to have withstood a siege by Artale Alagona for five years.

When King Louis died at the age of eighteen in 1355, reportedly from the Black Death, he was succeeded by his younger brother, Catanian-born Frederick "the Simple," whose nickname tells us much about him. Frederick was barely thirteen; his regent during his minority was his elder sister, Euphemia, who died in 1359. He wed his cousin, Constance, daughter of King Peter IV of Aragon, who gave birth to a daughter, Mary (Maria). Constance died in Catania in 1363, probably giving birth to Mary (although it is possible she died from the plague).

Queen Mary

Frederick's unflattering appellation seems merited, for he was hardly intelligent or enlightened; indeed, he may have been quite stupid. In 1369 he egregiously decreed that all Sicilian Jews were to wear a small badge of bright fabric the size of a large coin or seal to indicate their religion. Fortunately, this abhorrent measure was not enforced for very long, if at all.

Many of the island kingdom's most distinguished physicians were Jews. A certain Vidimura of Catania was the first Sicilian woman known to have practiced medicine professionally and openly, as a doctor rather than a midwife or nurse. Her husband was also a doctor, and such evidence as exists suggests that both spouses were Jewish.

Frederick fathered a son outside marriage, but Mary was his only legitimate child to survive into adulthood.

As we have seen, in the absence of a son as heir, a king's daughter might be considered his heiress apparent, effectively his hereditary "repository," and the man she eventually married could claim to rule in the name of her patrimony. This was to complicate young Mary's life.

With the death of the ignominious Frederick the Simple in 1377, the orphaned girl was effectively "kidnapped" by the so-called "Four Vicars." These were none other than Manfred Chiaramonte, Artale Alagona, Francesco Ventimiglia and William Peralta, who had set aside their differences when they realized that they might control the entire island unopposed during an interregnum.

Who young Mary wed was a matter of paramount importance in their designs. News of the Four Vicars' misdeeds soon reached Barcelona, where King Peter IV of Aragon, now arguably the most viable claimant to the Crown of Sicily, was not amused at the manipulation of his granddaughter by a pack of unruly barons.

In 1379, perhaps acting on King Peter's orders, William Moncada, a Catalan rival of the Four Vicars, rescued Mary from Catania Castle, ostensibly to prevent her planned marriage to the Duke of Milan. She then resided at Licata until

1382, when she was retrieved by an Aragonese fleet. Following a sojourn in Sardinia, she was taken to Catalonia, where she wed, in 1390, her cousin Martin "the Younger." Martin ruled, in effect, by right of his young wife, who was also Duchess of Athens. By now, King Peter was dead, succeeded by his eldest son, Martin's uncle, John.

With Martin the Younger and his father (also Martin) Mary returned to Sicily in the Spring of 1392 to rein in the disloyal Sicilian barons who had violated their oaths of homage and fealty to the Crown, eroding the island's economy in their private civil war.

Legend has it that the rebels betrayed Andrew Chiaramonte, the most powerful of their number. Obsequiously receiving Mary and the two Martins at Trapani, the opportunistic barons blamed Chiaramonte and his family for all of the recent problems, claiming to have collaborated with him under duress. Whether the royal family truly believed these entreaties is moot; more immediate was the need to restore order.

Following a naval assault and a long siege, Chiaramonte was beheaded in June 1392 in front of his family's Steri, which became King Martin's residence.[27]

In 1395, the elder Martin succeeded his brother, John I (eldest son of the late Peter IV), to the Crown of Aragon.

In Sicily, Martin the Younger, seeking to placate the restless nobility, convened a parliament at Catania in 1397 and another in Siracusa in 1398. Mary died at Lentini in 1401. She and Martin had a son, Peter, who died very young.

King Martin the Younger, Mary's widower, is remembered for ordering the construction of a network of coastal watch towers around Sicily. He died in 1409. Anomalously, he was succeeded by his father, Martin the Elder, who would not live much longer.

At this point the eligibility of young Frederick, Count of Luna, an illegitimate, Sicilian-born son of Martin the Younger by the Catanian noblewoman Tarsia Rizzari, was advanced by proponents in Sicily and Aragon. This proposal was not entertained seriously enough even though there was an effort afoot to legitimize the boy before his grandfather Martin's untimely death, from choking (or from spasms brought on by laughter), in 1410, aged fifty-three. Frederick went on to pursue a successful career as an admiral. Had he been legitimized, and then acclaimed King of Sicily, history might have been written very differently.

The old animosities between Catalans and Latins died a slower death than Martin the Elder. For generations, they were both subtext and pretext for bitter feuds. One of these involved the Luna family brought to Sicily by the Aragonese (Maria Lopes de Luna was the wife of Martin the Elder). At Sciacca, the Catalan Lunas and Latin Perollos enlisted the support of private armies in a running war they waged against each other from 1455 until 1529. William Shakespeare drew his inspiration for *Romeo and Juliet* from the feuding clans of Verona, but the Bard would have done better to look to the vindictive nobles of Sicily as his model. The violence in northern Italy was tame by comparison.

The House of Castile

With the extinction of the House of Aragon, Sicily found herself in another interregnum. Mercifully, this one lasted only two years. The solution, subsequently known as the "Caspe Compromise," revealed itself through dynastic inheritance along legitimate lines. Eleanor, a daughter of King Peter IV of Aragon, wed John I of Castile, of the House of Trastámara. Their son, Ferdinand, became King of Aragon and Sicily in 1412. Upon his death four years later, he was succeeded by his own son, Alfonso, known as "the Magnanimous."

This ushered in the age of viceroys. The first was Alfonso's younger brother, John, who was destined to become King of Sicily, but after his term the viceroyalty was usually entrusted to men of the high nobility of Sicily or Spain, sometimes to bishops. These were not simply regents; the rank and office of viceroy entailed specific prerogatives and duties.

With the help of the Sicilian barons, Alfonso waged war against Naples, which the childless Queen Joanna II had left him in her will, having adopted him. Repulsed in 1424, he retreated to Sicily. Following a series of battles and intrigues, he retook the Kingdom of Naples in 1443, for good measure adding Sardinia three years later. At Papal urging, he willed the Crown of Naples to his illegitimate son, Ferdinand (or Ferrante). By now, the Papacy preferred to keep Naples and Sicily separate.

To defray the cost of these military adventures, Alfonso levied in Sicily the tax known as the *donativo*, which supplanted the medieval *collecta*. Before long, the *donativi* were being collected ever more frequently, almost regularly. Not all the funds found their way to the royal coffers. Some viceroys were infamously corrupt, embezzling much tax money for themselves. The barons, for their part, resented a tax that could be imposed at royal whim, often on short notice.

In spite of this, they seemed willing, for now, to pay more taxes to a king they viewed as an ally willing to grant them all kinds of concessions. Giovanni Ventimiglia's county of Geraci was elevated to a marquisate, until then a title unknown in Sicily. With this advancement in rank came virtually unlimited powers to administer justice in his extensive holdings. This *ad personam* right did not extend to every nobleman on the island, but it initiated a trend. Worse yet, it came to reflect the attitudes of viceroys and judges.

In 1446, some shepherds prevented by a baron from grazing their flocks on public pasturage sought legal recourse and, surprisingly, won their case. This was exceptional. More often, the increasingly complex *corpus* of law was manipulated by the wealthy, especially the aristocrats.

Rarely has Alfonso himself been characterized as lacking in a sense of justice, but his policies in his Spanish dominions did not always extend to Sicily.

Alfonso was a steadfast supporter of George Kastriota "Scanderbeg," the Albanian leader who was waging a defensive war against the Turks advancing into the Balkans. In 1448, Scanderbeg had sent him help to subdue some rebellious Neapolitan barons.

Significantly, Sicily was now little more than an appendage of what was to evolve into the Spanish Empire. This was to determine everything from the island's culture to its economy. Sicily was in free fall, even if the Sicilians were by now acclimated to the environment in which they found themselves. Long ago, the island's *sui generis* golden age had decayed to a vermeil vestige of its former self, forgotten in its details.

Alfonso was a noted patron of the arts and education. In 1434, he founded Sicily's first "public" university, at Catania, partly to stem the "brain drain" of intellectuals who were fleeing Sicily in droves.[28]

Yet ignorance reigned supreme. The architects working to add a Catalan Gothic portico to Palermo's Norman-Arab cathedral found some suitable pillars embellished with faintly Fatimid motifs. Not recognizing an inscription on one of these as a Koranic sura in decorative Arabic script, the monoglots used it as a supporting column. It once belonged to a mosque.

The Genoan merchants and bankers were an important commercial element, a force for good in an essentially agrarian economy; their Church of Saint George still stands in Palermo. Spanish merchants also held an important place in the Sicilian economy. Catalan cloth, for example, was traded for Sicilian durum wheat. The problem here was that entire sectors of Sicily's manufacturing economy were dependent on foreign trade, while domestic industries (based on artisanal crafts) failed to develop as they should have. This disadvantage would haunt the island for centuries to come because, on the one hand, it was difficult to compete with the established foreigners while, on the other, the aristocracy was unmotivated to invest in manufacturing. Such an environment stunted the growth of a true middle class.

The greedy nobles were unwilling to invest much even in agriculture. By the middle of the century, Sicily's wheat, its chief export, was traded at prices higher than the rate prevailing in the Mediterranean market. This helped nobody.

Even the logistics of trading in the Mediterranean presented certain challenges. As a simple consequence of geography, much of Sicily's trade, particularly the export of wheat, was oriented toward the south and east of the island. It would have been opportune to sign better trade treaties with those governing these regions, but for the most part the devoutly Catholic Spanish kings were reluctant to negotiate with the Muslims ruling these states.

At the same time, an important mint was established in what is now Palazzo Cefalà in Palermo's Via Alloro, the street's name deriving not from the modern noun for "laurel" but from the phrase *all'oro,* "of the gold." Another mint was operated at Messina. (Palermo was home to a mint until 1836.)

End of an Era

Some historians date the end of the Middle Ages to the conclusion of the Hundred Years' War, coinciding with the fall of Constantinople to the Ottoman Turks, both in 1453. But in Sicily the Middle Ages seemed to continue for a few more decades, socially and even architecturally.

Elsewhere, it was an age of inspiration. Johannes Gutenberg printed the Bible and the Renaissance was flowering.

In Sicily, the Renaissance boasted early exponents in the painter Antonello da Messina, the sculptors Francesco Laurana and Antonello Gagini, and the poet Antonio Beccadelli, nicknamed "Panormita." They were rare exceptions. The movement found its greatest expression in central and northern Italy.

King Alfonso, who lived and reigned until 1458, was an enlightened monarch, but his immediate successors, John "the Faithless" and then Ferdinand "the Catholic," were nothing of the kind, and before long the Sicilians were the chronic victims of a repressive, reactionary dystopia.

At a parliament in Caltagirone, King John acquiesced to outrageous baronial demands, reducing feudal military obligations (scutage and the defrayal of general expenses) while granting barons the right to veto royal requests to impose the occasional *donativo*. In some countries, such measures might be seen as concessions to requests for local control of government. Here they reflected little more than the selfishness of a single socio-economic class.

In the palpable pathos, Jews were barely tolerated. In 1474, three hundred of them were massacred at Modica for refusing to pray in a Catholic church. This was a foretaste of the bitter fate awaiting the Jewish population. Outside the aristocracy and the clergy, the Jews were the best-educated social class in the Kingdom of Sicily. As we have seen, a great number of physicians were Jewish; so were many accountants, dyers, weavers and metalsmiths. By the fifteenth century a very few Jews, by virtue of their feudal tenure, belonged to the minor nobility.[29]

In 1478, the barons refused to pay a proposed tax meant to defray the cost of a Spanish campaign against the Turks. Such a war (as we saw earlier) ran counter their commercial interests. Closer to home, the Sicilians traded with the Hafsids of Ifriqiya (Tunisia) despite piracy emanating from that region.

As the nobility grew more powerful, the Church grew more overtly repressive. The same year the barons refused to pay for the war against the Turks, the Spanish Inquisition was founded.

The Inquisition, with its horrors, nourished the most extremely reactionary elements of the prevailing social milieu. Discouraging free thought in any form, it hindered the development of a true intellectual class. The Inquisition partially accounts for the kind of widespread suspicion and clannishness for which (unfortunately) the Sicilians have come to be known. The Sicilian social culture we see today is largely the product of this period.

Scarcely anybody was safe from the long arm of the Inquisition, established to root out "heretics" of all kinds.

History has painted the Inquisition as a secretive phenomenon. This it was, but some of its actions were all too public. The most spectacular was the *auto-da-fé*, the inappropriately named "act of faith" attended by thousands of citizens for prayers followed by executions. The highlight was the burning of condemned heretics. A favorite place for this was the square next to Palermo Cathedral, where the archbishop could watch the entertainment from the comfort of his residence without rubbing shoulders with the hoi polloi.

In Sicily the Inquisition lent itself to the most evil corruption. A man might denounce his neighbor as a heretic in order to obtain his land. As nobody was exempt from prosecution, the Church occasionally used the Inquisition to control the Sicilian nobility.

Ferdinand the Catholic was one of the forces that managed to forge Spain into a united nation. This he achieved with his wife in 1492, the year Christopher Columbus reached America and the year that Judaism was outlawed in Spain and Sicily.

A number of Albanian refugees fleeing the Ottomans were permitted to settle in rural Sicily, and to keep their language and Byzantine Rite. They arrived just as the Jews were leaving. The edict against Jews, the "Alhambra Decree," forced widespread conversions and some emigrations when it became effective in 1493; its implementation had been delayed by a few months so that one last tax could be levied on the departing Jews. The departure of the prosperous Jews, who often lent money to merchants and tradesmen, left a gaping hole in the fabric of the Sicilian economy.

The Teutonic Knights were politely retired from Sicily, leaving only the Hospitallers among the old knightly orders. Church and Crown had often been at odds. Now they would work together.

In 1497, the Inquisition set up a permanent Tribunal in Palermo, eventually finding a home in the Chiaramontes' Steri. For nearly twenty years, Inquisitional cases in Sicily were heard in either civil or ecclesiastical courts, depending on geographic jurisdiction; this move regularized procedures, lending a ruthless efficiency to an evil institution.

Somebody had to pay for this ballooning bureaucracy. The *donativo* was always expedient. In theory, it could be imposed on the nobility, and passed along to all citizens, whenever the Crown needed money, but (since 1459) only so long as the barons approved. The local and personal record (or declaration) of each *donativo* was the *rivelo,* so named because it "revealed" the assets of each citizen, male or female, who was head of a household. The *donativo* was based on the value of land and certain possessions, such as livestock. It was, in a sense, a "wealth tax" from which monasteries were partially exempt. Although the *latifondi,* the largest estates, were held by nobles, most ordinary families living in rural areas owned their own homes and at least small parcels of land — an olive grove, a citrus orchard, a vineyard, a large garden.

Not that most families were by any means affluent, but these tax rolls, most of which are still preserved (being an invaluable aid in genealogical research) provide a clear idea of who owned what, putting the lie to the tired cliché of The Landless Peasant.

Even the earliest *riveli,* issued around 1500, were recorded in a language very similar to Tuscan Italian, albeit with a few Sicilian and Latin words sprinkled throughout the text. Latin was falling into disuse for official documents, though it was still used in ecclesiastical records and in liturgy. Sicilian was by now a spoken language that one found written only rarely. Much as we might presume to encounter official documents issued in Spanish, these were a rarity except in correspondence with Spain. Indeed, Italian was fast becoming the written and spoken language of the educated classes, not only in Sicily but in Sardinia, Calabria, Abruzzi and Basilicata. True, an aristocrat would have to speak Sicilian to communicate with the majority of people he encountered daily, as the *ferraro* (blacksmith) who shod his horses was known as a *maniscalco* in Palermo, but the language the baron spoke with magistrates and bankers was Italian.

The social effect of this phenomenon is that Modern Sicilian, with its various local dialects spoken by 1600, became the tongue of the comparatively uneducated masses who did not master Italian or Latin. This unfortunate stigma was not unique to Sicilian; it was part of a wider trend that touched "regionalized" languages in many parts of Europe, including Spain, where the dominant language was Castilian. The fact that most Sicilians were unschooled formally, and that they were raised speaking an unwritten language, only served to keep the great majority of people illiterate for many generations to come.

Keeping the greater number of people illiterate and ignorant may not have been the intended objective of a planned "social policy," but it nonetheless served at least some of the purposes of Church and State, and indeed the entire ruling class. A man could barely stand up for his rights, such as they were, if he couldn't even read a publication outlining them. Moreover, the poor could not afford lawyers. By 1500, the law, being a conglomeration of every royal decree and parliamentary statute haphazardly issued over the last century, pasted onto what already existed, was becoming unwieldy, with many contradictory statutes and principles. This lack of cohesion led to inconsistency in legal decisions, and as there was no "common law" (verdicts establishing precedent), two judges might rule similar cases in completely different ways. It was to continue this way for another three hundred years.

In such a poorly administered bureaucracy, reliable statistics are nowhere to be found, but the best estimates place Sicily's population at around 600,000 in 1505, about 800,000 in 1548, and close to a million in 1570.

The Forgotten People

Strewn along the tottering bridge spanning — if rarely defining — the invisible chasm between Sicily's medieval and modern epochs are people mentioned only cursorily in the annals of history. Among the forgotten are religious minorities and, more generally, women. The experience of a convert to Catholicism tells us much about the bizarre social atmosphere of Sicily at the dawn of the sixteenth century, when nothing could compare to the isolation felt by a Jewish mother.

She is not known to us by the name she was given at birth around 1460. Caterina de Monteverdi was the daughter of Jews in the western coastal city of Mazara, where the *Giudecca,* or Jewish Quarter, was then a labyrinth of narrow, winding streets. Evidence suggests that the first Jews arrived in Mazara, perhaps from Tunis, in the sixth century during Sicily's Byzantine era. By the fifteenth century, they were part of Sicilian society.

Mazara was an important port, and a gateway to Africa, but its maritime traffic probably consisted principally of fishing boats. There were occasional pirate raids along the coast, although these were rarely grave enough to upset life in the city.

One imagines Caterina's girlhood being normal and serene. In her time, Jewish girls were more likely to be taught to read than Catholic ones, who might receive very little formal education at all unless their parents could enroll them in a convent school. It is possible that a few of Caterina's friends were Gentiles.

Caterina was already married in 1492 when it was decreed that the Jews in Sicily would have to convert to Christianity or leave. This was a traumatically difficult decision for the Sicilian Jews. Those who left Sicily ended up in various parts of the Mediterranean and in Rome, where they established a Sephardic congregation with its own synagogue. Some crossed the Strait of Messina and went to Calabria, but within two decades they were forced to make the same decisions that had confronted them in Sicily.

Those of us raised in today's pluralistic societies, where citizens can readily abandon one faith for another, or even forsake religion altogether, may not fully empathize with such a plight. Like the *conversos* of Spain, the Sicilian converts, called *neofiti* (literally "neophytes"), faced great hardship. Many Jews, who they might never see again, regarded them as turncoats or opportunists, while some Catholics were reluctant to embrace them as brethren.

The state was suspicious of the converts. In 1499, the civic administration of Trapani, seeking to tax property owned by former Jews following the mass expulsions of 1493, still referred to the converts as "former Jews." In many cases, the converts and their descendants continued to live in the *Giudecca* for centuries.

In Jewish law, the converts and their children came to be known as *anusim*, literally "the coerced." A few, like Caterina de Monteverdi, sought to continue their traditional Jewish observance secretly after conversion.

Almost overnight, their communities ceased to exist. Friends and relatives departed, to be lost forever. Synagogues were destroyed or turned into churches. In Syracuse, the mikveh, located in a hypogeum in the Jewish Quarter, was hastily, covertly filled with vast quantities of sand and soil, to be discovered five centuries later following a long sleep. Its very existence was one of the best-kept secrets of Sicilian history. Ritual bathing played a part in the trial of Caterina de Monteverdi.

Upon baptism — which signalled their conversion — the converts literally chose new identities, at least publicly. Christian given names were assumed, along with Latin-based surnames. *Caterina* was one of the more popular baptismal names for converts. *Monteverdi* simply means "green mountain." Converts sometimes took the surnames of their godparents or sponsors. Several families bearing the surname *Monteverdi* flourished in Mazara into the eighteenth century.

Pietro, Caterina's husband, was accorded the Sicilian title *mastro*, "master artisan," and had an apprentice. He was a metalsmith.

The only information about Caterina known to us comes from a court record of 1495 (the trial began in 1494) which actually speaks to the conduct of all the city's converts, although Caterina and her husband are the only ones mentioned by name. This was an ecclesiastical hearing before the local bishop rather than a trial by the Inquisition, and the accusations were similar to those brought against some *conversos* in Spain during the same period. The reason the trial was ecclesiastical rather than civil was that the Mazara district, by tradition, appertained to the Queen and was therefore outside the Inquisition's jurisdiction at that time.

The gravest charge against the couple was the vague but real offense of "Judaizing." This was a crime akin to heresy and blasphemy but somewhat less serious. Specifically, it referred to the persistent, overt belief in Judaism by a professed Christian, typically a convert from Judaism.

Clearly, Caterina was an irresolute convert, but her conscience might have remained a private matter if not for her intrusive neighbors, whose houses stood nearby. Located in the *Giudecca*, these houses were two stories high, built around a common courtyard that made complete privacy virtually impossible.

The troublesome women who complained to the Church authorities were converts themselves. These were the cunning Margarita, the wife of Bartolomeo de Marrono, and a certain Betta, whose baptismal name was Elizabeth. It was clear to all, including the episcopal court, that these two women had never been especially friendly to Caterina. Betta was described by the court as a woman of lax morality, even a prostitute, a fact which eventually excluded her testimony from the record. On at least one occasion, Margarita literally forced her way into Caterina's house to see what her neighbor was doing.

Caterina had recently given birth to a son who was circumcised. This formed the material evidence of the main accusation against her, but it was not the only complaint lodged by her detractors.

She habitually bathed weekly in the traditional Jewish manner, full immersion in fresh water. Since the local mikveh was closed, Caterina continued this practice at home. Somehow Margarita and Betta must have come to discover it, along with the fact that Caterina donned fresh undergarments after bathing.

This was not the only incident of its kind. On another occasion, the Inquisition tortured a young woman for changing her undergarments every Saturday, that being the Jewish Sabbath; she swore that she was not engaging in a Jewish custom but rather something that her mother had taught her to do.

Caterina failed to observe Christian holy days. In other words, she worked on these days, including Sunday, but never on Saturday. When one of her neighbors reminded her that she should not be spinning on a holy day, Caterina responded that she needed the thread, and continued her work. Clearly, Caterina's devotion was grudging at best.

Pietro, her husband, was aware of her behavior and apparently did too little to dissuade her, actions which made up the essence of the charges against him, namely "collusion."

It was Caterina's continued kosher dietary observance that aroused the greatest suspicion. To the modern mind, the fact that one's dietary choices could bring about public censure is frightening indeed, but that is exactly what happened to poor Caterina.

It was serious enough that she refused to eat rabbit or starlings (neither is ever kosher), but it was Caterina's reluctance to consume pork that provoked the greatest condemnation. Here it seems that Pietro, wishing to appear as "Christian" as possible, wholly adopted the typical Gentile diet. On one occasion, when he brought home pork sausage, Caterina declared very bluntly that "Jews don't eat pork," and threw it out.

Undeterred, Peter waited for another occasion to "encourage" his wife to change her culinary ways. This he attempted by bringing home half a pig, sharing the other half with a neighbor — possibly a fellow convert — who made sausages and rendered the fat. Obdurate Caterina was no more willing to eat pork chops and bacon than sausage, and before long her invasive neighbors saw her feeding small pieces of fried pork to some grateful dogs.

They also noted that Caterina invariably cooked with olive oil but never with animal fat. This observation was likely more olfactory than visual. One imagines the heavy aroma of sizzling lard wafting across the small courtyard from everybody's kitchen except Caterina's.

The couple was also accused of failing to share meals with their neighbors. This is unsurprising because, on the one hand, Caterina was unlikely to eat pork or other non-kosher foods offered by her hosts while, on the other, she certainly would not have prepared such dishes for her own dinner guests. The accusation itself implies that the neophyte de Monteverdis were invited to dine with other converts but refused. Here we might imagine Margarita and Betta tempting their reluctant neighbor with an enticing seafood dinner featuring grilled red prawns fished from Mazara's waters. Or perhaps they would simply opt for a communal pig roast, inviting everybody whose house bordered the courtyard. In either case, the meal would be meant to test Caterina's Christian conviction. Apparently, she was unwilling to abandon *kashrut*, Jewish dietary law.

It was obvious that Caterina was not an obsessively devout Catholic, and she refused to kneel and pray when Mazara's church bells pealed every evening. This did not go unnoticed by her two "friends."

She had been seen in church, and we can presume that her son was baptized in infancy, but at one point Caterina may have abjured prayer altogether. Pietro was known to have struck her in an attempt at inducing some semblance of piety. He once struck her hands when she refused to pray. On at least one occasion, he did so with a stick.

Caterina continued to make unleavened bread during Passover, coinciding with Lent. This might not have attracted attention had she not imprudently borrowed her neighbor's oven for the task, saying that "this is the season of unleavened bread."

For his part, Pietro continually sought to demonstrate his Christianity openly despite his wife's obvious reluctance. Perhaps he wanted to convince his neighbors of his religious fervor while discouraging their suspicion of Caterina. In an open expression of piety, he brought home an icon of the Virgin and hung it on the door.

This gesture enraged Caterina, who launched ripened, juicy oranges at the icon as if it were a target. Unfortunately for Caterina, this creative use of citrus fruit was witnessed by the meddlesome Betta.

Yet there was never any suggestion that Caterina was cruel or unkind. The accusations against her were nothing more than allegations of her failure to practice her new religion with the required zeal. In a society that made no distinction between sin and felony, these were "crimes of omission" rather than commission. Some of Caterina's actions were probably little more than the result of falling into certain habits over the course of her life.

The trial of Pietro and Caterina de Monteverdi began in October 1494. With their acquittal in June of the following year, the couple was released (it is unclear whether they were imprisoned during the entire duration of the trial), and in July the court's verdict was made public. The case seems to have drawn a certain amount of local notoriety. The court's exclusion of the evidentiary testimony of Caterina's nasty neighbors, Margarita and Betta, was a decisive factor in the couple's exoneration. A trial by the Inquisition itself might have been more vicious than this one by a comparatively benevolent ecclesiastical court.

Nevertheless, in 1525, a few years after his death, the bones of Pietro de Monteverdi were exhumed by the Inquisition and cremated, the deceased convert accused retroactively of Judaizing, a charge that rings hollow in view of the verdict of 1495. This may not have been an actual trial. However, the practice of trying and convicting the accused in effigy, or even as a corpse, was not unknown.

We do not know what became of Caterina de Monteverdi.

It seems that around 1514 a certain Pietro Jacobo de Bologna brought together a group of Crypto Jews in a secret, makeshift synagogue in Palermo, but few details are known of this.

A number of converts and their children would be tried for heresy over the next few decades, until 1550. A few were executed.

CHAPTER 8

Hapsburgs and Bourbons

"To God I speak Spanish, to women Italian, to men French, and to my horse German."

— Charles V, Holy Roman Emperor, King of Sicily

Spain had been united dynastically through the marriage of Ferdinand and Isabella, who each brought some Iberian regions with them to form an alliance, but it was not yet unified politically, legally, as a single nation. Ferdinand's son and heir apparent, John, predeceased him, leaving no children. This left a daughter, Joanna "the Mad," as heiress presumptive upon the Spanish monarch's death. She was married to Philip of Hapsburg, son of the Holy Roman Emperor Maximilian I, by whom she had several children. There is no conclusive evidence that Joanna, despite her nickname, was insane; she was given to fits of anger in reaction to her cruel husband's mistreatment of her. Philip died in 1506. Raised in the Low Countries, Charles, the couple's eldest son, was destined to become King of Spain.[30]

In 1516, Sicily's barons balked at the viceroy's request for money. These disgruntled nobles may have instigated the revolt at Palermo that lasted nearly a year.

Europe's Last Medieval Knight

The same year, Charles succeeded Ferdinand, his mother's father, as King of Spain and Sicily. In 1519, he succeeded his father's father, Maximilian, as Holy Roman Emperor and Archduke of Austria.

It was a corrupt Sicily that greeted the reign of Charles V. By now it was *de rigueur* for wealthy suspects in criminal cases to pay for light sentences or outright dismissals. In 1523, a parliamentary commission found that judgeships were being bought. It seems that the same judges, in turn, were passing this expense on to rich suspects who sought, quite literally, to purchase justice. Nepotism and clientelism were fast becoming a way of life; adding bribery to the mix only made matters worse.

Corruption wasn't the only plague visited upon Sicily. From 1521 to 1530, an outbreak of bubonic plague claimed many lives. (See note 32.)

Charles had to dedicate much of his reign to the "Italian Wars" against the French kings who sought control over northern Italy. This led to the bizarre Franco-Ottoman alliance against him.

Suleyman the Magnificent conquered Hungary in 1526 after defeating the Christians at the Battle of Mohács, but his advance was stopped at Vienna by Charles' armies a few years later.

In opposing the Reformation — yet maintaining peace with England — Charles challenged several popular movements, such as the Peasants' War in Germany, and the Protestant federation known as the "Schmalkaldic League." As a result of this experience, and hoping to discourage Protestant power, he supported the Council of Trent, signalling the beginning of the Counter Reformation.

Though devoutly Catholic, Charles was no slave to the Papacy and personally wished to reform the Church in some ways. Most of his wars, both ideological and military, were arguably defensive.

In the years immediately following his mutinous army's sack of Rome in 1527, his influence seems to have been instrumental, if not decisive, in discouraging fickle, spineless Pope Clement VII from annulling the marriage of Henry VIII of England to Charles' aunt, Catherine of Aragon. (As a Medici, Clement was a born opportunist who might well have granted Henry's request under other circumstances.) Here perhaps was the umpteenth "unintended consequence" of one event acting upon another. If so, this one was monumental, prompting Henry's Act of Supremacy in 1534. The Dissolution of the Monasteries followed, along with Henry's excommunication.

Whatever the cause of this religious schism, the current status of England, which had yet to emerge as the global power it would become, made it easy for some European sovereigns to dismiss these "domestic" developments in a nation on their Continent's periphery. Such reasoning was myopic. By 1560, the *Ecclesia Anglicana* was completely independent of Rome.

In 1530, Charles granted the islands of Malta and Gozo as a fief to the Order of Saint John, the Hospitallers, to establish a bulwark against Ottoman naval activity. Without ceding sovereignty, the King of Sicily required that the knights render to the Crown the annual feudal tribute of a falcon.

The Maltese maneuver was only a prelude for what was to come. In 1535, as part of his attempt to free the central Mediterranean and the Sicilian coasts from the raids of pirates and the underlying threat of Ottoman attacks, Charles led an army to Tunis, which he conquered.

Returning from Tunisia, Charles visited Sicily, arriving at Trapani in August 1535, then stopping at Monreale just in time for the Feast of Saint Louis (whose heart is preserved there) *en route* to Palermo where, to much fanfare, he opened parliament at the Steri in September. A medieval-style joust and other festivities marked the occasion.

In Palermo, Charles did not stay at the Steri Palace, the administrative center which housed his viceroy, Ferrante Gonzaga, but rather at the home of Baron Aiutamicristo near the "Old Fair" (now Piazza Rivoluzione). Like other homes built in the same Catalan Gothic style — the Brancifortes' Palazzo Abatellis comes to mind — this was a residence fit for a king or even an emperor. He toured the city, attending services at the Magione.

Charles ordered high defensive walls built to protect the important coastal cities, including Palermo, Catania, Messina, Siracusa, Trapani and others. Segments of these walls still stand today.

He remained in the capital until the middle of October, when he commenced an inspection tour of the island. Charles stayed in Sicily into early 1536, visiting the eastern provinces before departing for his mainland dominions.

Enlightened as he may have been, Charles failed to abolish the practice of prisoners of war being pressed into servitude, and he expressed no opposition to what became the Atlantic slave trade. A social war between clergy and aristocracy worsened during his reign, with the Inquisition fanning the flames and introducing torture. Feuds were pursued by noble families contesting the control of cities and important estates, while banditry became rife. The viceroys sent from Spain had ambivalent relationships with the Sicilian nobility.

Church and People

Charles personally defeated the Protestants at the Battle of Mühlberg in 1547, but in 1555 he signed the Peace of Augsburg, formally ending the war that had raged between Germany's Catholics and Lutherans. This legalized Lutheranism within the

Holy Roman Empire. But the Inquisition saw to it that Protestantism was outlawed in Sicily and Spain. Unfortunately, religious conflicts continued to simmer in central Europe.

The Jesuits, a missionary and teaching order formed in Spain during Charles' reign, arrived in Sicily officially in 1549, having founded their first *studium* at Messina under a royal charter the previous year. That school evolved into Messina's university.

This *Society of Jesus* was in part an attempt to respond to Protestantism peacefully and intellectually but, like the Dominicans, the Jesuits often collaborated with the Inquisition, whose methods sometimes included coercion and, as we have seen, torture. Although the Jesuits came to be closely identified with the Counter Reformation movement, simple evangelization and education were their chief pursuits. The concurrent growth of the Spanish Empire facilitated their progress, enabling them to constitute a global network far wider than those of contemporary religious orders lacking the patronage of a powerful Catholic monarch. Before long, the zealous Jesuits were present in the Americas, China and the Philippines. Their missionary efforts often imposed European Catholic values on the local populations, effectively repressing indigenous cultures, although there was occasional accommodation for localized customs. Rightly regarded as intellectuals, the Jesuits — for better or worse — were a key element in the propagation of Catholicism around the world. No Protestant missionary organization was ever so successful as the Jesuits when it came to converting entire continents.

One of the first Jesuits to serve as the order's Superior General in China was a Sicilian, Nicolò Longobardi. In Vatican circles another Sicilian cleric, Scipione Rebiba, was destined to cast a long shadow. Every Pope elected since 1724 traces his line of apostolic succession through Cardinal Rebiba, who was born at San Marco d'Alunzio in 1504. Indeed, this *Rebiban Suc-*

cession accounts for nearly all of the episcopal lineages of consecration in the Catholic Church.

In 1552, the *tavola* was founded in Palermo. This was a publicly-operated bank that extended small loans to craftsmen. Its unstated purpose was to fill the void left in the domestic economy when the Jews, some of whom lent money, were expelled six decades earlier.

Suffering various ailments, Charles abdicated his titles via a series of decrees between 1554 and 1556, retiring to seclusion in the monastery of Yuste in Extremadura. His son, Philip, succeeded as King of Spain (as Philip II) and Sicily, while Charles' younger brother, Ferdinand, succeeded as Holy Roman Emperor. Charles died in 1558 from a severe case of malaria and is buried in the Saint Laurence monastery in the Escorial.

The traditional Sicilian view of Charles V is quite sympathetic. Viewed from this distance of time, it seems downright adulatory. The Sicilians' plaudits are too generous.

Sicily was largely overlooked and generally overtaxed during his reign, even if the nobles were placated with the occasional parliament. The New World moved toward center stage, leading to the obvious decline of Sicily's importance in relative terms. True, Charles visited the island, but this resulted from such events as his Tunisian campaign rather than from any obligation he felt to the Sicilians, who provided troops, ships and money for his adventures abroad.

They also provided most of the wood to build the ships. Yet forests were ever fewer, and land management was mediocre at best. Rivers dried up, and crops like sugar cane were no longer cultivated as widely as they once were. Foreign trade suffered.

But Philip was worse. In 1564, he imposed a crippling tax, the *macinato,* on the milling of grain into flour.

Sicily was the least of his concerns. The same year, he married, as his second wife, his cousin Queen Mary I of England.

She died childless in 1558, succeeded by her half-sister, Elizabeth I, "the Virgin Queen," the last Tudor monarch to rule England.

In sixteenth-century Sicily, it was rare for a woman to rule her own life, let alone a kingdom. When Laura Lanza, Baroness of Carini, was killed by her wicked father for cuckolding her husband, the murder was touted as a defense of family honor rather than an overzealous punishment for adultery. It was axiomatic that the man orchestrating such a homicide would be pardoned or otherwise absolved by the courts. The modern terms are *femicide* and *honor killing*.

These were violent times.

Just beyond the horizon, the Hospitallers repulsed a bloody Turkish siege at Malta in 1565. Undeterred, the Ottomans reclaimed Tunis four years later.

Led by the Spanish, the naval Battle of Lepanto of 1571 resulted in a Christian victory. In its wake, the Turks lost Tunis to John of Austria, an illegitimate son of Charles V, two years later. They returned in force in 1574, definitively annexing Tunisia to the growing Ottoman Empire.

Piracy and coastal raids on Sicily resumed. This would be a chronic problem for a long time as the "Barbary" pirates often abducted Sicilians living in isolated areas along the coasts, selling the prisoners into slavery. As a means of protection, the network of coastal towers constructed early in the fifteenth century was extended, but it was far from adequate.

The Ottomans and their governors would control this part of northern Africa for centuries, and for centuries Sicily would suffer. Philip's navy was preoccupied in other seas.

Spanish Power

Named for King Philip himself, the Philippines fell into the Spanish orbit with the arrival of Ferdinand Magellan, whose expedition was the first to circumnavigate the globe; Magellan himself was killed during fighting on the island of Mactan. One of the first navigators sent to the islands by Philip was Sebastian Cabot (Caboto), a Venetian who had sailed to Canada in 1497 with his father, John, who was in the service of England. His mission was less than successful, but others followed, and Manila was occupied in 1574, given the appellation *Insigne y Siempre Leal Ciudad de España*, "Distinguished and Ever-Loyal City of Spain." In November of that year, the Spanish successfully defended the city against a Chinese invading force.

Sicily, meanwhile, had to contend with a major epidemic of plague, the worst effects of which were seen at Messina and Palermo.

One of the few men who understood such things was the physician Giovanni Filippo Ingrassia. A student of Vesalius, Ingrassia taught anatomy and medicine at the University of Naples. In 1563 he was appointed *Promedico* of Sicily, effectively the chief administrator of hospitals. Published in 1576, his book *Informatione del Pestifero et Contagioso Morbo* described the disease in detail, outlining the development of its recent outbreak. It is the first known work ever to recommend effective countermeasures to prevent the spread of such diseases. Two years later, he wrote *Methodus dandi Relationes pro Mutilatis Torquendis,* an analysis of the torture methods used by the Inquisition. This, of course, was banned, to be published only centuries later.

During Philip's reign, Spain boasted the most geographically extensive empire in the world. In Florida, the Spanish founded Saint Augustine in 1565. Sicily was just a tiny part of "the empire over which the sun never set."

For the Sicilians, the only obvious benefit of this imperialism was the introduction of fruits and vegetables from the Americas, with tomatoes, potatoes, prickly pears, tobacco and cacao being the most obvious examples. An old recipe is still used in the making of Modican chocolate, from the Aztec *xocolatl*.

This, however, was of no help in the famine of 1582. In response to the Syracusans' prayers to Saint Lucy, their heavenly patron, a ship full of grain arrived at the city's port. So hungry were the people that they simply boiled the wheat berries. This gave birth to *cuccìa*, a sweet pudding served on 13 December, Saint Lucy's Day.

Philip's escapades on the high seas were not undertaken just to discover a few new culinary delights. In 1588, during the undeclared "Anglo-Spanish War" (1585-1604), the Spanish Armada was defeated off the coast of England. Sicilian taxes helped to pay for such expeditions. At the same time, less money was being invested to defend Spain's interests in the Mediterranean, leaving Sicily still more vulnerable to pirate raids along its coasts.

In 1592, still another famine struck, with particularly severe effects in western Sicily.

American gold and silver helped the Spanish economy while destabilizing Sicily's. Taxes on exported manufactured goods, such as silk, didn't help. As the production of silk and cotton gradually diminished, the economy became increasingly reliant on grain. This lack of diversification was not a good sign.

The Winter of Europe's Discontent

As if economic problems were not serious enough, the seventeenth century ushered into the public consciousness a seemingly endless succession of wars that touched Sicily to one degree or another, some intimately and others indirectly.

Crowns and countries were swapped between dynasties like cards from the stack at a crowded poker game. Only rarely did

Sicily draw a good king, and she never seemed to have an ace up her sleeve. She was not even a major player.

There were wars for territory (the usual scenario), wars of religion (less usually), and "civil" wars between subjects of the same sovereign (rather rarely). There were wars that eviscerated entire regions and wars that spilled into distant colonies, decimating populations that barely knew why they were fighting in the first place. There were wars for which the causes are still the object of spirited debate.

There were at least as many pretexts for war as there were European monarchs; it was not unknown for a zealous sovereign to formulate two or three reasons to justify a contemplated war. Kings and emperors great and small were still fighting each other into the early years of the twentieth century, during the First World War, whose tanks and airplanes banished the cavalry — and any shred of chivalry associated with it — to the darkness of obsolescence.

Often tendered but rarely substantial, the justifications for war are myriad. True, a purely defensive war might well be justified on the grounds that sovereign nations don't usually choose to be attacked, invaded, conquered or annexed, and must necessarily defend themselves. But in the complex annals of history, obscured by the smoke that rises from the battlefield, it is sometimes difficult to discern the victim from the aggressor, the pitied from the pitiless. This is partly explained by the continuous state of acrimony that led, over decades, from one war to the next, blurring the lines that might otherwise separate conflicts.

War became an evil continuum, relished by a few opportunistic princelings, bankers and generals but detested by everybody else. Alliances changed frequently. The English and Austrians might be friends one year, enemies the next.

A small minority of people, most of whom happen to be men, truly enjoy the killing entailed in modern warfare, deriving from it a perverse pleasure that transcends raw emotions such as the satisfaction elicited by a football victory. These men are known variously as sadists, terrorists and lunatics. History is full of them.

If some wars are treated cursorily in the following pages, it is only because lengthier expositions would be tedious; we are more concerned with the effects of these conflicts on (and in) Sicily than globally.

By 1600, Sicily was the underprivileged handmaid of history.

The Baroque Kingdom

Philip II of Spain (Philip I of Sicily) was succeeded in 1598 by his son, another Philip (who ruled as Philip III of Spain). The king's name didn't change, and neither did much else except the viceroy. Bernardino de Cardines of Maqueda was without doubt one of Sicily's best viceroys, but his term lasted only three years.[31]

Known to posterity as "Philip the Pious," the new monarch reigned during a pivotal period of history but, despite being reasonably intelligent, relied excessively upon his ministers. In some respects this was logical, for the Spanish Empire was now larger than ever.

In Sicily, a bad harvest resulted in grain shortages in 1606.

In 1609, Philip III resolved a clash of cultures in the Netherlands rooted in differences between Protestants and Catholics. This was later referred to as the "Twelve Years' Truce." In Spain, he expelled the *Moriscos,* Catholic descendants of the Moors who maintained their ethnic culture. This outrage perpetrated against Philip's own subjects was consistent with the Spanish treatment of the native peoples in the American regions Spain conquered.

While these events had little direct effect on Sicily, they reflected a *laissez faire* attitude in the ethical treatment of the great majority of people where Philip ruled. In Sicily, lack of efficient law enforcement meant that local families could pursue their own feuds in remote towns. By now, the *corpus* of law was so complex that it was nearly impossible to enforce any statute, even a law against robbery or murder. Adding to this disgrace, the bureaucracy and judiciary were hopelessly corrupt. The absence of law, coupled with the presence of poverty, made brigandage and frequent revolts seem normal.

In this social chaos, the barons were reluctant to relinquish their power. In 1621, the Crown began to permit nobles the purchase of "jurisdictional rights" on their vast estates, meaning that they could prosecute more serious cases previously reserved to the authority of the royal courts.

Seeking greater representation in parliament, some barons were granted charters to found new towns. In some cases this meant, in effect, splitting an older town in two, or establishing a new town just outside an existing locality. In other cases, a baron might coax peasants to "colonize" a new town he built in desolate country far from roads and rivers so long as it gave him an extra vote in parliament. Of course, many of these charters were purchased with bribes.

In connection to this proliferation of titles, for the baron of town X was now also the baron of town Y, nobles sought ever more illustrious titles. In this environment, only the humblest baron was content with his rank, perhaps because he lacked the money to buy a higher one. Wealthier barons wanted to be counts, even if the feudal land they held was not very extensive. Marquisates and dukedoms were more prestigious than counties and baronies, affording their holders precedence at court. Seeing in this unabashed social climbing an opportunity to generate revenue, the Crown began to tax titles — the higher the title the higher the tax. This phenomenon may not have seemed too bizarre in the case of a man whose estate was a vast *latifondo* of endless orchards and fields, but it was ridiculous when a tiny manor became a marquisate overnight.

While their economic freedom was limited, the peasants, as we have seen, were not serfs tied to the land. Slavery in the modern era consisted chiefly of the practice of prisoners of war, mostly from the Barbary coast, being pressed into servitude by aristocrats rather than detained indefinitely in prisons as captives. Another development was Spain's transatlantic slave trade. The Sicilian market for slaves paled in comparison to what existed elsewhere.

The Thirty Years' War

The Peace of Augsburg signed by Charles V sought to achieve lasting peace between Germany's Catholics and Lutherans. This was not to be. The question of religious diversity was not confined to one country, while the Holy Roman Empire itself was, in reality, a conglomeration of numerous states, some predominantly Catholic and others increasingly Protestant.

The spread of Calvinism, which was not covered by the Peace of Augsburg, complicated the religious landscape. In the face of Catholic hostility, many French Calvinists, the early Huguenots, were forced to flee despite the Edict of Nantes, an effort to protect their rights.

By now, the politics of the Holy Roman Empire were of only tangential concern to Spain, but Philip's territories in the Spanish Netherlands were important. There was also the so-called "Spanish Road," a network of military and trade routes running over land from Naples and Rome northward through Genoa and Milan to Flanders. At all events, Spain was prone to support allies to which she was bound by ties of faith and blood.

Here blood, much of it spilled, was a key element. By 1618, Europe was embroiled in a major war of religion between Christians.

Why? It is in our human nature to search for reasons. Simple intolerance was the root cause of the discord. By 1618, the putrid vat of hatred had been fermenting for a century, ever since Martin Luther's Ninety-Five Theses. There was no longer a single reason for the enmity. It simply thrived, nourished by its own odious stench. *Christianity* and *brotherhood* had become little more than words.

In this morass of misanthropy, the accession, in 1621, of still another Philip to the thrones of Spain (as Philip IV), Portugal, the Netherlands and half of Italy went all but unnoticed. The war continued unabated.

Neither side was without fault, but in the dark shadows of an eternal city on the Tiber lurked a vindictive spirit who had long ago forgotten his Savior's every word.

In the medieval past, Papal Rome instigated war after war, usually with little regard for the lives claimed by the violence. This was worse. Modern warfare, with its sophisticated artillery and ordnance, raised the stakes. Here the widespread death and destruction reached a point never envisaged in the bygone Middle Ages.

War wasn't the only thing that claimed lives. In Palermo, a plague epidemic ended when the bones of Saint Rosalie were discovered in 1624. She was adopted as the city's patron saint.[32]

Unfortunately, the Sicilians had forgotten the lessons learned from Ingrassia about containing the spread of the disease.

Meanwhile, the protracted war saw the Hapsburg allies, namely Spain, Austria, Poland and the Holy Roman Empire, on the Catholic side, pitted against several nations supporting the Protestant cause. Saxony, Prussia and, eventually, France, Sweden and England were in the Protestant camp. To the east, the Russians and Ottomans lent support to the Protestant side; each had a few axes to grind with the Catholics, and both might benefit from the conflict by annexing a bit of Hapsburg territory to their growing dominions. Geographically as well as politically, the Catholic powers in German Europe were surrounded. Spain's help was sorely needed.

So was Sicily's. Initially, this was provided in the form of manpower and ships. By 1638, with the war entering its third horrific decade, the Crown decided to impose a special tax to defray its mounting costs.

In theory, this "head tax" had to be paid by every adult subject. In practice, of course, that was impossible. It had to be remitted by the civic administration of each demesnial and feudal town. In the latter, the tax burden fell to the feudal nobility.

The immediate problem was that many counts and barons, with their *palazzi,* town houses, mistresses, gambling and general profligacy, had been spending money as if there were no tomorrow, in the process accumulating huge debts. Frugality had come to be regarded as a vice rather than a virtue. The Crown, for its part, could not afford to be indulgent with these spendthrifts. Clearly, Sicily's Genoan bankers couldn't extend loans to everybody.

Here many nobles turned to private lenders. Some were merchants, others owned profitable mines. A few were thrifty barons who had resisted the temptation to live beyond their means. In Cammarata, for example, Count Branciforte borrowed from a family of the minor nobility that operated a limestone quarry.[33]

With the Peace of Westphalia in 1648, a heavy marble lid was placed atop the Pandora's box of holy war. One or another tyrant tries to prise it off from time to time, perhaps at this very moment.

Life in Sicily

The Sicilians were suffering enough without warfare. Here mediocre agricultural policy was taking its toll, and food riots broke out in Palermo in 1647. In this case, there were several immediate, natural causes for the lack of flour.

Early in a year tainted by extreme weather, heavy rains washed away or rotted a great deal of the seed that had been sown. There may not have been much seed for a second planting, and in the event a severe drought made short work of what little sprouted. Only rarely were there sufficient reserves for such emergencies, and Sicily had grown dependent on wheat when other crops should have been encouraged as well.

Wheat, naturally, was a commodity, and retail bread prices had long been regulated to discourage speculation. Inevitably, the great underclass, the *popolino,* was distrustful of the motives of the viceroys, the nobility and the clergy. In the crisis there was widespread suspicion that some merchants were hoarding grain or flour in an attempt to sell it on a kind of black market.

A sign of the times was what in Sicily came to be called the *cuccagna,* a festival of free food offered every once in a while by the Crown or important nobles to the *popolino* in the largest cities. Coinciding with important local feasts or events such as coronations, this cruel form of charity sought to placate the urban population in an age of chronic food shortages. Typically, all manner of culinary delights would be prepared and placed on large, sturdy tables in a vast public square. At a certain moment guards would permit the hungry crowd to throng the tables. The occasional generic distribution of uncooked food to crowds of poor Palermitans or Catanians also came to be known as a *cuccagna.*

The weather, of course, was beyond human control, but deforestation and the loss of what little water flowed in the island's diminishing streams certainly did not help to alleviate the situation. Neither the nobility or the government confronted this problem. Few trees were planted and few dams were ever constructed.

Nor did the Crown encourage the diversification of agriculture. Even exports were being taxed. As recently as 1651, what little sugar was still being produced in Sicily for shipment abroad was taxed beyond reason. However, the death knell of this particular industry was competition from the Caribbean sugar cane plantations, where the crop was cultivated by slave labor. By 1684, Sicily was purchasing sugar from the Spanish colonies, and the product was highly taxed. Very little cane was grown in Sicily, and it was sold exclusively in the local market.

Despite the growing competition from abroad, agriculture might have been managed better if the major landholders, the *latifondisti,* spent more time on their farms instead of gambling and womanizing in the cities.

However, not all the nobles were philistines. Some commissioned works by painters like Pietro Novelli and his talented daughter, Rosalia, whose styles were not unlike those of Caravaggio and Van Dyck, masters who spent time in Sicily.

Yes, the island could still inspire. Two of Shakespeare's works are set in Sicily, namely *Much Ado about Nothing* and *The Winter's Tale.*

The flight of the wealthier nobles from their rural estates to the larger cities was becoming a general trend. Those who held numerous towns had always been constrained to spend more time in one or the other, but the newly-minted dukes and counts now began to build sumptuous *palazzi* in Palermo, Messina, Catania, Siracusa, Trapani and elsewhere. Naturally, these lavish residences were paid for with the toil of the poor peasants working the aristocrats' estates, but the trend provoked equally grave problems that were to plague Sicily for centuries.

The absentee landholders were inclined to leave day-to-day administration to estate agents, the infamous *gabellotti,* who were easily corrupted. Many of the *gabellotti* were probably dishonest to begin with, and the landholders' complete lack of supervision over them made embezzlement easy. Some actually rented the estates from the landholders; others were intermediaries who hired farmers to work the land.

By no means were major landholders like the feudal nobles and *latifondisti* beholden to the *gabellotti,* but many poor people were.

Endemic in officialdom, corruption now infiltrated the private sector. Sometimes working in tandem, the bandits, brigands and *gabellotti* of the hinterland thrived in a setting virtually devoid of police and other checks on their local power. Tilling the soil of the peasants' chronic suspicion of official authority, they created a fertile environment for what eventually evolved into the Mafia even if "modern" organized crime, with its extortion and murder, was still some centuries away.

In 1665, the coronation of a new monarch, Charles II of Spain, at just three years of age, failed to prompt great changes in administration. The government wished to maintain the *status quo* during the young king's childhood. At the time, Spain's economy was as stagnant as Sicily's.

In Summer 1669, a major eruption of Mount Etna destroyed several towns. The lava flowed down to the Ionian coast. At Catania, it extended the shoreline beyond Ursino Castle, erected as a coastal fortress. Preceded by a series of earthquakes, it was the most devastating eruption ever recorded. An attempt to divert the flow of the lava by digging trenches was probably the first such effort in history.

A localized social cataclysm followed in 1672 as some guilds of Messina revolted against the city's oligarchs. This protest against civic administration, which did not question the authority of the Crown, was hijacked by some of the city's nobles in July 1674. Knowing that Spain was now at war with France (in the brief Franco-Dutch War), they made the local revolt into an "anti-Spanish" protest. This rebuke to authority may have merely been a pretext for other objectives. Even so, the local garrison was overpowered and the Crown lost control of the city and its environs. In early 1675, when their cause seemed all but lost, the insurgents were relieved by a French fleet and an allied Dutch squadron. What ensued was a series of naval battles around the island, without a single Spanish victory.

Spanish naval forces were first defeated at the Battle of Stromboli. In April 1676, the French won a naval battle off the coast of Augusta, followed by a skirmish near Palermo in June.

In 1678, when a truce was negotiated in the wider conflict (resulting in Spain's loss of its territory in the Netherlands) with the Treaties of Nijmegen, the French pulled out and Messina was placed back under the control of young King Charles. Fearing punishment, the patrician leaders of the revolt fled. This war was at an end.

An attempt was made to gain an edge in the war on poverty, especially in the cities, and Palermo took control of the local bread market, guaranteeing bread to the poor at a fixed price.

But the Sicilians' wars against natural disasters continued. In 1693, an exceptionally destructive earthquake struck the island's far eastern region, wreaking havoc from Catania southward to Noto and Ragusa. The loss of life was unspeakable, the destruction horrendous.

In the wake of this calamity, engineers undertook to rebuild homes and churches with anti-seismic measures in mind. The latter were designed in a new, ornate Sicilian Baroque style that stood out from the conventional Spanish architecture in vogue for decades. In Catania, a bustling metropolis, wide streets and large squares were designed to accommodate a new monumentality.

It wasn't only nature that terrorized the Sicilians. The landed nobility still exploited the poor, while the ubiquitous Inquisition, supported by the state and several religious orders, was as repressive as ever. Small and powerless, the intellectual class rarely rebelled. A certain censorship meant that books and pamphlets reflecting views contrary to those of the Church could only be smuggled into Sicily, never distributed or read openly, and the penalty for possessing such contraband was severe. Obvious targets of this policy were works advocating Protestantism and other "heresies." A particular proscription was placed on the work of the Enlightenment's most prominent philosophers: Francis Bacon, René Decartes, John Locke, Baruch Spinoza, Pierre Bayle. And of course Voltaire.

In reaction to this, an elite anti-Inquisitional movement (of sorts) took root in Palermo. It was informal, always small and necessarily secretive, serving merely as an intellectual network for those men, and perhaps a few women, who wished to keep themselves abreast of ideological developments in the wider world. They sought merely to discuss in private what their English counterparts could discuss openly in London's coffeehouses. They were not openly revolutionary. Shrouded in legend, this loose organization has been known by various names.

In fanciful literature, it was called the *Beati Paoli,* its confreres meeting at night and making use of secret underground passages to move around the city. There may be a grain of truth in this; a few such tunnels between *palazzi* were discovered during restorations following the Second World War. Little will ever be known of these intellectual rebels. They probably never numbered more than two or three dozen young Palermitans of the aristocracy and bourgeoisie, rarely meeting in groups of more than seven or eight. Their names, but not their spirit of defiance, have been lost to time.[34]

Viceregal administration was never too efficient. By 1700, the Spanish government of the island was not very obviously different from colonialism except that Sicily had a parliament and an entrenched aristocracy. Nevertheless, whatever vicissitudes the Sicilians faced, dynastic rule from Spain was — if nothing else — a sign of continuity. Sicily endured banditry, repression and innumerable revolts, but no major warfare of the kind seen in central Europe during the terrible Thirty Years' War.

The arts flourished in the cities. Alessandro Scarlatti, one of the greatest composers of his age, was born in Palermo and later worked in Naples and Rome. He is best remembered for his operas and cantatas.

Filippo Juvarra, a native of Messina, was one of the most creative Baroque architects of his time. He designed the royal palaces at Madrid and Turin.

Giacomo Serpotta, a sculptor, achieved fame for his statues in stucco, which can be seen in several of Palermo's churches. He is credited with inventing a unique polishing technique that imparted to these figures a lustre not unlike that of stone.

Three Kings

Frail King Charles II was not made of stone; his health was fragile, and when he died in 1700 the Spanish Hapsburg dynasty was extinguished with him. At the end, his relations with other monarchs were cordial; three years earlier, Spain was a signatory to the Treaty of Ryswick, by which France ended its Nine Years' War against the Grand Alliance (the Dutch, English, Spanish and Germans). Yet some of these Allied leaders were concerned about who would eventually succeed the sickly, childless Spanish king. Hoping to resolve this potential problem, Charles willed the Crown to his grandnephew Philip, grandson of his half-sister Maria Theresa, who was the first wife of Louis XIV of France.

Reigning as Philip V of Spain, he was the son of King Louis' son, "Louis, the Grand Dauphin," so-called for being the French heir apparent for many years until his long-reigning father survived him.

This dynastic choice was not so clear as it might seem, for

there were other candidates. Charles' sister Margaret had married a cousin, Leopold I of Austria, who also claimed a place in the succession as a grandson of King Philip III of Spain. Leopold himself had a son and heir, the future Charles VI of Austria.

The genealogical crux of this dispute between descendants of Philip III (who died in 1621) was that Philip V (a Bourbon) and Charles VI (a Hapsburg) were second cousins one generation removed, and obviously not "kissing cousins." Further afield, other descendants claiming dynastic rights through the Spanish Hapsburgs included Joseph Ferdinand of Bavaria and Vittorio Amedeo of Savoy.

As a condition of his succession to the Crown of Spain, young Philip V renounced any claims to become King of France. Despite this, King Louis left his young grandson in the French line of succession, something which could someday leave Philip ruling much of Europe as well as vast colonial territories abroad. Having reneged on certain terms of the Treaty of Ryswick, Louis came to be viewed — or at least characterized — by the powers of the Grand Alliance as duplicitous. There were already grave misgivings about too much power falling into the hands of a single monarch, and these now bubbled to the surface.[35]

What ensued in 1702 was the War of the Spanish Succession. Here Sicily found herself caught in the middle of a conflict involving most of western Europe, with the island's fate hanging in the balance in a wider war that reached as far as the Americas.

Favoring Charles of Austria, a new Grand Alliance of Germany, England and the Netherlands fought against France and Spain. In 1707, Austrian forces were at Calabria, the gateway to Sicily. Needing a loyal professional army to defend the island, Philip stationed French and Irish troops at Palermo, raising the likelihood that the Palermitans themselves would bear the cost. This set off riots that lasted for a solid month. Here the guilds seemed to lead the insurrection, and they managed to convince the viceroy to send the foreign troops to Messina.

From Messina to Mazara, enemy ships raided the coasts, but nothing like an invasion seems to have been contemplated. Indeed, the attacks were rather similar to those of 1676, but under a different flag.

The war ended in 1713 with the Treaty of Utrecht. Restoring what was perceived as Europe's "balance of power," this agreement gave the island to Vittorio Amedeo of Savoy, who happened to be the father-in-law of Philip V of Spain, Sicily's erstwhile king. Sardinia, another of Philip's dominions, was given to Charles of Austria. Among the sundry territories ceded to Britain was Gibraltar, which an Anglo-Dutch force had captured in the name of Austria during the previous war.[36]

The Duke of Savoy ruled Piedmont, Savoy and some adjoining territories from Turin, his capital. Despite the decline of its economy, Sicily was potentially wealthier than these regions. In late 1713 Vittorio Amedeo arrived in Sicily with an English fleet. Now he was a king. With him were six thousand northern Italian soldiers to replace the Spanish garrisons. He remained on the island for a year, reopening the University of Catania and attempting to improve general and local administration.

As the Spanish had depleted the treasury, the new monarch's first decision was to levy taxes on the Sicilians, including a *donativo* in 1714, and to seize what little gold was left in the national accounts.

Vittorio Amedeo II is sometimes depicted in modern Italian hagiography as efficient and austere. He was also bloodthirsty. In 1686, as a young monarch acting on the advice of reckless ministers, he ordered a ruthless suppression of Waldensians that led to thousands of deaths, either directly or through imposed starvation in Savoyard prisons. In Sicily, he ensured that the censorship of "forbidden" books was more avidly enforced than it had been under Spanish rule.

Nevertheless, sincere efforts were made to improve the government while discouraging bribery and embezzlement. Part of the solution was the appointment of Piedmontese officials. Excise taxes on tobacco, salt and other products were increased. Laws against murder and manslaughter were rewritten and enforced.

A strange case involving the Bishop of Lipari tested the traditional Legatine rights of the King of Sicily. In 1711, the bishop had excommunicated several officials who erroneously taxed some produce destined for the Church. This was clearly overzealous. When the excommunications were lifted by a royal office claiming to represent the Crown's apostolic authority, the bishop sought recourse with the Pope. This jurisdictional conflict was not of Vittorio Amedeo's making; he had inherited it from his predecessor, Philip, whose viceroy was seeking to apply an obsolete medieval law to modern circumstances.

In response, the Papacy formally revoked the Legateship in 1715. (See note 15.) For good measure, to show that Popes still had teeth with which to bite insolent kings, Rome absolved Sicily's clerics from paying the most recent *donativo*. In response, many were arrested, and there was a dearth of priests to celebrate mass in parish churches. This discord probably delighted Philip, who was doubtless monitoring developments from Madrid, even though it was he who had instigated the dispute over the Legateship four years earlier.

Philip was already plotting to reclaim Sicily even as he expressed public support for Vittorio Amedeo. His wife, Vittorio Amedeo's sister Maria Luisa, was now deceased. In 1714, Philip wed Isabella (Elisabeth) Farnese, of the family of the Dukes of Parma. He need no longer feel bound to Vittorio Amedeo of Savoy by the strictures of genealogical affinity. Indeed, his ambitious second wife was encouraging him to reclaim Sicily and much more.

Many in Europe already suspected the machinations of Philip, his ministers and his avaricious Italian wife. When King Louis XIV died in 1715, his only legal heir was his infant great-grandson, Louis XV. Philip made it known that he would reclaim a place in the French succession, and this assertion didn't set well with the French. In early 1717, they joined the Dutch and the British in a Triple Alliance intended to thwart Spanish ambitions in France and Italy. They didn't have to wait long for Philip to make the first move.

In August, the Spanish invaded Sardinia while the Austrians were occupied with a war against the Turks in the Balkans. That island was completely conquered by November. By then, the Austrians had decided to join France, Britain and the Netherlands to form the Quadruple Alliance. By now, Philip's intentions should have been obvious.

In July 1718, a large Spanish fleet appeared off the Sicilian coast. Lacking baronial support, the Piedmontese viceroy eventually departed in the face of a landing by more than twenty thousand troops. The developing predicament was bigger than anything he was prepared to confront.

Vittorio Amedeo appealed to Europe to restore his rights in Sicily since his own Piedmontese navy was not sufficient to engage the Spanish. At the same time, he made it clear that he would accept another island, Sardinia, in exchange for Sicily if it would permit him to retain the title of king. His wish was granted with the Treaty of London.[37]

Sicily was given to Charles of Austria, but he would have to work to possess it.

The first Mediterranean encounter leading up to the War of the Quadruple Alliance occurred in August when a British fleet defeated the Spanish at the Battle of Cape Passaro involving some sixty vessels, threatening Philip's ability to reinforce his troops in Sicily. In December, France, Britain and

Austria declared war on Spain; the Netherlands joined them the next year.

In depriving the Spanish of their control over Sicily's eastern coasts, the British victory at Cape Passaro cleared the way for the Austrians to land. Crossing the Strait of Messina from Calabria, they attacked Spanish positions in a series of battles between Messina and Catania. The key to their success was that they were supplied by their British allies with armaments and victuals, while the Spanish began to run low on both.

In October, a large battle was fought at coastal Milazzo. The Austrians numbered about six thousand, the Spanish three thousand more. This was a Spanish victory in as much as the Austrians had to retreat. What was important was that they would live to fight another day.

There were battles around western Europe. In Scotland, the Spanish supported an ill-fated Jacobite rising at the Battle of Glen Shiel in June 1719.

Later in the month, the next major ground engagement in Sicily was the Battle of Francavilla, thought to be the largest battle on Sicilian soil since antiquity. Here, with a total of some fifty thousand men on the field, the Austrians and Spanish met head-on in a large plain along the Alcantara River. Spanish artillery won the day, but a series of smaller battles followed around Messina, which the Austrians occupied following numerous attacks.

The war ended with the Treaty of the Hague in February 1720, and Sicily came under Austrian rule.

By this time, most Sicilians had ceased to care who ruled their island. Whether the viceroy spoke Spanish, French or German made little difference. Cultural continuity came from the Church. Social networks were built around families. Everybody else was an outsider.

Like his predecessor, Charles VI sought to bring some order to Sicily, and, like him, he found many obstacles. To placate some obstinate nobles, he created them Princes of the Holy Roman Empire, as if there were not already a glut of exalted titles of nobility in use. He imposed a number of *donativi* over the next few years. Soon it was clear that much of this money was not actually being received from the nobles who had collected it from the people in their districts.

The Anglo-Spanish War (1727-1729), which involved Spain's efforts to retake Gibraltar, did not touch Sicily. The Treaty of Seville officially ended the hostilities, but it hardly represented a bond of eternal amity between the British and the Spanish, and the dispute over Gibraltar continued to fester.

Charles curried favor with the Church, and in 1728 a new Pontiff, Benedict XIII, granted a milder version of the Papal Legateship that had been rescinded in 1715.

Feudal tax rights were now being sold more frequently as a means of raising money. For example, a man might purchase the right to levy an excise at a port on all outgoing grain. These rights were usually attached to nobiliary ranks, so we find such strange titles as the "Baron of Two Onze of the Port of Trapani." At the same time, he lowered duties and excises at the Port of Messina, but here any beneficial effect was offset by port taxes imposed locally.

Industry seemed all but moribund. The last sugar refineries closed, and by now many products, including silk and glass, were imported. This was even true of much of the paper sold in Sicily.

The Inquisition continued unabated, but 1732 was the last year to see a Sicilian burned alive in a public spectacle.

Catania was beginning to rival Messina in importance as Sicily's "second city." Inspired architects like Girolamo Palazzotto and Giovanni Battista Vaccarini designed glorious Baroque churches and residences along broad squares and streets. The city's cathedral still housed the relics of Saint

Agatha, its patron, and the remains of King Frederick, who agreed to the Peace of Caltabellotta in 1302, as well as his grandson King Louis of Sicily, who died in 1355.

The House of Bourbon

In Spain, King Philip's immediate heirs were his two elder sons by his first wife. This left no obvious Spanish patrimony for his sons by his second wife, the ambitious Elisabeth Farnese. With the death of her brother, Antonio, Duke of Parma, in 1731, Elisabeth became the universal heiress of that small Italian state, already acknowledged as the birthright of her eldest son, Charles.

The young prince might have been content with this modest inheritance, but a greater opportunity presented itself in 1731 when the Treaty of Vienna brought about the end of a tenuous Anglo-French Alliance forged a few years earlier. It marked the birth of a new Anglo-Austrian Alliance. Spain and France were again united, while Austria found herself comparatively isolated in the power structure of western continental Europe. Significantly in the fickle politics of northern Italy, Piedmont was also allied with the Spanish and the French.

The recent treaties confirmed the international recognition of Charles' right to rule Parma, a tiny state of little concern to the great powers. Before long, he was on his way to Italy. He was fifteen.

In 1733, the War of the Polish Succession tested the military alliance between Spain and France. The Treaty of the Escorial between Philip V of Spain and his nephew Louis XV of France formed part of the Bourbons' first *Pacte de Famille*, agreements that would remain in effect for decades.

Exploiting Austrian vulnerability in southern Italy, Charles marched with an army of some forty thousand across Papal territory to Perugia and then into the Kingdom of Naples, where he encountered minimal opposition. To allay chronic European fears of the concentration of power in a single monarch, Philip V ceded his claims in Italy to his adventuresome son, who was crowned at Naples in 1734. A coronation followed at Palermo the next year.

The change could have made little immediate difference to the ordinary subject or even to the ordinary aristocrat. Charles Hapsburg was replaced by Charles Bourbon.

With the Peace of Vienna of 1738, the European powers permitted the latter to keep Naples and Sicily while ceding Parma and Piacenza to the former. The young king had to renounce his claim to Tuscany, which he had been willed by the enlightened but childless Gian Gastone de Medici, his distant kinsman. This treaty iterated the principle that Charles, in the event of succession to the Spanish Throne, would have to abdicate the Crowns of Naples and Sicily in favor of one of his sons.

Despite its determining impact throughout Italy, the war had been initiated on the pretext of a disputed succession to the Throne of Poland. In its aftermath, Augustus III was recognized as King of Poland, and his daughter, young Maria Amalia, was betrothed to the new King of Naples and Sicily.

Significantly, Charles de Bourbon resided in the sovereign state he ruled, establishing his residence at Naples. For too long had the twin kingdoms of Naples and Sicily been ruled by absentee monarchs. Naturally, King Charles couldn't be in Palermo and Naples at the same time; some tasks would always have to be handled by delegates, be they called "lieutenants" or "viceroys." But government at least approximated what the British, with special reference to Ireland in a later time, called "home rule." Sicily's parliament had never ceased to exist, but now it would meet more frequently; it might even be more accountable than in the past.

Charles immediately set about revising the legal and bureaucratic organs of his twin kingdoms while encouraging economic growth through trade and industry.

Among his more monumental construction projects would be the royal palace at Caserta, "the Italian Versailles," and smaller palaces at Portici and Capodimonte, but these were simply the most obvious of many undertakings. The most impressive Baroque churches and aristocratic residences we see in Palermo, Naples and other large cities, as well smaller localities, were erected during the eighteenth century. This reflected a certain affluence, at least in ecclesiastical and aristocratic quarters. Unfortunately, the prosperity sometimes precipitated the defacement or destruction of splendid medieval churches and castles, which found themselves replaced by "modern" Baroque monstrosities.

Tuscan Italian was by now widespread in literature and communication. It was regarded as a formal language that unified the peoples from Turin to Palermo, even though each nation or region also had its language and local dialects, which (like Sicilian) were not usually written. Piedmontese was strongly influenced by French, while Neapolitan was probably the Romance language closest to classical Latin in pronunciation and syntax. "Italy" was a vague geographic term; rare was the Milanese, Roman or Catanian who referred to himself as "Italian."

The children of Charles and Maria Amalia seem to have spoken Neapolitan as if it were their mother tongue, but they were tutored in Italian, French, Spanish and German. French, of course, was the language of international diplomacy, while some scholarly texts were still published in Latin. The Church clung to Latin in liturgy, but many everyday prayers were learned in Italian.

If Charles was progressive, it is clear that most of his aristocratic subjects were reactionary.

In 1740, he decreed that Jews would again be permitted to

live and work in his kingdoms, but both bishops and nobles protested against this and the act had to be repealed a few years later.

A series of minor disputes with the Papacy was resolved with a concordat signed in 1741. This permitted taxation of some ecclesiastical estates, limited the number of clergy in the Kingdom of Naples and reduced the extent of clerical jurisdiction.

The new Pope, Benedict XIV, appreciated the arts and sciences. His pontificate was a progressive one. One of his first acts was to formally condemn the enslavement of indigenous peoples around the world. He spoke against the Latinization of Byzantine Catholics, numerous in the Albanian communities of Sicily and Calabria. He issued an encyclical in defense of the Jews in Poland.

Naples and Sicily each retained their own institutions and laws. Between parliamentary sessions, which were called every three or four years, government was administered by the *Deputazione del Regno di Sicilia* based at Palermo. Baronial interests formed the basis of its activity. *Plus ça change, plus c'est la même chose.*

Though devoutly Catholic, Charles seems to have been no slave to the principle of rule by divine right. Indeed, he has come to be identified with a form of what is now called "enlightened absolutism." In this he is sometimes compared to his contemporary, Frederick the Great of Prussia, another enlightened despot.

He ordered construction of the Teatro San Carlo (dedicated to his patron saint), which opened in Naples in 1737, decades before the great opera houses of Milan and Venice. He granted permission for the archeological excavations at Herculaneum in 1738, and at Pompeii a decade later. He founded the Capodimonte porcelain works in 1743. The Naples archeological museum and numerous institutions of higher learning were founded at his initiative.

His reign was nothing less than a mini-renaissance. His popularity in Naples soared.

Whether he could boast the same popularity in Palermo remains to be seen. His greatest achievements, and his greatest reforms, took place on the mainland.

Yet some policies and programs improved the situation of both kingdoms, Sicily as well as Naples. In this regard, better trade with other nations was a constant objective. This included a series of navigation and trade agreements in 1740 with the Ottoman Empire, implying that Charles was not the isolationist that some have suggested, at least not where commerce was involved.

Nature conservancy was an important concern. Charles approved legislation to protect forests and lakes.

In 1742 the population of the city of Naples exceeded three hundred thousand, and this figure might well have reached a half million if the neighboring towns and those around Mount Vesuvius were included. The prosperous capital was becoming a magnet for people throughout central and southern Italy, and it boasted a growing international community. Before long, its population would be rivalled in Europe only by London and Paris.

He initially sought to stay out of the War of the Austrian Succession that erupted in 1740 upon the death of Charles VI of Austria. His decision was poorly received in Paris and Madrid. Fate forced the issue with advancement of an Austrian army down the Italian peninsula in Spring 1744. From Abruzzo, Charles personally led an army of twenty thousand men. On 11 August, a combined Neapolitan-Spanish force defeated the invaders at the Battle of Velletri in the Alban Hills outside Rome, a victory commemorated in Giuseppe Verdi's *La Forza del Destino*.

Apart from its strategic and political significance, this

earned Charles a certain respect in the eyes of other European monarchs. He was equally popular in Naples, where he released the political prisoners of the former regime from hellish jails.

Serious efforts were made to care for the poor. The *Albergo dei Poveri,* a large hospice, was begun in Palermo in 1746, thanks in part to the efforts of the Prince of Palagonia years earlier. In 1751, work began on an even larger hospice of the same name in Naples. (Due to the discovery of traces of Carthaginian civilization at the Palermo site, the hospice in that city was completed only in 1772.)

By 1750, Charles had balanced the budgets of both his kingdoms, and that year he renounced collection of another *donativo* in Sicily, the last one having been imposed just two years earlier (and still not entirely collected). The surplus in the treasury would be put to good use.

In 1754, he established the first university department in Italy dedicated to the study of economics as a science, where the brilliant economist Antonio Genovesi lectured in Italian instead of the traditional Latin. A proto-socialist, Genovesi suggested the reform of agriculture and the redistribution of wealth, particularly in the form of land. Charles protected the professor's right to advocate such views.

Another important Neapolitan thinker of this era was Giambattista Vico, author of *Principi di Scienza Nuova,* published in Naples in 1725. Part of a wider treatise on natural (or universal) rights, a concept consistent with Enlightenment ideas, it was influential on the philosophy of history.

The university curricula were updated. Apart from economics, fundamental principles of the new science of electricity advanced by Jean-Antione Nollet (who pioneered endosmosis) were taught. Departments in botany, chemistry, physics (originally a sub-field of chemistry) and astronomy were established or expanded, and these studies encouraged. The state's promotion of fields of study like jurisprudence and scholastic theology, formerly favored by the lion's share of students, was cut back.

The great majority of university students were men, but women were not absent from the intellectual elite of Naples. Maria Angela Ardinghelli maintained a running correspondence with Nollet on electrical theory and translated the works of Stephen Hales into Italian. Giuseppa Barbapicciola, a student of Giambattista Vico, translated Descartes' *Principles of Philosophy* into Italian.

Charles proved that a devout Catholic need not fear novel ideas; Pope Benedict proved that a universal Church could embrace them.

In this golden age, benefactors were inspired by their king's example. One nobleman opened his personal library to the general public, another established a public museum dedicated to numismatics and finds from ancient Greek and Roman sites.

The phrase *the Two Sicilies* came back into vogue. People spoke of its "thousand cities."

Thanks largely to the efforts of King Charles, wondrous Pompeii, Paestum and Naples became stops on the "grand tour" that formed part of the foundation of the cultural education of aristocratic Europeans. The itinerary eventually reached across the Strait of Messina to Sicily, of which Johann Wolfgang von Goethe wrote in his *Italienische Reise,* "To have seen Italy without having seen Sicily is to not have seen Italy at all, for Sicily is the key to everything."

Charles was highly adept at delegating authority. This left him more time to indulge his passion for hunting. While many kings spent as much time bedding mistresses as bagging prey, Charles was exceptionally faithful to Maria Amalia, who bore him thirteen children.

The exceptional king had an exceptional queen. Maria Amalia, who was born and raised in Dresden as a princess of

Saxony's House of Wettin, found time to oversee construction of the palace at Caserta, begun in 1752. She served on the council of state. It is said that she convinced Charles to stay neutral at the outset of the War of the Austrian Succession, which Naples was eventually forced to enter.

In an age of petty territorial wars, Naples and Sicily were spared the addictive vice of expansionism. "We have no ambitions," was how Charles expressed this in 1756. By then, he had transformed a languishing metropolis into a splendid royal capital.

Vedi Napoli e poi muori, said the city's visitors. "See Naples and die."

When his elder half-brother, King Ferdinand VI of Spain, died in August 1759, Charles succeeded him as Charles III of Spain. This meant abdicating the twin thrones of Naples and Sicily in favor of one of his sons.

Philip, the eldest, born in 1747, was excluded from the succession for his diminished mental ability. Charles, the next oldest, born in 1748, would accompany his father to Madrid as heir apparent to the Crown of Spain. This left young Ferdinando, born in 1751, as King of Naples and Sicily.

Viva o' Re, cheered the Neapolitans to welcome the reign of the boy king. They could not know that the end of Charles' reign signalled the end of an age.

CHAPTER 9

The Two Sicilies

"I devote all my attention to improving the welfare of my subjects, since I wish to save my soul and go to Heaven."

— King Charles de Bourbon of Naples and Sicily

Charles de Bourbon was the greatest king to reign in Italy after 1700. Unfortunately, his ethos, his singular perseverance of effort, was not shared by his successors. The grit of a man who must forge a great enterprise, be it a business, a university or a nation, is not always inherited by his children, privileged to live off the fat of the land.

The Pragmatic of 1759 (see the appendix) laid the groundwork for the foundation of the Kingdom of the Two Sicilies which would be chartered later in Ferdinando's long reign. More immediately, it reinforced a national sovereignty which, on paper, had never ceased to exist since 1130. In practice, as we have seen, this sovereignty was sometimes attenuated by the complexities of rule from abroad by monarchs who were also kings of Spain or other nations but rarely set foot in Sicily. The Pragmatic also established the Bourbons of Naples and Sicily as a dynasty juridically separate from the royal houses of Bourbon in Spain and France. This dynastic principle was perhaps more subtle than the obvious matter of political independence, yet inextricably connected to it, for it meant that the crowns of Sicily and Spain were not to be borne by the same monarch.

The Seven Years' War, which ended up involving many countries and their territories on several continents (to Americans it was the "French and Indian War"), began toward the end of Charles' reign in Naples. Although he managed to keep Naples and Sicily out of this conflict, it was something that awaited him in Madrid. For Spain and her empire, it was unavoidable. In the years to come, Charles attempted to maintain Spain's influence in the face of encroachment by other colonial powers. His efforts were generally successful, and he is credited with preserving the Spanish Empire in a minor resurgence.

Charles was as autocratic as any absolute monarch of his age, but he made absolutism palatable.

As King of Spain, he was one of the first monarchs to recognize the fledgling United States of America, where he sponsored the construction of New York's first Roman Catholic church.

We should resist the temptation to ignore Charles III of Spain after 1759, for he was to be the invisible hand in the life of his young son living in Naples, who would not reach the age of majority until 1767. The visible hand would be Bernardo Tanucci, head of the council of regency.

Charles had brought Tanucci with him to Naples from Tuscany, appointing him to a succession of posts. Like Charles, the man now acting as regent advocated what later came to be called "enlightened despotism." Indeed, he had been instrumental in bringing about many of the changes Charles implemented during his Italian reign.

Commerce and Kleptocracy

What had not changed very much was the basic economy of Sicily, which was still overwhelmingly dependent on exports of grain, a commodity whose price was increasingly influenced by greedy brokers and fickle factors in the market. By 1760, just a few brokers from Genoa seemed to be controlling the entire export market for the Sicilian supply. Price fixing and corruption were rife. Smuggling wheat shipments out of Sicily as contraband was a normal practice.

The harvest of 1763 was disastrous, leading to what can only be described as a famine. The next year's harvest was better, and this brought about a decrease in the domestic prices of wheat and flour for use in Sicily. The harvest of 1765 was still more bountiful, even though growers and export agents attempting to fix grain prices initially sought to convince everybody that it wasn't.

In another detrimental trend, Sicily's hard wheat was falling out of fashion abroad, where easily-milled soft wheat was preferred, but for now it still had buyers in the Ottoman and British empires.

Unfortunately, taxes, transportation (Sicilian roads were terrible), bribes and other costs kept the price of the Sicilian product high, making the international market for the island's wheat extremely vulnerable to foreign competition. An unforeseen blow came in the form of Ukrainian grain when Russian ships were permitted passage through the Bosporus and the Dardanelles into the Mediterranean beginning in 1774.

In a bizarre twist, Sicily began importing wheat from the Russian Empire. While the effect of this development should not be exaggerated, it represented an economic turn for the worse. Sicily might still be able to feed her people, but corruption, bad public policy and poor management were destroying the island's economy. There were early signs of the advent of the Industrial Revolution on the mainland around Naples and Salerno, but not in Sicily.

Sicily may have been exporting less grain, but she managed to export the charlatan Giuseppe Balsamo, known as

"Cagliostro," an occultist and swindler whose travels took him across Europe. Goethe wrote a comedy based on his life. Balsamo, who died a Papal prisoner, is little more than a colorful footnote to history, but his fame exemplifies the Sicilians' enduring fascination with charlatanry and the social craft of *furbizia,* slyness. Sadly, this trait is something with which the Palermitans, in particular, have come to be strongly identified since the eighteenth century, even if it was never an exclusively Sicilian phenomenon.

In Cagliostro's time, *furbizia* was reflected in the efforts of grain brokers to fix prices. In ours it is a widespread, if not immediately apparent, social ill that has infiltrated the worlds of government, politics, business and even academia on many levels. Bribes, payoffs, embezzlement, cronyism, nepotism and mediocrity (incompetence among doctors, lawyers and professors) are its by-products, and its tentacles have stretched beyond Palermo to Milan, Turin, Venice and Florence.

In the countryside, the most *furbi* Sicilians were the *gabellotti,* who we met earlier. By the end of the eighteenth century these estate agents for absentee landlords formed part of the corrupt socio-economic *milieu* that nourished widespread criminality. A greedy mayor might conspire with a *gabellotto* to control the local water supply or to impose illegal "tolls" on the farmer who had to cart his produce down a local road.

Complicit in this phenomenon was a widespread distrust of authority, which the ordinary person saw embodied in the local baron and his *gabellotto*. As often as not, the police colluded with the landholders. The police were more interested in maintaining order, keeping the masses under control, than enforcing the law, which anyway favored the rich.

Justice was stacked against the poor. It became expedient for a cattle rustler to steal a flock of sheep in the dead of night and demand a ransom for it from the shepherd the next day. On top of this, the thief might require payment, "protection money," to guarantee that the flock would be safe from theft in the future. To whom could the victim turn? Even if the police investigated, the entire case was based on the victim's word against that of the thieves.

A reliance on whatever local power structure existed was only natural. Some people sought relief from prominent local men rather than the ineffective police or the absent landholders. Most of these local "men of honor" were themselves criminals; some were *gabellotti*. Here we find the insidious beginnings of organized crime, the Mafia. Over time, Calabria, Apulia and Campania fell prey to the same thing.

The earliest Mafia activity seems to have begun in Sicily's central and western regions, in localities amidst the vast *latifondi* where wheat was the main crop, but the rangers guarding the Madonian and Nebrodian forests of the northeast could be just as corrupt as any *gabellotto*. As the Mafia's early growth was sporadic and uneven, historians disagree about its date of origin and the mode of its development. Until the twentieth century it was, at best, a loose network rather than a centralized organization. (See note 22.)

It was always about money and wealth. The murders, vendettas and feuds were incidental evils necessitated by the chief objectives.

While the authorities might successfully prosecute an individual *mafioso* for a specific crime, it was difficult to attack a covert activity that could barely be identified.

Others made easier targets. One of these was a powerful religious order in possession of numerous edifices, a seemingly endless patrimony of rural estates, plenty of gold and an international network spanning the Spanish Empire, much of Europe and part of Asia.

The Jesuits were a highly influential institution that might arguably be described as corrupt. Enjoying the support of the state, they worked in tandem with the Inquisition. The order owed its very existence to the Spanish Crown.

Many had grown suspicious of the order's excessive influence in the Church. In Madrid, the ministers of Charles III came to view the order's power as dangerous. Like the erstwhile Templars, the Jesuits had become, in effect, a state within a state. They were bolstered by the Inquisition, virtually a law unto itself. This intolerable condition led Portugal and France to take measures against them. Now Charles would follow suit.

In 1767, the order was suddenly and unequivocally suppressed in the Bourbon kingdoms of Spain, Naples and Sicily (along with Malta), where a single day saw the arrest and deportation of thousands of Jesuits and many of their retainers. It was an exercise in efficiency, with local officials opening sealed orders on a designated day. With the expulsions came the confiscation of Jesuit property. This left the Dominicans as Sicily's largest, most powerful religious order.

King Ferdinando I

In the same year, Ferdinando (for the first part of his reign he was Ferdinando IV of Naples and Ferdinando III of Sicily) reached the age of majority. While he was not lacking in intelligence, he seems not to have absorbed much of the enlightenment of his mentor, Tanucci, or perhaps he simply rebelled against what the regent occasionally tried to instill in him. It is thought that the overbearing Tanucci gave in to a dark side, indulging the young king's idleness and hedonism while ignoring his education. The results of this could not be good.

Ferdinando's first important act as king was the expulsion of the Jesuits, something his father and others had been planning for some time. His marriage to Maria Carolina of Austria had also been planned.

True to her parentage, Maria Carolina, who was guaranteed a place in the council of state, advocated for Austrian interests over those of Spain. When Tanucci protested this, he was summarily retired. Ferdinando didn't seem worried at being distanced from the father he barely knew.

What emerged from this political metamorphosis was a rapprochement with Great Britain and Austria. Naples and Sicily, to paraphrase Charles III, had no political ambitions in either the Old World or the Americas, so Ferdinando's accommodation of foreign interests was not a matter of great international importance.

There could be no doubt that Ferdinando's Italian dominions stood to be exploited by Britain and Austria, both imperial powers. On the other hand, one could just as easily argue that Sicily had long been exploited by Spain, which took the island for granted.

Despite its slow economic decline over the last few centuries, Sicily had much to offer, some of it from the land itself.

Sulfur, the Biblical brimstone, was an essential element in gunpowder long before 1777, when Antoine Lavoisier convinced the world that it was an element rather than a chemical compound. However one defined it, sulfur was needed for Britain's burgeoning Industrial Revolution. The golden mineral was abundant in Sicily, where it was more easily mined than elsewhere. Before long, Great Britain enjoyed a virtual monopoly on Sicilian sulfur, which at first was extracted from open pits.

Visiting western Sicily in 1773, John Woodhouse, an English merchant, immediately realized that the grapes and climate were similar to those of Portugal and Spain. Here he could produce a fortified wine similar to Port, Madeira and Sherry, for which there was an unslakeable demand in Britain. Moreover, the British did not wish to rely on their fragile relationship with Spain for their supply of fortified wine; these concerns were substantiated a few years later by the outbreak of the "Anglo-Spanish War," part of a wider conflict, the American Revolutionary War.

Before long, Marsala was being shipped as far as the United States, where it was served in the White House by President Thomas Jefferson. Competition eventually arrived from Benjamin Ingham and his nephew, Joseph Whitaker.

Sicily also provided Britain a convenient base for its Mediterranean naval operations, and here Ferdinando's amenability facilitated the negotiation of several military agreements. An Englishman, John Acton, was enlisted to reorganize the navy and the army. These efforts met with mixed success, but Acton eventually rose to the rank of prime minister.

While Woodhouse was enjoying the sunshine of rural Sicily, Palermo suffered a long revolt that began as a food riot but quickly turned into a rebellion against an unpopular viceroy (or "lieutenant") who had increased local sales taxes. Most of Ferdinando's ministers, unfortunately, seemed to learn too little from this experience.

There was greater social progress on the mainland. In 1778, Italy's first public housing estate, San Leucio, was built near Caserta. This became the cornerstone of an industrial town dedicated to the silk trade. One of the advisors on this project was Domenico Caracciolo, who had lived as a diplomat in London and Paris, where he assimilated some principles of the Enlightenment.

The very antithesis of his reprobate predecessors, Caracciolo became Sicily's viceroy in 1781. His first major act was to suppress the Inquisition the following year. It was good to finally be rid of the "Holy Office." An inspired reformer, Caracciolo attempted to enforce laws and curtail baronial privileges. The barons' displeasure can be imagined. Accustomed to purchasing justice, they resented being called to book for their crimes and corruption.

One of Caracciolo's greatest humanitarian challenges was

responding to the Messina earthquake of 1783.

In 1785, he anonymously published a treatise on the Sicilian economy and its failing agricultural policy in response to widespread malnutrition during a famine the previous year. Some years earlier, he had written about water management in Sicily.

At least a few changes survived the end of his term, which came in 1786. The following year, a school of agricultural science named for the gifted Paolo Balsamo, who advocated many practical reforms in his field, was established at Palermo's Royal Academy of Studies, precursor of the university. In connection with this, a department of botany was set up, complete with a large botanical garden (the public gardens would open later). An attempt was made to introduce agricultural ideas from England. Some concepts, such as crop rotation, were rudimentary, but the stagnant mentality of the landholders impeded significant progress.

Elsewhere, seeds were sprouting with uncommon alacrity. They were seeds of revolution.

The French and the British

The French Revolution broke out in 1789. Not without reason, monarchs across Europe watched in fear as events unfolded.

Ferdinando, of course, was a cousin of King Louis XVI. Queen Maria Carolina was the sister of his wife, Marie Antoinette. The French king and queen were executed in 1793. By then, Ferdinando had joined the many nations of the First Coalition arrayed against France and her expansionism.

On the domestic front, Ferdinando's advisors suggested that he curtail reforms of the kind advocated by Caracciolo.

The republican animus reached Sicily in a series of revolts, but even the largest, led by Francesco di Blasi in Palermo in 1795, was underwhelming. The response to this revolutionary riot, with its treasonous overtures, was uncompromising; its leader was tried and executed as surely as the French had beheaded *citoyen* Louis Capet.

As the revolutionary spirit, which the *ancien régime* viewed as a lethal virus, spread across Europe, anything seemed possible. At the very least, serious reforms might be demanded. Ever reactionary, Ferdinando and Maria Carolina were resolute in their opposition to political change in any form. It would be conceded only over their dead bodies.

Yet Ferdinando chose this moment to recognize another nation founded in revolution, the United States of America, whose president, George Washington, sent a consular agent to Naples in 1796. Here there were no diplomatic intricacies; quite simply, Ferdinando acted only after his British ally, King George III, approved "Jay's Treaty," which the United States Senate had ratified the preceding year. Although President Thomas Jefferson sent a consular agent to Palermo in 1802, the kingdom's full diplomatic relations with the young nation across the ocean would be established only much later.

Popular revolts were not the only outgrowth of France's revolution. Before long, the rise of a faction led by charismatic Napoleon Bonaparte was exporting its ideas by force. Like the Punic Wars of yore, the incessant Napoleonic Wars spawned myriad complexities, constantly reshaping alliances and borders.[38]

Over the next two decades, most European rulers were dragged into this quagmire. The King of Naples became one of them. A factor that made matters worse for Naples was that Ferdinando was more easily manipulated than his counterparts who ruled other nations.

Notwithstanding that Ferdinando had made peace with the current French government, the Directory, two years earlier, Napoleon Bonaparte seized Malta *en route* to Egypt in June 1798, evicting the Knights Hospitaller from the fief they held from the Sicilian Crown. It is quite possible that the French (like many in Europe) inferred that the Hospitallers' possession of Malta and Gozo was tantamount to sovereignty, without realizing that both were legally part of the Kingdom of Sicily. At all events, the islands now joined Napoleon's rapidly-expanding empire.

In August the British defeated the French at the Battle of the Nile. Within weeks, Britain commenced a blockade and siege of Malta.

Ferdinando was more immediately alarmed by events transpiring to the north of Naples. The French had occupied most of northern Italy.

In November, acting impetuously instead of waiting for promised support from his Austrian allies, Ferdinando marched on Rome, where his army was handily defeated by the French forces. Following this debacle, he retreated to Naples, where he and his family boarded a British warship for Palermo. The French, meanwhile, made their way southward.

In January 1799, the French marched on the city of Naples which, despite fierce resistance from the loyalist faction, fell to the invaders, who established the Parthenopaean Republic on behalf of some local revolutionaries, stationing a French garrison there. That this new republican state was a French puppet did not seem to bother its Neapolitan founders.

Ferdinando's rashness had cost him one of his kingdoms, at least for the moment.

Before long, the greater part of the overextended French army was recalled to northern Italy. This offered Neapolitan troops, led by the intrepid Fabrizio Ruffo — aristocrat, politician and cardinal — the chance to take back the Kingdom of Naples. In June his army reached the city of Naples, where it was aided by Horatio Nelson's formidable naval forces. Deprived of French military support, the Parthenopaean Republic crumbled.

Although Ferdinando returned to Naples on a British warship, he did not immediately take up residence in the city, choosing to wait until the revolutionary dust settled. Some of the revolution's leaders were tried but most were eventually granted amnesty.

In September 1800, the French garrison at Valletta capitulated. By now, the Maltese were disillusioned, having come to view the French troops as arrogant, but Napoleon Bonaparte, the modern Caesar, had brought more than an army to Malta. The French freed slaves and political prisoners, abolished the rights of the nobility and introduced democratic principles. All Maltese were to be equal before the law, and the few Jews were given permission to erect a synagogue. It was enough to make despotic kings tremble in trepidation.

The British retained most of these reforms but refused to restore the Maltese islands to the King of Sicily, who likely would have suppressed the islanders and reinstalled the nasty knights. Malta, the Diego Garcia of the Mediterranean, would make a useful base of military operations. Unlike Sicily, where Britain's Royal Navy enjoyed specific port privileges accorded it by treaty, this became a British possession. Ferdinando's strenuous objections fell on deaf ears.

In 1802, the Peace of Amiens brought a brief respite from French expansionism. Before leaving Sicily, Ferdinando sought to put the island's affairs in order. He called a parliament where Gaetano Cottone, a nobleman, adamantly urged the adoption of a constitution. This proposal was ignored.

Cottone wasn't the island's only intellectual to support reforms. Another was Giuseppe Piazzi, an astronomer who discovered the first known dwarf planet, Ceres, in 1801, based on observations made from Palermo.

Back in Naples, the government imposed austerity measures in view of a national budget saddled with extraordinary deficits resulting from the French occupation that bolstered the republican revolutionaries. Compounding the crisis, a bad harvest necessitated the importation of grain from abroad. In March 1803 there was a run on the Neapolitan banks.

French power in the region may have dissipated, but it had not disappeared. Indeed, the French encamped some troops in coastal regions of the Kingdom of Naples after being ejected from Malta by the British and Corfu by the Russians. Ferdinando now sought to avoid involvement by keeping his kingdoms neutral.

In 1804 the Pope permitted the return of the Jesuits in the kingdoms of Naples and Sicily, an action that antedated by a decade their general restoration around Europe. The order's influence in Sicily, where the Jesuits reacquired only a fraction of their former property, was to be muted.

In late 1805, the bloody Battle of Austerlitz resulted in a French victory over Russia and the German states. This "Battle of the Three Emperors" precipitated the dissolution of the Holy Roman Empire while effectively ending the Third Coalition uniting Britain, Russia and Sweden.

Having consolidated his position to the north of the Alps, Napoleon dispatched an army to conquer the Kingdom of Naples despite having recognized its neutrality.

In advance of the arrival of the French, Ferdinando left Naples, which the invaders occupied following token resistance in February 1806. For the second time, he found himself in Palermo. This sojourn would be longer than the first one.

This time he already had a place to stay. The Ficuzza Hunting Lodge was located amidst a woods in the Sicanian Mountains near Corleone. On the edge of Palermo, in the Favorita hunting reserve, was the Chinese Villa. Both were built in 1799 to designs by Giuseppe Venanzio Marvuglia.

Napoleon also had designs on Sicily — military ones. As the island's army and navy were underdeveloped, there was no choice except for the British to defend it.

For the most part, Ferdinando stayed at Ficuzza with his

courtiers and his mistresses, while Maria Carolina preferred Palermo, where she could intrigue against the British, who she regarded as natural enemies.

A ray of sunlight came with the marriage of her daughter, Maria Cristina, to Carlo Felice of Savoy in the Palatine Chapel of Palermo's Norman Palace in March 1807. Maria Cristina became Queen Consort of Sardinia when Carlo Felice was crowned in 1821; she lived until 1849 surviving her husband by eighteen years.

In Naples, the French were laying serious plans to invade Sicily. Appointed king by his brother, Joseph Bonaparte amassed a large army but lacked enough suitable ships to effect a safe crossing to Messina, where the British beat back an attempted landing by a small contingent.

In 1808, Napoleon replaced Joseph with Joachim Murat, who was married to his sister, Caroline Bonaparte. An able administrator, Murat instituted civil vital statistics records and undertook a number of measures to curtail the influence of the Catholic Church in daily life.

If there were ever any doubt in the past, by now it was becoming painfully obvious to the British in Sicily that Ferdinando was anything but competent. Whenever it was possible, they preferred dealing with his son and heir apparent, Francesco. In January 1810, Francesco's wife gave birth to a son, christened Ferdinando Carlo. He was to be the last King of Sicily born on the island.

The British were loath to interfere in local politics, but Ferdinando left them little choice. When parliament rejected the Crown's request for a *donativo* that was viewed as an excessive imposition, the compromise was a fixed rate tax of one percent on certain financial transactions. In July 1811, William Bentinck, an experienced governor, arrived to take command of the British forces and he effectively took control of Sicily.

At Bentinck's urging, Ferdinando named Francesco his

"Prince Vicar," or regent, in January 1812. Great changes were in the offing.

Evolution and Constitution

Bentinck proposed a constitution loosely based on the British model. Ratified in July, it had several significant effects, the greatest being the modernization of government based on democratic principles. It sought to bring Sicily out of the social morass of the Middle Ages, in the process stemming the tide of revolution.

It established that only parliament, consisting of two chambers as in England, was to propose laws and levy taxes. The infamous *donativo,* imposed at royal whim, was categorically abolished. Parliament was to be called at least once each year.

Here the *vox populi* came to life in a constitution for the people. Freedom of speech and freedom of the press were formally recognized, even though restrictions were placed on direct criticism of Church and Crown. Torture was abolished, and citizens were to enjoy equal rights before the law. Nobody would be denied due process, or detained without being charged. *Habeas corpus* became a reality. (The constitution's chief elements are outlined in an appendix.)

Feudalism was abolished. In its stead, the feudatories whose estates had the highest tax base were accorded seats in a Chamber of Peers similar to Britain's House of Lords. This is usually cited as the most significant element for several reasons, not the least being that it was one of the few reforms to survive the constitution's suppression a few years later. In practice, it meant that any vestige of feudal privilege disappeared overnight. Anachronistic rights of taxation were abolished.

Land holdings large and small became "freehold" properties for which only the owners or the state could claim rights to water and minerals. Now the owner of a sulfur pit or salt mine located on heretofore manorial land became its absolute proprietor.

Because the largest estates, the *latifondi,* remained in existence, the major landholders still wielded power, but certain areas used by the general public, such as major roads, became the property of the state. No longer was it possible for a feudatory to literally own an entire town.

While the social order did not change immediately, the status of the nobility itself evolved. Until now, most nobiliary titles were feudal. Purchase of a county brought with it feudal rights and also the title of count. By 1800, Sicily's largest manorial estates were princedoms and dukedoms. Many *gabellotti* purchased baronies — typically smaller than marquisates and counties — in the decades immediately before 1812, and this explains a certain snobbery toward barons on the part of Sicily's princes, dukes, marquesses and counts. Since peerages were based on revenue rather than title, a few wealthier barons obtained parliamentary seats (see the list in the appendix).

In view of feudalism's abolition, titles of nobility became personal, to be inherited based on blood rights, with no connection to feudal tenure. Dukes and counts could, in theory, be landless.

With the help of astronomer Giuseppe Piazzi, twenty-three administrative districts analogous to provinces were established based on topography, and some local officials would be elected. Initially, only literate landholding males were eligible to vote.

Some constitutional principles deal with dynastic law. In the absence of male heirs among descendants and collaterals, a woman can succeed to the Sicilian Throne. If there are no heirs whatsoever, parliament may elect to nominate a King of Sicily from a reigning European house, and not necessarily from one of the houses of Bourbon.

The British were not the only ones encouraging modern

constitutions and elections in Italy during this period. The constitution drafted in Bologna in 1796 was of French inspiration, and so was the Italian tricolor flag.

Alas, the life of Sicily's constitution was not destined to be a long one. Palermo would never be Westminster or Washington, but a sincere attempt had been made to achieve what existed beyond Sicilian waters.

The state might create institutions, but the one most citizens knew best was the family.

Women

Until very recent times the few Sicilian women known to us as anything more than names were abbesses and aristocrats.

Most Italian marriages in the nineteenth century were arranged by the spouses' parents, or in any case contracted only with parental consent, just as they had been for centuries. The new vital statistics laws formalized the betrothal process.

Two customary practices among common folk represented opposite approaches to betrothal. Being *fidanzati in casa* was an engagement, sometimes before the future bride had reached the age of majority, where the parents of the future spouses would formally agree to the marriage.

Conversely, the *fuitina* was essentially an elopement in cases where the young woman's parents did not approve of the marriage, or perhaps could not afford to defray the cost of the wedding and therefore tacitly condoned the elopement. More precisely, in the *fuitina,* from the Sicilian word for "fleeing," the couple "escaped" together for a few days, and upon their return an immediate "reparative" wedding was deemed necessary to avoid further scandal because the young woman was presumed to have "lost her honor" during the sojourn.

Apart from these perennial practices, courtship, such as it was, might entail chaperones to ensure that the couple was never alone. On average, husbands were around eight years older than their young brides. Dowries and other details could make betrothals quite complicated.

The generic description of such a social hierarchy as "matriarchal" is specious at best. Nevertheless, the salient role of Sicilian women as wives, and especially as mothers, must not be overlooked. Into the early decades of the twentieth century, the ordinary Italian mother raised a large family — five or six children on average — on meager means in what was essentially an agrarian society all but ignored by the Industrial Revolution.

Sicilian mothers were not the only women of fortitude. By 1812, Queen Maria Carolina had become famous, or infamous, in British circles for her outspoken opinions and endless intrigues. This led to her "self-exile" to Austria. In Vienna in early 1814, she met with Klemens von Metternich and her nephew, Francis I of Austria, to discuss the details of the royal family's restoration in Naples in view of Napoleon's recent defeat at Leipzig. Her death in September ended these negotiations.

Two Crowns in One

The death of Maria Carolina coincided with the beginning of the Congress of Vienna. With France's defeat, Europe sought to restore some semblance of the *status quo ante bellum* to the Continent while laying the foundations of a cohesive policy that might prevent the likelihood of a major war breaking out again in the near future. This met with success if we consider that Europe enjoyed a respite from an extensive, multinational conflict for a solid century. Conversely, the Congress failed to address most of the underlying social problems that existed *within* the signatory nations, things that fed a general discontent among citizens.

German unity of a kind was recognized in the form of the

German Confederation. Italy, which Metternich famously described as being little more than "a geographical expression," remained a checkerboard of monarchies ruled by the Pope, the Bourbons and the Savoys, with Lombardy and Venetia under Austrian control. Here the borders were nearly identical to what they were before the beginning of the Napoleonic Wars a quarter-century earlier.

Ferdinando was now free to decamp to Naples, which he much preferred to Palermo. Aside from an attempted invasion during the brief "Neapolitan War" by Murat, who was executed in Calabria in May 1815 by the people he sought to liberate, Ferdinando found himself unchallenged.

Others found him unintelligent, unschooled and uninspired. He was growing more cynical with every passing day. In 1816, he abolished the Sicilian Constitution of 1812, justifying this by uniting the states of Naples and Sicily that had been institutionally separate since the War of the Vespers. This new state would need a new constitution, but Ferdinando had no immediate intention of granting one. The neoteric Kingdom of the Two Sicilies owed its name to the Angevins and Aragonese, and its territorial legacy to the Greeks and Normans, but it was far from a restoration.

The Jesuits' general restoration in 1814 alarmed many, and not only in Europe. Across the ocean, John Adams wrote to American President Thomas Jefferson in 1816 that they "merited damnation."

While his counterparts around Europe were scrambling to institute reforms and accommodate popular demands, reactionary Ferdinando resumed the role of doctrinaire despot. Feudalism, however, was not restored, and a few laws established by the French on the mainland were retained.

Here one cannot help speculating how different things might have been were the Sicilian Constitution not abrogated but, instead, adapted for the entire Kingdom of the Two Sicilies.

This, however, was not a question merely of constitutional law. Only with the greatest effort would old ways of thinking ever be pushed aside.

Over the next few years, a liberal movement gained steam around Italy. To describe this as a "grass roots" effort would be imprecise. Like the recent European uprisings, it was essentially a bourgeoisie movement supported by intellectuals, even if it had its "popular" faction of tradesmen and farmers. It did not have a very specific political agenda beyond the dream of democracy and the implementation of some liberal principles. It did, however, enjoy exceptionally wide support, and many of its proponents advocated a republic over a monarchy. Some desired a unitary Italian state. Clearly inspired by the French Revolution, one of these loose knit organizations emerged in southern Italy.

The *Carbonari* (literally "coal burners") formed a secret network whose *modus vivendi* of covert activity was probably patterned after certain practices common in Italian freemasonry while being vaguely reminiscent of the clandestine *Beati Paoli*. With its membership rites and code of conduct, it had all the trappings of a sect. As a first step toward greater reforms and perhaps a republic, many of its members were willing to accept a constitutional monarchy.

By 1820, the insurgents had gained enough support to foment open revolts in Naples and other cities, compelling Ferdinando to call a parliament and grant a constitution. Palermo saw months of violent protests by groups which, if not allied with the *Carbonari,* certainly shared some of their objectives, although here the ringleaders were aristocrats. The next year, the *Carbonari* marched on Turin.

In February 1821, the Holy Alliance (a military coalition of Russia, Prussia and Austria) sent troops to crush the uprisings in southern Italy.

With the Austrians came Carl Rothschild, who set up a bank in Naples. (This operated until, in view of the decline of the local economy with the annexation of the Two Sicilies to the Kingdom of Italy, it was forced to close in 1863.)

Meanwhile, in Piedmont, Vittorio Emanuele I abdicated in favor of his brother Carlo Felice, who sought and received Austrian military intervention to suppress the protests. This ended *Carbonari* activity for the time being. In September, Pope Pius VII condemned the *Carbonari* as a masonic secret society, imposing excommunication on its members.[39]

The Italian kings weren't the only monarchs sucked into this vortex. Spain was equally unsettled. The epoch of absolutism was nearing its end.

At his death following a hunt in the first days of 1825, Ferdinando I had reigned sixty-six years, far too long for a reactionary despot. His intellect and capacity were abysmal, with tragic results for the people he ruled. The antithesis of social progress, Ferdinando never missed the opportunity to miss an opportunity. Nary a tear was shed for the crowned nemesis of constitutions. Once, responding to citizens' request for one, he cynically replied that, "Yes, my children, I shall give you a constitution, I shall even give you two."

Francesco I and Ferdinando II

Francesco I, his successor, seemed to be a slight improvement. Nearing fifty, he understood the importance of science and industry, and even founded an order of knighthood to recognize these, but his government was just as stagnant as his father's had been. Some of the most deplorable social practices known in Francesco's time are still with us in Italy today.[40]

Having served as Ferdinando's Vicar in Sicily, the new monarch was familiar with government. Given his age and experience, he should have been prepared to reign. Perhaps he was. Francesco was endowed with the gift of certitude. So far as we can tell, the shadow of dilemma never crossed his mind.

By contrast, the nation he inherited was full of unresolved conflicts and unrealized ambitions. Few knew precisely what these were. Fewer seemed to care. Daily life was challenging enough. The rebels were a small but vocal minority.

Austrian troops were still present. Not only was this costly, it made the kingdom seem like an occupied nation. Francesco wanted order maintained by national forces, so the Austrians left in 1827.

The new king granted a general amnesty for those involved in the recent revolts. This facilitated the return of political exiles.

Inspired by a French organization of the Napoleonic era, a group called the *Filadelfi* was revived in 1828 beyond the largest cities, especially in the Cilento region (around Salerno). These revolutionaries sought the restoration of the constitution enacted in 1820, which was based on the Spanish model. Like the *Carbonari,* who they predated, the *Filadelfi* had a masonic type of hierarchy. These revolts were suppressed, some ruthlessly, by Neapolitan forces. Dissension seemed dead.

Francesco I was dead by the end of 1830, succeeded by his Sicilian-born son, Ferdinando II.

Revolution was still in the air, its winds blowing across the Alps from France. The July Revolution of 1830 blew another gust of dissent into Italy.

Despite some renewed activity in central Italy around that time by the *Carbonari* or allied groups sharing their sympathies, the *Carbonari* movement itself was destined to dissolve into the ether because, realistically, it would always lack the means to bring about change by force. Something less "militant" might be more effective, even preferred, at least for the time being. In northern Italy, Giuseppe Mazzini, a young Genoan intellectual who advocated Italian unification under a republic where Papal power would be marginalized, organized *Giovane Italia*. Some former *Carbonari* eventually joined this new organization. As one can imagine, Mazzini was no more beloved by the

Savoys in Turin than by the Bourbons in Naples. At first, he would prove a thorn in the side of the Piedmontese. While the survival of *Giovane Italia* depended on secrecy or at least discretion, it was not, strictly speaking, a sect or "secret society."

One of the first acts of young King Ferdinando II of the Two Sicilies was a proclamation promising to guarantee justice to all citizens. He made an early attempt to root out corruption while encouraging fresh ideas by replacing jaded bureaucrats and aged personnel. In the end, this was only partly successful. However, cutting expenditures while encouraging commerce led to a reduction of the national debt.

For the moment, the frequent protests, though a matter of grave concern, were hardly tantamount to general civil strife. The economy of the Two Sicilies made it the most prosperous state in Italy. (In fairness, it must be observed that it was also the largest and most populous.) According to a royal decree issued in January 1831, the balance of the state's assets was substantial enough to justify reduction of certain taxes, such as those on flour.

To direct tangible assistance to the poor while instituting safeguards to prevent these funds ending up in the pockets of corrupt bureaucrats, Ferdinando established the Royal Charity Commission.

The brief emergence of Ferdinandea, a volcanic islet in international waters in the Sicilian Channel between Sciacca and the island of Pantelleria, incited a minor diplomatic row. Surveyed by the British, who named it "Graham Island" and claimed it for themselves, it submerged early in 1832, to arise again briefly in 1846. It is part of an active submarine volcano.

Turning to address concerns expressed by privileged citizens on dry land, Ferdinando established a Commission for Titles of Nobility. This was not as superficial or elitist as it might seem, for it curtailed the avaricious claims still entertained by some aristocrats long after the abolition of feudalism, all the while discouraging the ambitions of a new class of social climbers.

Ferdinando wed Maria Cristina of Savoy in 1832. The youngest daughter of King Vittorio Emanuele I of Sardinia was a kind, devout girl. She was pretty and shy. Maria Cristina may have found Naples and its court more stifling than the austere ambience she knew in Turin, but here, despite her natural modesty, she was a queen.

It is worth noting a fact conveniently overlooked by Italian-born historians writing after 1860, namely that for many years the Bourbons in Naples had cordial relations with the Savoys in Turin. Indeed, both Italian dynasties shared a sense of solidarity in confronting the revolutionary spirit that threatened to topple them from their lofty perches.

The year he was married, Ferdinando proposed a "League of Italian States," a federalist union that would include the Two Sicilies, the Papal States, Piedmont and Tuscany. This was anathema to the Austrians, Germans and Russians, who saw in it a violation of the terms of the Congress of Vienna and the potential foundation of a new power. Leopoldo II in Florence seemed indecisive while Carlo Alberto in Turin was evasive, perhaps viewing it as a reflection of Ferdinando's personal ambition to rule the whole of Italy.

Pope Gregory XVI objected pre-emptively. This may have seemed unreasonable but it was not surprising. Gregory was a rabid reactionary who feared that the introduction of such inventions as railways and gas lighting in the Papal States might promote commerce and therefore empower the bourgeoisie. More immediately, he wanted to retain his grip on a third of the Italian peninsula.

In Naples, Queen Maria Cristina urged that offerings be made to the poor in lieu of nuptial festivities to be held around the country to mark her wedding. Unwavering in her religious devotion, she influenced Ferdinando to release inmates from the debtors' prisons, to forgive debts of less than twenty ducats, and to grant amnesty to convicts serving terms for lesser crimes. The municipal pawn brokerages in Naples and Palermo were ordered to return to the owners items having a pawn value of six ducats or less.

Young, sweet, innocent Maria Cristina of Savoy, Queen Consort of the Two Sicilies, would be Italy's last fairy-tale princess.

She died in 1836 shortly after giving birth to a son, Francesco. She was twenty-three years old. The death of the saintly Maria Cristina (she was beatified in 2014) seems to have had a profound effect on Ferdinando, who was just two years her senior. A king's personality change, if such it was, would not be a determining factor in the running of a constitutional monarchy, but it might well exert an adverse impact on a state ruled by an absolute monarch. A nation that was soon to face great challenges.

The fairy tale was over.

In 1837, a terrible cholera epidemic struck Sicily and part of the peninsula, leading to the deaths of many thousands. The larger cities were hit especially hard. Revolts erupted at Siracusa and Catania. Although these were not initially political, they were exploited by revolutionary elements. In the face of widespread suffering and death, the insurgents diffused the notion that the cholera was in some way the fault of King Ferdinando. The idea was popularized that a poison was somehow responsible for the epidemic.

Along the way, the Crown was enjoined to invoke the lost constitution. The entreaties were ignored.

Unprepared, the local authorities found it difficult to suppress violent uprisings fed by rumors and conspiracy theories, and now political demands. The worst violence was seen in Catania, where troops sent from Naples put down the rebels with the same overzealous brutality they had used against the *Filadelfi*.

During a visit to Sicily in 1838, Ferdinando granted amnesty to a number of prisoners. He also granted the major part of Sicily's sulfur mining licenses to a French firm. As Sicily provided around eighty percent of the world's sulfur, this did not set well with the British. Indeed, it conditioned Britain's attitude toward Ferdinando over the next two decades.

More immediately, the British threatened a blockade of the Sicilian ports that exported most of the sulfur, along with the seizure of ships carrying it. In 1840, after a protracted series of diplomatic maneuvers, the British were restored to their former primacy in the market, but much mutual bitterness remained.

At the same time, the government sponsored industrial projects that placed the Two Sicilies at the vanguard of the day's technology. This trend saw, for example, the first railway in Italy connecting Naples and Portici in 1839.

To observers, it seemed that Ferdinando was using one hand to introduce industry, and the other to slap down the population. Perhaps he contemplated using technology to subdue the people.

The next few years were comparatively peaceful, but the pot of discontent continued to simmer. It wasn't very appetizing.

To the *popolino*, Ferdinando II came to be known for *feste, forche e farina* (festivals, gallows and flour).

Arts, Culture and Science

Yet the arts flourished. Composer Vincenzo Bellini, born in Catania in 1801, was known for his *bravura* works during opera's *bel canto* era. Another Catanian, Giovanni Verga, was a writer of the realist school. His *Cavalleria Rusticana*, later adapted to opera by Pietro Mascagni, was based on events said to have taken place in Vizzini.

Giuseppe Verdi composed *I Vespri Siciliani* about the War of the Vespers. His contemporary, Richard Wagner, composed *Parsifal*, his last opera, during a sojourn in Palermo. In folk art, Sicilian marionettes were inspired by the same medieval culture.

Majolica, tin-glazed earthenware, was already popular in Sicily by the nineteenth century. Its origins may reach into the island's Aragonese era.

Sicily had scientists besides the astronomer Giuseppe Piazzi. Stanislao Cannizzaro was a chemist whose work took him to the vanguard of the new field of physics, which he taught at the University of Genoa as "theoretical chemistry." He was one of the first scientists to clearly distinguish between atoms and molecules and define valence. His work led to the development of the periodic table of elements.

By the middle years of the nineteenth century, Sicilian cuisine was well established as a medley of influences formed into a distinctive order. The wines and spirits, the cheeses, the breads, the recipes known today were already popular.

Food was the basis for *sagre* that celebrated local cuisines based on the seasons. Some were harvest festivals. One town might celebrate artichokes, another almonds. Products like ricotta would be celebrated during the Spring.

Oenicultural festivals were rare. Sicily's wine country straddles a series of graceful hills between Salemi and Marsala. Following in the footsteps of John Woodhouse, the Inghams and Whitakers greatly increased the scale of Marsala wine production. Until then, the principal crop in this part of Sicily was wheat. Except for Marsala, very few Sicilian wines were produced for sale. Varietal vintages emerged following the Second World War as wineries were established on farms around Sicily.

A few entrepreneurs stood out from the crowd. Apart from vintners, one of the first food exporters was the innovative Vincenzo Florio, who sold tuna in jars. In 1840 he signed a partnership with the Inghams, founding a small steamship line.

Every town or quarter had its chief religious festival held on the feast day of the local saint. The festivals of Saint Rosalie (Palermo), Saint Lucy (Siracusa) and Saint Agatha (Catania) were week-long celebrations.

Apart from holidays like Christmas, numerous holy days filled the calendar. In the course of a year, there might be twenty or thirty days of festivals. (Italy's "beach culture" is a more recent development.)

None of this is to suggest a kingdom in a constant state of joviality. It is difficult to ascertain with much precision the quality of life of most people living in Sicily during this era. John Goodwin, a British consul who reported on social progress in the Two Sicilies in the years leading up to 1840, was cautiously optimistic.

We may speculate that life was better in the country than in the cities. Italy, where the effects of the Industrial Revolution were minimal, has nothing comparable to critiques like those of Friedrich Engels, who wrote *The Condition of the Working Class in England* in 1845.

Winds of Change

In 1844 around a hundred armed rioters sympathetic to the ideas of Mazzini were arrested in Cosenza, in Calabria. A number were tried and a few executed, but some of the sentences were commuted.

The following year, Ferdinando hosted a major scientific congress in Naples. Like similar congresses held in other cities, this one had its political side.

If Ferdinando lacked encouragement of his suspicions about social progress, it arrived in Palermo in the person of Tsar Nicholas I of Russia, the quintessential autocrat. Here was Ferdinando's kindred soul, an equally conservative monarch equally willing to quash dissent.

Apart from its excellent commercial relations with Russia, the Two Sicilies negotiated sound trade treaties with Britain, France and the United States.

Commerce itself may have been good, but agriculture was

as fickle as ever, and governments were rarely prepared for nature's caprices. The terrible potato blight that struck Europe was unforeseen. While its effects in Italy were minimal, Ireland, which depended on this crop, was hit hard. The result was a lethal famine that decimated the population.

Sicily depended as much on grain as Ireland depended on potatoes, and a Europe-wide drought lasting several years resulted in a critical reduction of wheat supplies. The very definition of the word *drought* varied from one region to the next; in comparatively arid Sicily a drought was worse than what the term implied in Germany.

Acting on sound advice, Ferdinando ordered a general ban on grain exports and began a tour around the country to ensure that starvation might be avoided. Arriving unannounced in the various provincial capitals, he and his suite of officials conducted inspections to uncover any cases of hoarding. In a land where price fixing and speculation were normal, corruption might, in theory, be punished when exposed in this manner. Nevertheless, the sovereign still found himself in the crosshairs of domestic critics, such as Luigi Settembrini, who penned an anonymous tract against the Crown.

The climate, both literally and figuratively, was perfect for another round of protests. The first was at Messina in 1847. This was planned some months in advance, and it coincided with similar insurrections in Reggio across the Strait of Messina. The use of artillery earned Ferdinando the enduring nickname *Re Bomba,* "King Bomb." However, he was not the only king to use such tactics during this era.[41]

The bomb of popular discontent was not going to be contained, restricted to just one city. On 23 January 1848 it exploded in Palermo.

There were several underlying causes for these protests. The paucity of grain was an obvious catalyst; food shortages and high prices made it easy to enlist the support of the common people.

In Sicily, a subtle independence movement was also at work; this reflected the desire for a constitution, and perhaps a separate king, for the island. Presumably, this revived "Kingdom of Sicily" would be governed separately from the mainland. This minority view by the intellectual elite probably belied the more banal grievances of the general populace, more immediately concerned with bread and taxes.

As usual, the list of demands was soon amended. A republic was placed on the agenda and a few prominent aristocrats jumped on board. These developments were perhaps predictable, or at least conceivable, but the Palermitans' rabid fervor portended incidents beyond Sicilian shores.

The mini-revolution at Palermo has been painted as the determining spark that ignited a series of revolts around Europe, as if this were a simple chain reaction. The true impetus was the revolt that began in Paris a month later. Europe's "hungry years" of high food prices and an industrial downturn made revolution seem attractive to a new generation.[42]

Even before the Sicilian riots, several revolutionary movements of a similar kind were in the planning stages across the Continent. It was only a matter of time before they became open insurrections. Nevertheless, there were French and British diplomats and merchants in Palermo to encourage the revolts on behalf of their fellow citizens back home, while reporting to Paris and London.

This time there was a new element in the revolutionary mix. It would change the world forever.

The telegraph, a novel technology zealously promoted by Ferdinando II, provided the network. It made possible fast communication between cities, and between the allied revolutionaries in those cities. Their *lingua franca,* the language of diplomacy, the second tongue of aristocrats and intellectuals, was French. Railroads made travel between European capitals easier than ever. Europe's autocrats had underestimated the power bestowed upon the citizenry by telecommunications and the steam engine. (The greatest beneficiaries of telegraphy in 1848 were those in central and western Europe; the impetus in Italy came with electric telegraph lines around Naples in 1852.)

Viewed as a trend, the scattered European protests defy simple description. One might loosely describe many as "nationalist" or "liberal." Some political theorists even characterize them as "proto-socialist." Apart from such labels, each assumed a local flavor. Their common element was a neglected population in search of change and a greater voice in government, things that might lead to more prosperity for all.

This had festered ever since the Congress of Vienna, for which many Europeans entertained high hopes, restored the social order to what it had been before the Napoleonic Wars. True, the borders drawn by the delegates to Vienna kept the peace among nations, but socially the Congress left a tattered legacy of unresolved issues because the nations themselves did not move with the times. This wave of popular dissent was the price to be paid in a Continent where, for the ordinary person, little had changed in fifty years. If monarchy were to continue, it would have to be constitutional, granting citizens a larger role in government. Nobody but a few selfish aristocrats, reactionaries and religious zealots wanted an absolute monarchy.

Alexis de Tocqueville saw "a world divided between those who had nothing joined in common envy against those who had everything joined in common terror."

Yet each regional protest had its peculiarities. In the German states, national unity was a key factor. In Poland, the rebellion was characterized by calls for independence. In Switzerland, the cantons sought and achieved greater autonomy. In Austria, many of the first protesters were students, while in allied Hungary the protests evolved into a call for independence from Austria. Romania also saw riots.

Unlike earlier revolutions, this one would not be quelled by tossing the peasants a few loaves of stale bread. In Denmark, where a new king granted a liberal constitution, real social change was coming. That was the exception in what has come to be called the "Springtime of Peoples."

In Lombardy, the initial lament seems to have been about tax increases imposed by the Austrians. In Piedmont, the revolt was an effort by the bourgeoisie to obtain a constitution.

Newly-elected Pope Pius IX was forced to flee Rome. He left as a reformer, he returned a reactionary.

Almost immediately, Ferdinando's response was to grant a constitution. In Turin, King Carlo Alberto followed suit, promulgating his *Statuto*. This became a point of divergence between the two Italian kingdoms, for the changes effected by Carlo Alberto would elude Ferdinando.

Following the revolts of 1848, the *Statuto* enacted in the Kingdom of Sardinia remained in force, even if its principles were not always applied with rigor. The one in the Two Sicilies was suppressed as soon as the protesters were placated. This earned King Ferdinando II the ire of many in Europe, especially in Britain. In the Two Sicilies, his obstinance played into the hands of detractors seeking the alternative model of a comparatively liberal — or in any case constitutional — monarchy elsewhere in Italy.

Unwittingly, Ferdinando and Carlo Alberto set the stage for an Italian dichotomy, a rivalry, even a regionalist antipathy, the infamous *divario* that taints Italy to this day, pitting Turin and Milan against Naples and Palermo, northerners against southerners. Although it was soon to be repressed in favor of a national unification movement, Sicily's aspirations to independence would resurface from time to time (notably in 1866 and again in 1944).

Ferdinando was demonized in the most emphatic terms. William Gladstone described his sclerotic policies as "the negation of God erected into a system of government." Others were no kinder. "Power tends to corrupt," railed Lord Acton, "and absolute power corrupts absolutely."

Such sentiments were doubtless sincere, but more broadly the political relationship with Britain was still complicated by such concerns as the sulfur industry. By 1850, this was a *sine qua non* of the rapport between the two nations. The lust for the yellow mineral vexed Britain just as major nations (in later centuries) resented less important states controlling the petroleum market.

It was not only British ideas that Ferdinando wanted to keep in check, but Britain's economic and military influence in the *Regno*.

Here was the consummate pragmatist, the inveterate survivor. The king who began his reign as something of a progressive was now a full-fledged, autocratic reactionary. This prompted a number of citizens to leave the Two Sicilies for self-imposed exile in northern Italy.

In 1856, the Congress of Paris was held to formally end the Crimean War. The Two Sicilies had nothing to do with this but Piedmont did. The Piedmontese representative, Camillo Benso di Cavour, exploited this opportunity to disparage Ferdinando's government in the south. By diplomatic standards, it was an underhanded tactic, especially if one considers that there was no Neapolitan representative present to defend Ferdinando. The same year, the French and the British recalled their ambassadors from Naples.

The next few years saw an effort by external forces to curtail Ferdinando's international influence, but isolating Italy's largest state would not be easy. For now, Ferdinando's detractors in Paris, London and Turin could only await his death, all the while thinking and planning.[43]

Unification

The *Risorgimento,* or "resurgence," was an intellectual movement that began long before the middle years of the nineteenth century. It was not born as an explicitly political effort to unify the Italian states but, for better or worse, that is how it has come to be identified in the popular mind. One could even say, with only the slightest hyperbole, that the movement, along with its name, was "hijacked" by opportunistic politicians, so what began as the humanistic *Risorgimento* ended with political unification.[44]

Although the idea had been broached decades earlier, Giuseppe Mazzini's *Giovane Italia,* the organization that enlisted some of the disenchanted *Carbonari,* was the first major political movement to advocate a unitary Italian state. Its leaders wanted a republic where Papal influence would be marginalized. It was largely covert, even conspiratorial, its members identifying themselves in correspondence by nicknames. No state in Italy would tolerate such a movement. In 1833, some members plotting a revolt in Piedmont were arrested and put to death.

Each passing year after the tumultuous revolts of 1848 saw a wider advocacy of Italian unification. Naturally, the greatest support for this came from the political elite of the smaller northern states, who were most likely to benefit from a united Italy. For the most part, this was the aristocracy and the middle class. It seems that most people were indifferent to the idea, but we have no opinion surveys to tell us what most people thought.

The revolts of 1848 left Austria weakened. Seeking to exploit this, Carlo Alberto of Savoy invaded the Austrian-occupied Italian regions bordering Piedmont in an attempt to expand his realm. This ambitious effort met with failure. Following his defeat by Austrian forces in 1849, Carlo Alberto abdicated in favor of his son, who ruled as Vittorio Emanuele II.

Despite this setback, Italian unification, in some form, was inevitable. What shape would it assume? A republic, a confederation of states, or a monolithic monarchy? Each concept of nationhood had its proponents.

Giuseppe Mazzini's anticlerical republican faction was the most "radical" element. Camillo Benso di Cavour, the Piedmontese cabinet minister and nobleman we met earlier, led another faction — initially defined as "liberal" — which sought to coexist with the established monarchical order; in time, the liberals came to embrace the "moderates" of the bourgeoisie, such as bankers and industrialists, who wanted political continuity but a free-market economy. It was these moderates and liberals, enjoying a certain degree of sympathy from the British, who would plot the course of Italian unification. To that singular end, Cavour was tireless in his backstage machinations.

The role of freemasonry, though real, was never more than peripheral. Freemasonry, of course, was condemned by the Papacy. The secretive nature of *Giovane Italia* and the clandestine methods of many unificationist proponents were probably inspired by freemasonry.

Apart from the diminution of Catholic influence in public affairs, the "anticlerical" facet of the unification movement as it manifested itself around 1860 was never quite so liberal or secular as its most vocal apologists subsequently claimed. It certainly was not atheistic, nor much inspired by the Enlightenment.

Although a number of disaffected southerners joined its ranks, the movement's founding leadership was northern; Mazzini was from Genoa, Cavour from Turin. Few of the northerners had spent much time south of Rome. To some extent, this influenced certain unificationist views of Italy's southern regions.

Nevertheless, as the movement gained ground, Ferdinando's cousin in Turin offered him the Crown of Italy if only he would agree to a federalist union, something vaguely conceived along the lines of the Holy Roman Empire and already proposed in 1832. This Ferdinando declined despite his earlier advocacy, explaining that he had no wish to infringe the rights, and the territory, of the Pope, who would never willingly relinquish Rome.

Foreigners, with Britons leading the charge, generally directed their criticism at the Two Sicilies as Italy's largest, wealthiest state, and the one that, at least superficially, seemed to suffer the most from outmoded laws and an entrenched, unenlightened ruling class. These criticisms of an obsolete ethos chained to the Catholic Church were not without merit. However, they must be considered in the context of the times.[45]

Closely allied with the Two Sicilies, the Papal State garnered its share of opprobrium, much of it deserved. The Catholic Church, of course, was a perennial target of Europe's more strident Protestants, but never more so than during the pontificate of sanctimonious Pius IX.

A case could be made that some states in pre-unitary Italy were at least marginally more socially progressive than others. Tuscany first abolished the death penalty in 1786 (only to reinstitute it four years later) and, as we have seen, Piedmont's *Statuto* of 1848 proved to be more enduring than the constitutions enacted in the Two Sicilies, however lofty their aspirations.

In such an environment, it was easy enough to paint the Two Sicilies as being somewhat more repressive than the comparatively "liberal" mini-nations of northern Italy.

But didn't the revolts of 1848 touch Turin as well as Palermo? Wasn't Roman Catholicism the official religion of the "anticlerical" Kingdom of Sardinia? Wasn't the Shroud of Turin venerated just as fervidly as the blood of Saint Januarius and the bones of Saint Rosalie, its provenance equally dubious? Was there not press censorship in Piedmont? Would a recalcitrant journalist in Turin go unpunished if, in his reckless *lèse-majesté*, he wrote an article calling for the deposition of the reigning Savoy?

It would be ridiculous to conclude that life in Sicily was any better than life in Piedmont, but ludicrous to conclude that it was any worse, or that Palermo was in some way backward compared to Turin. There are no precise figures for annual household income outside the aristocracy, but in Sicily proper the *riveli,* referred to elsewhere, provide a general indication of taxation based on familial assets to pay the *donativi.* (The appendix gives figures regarding university enrollment circa 1860, as well as various social and technological achievements before the annexation.)

Sicilian political dissentients went to Piedmont. Where were the Piedmontese dissidents? Where did *they* go?

To America, of course.

The first major wave of Italian immigrants to make their way across the ocean were Piedmontese and Genoans.

While few of these emigrés were political exiles *per se,* it is obvious that they made the long journey to a strange land for a reason. Even if their motivations were purely economic, that begs a number of questions about life in happy, prosperous, democratic "Savoy Land" where, to read the writings of some apologists — Italians and Britons alike — everyday existence was one giant, continuous bacchanal of Barolo and Spumante consumed with bresaola, risotto and truffles.

A transitory expatriate was sometime general Giuseppe Garibaldi, a native of Nice (under Savoy rule since 1814) who had fallen out of favor in Turin but would live to play a pivotal role in Italy's unification. Arriving in New York in 1850, he befriended Antonio Meucci, a Tuscan inventor best known today for his rudimentary experiments in the field of voice transmission via electrical signals over wires.

The truth is that until unification, and indeed for some years thereafter, the greater part of Italy's emigration came from the regions to the north of Rome, not from the south.

Statistically speaking, the people living in Piedmont, Lombardy, Liguria, Venetia and Tuscany were every bit as impoverished and illiterate as those in Abruzzi, Calabria and Sicily. In rural Piedmont, rice had been planted and harvested the same miserable way for centuries, by women wading through the water, all the while being harassed by the merciless mosquitoes.

Some unification apologists chose to focus on the movement's "political philosophy." But what was actually promoted to the majority of people in the middle years of the nineteenth century had very little to do with political theory as such. It was all about the purported benefits of unification.

Were the "philosophical" issues in Italy any more complex than the contemporary questions of serfdom in Russia or slavery in the United States?

Among political theorists, Karl Marx was especially critical of the movement after it transpired because it did not represent, in his view, a step forward. If one were to create a new nation, why a monarchy? Why not a republic like France or even the United States? In the end, Marx was as critical of some of the men who forged the new state as he was of the unitary kingdom they erected upon the embers of the monarchies of the Two Sicilies, Tuscany, Parma and Modena. They were a disappointment. To be fair, Marx in his later years was critical of almost everybody, but many commentators came to agree with his sentiments about Italian unification.

The road to Hell is paved with good intentions, says an old aphorism. Mazzini and Cavour entertained some good ideas about great things the "New Italy" was going to do but, in the end, never achieved. The former was cast aside, and the latter died soon after the Kingdom of Italy was proclaimed. Deprived of the guidance of such intellectuals, the nation floundered along a self-destructive path these thinkers never foresaw.

Once the united Italy became a reality, many of the ideas espoused by the unification movement's intellectuals were ignored, even disparaged. Its shadowy democracy never fostered the freedom one found in France, Britain or the United States. (The foibles and fiascoes of the Kingdom of Italy are set forth *ad infinitum* in the next chapter.)

However noble its ideals may have been in the beginning, the unification effort, like many political movements, took on a life of its own with the passage of time. By 1860 it would be something slightly different from what it was ten years earlier.

While the Two Sicilies didn't need Piedmont, it is clear that Piedmont needed the Two Sicilies, or at least its gold reserves. Based on this measure alone, the wealth of the southern kingdom eclipsed that of all the other Italian states combined, while its national debt was a mere fraction of Piedmont's. This was a matter of public record. Somebody in Turin wanted the gold in Naples. And they were willing to kill for it.[46]

Ferdinando's refusal to accept the Italian Crown left a Savoy as the next logical candidate. For the moment, Ferdinando was an implacable roadblock. He commanded Italy's largest standing army. More importantly, he was willing to use it, to lead it himself if needs must, even — as he had already shown — against his own people. Of course, redoubtable Ferdinando wouldn't live forever.

On the wider stage, the one that counted internationally, stringing together a few Italian monarchies was never a matter of global import. It was, at its best, a sideshow. True, commingling yet another major state with the existing European potpourri could alter the balance of power, as the united Germany eventually did, but Italy never had the population or industrial might of the *Reich,* and nothing that happened anyplace in Italy during the nineteenth century had global consequences, despite what a few rabid Italian nationalists would have us believe. Russia and the United States spanned entire continents, while Britain's empire linked one sea to another in a chain encircling the globe. Whatever pretensions she eventually entertained, and at whatever cost, little Italy was not destined to be the mouse that roared, or the tail that wagged the dog.[47]

The Undeclared War

Ferdinando II died in May 1859. Francesco II, the son of Ferdinando's first wife, saintly Maria Cristina of Savoy, was a very devout young man. That would be his undoing.

The young king lived under the spell of dogmatic, intransigent Pope Pius IX. Zealous Pius was a Pontiff given to pontificating. Too much of it, in fact. Not enough has been written about the influence on Italian unification by the most pertinacious man since 1800 to occupy the See of Saint Peter. If Cavour and his confederates orchestrated the unification, it was Pius IX who provided its instruments, setting the stage for a pathetic performance.

Pius wasn't always opposed to Italian unification; early in his pontificate, during his ephemeral liberal phase, he was willing to accept an Italy united under the Papal tiara. The obvious defect in such a proposal is that no king with any knowledge of history was ever going to accept it!

A true reactionary, Pius came to defy social progress in all its forms. For the times in which he faced adversity, Francesco could not have chosen a worst mentor.

In some countries today we find military chaplains holding officer rank. Even in the Middle Ages, there were bishops and imams who commanded armies, but they were the exception rather than the rule. For most men, the path that leads to soldiery is not the one that leads to priesthood. A good king must be a good leader, and that sometimes means spilling blood in defense of his subjects' lives. This is never pretty, but it's a fact of life — or death. Such a terrible task, undertaken only after the most judicious consideration, may spell the difference between a people's survival or its subjugation. Francesco's fatal flaw was a conflict between competing vocations. Heaven might welcome him, posterity would curse him.

In Turin, the Savoys knew that their newly-crowned Neapolitan cousin was unlikely to be as ferocious as his father, and they knew something of his piety. Nevertheless, it would be imprudent to risk a major military invasion against a state boasting the largest army on the Italian peninsula. A few zealous Neapolitan generals might actually annihilate a Piedmontese regiment or two. Initially, therefore, support was sought from within the Kingdom of the Two Sicilies. The most efficacious tools were old-fashioned bribery, treason and sedition.

It was never difficult, anywhere in Italy, to find a few disgruntled generals. This discontent was not, for the most part, political so much as personal. Perhaps it was born of an Italianate apathy in response to too many conquests. Whatever their root cause, the lamentations were many, reflecting a lack of *esprit de corps* that would plague the armies of the Kingdom of Italy for the whole of the monarchy's existence. In the decades to come, Italian generals prosecuting campaigns from Africa to Austria regularly blamed their failures on their troops rather than themselves; military training of conscripts was rarely more than mediocre, and a lack of morale came to define the downtrodden, often indolent, Italian soldier, making him the object of condescension.

Apart from their more obvious efforts to sow the seeds of sedition among the populace, Piedmontese agents had sought to incite treason among Neapolitan generals for some years, ever since Ferdinando II rejected the Italian Crown.

The extent to which they succeeded is a matter of historical debate because supporting documents and reliable accounts are scarce. Be that as it may, the fact that a tendency toward indifference prevailed by 1860 is beyond disputation. Equally indisputable was Britain's support for the unification. This would come in handy.

As early as the Plombières Agreement of 1858, Cavour was sounding out the French and the British about cooperating in a hypothetical invasion of Sicily he knew Piedmont couldn't achieve on its own.

The Crown of the Two Sicilies was never Vittorio Emanuele's to win, it was Francesco's to lose.

Yet the Piedmontese ministers didn't want to risk their own troops, and they didn't want to be accused of starting an unprovoked war even though, like other European sovereigns, the Savoys had participated in quite a few. The solution arrived in the person of Giuseppe Garibaldi, a sometime general and occasional mercenary with a checkered past who was willing to fight such a war. As it was known that Garibaldi had not always enjoyed the good graces of his Savoy masters, he could be supported tacitly, surreptitiously, and in the event of either a military or diplomatic disaster Cavour could simply deny having ever authorized an attack by a man who didn't even hold an active, formal commission as a Piedmontese general. This meant that Garibaldi and his assemblage of ragtag volunteers were expendable. Whatever the outcome of an invasion, Piedmont's ignoble "plausible deniability" would be a useful political tool where Piedmont lacked a clear justification, a legal *casus belli*.

Cavour wanted unification but he wanted it on his terms, not Mazzini's, and he was suspicious of Garibaldi.

"War is merely the continuation of policy by other means," said Carl von Clausewitz. The first order of business was the occupation of the tiny duchies of Parma and Modena, along with the larger Grand Duchy of Tuscany in early 1860. Here there was little resistance to the overwhelming numerical superiority of the Savoyard forces. Sicily would be left to Garibaldi, with Turin's tacit approval.[48]

In late April, the military command at Messina received news of Garibaldi's impending arrival someplace in Sicily. Further intelligence referred to the transportation of armaments and additional troops, possibly with British logistical support. Acting on these reports and others, Paolo Ruffo, the Lieutenant of the Realm for Sicily, alerted some port officials in the major cities. Cavour ensured that Garibaldi's ships were shadowed along most of the route to Sicily by Piedmontese warships; in effect, they had an "unofficial" military escort.

On 11 May, Garibaldi's two large vessels landed at Marsala while the commanders of the two British warships stationed there stood by and watched. Indeed, it appears that the British may have actually assisted the landings of the "red-shirts" directly, probably by maneuvering into position between them and the Sicilian forces, but this is not known with certainty. In the confusion that followed, overpowering Marsala's garrison was not extremely difficult, and naval relief for the Sicilian troops arrived too late to save the day. The city's British wine merchants raised the Union Jack.

Four days later, the garrison at Calatafimi surrendered following what some have described as token resistance. Several "political" prisoners, mostly aristocrats, were released from the local prison. Here is where wholesale desertion began, swelling the ranks of Garibaldi's army. Before long, Salemi, Alcamo, Partinico and other towns had fallen to the invaders.

Garibaldi's army enlisted more men *en route* to Palermo, where a bloody battle raged in the streets for days. Here the hostilities continued until early June. Traditional unificationist accounts paint the picture of a popular insurrection leading to an "easy" victory over the "cowardly" Sicilian troops who "abandoned" the city. The real pictures, the photographs, tell the story of a highly destructive series of bloody engagements similar to urban guerilla warfare, their death toll surpassed only by the aerial bombings of the Second World War.

The defenders did not lack the courage to fight; what they lacked was courage of conviction. They did not abandon king and country; they were abandoned by generals who failed to act in unison against a common enemy. It's that simple.

Rationalists are wary of conspiracy theories (and none shall be advanced here), but there are a few details of the Palermo campaign that are likely to spark suspicion in the mind of any scientific, critical thinker. The events suggest, at the very least, covert planning if not a wider cast of international players lurking offstage just beyond view. In early April, weeks before Garibaldi's landings, there was an attempted revolt by insurgents, amply supplied with guns and ammunition, at the Gancia monastery. Francesco Crispi, a dissident, is thought to have masterminded this.

Loquacious Giuseppe Garibaldi was the darling of the foreign press, especially fawning Britons (some of whom still pen whimsical narratives of the invasion). A few foreign journalists even met him at Palermo. It was in Sicily that Garibaldi's apotheosis began.

Whether General Ferdinando Lanza's surrender was the result of something other than a looming military defeat is still hotly debated; following a brief truce arranged with Garibaldi on a British ship, Lanza's army resumed fighting for a few days before suddenly capitulating. Less polemical is the fact that in June, following the Battle of Palermo, British ships sent from Malta supplied rifles, and American ships arrived full of arms and northern Italian troops. That the war soon assumed the character of a multinational invasion bolstered by foreign navies is beyond cavil.

Garibaldi had taken to wearing a Piedmontese general's uniform when it suited him, especially when meeting with high-ranking officers of the Two Sicilies or Britain. While in Palermo, the general found time to be promoted to the thirty-third degree of freemasonry during a ceremony at the *palazzo* of Count Federico.

The war continued eastward across the island. During the torrid Summer, the troops of the infamous Nino Bixio massacred part of the population of Bronte, a town of little strategic importance associated with the Nelson family, which had asked that it be protected. By the end of August, Garibaldi's troops had crossed over to Calabria. It wasn't long before the growing force was making its way toward Naples.

Wishing to avoid a civilian slaughter, Francesco and Maria Sophia left the capital in favor of the coastal stronghold at Gaeta to the north. This was a strategic error, and Garibaldi entered Naples in early September. British warships anchored in the Bay of Naples stood by, just in case Garibaldi's troops needed assistance.

The Battle of Volturno, a series of engagements into early October, some led by Francesco's younger brother, Alfonso, made it clear that there were still people willing to defend the realm.

The royal family left behind all its personal assets, including accounts in the Bank of Naples. All were confiscated by the occupiers.

On 26 October, Giuseppe Garibaldi met King Vittorio Emanuele II at Teano, between Naples and Gaeta, formally recognizing him as the ruler of the conquered territories. The old state was gone, the new one stillborn.

Appearances aren't everything, but both king and general were short and stout, so depicting them with any verisimilitude proved challenging for painters, sculptors and photo retouchers seeking a heroic national archetype.

The withdrawal of French ships anchored in the Gulf of Gaeta made it possible for the exigent Piedmontese to bombard the fortress from the sea, and Francesco surrendered it on 13 February 1861. The anschluss was complete, even though a piece of Sicily fought on for another month.

The last Sicilian resistance held out at Messina's massive citadel until 13 March, when it surrendered to the Piedmontese army. So long as the Two Sicilies' flag flew, a tiny fragment of Sicily could claim to be a sovereign territory loyal to its own king, even if he had been deposed. Now, after seven centuries and three decades, it was over.

Never again would the island's toponym find itself part of the name of a sovereign country. The *Regnum Siciliae* and the *Regno delle Due Sicilie* were gone forever.

Tempus edax rerum. Time consumes all things.

But there would still be kings. Monarchy's requiem had yet to be sung, its epitaph yet to be written.

The Italians, for such they became, finally got their unitary monarchy and the British would have their Sicilian sulfur. Southern money and new industries would enable Milan and Turin to overtake Naples and Palermo economically. Nobody in Britain could contemplate a war against a future Vittorio Emanuele forcing a stalwart, half-American, cigar-chomping prime minister to dismember the Empire to secure a new alliance that might defeat an axis of evil.

CHAPTER 10

Postlude: Italian Sicily

"We have made Italy. Now we must make the Italians."

— Massimo Taparelli d'Azeglio

Would that we could revel in the advent of the Kingdom of Italy. In vain do we search for its virtues. The Kingdom of the Two Sicilies was far from perfect, but for the great majority of Sicilians life in the unitary state that succeeded it was nothing less than tragic. Now, more than ever, poverty and suffering were to be the order of the day. Very little that is edifying can be said about the Kingdom of Italy. Its history makes for uncomfortable reading; this exposé shall be mercifully succinct.

Elections and Insurrections

A plebiscite held in the invasion's aftermath — but before the besieged fortress of Messina surrendered — confirmed Savoy rule with an astounding ninety-nine percent of eligible Sicilian voters favorable to the new regime. Were this a legitimate balloting, its results would be studied around the world as a rare electoral phenomenon, for how many elections are ever won with such a majority?

Of course, the referendum of 1860 was fraudulent. Only

the most inscient among us would claim otherwise. Even though the paper ballots were ostensibly "secret," the election officials, who already saw the fall of the Two Sicilies as a *fait accompli,* would know who the local dissenters were most likely to be. In the event, such evidence as exists suggests that the officials simply "corrected" any dissenting ballots to reflect approval. The only eligible voters were literate males of at least twenty-five years of age who declared a certain taxable income, and this was but a fraction of the adult male population (the literacy rate was twenty percent at best).

The result most often cited in Sicily is 432,053 votes favorable to annexation and a mere 617 in opposition, in a general population (including men under twenty-five, women and children) estimated at approximately 2,232,000. Moreover, the figure (equal to some twenty-five percent of the *total* adult population, including men under twenty-five years of age *not* entitled to vote) suggests a far higher level of literacy and taxable personal income than there actually was, rendering voting by any more than 300,000 literate, taxable men over the age of twenty-five mathematically impossible. That there might be so many eligible voters is altogether untenable in view of the most rudimentary statistical analysis.

Throughout Italy, region after region confirmed the annexation in referenda resulting in majorities invariably comparable to that claimed for Sicily. Not everybody was taken in by this ruse. Massimo Taparelli d'Azeglio, formerly prime minister of Piedmont, observed:

"At Naples we overthrew a sovereign in order to set up a government based on universal suffrage. Yet we still today need sixty battalions of soldiers to hold the people down, or even more, since these are not enough, whereas in other provinces of Italy nothing of the sort is necessary. One must therefore conclude that there was some mistake about the plebiscite. We must ask the Neapolitans once again whether they want the Piedmontese or not." [49]

Naturally, no such query was ever posed to the populace, at least not officially. What emerged in the new Italy was an ingrained disdain for southerners.

The former Two Sicilies was an occupied country in everything but name. Atrocities were not unknown. In August 1861, two southern towns, Pontelandolfo and Casalduni, suffered murder, rape and destruction at the hands of Piedmontese troops for two long days. This was even worse than the crimes Nino Bixio's troops had committed at Bronte.[50]

Other occurrences during this period were equally surreal, if less violent, and a particularly sobering incident said much about the credibility of the new Italian state in the eyes of the world. In November 1861, a Marseille court upheld King Francesco's earlier sale of two Neapolitan ships despite a vociferous protest from the hubristic Italian ambassador, who claimed that the vessels belonged to Italy. The splenetic reasoning advanced for this idea was that Francesco was no longer a reigning monarch when the ships were sold, and his former kingdom was by then part of the Kingdom of Italy. (History would repeat itself nine decades later when Great Britain refused to relinquish to the Italian Republic several million pounds that the "patriotic" Savoy kings had stashed in British banks.)

Following the fall of Gaeta, Francesco and Maria Sophia resided in the family's Farnese Palace in Rome until that city's occupation by Italian forces a decade later. It was there that their only child, a daughter, was born. She died in infancy. Francesco's dynastic heirs are descended from his younger half-brother, Alfonso, Count of Caserta.

In the wake of the lost war, a number of military officers who had loyally fought against the Piedmontese invasion in mainland Italy, particularly around Gaeta, found themselves incarcerated, along with numerous partisans — often branded as "brigands" by the new government — who continued an armed resistance in the countryside. A few were Sicilians, though most were from Naples and such regions as Calabria and Basilicata. Fenestrelle, an Alpine fortress converted into a prison, thus became Italy's first concentration camp in 1862, eventually housing some three hundred political prisoners. In most cases, their only "crime" was to have supported the crown and country they were sworn to defend. Others, tried as "war criminals" by the new regime, were pardoned or received suspended sentences.

Before long, a series of "extraordinary" taxes were levied on the residents of the former Two Sicilies to defray the cost of the undeclared war, the invasion, of 1860-1861. Of course, the treasury, holding more gold than what was held by all the other pre-unitary states combined, had already been pillaged.

The Rothschilds were forced to close their bank in Naples in 1863 in view of the precipitous decline in the economy following the annexation. (Historian Cyril Toumanoff used to infer the prosperity, or at least the wealth, of the Two Sicilies from the fact that the Rothschilds operated a bank there; many shared his view.)

In a sense, the pro-Bourbon revolt that broke out in Palermo in September 1866 was not unlike the pro-Hohenstaufen rebellion, the Vespers, six centuries earlier, except that Charles of Anjou never claimed to have been "elected" king. Leading to martial law and suppression by Piedmontese troops, the riots prompted many in Turin besides Massimo d'Azeglio (quoted above) to question how such a protest was possible in view of the Savoys' phenomenally high "approval rating" a few years earlier. Tellingly, some leading the revolts, which broke out in a number of towns around Palermo as well as the city itself, were aristocrats and public officials. In Sicily that was often the case throughout history.[51]

Life in the New State

Attempts to disparage the exiled Bourbons were undertaken with uncommon zeal. All manner of defamatory material was published, from cynical caricatures of the "foreign tyrants" to retouched photographs depicting a nude, "promiscuous" Maria Sophia. Every effort was made to discredit the dynasty and the kingdom in the popular mind. Such revisionism, or "historical denial," was part and parcel of the new state, which advocated a feeble *Italia über alles* nationalism.

There was never any grand conspiracy, for such planning requires concerted effort and courage of conviction. There was no coherent philosophy, no apologetics, indeed nothing more than a vague proclivity for expedience. In the Kingdom of Italy, propaganda was never much more than the pernicious result of improvised censorship supported by politicians and their shills. Like the spoiled boy caught with his hand in the cookie jar, unable to remove his chubby paw, they tried to deny what they had done, but never very convincingly. Destroying evidence while concealing facts was their *modus operandi,* but some *biscotti* crumbs always remained: witnesses, bodies, documents, foreign newspaper reports, a few collective memories passed from one generation to the next.

In 1869, a great deal of church property was confiscated. For the most part, these were monastic estates. Many included schools, and as these schools operated by the religious orders had been the chief means of educating young children, Sicily's literacy rate actually declined somewhat over the next decade. Compulsory public instruction for children in primary grades was instituted in 1877 (mandatory education to the age of fourteen years was made law in 1962), but very few public (state) schools were built in Sicily before 1900. The first state schools established by this law opened in Tuscany, Piedmont and other regions north of Rome.

A few monastic schools survived the divestiture of church property. The Dominicans were especially resilient. In rural monastic schools, far from the censors of the cities, the boys were taught two versions of history — the "official" one in the authorized textbooks and the traditional (oral) one which explained the facts of Bourbon rule and the invasion of 1860 in blunt terms. Such lessons became rarer as time passed and the Bourbons were all but forgotten.

The school history texts were bereft of all rhyme or reason. Sicily's every shortcoming was starkly highlighted while none of Piedmont's were even mentioned. A glaring omission was the infamous Piedmont Easter Massacre, which saw some 1700 Waldensians slaughtered by Savoyard troops in 1655, followed by another bloody suppression in 1686.

Deception of this kind might have been dismissed as risible were there not millions of Italian lives involved. Based on the *Statuto,* Carlo Alberto's "Albertine Statute" of 1848, the new state's constitution was trumpeted as an achievement comparable to the drafting of England's *Magna Carta* and the American Bill of Rights. In a land where few were conversant with traditions beyond their own borders, or even their own localities, such sleight of hand was quite credible, even convincing, but foreigners didn't take it too seriously.

Unfortunately, like many other regions, beginning around 1880, Sicily was attacked by the phylloxera louse and most of the island's vines were destroyed. Only those on Mount Etna were spared, probably due to the presence of sulfur in the local volcanic soil.

In 1882 the first deep sulfur mines opened in Sicily. These were tunnels and shafts, as opposed to the open-pit "strip" mines that had been used previously. Too often, children were pressed into labor as miners because few adults were skinny enough to get through the narrow passages. What resulted can only be described as slavery, but the government made little effort to prevent it. Although other reasons were cited as a pretext, Philip Carroll, the United States Consul in Palermo, was expelled from Italy in 1890 for exposing these inhumane conditions in a detailed report written two years earlier on Sicilian sulfur mining.

Italians

The surfeit of Italy's grandiose political propaganda did nothing to change reality.

By this time, most Italians were virtually destitute. Some emigrated, identifying themselves firstly as Sicilians, Calabrians or Neapolitans, and only secondly as "Italians." Until now, most Italian emigration was from the North, not the South. True it is that poverty existed elsewhere in Europe, but Italy's level of indigence, coupled with illiteracy, was not commensurate with the population in what was ostensibly an industrialized society, or even a sophisticated agrarian economy. Around the country, pellagra and goiter were as frequent as ever, and perhaps increasing. The childhood of Angelo Roncalli, the future Pope John XXIII, is instructive; he was born and raised near Bergamo, in the heart of Lombardy.

Francesco Crispi, a bigamist, became Italy's first Sicilian prime minister in 1887, but this did not help his fellow Sicilians. In 1894, during his second term in office, the *Fasci Siciliani,* a rural workers' movement, was brutally suppressed, resulting in lengthy prison sentences for the leaders. Nevertheless, Crispi and others acknowledged that problems existed in farming and mining. Prison terms were commuted but political attempts at reform failed.

The same year, King Francesco II died at Arco in Trent, which was then part of Austria, and Federico De Roberto's novel, *The Viceroys,* chronicling the life of a Sicilian family in the years immediately following unification, was published.

Two years later, the Crispi government fell when Italian forces were defeated at Adwa, in Ethiopia, during an ill-fated, imperialist campaign. The diplomatic chicanery that led to this disaster was typical of what passed for foreign policy in the Kingdom of Italy.[52] In the event, the unforeseen thrashing of Italian troops led the nation's army to be ridiculed internationally for generations. Yet it was domestic incidents that earned the Royal Italian Army the enmity of Italians.

In early May 1898, a series of mass protests broke out around the country over the scarcity and high price of bread amidst what was rapidly becoming a full-fledged famine. Even before the food shortages, many Italians lived in conditions bordering on debt peonage. In Milan, over a hundred demonstrators were killed by the army in the infamous Bava-Beccaris Massacre. Italians grew indignant when King Umberto I knighted the general responsible for this bloodbath.

The ever-present propaganda was ridiculously transparent. "Outside elements" were a frequent scapegoat. Born and raised in Tuscany, and then resident in the United States for just six years, anarchist Gaetano Bresci, who assassinated King Umberto in retribution for the carnage that took place in Milan, was portrayed as "an American," as if New Jersey were a breeding ground for regicidists.

The New Century

With the arrival of a new century and, as fate would have it, a new sovereign, King Vittorio Emanuele III, it was clear that little had changed over the years, at least not for the better. In this sisyphean setting, opportunities were ever in sight and always missed. Some kind of land reform was necessary to wrest control of the Sicilian *latifondi* from the nobility, but these were effected only later, in 1949, after the monarchy was abolished.

Rome responded inadequately to the catastrophic earthquake at Messina in 1908, the first major natural disaster to confront the Kingdom of Italy and an event that revealed the country's woeful state. To her credit, Queen Elena accompanied her husband to the city to do what she could. Montenegrin by birth and upbringing, she was the only queen consort of Italy who could be said to have found favor among the common people.

The lives of the common people were miserable. Following a visit in 1910, Booker T. Washington, an American born into slavery, wrote that, "the condition of the colored farmer in the most backward parts of the southern states in America, even where he has the least education and the least encouragement, is incomparably better than the condition and opportunities of the agricultural population in Sicily."

With the dismemberment of the Ottoman Empire, Italy occupied Libya in 1911. This is where the nation's worst war crimes began, as indiscriminate massacres in small villages. As the Ottomans retreated, the Italians also seized the island of Rhodes. Like its domestic policy, Italy's imperial policy was based on ineptitude.

Although Italy found herself on the winning side in the First World War, which she entered belatedly in 1915, the cost in Italian lives was high. A disproportionate number of draftees were from the South; many northerners obtained exemptions by working in factories built in the North, often with government support, while the South languished in poverty.

Combat is always hellish, but the morale of the typical Italian conscript was abysmal at best, spawning such sayings as "better a pig than a soldier." Trench warfare on the Austrian front found Carabinieri snipers a hundred meters behind the Italian lines, posted there to shoot deserters.

South Tyrol was formally, and legally, annexed to Italy in

1920, with the Istrian peninsula annexed less legally four years later. By that time, Italy was governed by a new regime.

Fascist Italy

Benito Mussolini's Fascists were placed in power by King Vittorio Emanuele III in 1922, and by the time of the Giacomo Matteotti murder two years later the nation was well on its way to becoming a nasty dictatorship. If most Italians were oblivious to the transition, it was only because the Kingdom of Italy, with its press censorship and repression of labor movements, already seemed like a police state. Throughout Italy, the provincial prefect was a figure somewhat similar to the commissar in Soviet Russia, sent to maintain order and ensure there was no dissension in the ranks of local officialdom; the Fascists instituted the additional office of *podestà*, a party official who "assisted" the local mayor in governing according to Fascist principles.

In 1925, Cesare Mori, the "Iron Prefect," arrived in Sicily to quell the Mafia. This had mixed results. Unfortunately, Mori's frequent solution, which was typical of the regime he served, was to jail every suspect he could find, sometimes without so much as the benefit of a show trial.

Queen Maria Sofia died in her native Munich the same year.

Alfonso, Count of Caserta, the heir of Francesco II of the Two Sicilies, maintained a quasi-diplomatic rapport with the Vatican in connection to the dynasty's Constantinian Order, an institution which enjoyed canonical status, until 1927. With an eye to signing a treaty with Italy, the Holy See let lapse the office of Cardinal Protector of this order of knighthood (see the appendix), normally a Papal appointment. The Lateran Treaties materialized two years later, belatedly ending what was, in effect, a state of war between the Kingdom of Italy and the Papacy. This addressed a number of legal anomalies, such as

POSTLUDE: ITALIAN SICILY

Roman Catholic marriages in Italy not being recognized by the Italian government and the longstanding claim of the Popes to a large part of Italian territory. It was typical of the Italian state to resolve such a matter only six decades following its occupation of Papal Rome.

During this trying period Sicily produced some of Italy's best writers; the poet Salvatore Quasimodo and the playwright Luigi Pirandello come to mind. The latter was an unrepentant Fascist. Vitaliano Brancati, on the other hand, came to despise the regime.

Only rarely was scientific achievement recognized, with Fascist sympathizers like Secondo Campini and Guglielmo Marconi being the favored exceptions.

Sicilian-born Giovanni Gentile, Fascism's chief ideologist, oversaw publication of the nationalist *Enciclopedia Italiana*. Here a lengthy entry credits Garibaldi's friend Antonio Meucci, whose name was scarcely known in Italy until 1930, with inventing the telephone, something Italian children are still taught today. The same entry casts aspersions upon the achievements of Alexander Graham Bell and Elisha Gray.[53]

Fascism's apologists sometimes cite old-age pensions and seemingly efficient public services in justification of the dictatorship, as if punctual trains were fair compensation for having censors at the Palermo post office open your mail, both incoming and outgoing.

But Fascism's faux rectitude was a fragile facade. Society at large was subsumed by the whims of an authoritarian state.

"Those who can make you believe absurdities," said Voltaire, "can make you commit atrocities." That is precisely what happened in Italy.

The depravity of Fascism is well-known. What is less widely known is that the invasion of Ethiopia of 1936 led to Italy becoming the first nation to acknowledge committing crimes against humanity (in addition to generic war crimes), and that

Italy eventually had to pay war reparations to that nation as well as Albania, Greece and the Soviet Union (Russia).[54]

In 1937, the year that Italy resigned from the League of Nations, physicist Emilio Segrè, working under primitive conditions at the University of Palermo, discovered the first "artificial" element, technetium (Tc). One of Segrè's colleagues was Ettore Majorana, a gifted young Sicilian whose sophisticated body of work included insightful theories on neutrino masses nearly a century before this became a popular line of research. Recognizing Majorana's landbreaking theories regarding electrons and positrons, important in nuclear fission and chain reactions (principles governing the function of nuclear power reactors and the first atomic bombs), Enrico Fermi praised him as a genius. Majorana disappeared in suspicious circumstances in 1938.

Italians may sometimes have been disparaged abroad, but within Italy some citizens were, to paraphrase Orwell, "more equal than others." The anti-Semitic laws of 1938 were particularly distasteful, if not altogether surprising in a dystopia that now sought to emulate Nazi Germany. Another phenomenon, now widespread, was the overt bigotry directed at "southerners," as residents of the former Two Sicilies were now called; northerners referred to these Italians with such derogatory slurs as *terrùn,* literally "dirt people."

Elvira Mancuso, of Caltanissetta, was an educator and writer, and the most famous of just a few Sicilian feminist activists in an era that viewed as anathema the notion of gender equality. Censored and silenced by the Fascist regime, she lived to see its demise, and the subsequent emergence of something approaching equal rights for Italy's women. Maria Messina followed in her footsteps.

Awash with platitudes, the regime offered very little for the typical Sicilian. Said Luigi Barzini: "If a man is intelligent and Fascist, he is not honest. If he is honest and Fascist, he is not intelligent." Fascism prompted the departure of the best and the brightest: Enrico Fermi, Arturo Toscanini, Maria Montessori, Emilio Segrè, Umberto Nobile.

They weren't the only emigrés. Most of the Italian citizens living in Great Britain and the United States when the King of Italy declared war on these nations were from Italy's southern regions. In becoming "enemy aliens," they risked incurring the antipathy of their hosts. The British imprisoned many Italian men; the Americans were more inclined to issue identity cards.

The Italians. The Germans. From Saxony to Sicily, the lands and peoples once united by the steadying hand of *Stupor Mundi* had given rise, centuries later, to nations and nationalities hatched in the minds of petty bureaucrats, united now only in their warped ambitions. Nationalism corrupts, and absolute nationalism corrupts absolutely.

The Lost War

Italy's invasion of Greece and the Balkans was a comedy of errors (and horrors) requiring German military support to bolster the inept Italian forces. Fascist attempts to bomb Malta and Gozo into oblivion could not compensate for the Italians' lack of radar, which left warships susceptible to nocturnal destruction by Britain's Royal Navy. El Alamein was a debacle that saw the Italians routed by the British. In a development not very unlike the imprisonment of Sicilians at Piedmont's Fenestrelle during the previous century, thousands of Italian troops taken prisoner in the failed invasion of Russia were repatriated only in 1955, the same year Italy was finally permitted to enter the United Nations.

Allied victories in North Africa paved the way for the invasion of southern Europe. The Allied military operations bore bluntly descriptive names like Mincemeat, Corkscrew and

Husky which few Italians could comprehend, the teaching of English having been, in effect, outlawed by the regime. Yet bombs speak a language of their own.

No war ever went very well for the hapless Italians, but the Second World War brought death to their doorsteps. It was horrendous. Italy's incompetent leadership left national territory as exposed and vulnerable as a lamb about to be slaughtered.

Here was the nadir of Sicily's existence.

The slaughter began on a February morning in 1943 when the first shells fell upon Palermo's Magione district, killing nearly a hundred civilians. In a subsequent raid a single massive bomb collapsed an underground air-raid shelter in the square behind the apse of Palermo Cathedral, killing two hundred.

And the slaughter continued.

Following this extensive "carpet bombing" of Palermo as well as Messina, the Allies landed in Sicily in the Summer of 1943. Not the faintest trace of equivocation tainted American General George Patton's declaration to his troops on the eve of battle, characterized by forceful words like these:

"Many of you have in your veins German and Italian blood. But remember that those ancestors of yours so loved freedom that they gave up home and country to cross the ocean in search of liberty. The ancestors of the people we shall kill lacked the courage to make such a sacrifice, and remained slaves."

The ensuing campaign proved highly destructive, with historical treasures like the Norman castle at Troina all but obliterated in protracted fighting between Americans and Germans.

If all wars are senseless, some are more senseless than others. In retrospect, it is difficult to make sense of this one. At all events, it was of Italy's own making; the Pact of Steel sealed the nation's fate.

Italian military leaders were rarely paragons of valor or exemplars of sage judgement, even when fighting on home turf. Alfredo Guzzoni, the general charged with defending the island, fled with his troops across the Strait of Messina, abandoning a piece of Italy. By then, most Sicilian Fascists were already burning their black shirts and party membership cards. Cut off from the party hierarchy, they had to think for themselves, some for the first time in their lives.

Anybody who ever saw in the Sicilians more than a modicum of nationalism was sorely mistaken. At Licata, as the authoritarian regime was swept away with the Summer sands blown in from Africa, local women on balconies launched rubbish onto the heads of Italian prisoners marched down the town's streets by the Americans.[55]

Led by Bernard Montgomery and George Patton, the Allies had won the day, and the century. Italy was emasculated, *quod erat demonstrandum.*

For their part, the occupiers were shocked at the abject poverty, the ubiquitous squalor, that confronted them — unequivocally and inescapably — on the conquered island. Despite having been forewarned of these realities, many were surprised that most homes lacked plumbing and electricity. Telephones and refrigerators were virtually unknown. Fleas and disease were everywhere. Illiteracy was rife. Ten percent of the population held seventy percent of the wealth. Women were little more than chattel.

Sullen and somber, Sicily was a forgotten land, utterly backward, cruelly forsaken by Rome's little king, pompous dictator and petty politicians, and perhaps even by God Himself. No wonder the invaders were greeted as liberators, delivering the Sicilians from two decades of Fascism and fourscore years as Italy's most neglected region.

Not for nothing did the title of Dwight Eisenhower's memoir about the war in Europe compare it to a crusade. Not since the days of Saint Louis had crusaders marched down the streets of Palermo. They had finally returned.

The irony of ironies was that many of the people welcoming the Americans and British as liberators had close male kin who had fought against the Allies in Africa and Russia, some never to return. Survival instincts and profit motives immediately supplanted faux reverence for king and *duce,* with young Palermitan men selling their sisters to American soldiers. Even where actual prostitution was not an issue, Sicilian fathers rushed to betroth their daughters to Americans. In Palermo and its environs, bands of soldiers wandered the labyrinth of narrow streets in search of pretty *signorine,* and a few were bold enough to knock on doors to find them.

Fed a steady diet of Fascist propaganda for two decades, the people were bemused at much of what they saw. The sight of men of color among the occupying troops left many of the Italians nonplussed.

It fell within the purview of the occupiers to feed the Sicilians. Having inherited a mediocre administration from the Italians, the occupation government had to contend with acute food shortages and every other kind of emergency. For the first time, the Sicilians had access to drugs to cure malaria.

On 8 September 1943, capricious King Vittorio Emanuele III announced Italy's armistice with the Allies and soon departed Rome for Brindisi with the royal family, several ministers and generals. This move bore an uncanny resemblance to Francesco's transfer of his court to Gaeta in 1860. Tactical withdrawals of this kind were nothing new; the problem was that in an age of faster communication the news media painted a leader's evacuation of his capital as something tantamount to a captain abandoning his ship. (During the war Britain's royal family remained in London rather than obtaining safety in Canada as King George was advised.)

Prince Umberto, the king's son and heir, wanted to stay and defend the capital but his request was curtly and categorically refused. Leaving the city virtually undefended, a few generals donned civilian attire and fled into the mountains.

What ensued was utter chaos, with German forces taking Italian troops prisoner in occupied territories like Greece. Within days, German divisions were pouring into Italy. Over the next year, the German occupation led to atrocities that were part and parcel of Nazi policy, such as the deliberate murder of civilians in reprisal for the actions of Italian partisans — Rome's Ardeatine Caves Massacre is the best known of these incidents in Italy — and the deportation of Italian Jews to death camps north of the Alps.

In Palermo, Stefania Mantegna, who was something of an anti-Fascist, hosted a ball for local aristocrats and American military officers at her sumptuous home, Palazzo Gangi. In this land of contrasts, a street a few blocks away became the scene for a much more desperate spectacle.

The Allies had left day-to-day police duties to the Italians. In October 1944, these Fascist-trained troops fired into a crowd of Palermitans protesting for food, killing twenty-four and wounding over a hundred in the *Strage del Pane,* the Palermo Bread Massacre. This was nothing if not an eerie reprise of the Milan massacre of 1898.

Meanwhile, the arduous Italian Campaign continued up the peninsula, mountain by mountain, valley by valley. Destructive battles like Monte Cassino have become infamous in the annals of modern history. In 1945, the Germans surrendered officially to the Allied Command headquartered at Caserta, the Bourbons' palace outside Naples.

"Uneasy lies the head that wears a crown," said Shakespeare's Henry IV. During his brief reign under Allied auspices in May 1946, King Umberto II was made by the victors to sign a decree establishing the island as Italy's first semi-autonomous region, something that would have shocked his great-grandfather, Vittorio Emanuele II, who embraced the creed of Italian unification. Little will ever be known about the precise machinations behind this maneuver, but it is clear that Italian emigré influences in the United States were at work.

Winston Churchill wanted to maintain the monarchy, Franklin Roosevelt wanted to institute a republic and Joseph Stalin wanted blood, which is to say war crimes trials. The month following Umberto's concession of Sicilian autonomy, a referendum, which saw Italian women vote for the first time, ousted the monarchy and exiled the royal family. There were irregularities in the balloting. As just one example, an American naval officer stationed in Rome's Quirinal Palace witnessed a leading communist politician and his cronies enter in the dead of night to tamper with some ballot reports.[56]

Nevertheless, this referendum was not nearly so outlandish as the plebiscite of 1860. Being traditionalists, most southerners voted in favor of the monarchy, but it was the republic that emerged victorious, if only by a narrow margin.

The End of Monarchy

The birth of the Kingdom of Italy was anything but auspicious, its death anything but glorious. Now no Italian monarch reigned.[57]

Like Francesco II of the Two Sicilies, Umberto II of Italy was devoutly Catholic, and highly esteemed by many, yet he was surrounded by a coterie of scarecrows. Umberto seemed to resent Fascists for the suffering they had wrought in his country. His reign ended up being shorter than Francesco's, and his exile would last longer. Like Francesco, he might have been a very good sovereign under less trying circumstances.

The next year, control of the nascent republic was ceded to the Italians with the Paris Peace Treaty of 1947. With this document, Italy guaranteed freedom of the press and freedom of religion to those living in the country. A new constitution was promulgated in 1948. As democracy arrived, few lamented the passing of the monarchy, and over the next decades vestigial nostalgia for kings and queens died with the older generation.

On the other side of the world, the Allies permitted a defeated people to keep their hereditary ruler. There was no referendum to expel him. The problem was that, unlike the Emperor of Japan, the King of Italy was not a deity.

Istria was lost, along with the nation's ill-won colonies. Italy's empire was no more. Her pretensions to great power were well and truly dead.

Saddled with debt, the new Italian Republic, with its poorly-written constitution, was not Plato's republic, but it was an improvement over the police state that preceded it. Even so, censorship continued.[58]

The war's end found the United States with the world's largest economy. For a few years, Italy was to be buoyed by American largesse in the form of the Marshall Plan and other programs. Over the next few decades, Italy became something of a client state. "When it rains in Washington," said the cynics, "you need an umbrella in Rome."

Emigration recommenced around 1950, with untold thousands of Italians seeking a better life in the countries against which they warred a few years earlier. Elsewhere — certainly in Japan — this would have been seen as the paradox of paradoxes. In the hearts of the beleaguered Italians, where there flickered not the faintest flame of loyalty to fallen *Italia,* it was considered normal, even mundane, a simple question of survival. An escape from penury. Once again, the Italians became part of a wave of people washed ashore by the ceaseless, indifferent tides of time.[59]

In Piedmont, Italy's most industrialized region, the women known as *mondine* might still plant rice by hand, but now they could finally vote.[60]

Italy would survive.

EPILOGUE

"Kings may be judges of the earth, but wise men are the judges of kings."

— Solomon ibn Gabirol

Monarchs reign by the tenuous, parsimonious Grace of God. The Neapolitan Bourbons' long exile ended as the Savoys' was beginning, and the dynasties finally made a formal peace with each other when neither house reigned. With the end of the world's greatest war, the descendants of the Bourbon kings were free to visit Naples and Palermo.[61]

In 1984, the remains of Francesco II and Maria Sophia, along with their daughter, Maria Cristina — named for Francesco's saintly mother Maria Cristina of Savoy — were interred in the family chapel in the Basilica of Santa Chiara, a splendid church built in Naples by the Angevins, a kindred Capetian dynasty.

When a few Bourbons made their way to Palermo a decade later to observe the solemn centenary of the death of Francesco II, the late Prince Giovanni, who the author had met some years earlier in New York, posed a simple question: "What's it like to live here?"

The historian's reply was couched in equal measures of complexity and diplomacy. Unkempt Palermo is a diamond in the rough. Or perhaps an old bronze artefact; one scratches the surface of its patina to find still another crusty layer. But something is always there. It need only be revealed. Siracusa,

Cefalù, Taormina and Erice are equally intriguing. Travel and tourism have become a lucrative business in Italy.

Inquisitors, dictators and bureaucrats no longer prevent our access to Sicily's history. The internet makes a mockery of censorship.

In 2014, the Bourbons and Savoys came together at Santa Chiara for the beatification of Queen Maria Cristina, a woman claimed by both families.

History is based on what happens, not on what might have happened. We cannot know with certainty that the Kingdom of the Two Sicilies, or perhaps the federation of united Italian states considered by irascible Ferdinando II, would have sidestepped the succession of blunders and calamities that plagued the Kingdom of Italy established in its stead. In view of the events that transpired after 1860, it is difficult to contemplate a worse fate befalling the Sicilians, or indeed any of the Italians, than annexation in such an imperfect union. Until its untimely demise at the hands of human forces greater than itself, the Kingdom of Italy was arguably one of the most backward of the major nations of western Europe.

The study of history is bittersweet. It is not history's responsibility to make us feel good. Facts can't be shaped to accommodate our every sensibility, and in the study of history anything other than fact is fiction, or at best hypothesis. It falls to historians to separate one from the other, even if it takes a few hundred pages (or years) to do so. We look to historians to provide us with accurate information, and we feel betrayed when that sacred trust is violated. Reading inaccurate history is like opening a gift wrapped in beautiful paper to discover that the box is empty. The emptiness disappoints.

Even a landscape dotted with temples and castles marking the paths of truths and legends cannot ensure that every experience lived will become a lesson cherished.

We study history so that we may learn from centuries past,

so that we will not repeat the mistakes of our predecessors. Let us study it well, that we may bequeath to future generations a worthy patrimony. Like kings and queens, we will be judged in death as in life.

We will learn from history as long as we remember it.

CHRONOLOGY

"The stream of time, irresistible, ever moving, carries off and bears away all things that come to birth, plunging them into utter darkness, both deeds of no account and deeds which are mighty and worthy of commemoration."

— Anna Comnena, *Alexiad*

Covering a thousand years, this chronology, like the main text, seeks to provide a general outline not only of the period under discussion (1130-1860) but of what came before and after the Kingdom of Sicily.

Kalbid Emirate

998-1019 - Rule of Ja'far al-Kalbi. Construction of Favara palace in Palermo is attributed to this Emir.

1000 - Norse civilization in northwestern France (Normandy) assimilates with local culture. Approximate period of Norse landings at L'Anse aux Meadows in Newfoundland. *Groenlendinga Saga* (the Greenlanders' Saga) and *Eiriks Saga* (Erik's Story) mention such sea travels.

1016 - Norman knights first participate in battles in Italy. First Turkish raids in Armenia.

1019-1037 - Rule of Ahmed al-Akhal in Sicily.

1037-1040 - Rule by Abdallah Abu Hafs, usurper.

1038-1042 - Byzantine forces of George Maniakes briefly occupy parts of eastern Sicily; army includes Greeks, Normans, Lombards and Norse Varangian Guard under Harald Hardrada.

1040 - Hasan as-Samsam begins his rule; deposed in 1044.

1044 - Island divided into four qadits. Rivalry among emirs worsens.

1053 - Following death of Hasan as-Samsam and extinction of Kalbid dynasty, three important emirs divide control of Sicily: Ibn al Hawas at Kasr' Janni (Enna), Ibn at Timnah at Syracuse and Catania, Abdullah ibn Hawqal at Trapani and Mazara.

1054 - Great Schism between eastern and western Christianity. Sicilian Christians initially remain "eastern" (Orthodox).

1056 - Arab poet ibn Hamdis born; leaves Sicily in 1078.

Norman Period

1060 - Unsuccessful Norman attack in coastal northeastern Sicily.

1061 - Battle of Messina. City and parts of Nebrodian and Peloritan region occupied; permanent Norman presence.

1066 - Battle of Hastings leads to complete Norman conquest of Saxon England. Battle of Messina forms partial pattern of this invasion of an island from a continent; some Norman knights fight at both battles.

1071 - Byzantines lose Battle of Manzikert to Seljuk Turks. Normans attack Palermo; Norman invaders are led by Robert de Hauteville, Arab defenders by Ayub ibn Temim.

1072 - Battle of Palermo ends in early January with Norman occupation under Roger and Robert de Hauteville. Greek Orthodox Bishop Nicodemus removed from authority over Christian community.

1081 - Suppression of revolt led by renegade "emir" Bernavert (Bin al Wardi) at Catania; another of his revolts is suppressed at Syracuse in 1085.

1083 - Roger I appoints Latin (rather than Orthodox) Bishop of Palermo and Gallican Rite is introduced in new churches.

CHRONOLOGY

1084 - Bruno founds Carthusian Order in Germany.

1087 - Ibn Hammud, Emir of Kasr' Janni (Enna), last major Arab stronghold, surrenders to Normans in 1087; Noto falls in 1091. Dozens of fortified Arab-founded (or repopulated) towns dot the island: Calascibetta, Caltanissetta, Caltagirone, Mussomeli, Marsala (Mars' Allah), Misilmeri, Cammarata, others.

1095 - Roger II, future King of Sicily, is born.

1096 - First Crusade begins; some Norman knights participate under Bohemond de Hauteville (later Prince of Antioch), brother of Roger I.

1097 - Odo of Bayeux, Earl of Kent, younger brother of William the Conqueror, King of England, dies in Palermo *en route* to the Crusade while visiting Roger I.

1098 - Roger I, as Great Count of Sicily, becomes Papal Apostolic Legate, with rights to approve island's Catholic bishops.

1099 - Crusaders conquer Jerusalem.

1101 - Roger I dies, succeeded by Simon, his eldest living, legitimate son, who is still a minor. Roger's consort, Adelaide del Vasto of Savona, is regent.

1105 - Roger II succeeds his elder brother Simon (1093-1105) as ruler of Sicily under Adelaide's regency.

1112 - Roger is knighted (this ceremony marks his age of majority and sovereign authority following "regency" under his mother).

1119 Knights Templar founded in Palestine. Preceptories in Sicily confiscated by Frederick II following Sixth Crusade. (Order suppressed definitively by Papacy in 1312.)

1123 - First Lateran Council forbids Roman Catholic clerics wives or concubines; until now Catholic priests were permitted to marry before ordination.

1130 - Roger crowned first King of Sicily (known henceforth as "Roger II").

1139 - Second Lateran Council makes celibacy mandatory for Roman Catholic priests, reiterating a canon established in 1123 but not widely enforced.

1140 - Assizes of Ariano, important legal code asserting royal authority, traditionally dated to this year.

1143 - Martorana church (Palermo) built in Norman-Arab style for Greek Orthodox community by George of Antioch. In this year Nilos Doxopatrios authors theological treatise.

1147 - Second Crusade begins but participation by Sicilian knights is very limited.

1154 - *Book of Roger* completed by court geographer Abdullah al Idrisi. Roger dies and reign of King William I "the Bad" begins.

1155 - Frederick Barbarossa crowned Holy Roman Emperor.

1158 - Qaid al Brun (Thomas Brown), treasurer at William's court, returns to England to reform exchequer of Henry II, thus influencing European accounting principles. He uses Hindu-Arabic numerals, later popularized in Christian Europe by Leonardo Fibonacci of Pisa (briefly a guest of young Frederick II in Sicily) in 1202.

1161 - Matthew Bonellus of Caccamo leads revolt of Norman barons. He is killed in the same year.

1166 - Reign of young King William II "the Good" begins under his mother's regency. Queen Margaret gives hospitality to exiled kin of Thomas Becket. Gradual Latinization of Sicilian language continues; Roman Catholic influence predominates in Christianity.

1169 - Major earthquake in Catania and southeast.

1170 - Benjamin of Tudela visits Sicily. Peter Waldo establishes evangelical Waldensian church, precursor of Reform (Protestant) movement.

1171 - Saladin defeats Fatimids in Middle East.

1174 - Work begins on Monreale Abbey in Arab village of Bal'at overlooking

Palermo. Style is Norman-Arab on Romanesque plan with Byzantine mosaic icons, including earliest holy image of Thomas Becket (canonized in 1173).

1177 - William II marries Joan, daughter of Henry II of England (sister of Richard Lionheart).

1184 - Bin Jubayr visits Sicily and records his impressions.

1187 - Saladin captures Jerusalem.

1189 - Death of William II. Succeeded by Tancred Hauteville.

1190 - Richard Lionheart, brother of Queen Joan of Sicily, occupies Messina with Philip II of France for several months *en route* to Third Crusade.

1193 - Death of Saladin.

Swabian Period

1194 - Death of Tancred. Holy Roman Emperor Henry VI von Hohenstaufen arrives. Teutonic Order of knights, accompanies him, establishing Saint Mary of the Germans (Messina) and obtaining Cistercian properties (the Magione in Palermo).

1198 - Frederick II, son of Henry, is king until 1250, weds Constance of Aragon. Swabian German influences in Sicily. Islam and Greek Orthodoxy permitted but practiced by ever-diminishing minorities. Emergent Sicilian language is Italic with Arabic and Greek influences.

1204 - Latins ("Franks") sack Constantinople during Fourth Crusade, establish "Latin Empire."

1206 - Mongols unite under Genghis Khan (Temujin), who conquers large parts of Eurasia.

1210 - Francis of Assisi meets Pope Innocent III; founds Order of Friars Minor (Franciscans). Albigensian Crusades begin.

1212 - Frederick II reaches age of majority.

1215 - *Magna Carta* in England. Dominic of Osma (of Caleruega, Spain) founds Order of Preachers (Dominicans or "Blackfriars"), confirmed by Papacy in 1216. By 1500 this is the leading monastic and teaching order in Sicily, supportive of the Inquisition.

1217 - Cleric and scientist Michael Scot (born 1175) translates *On the Sphere* by the Arab astronomer Al-Bitruji (or Alpetragius, who died circa 1204). Fifth Crusade begins.

1220 - Frederick issues Assizes of Capua.

1223 - Following execution of Arab rebel leader Morabit (in 1222), thousands of Arabs from Iato area, who had revolted with their leader Ibn Abbad (or Benaveth), are deported to Lucera in Apulia. Many Muslims have already converted to Catholicism. Jews from occupied Jerba (in Tunisia) invited to Sicily.

1224 - University of Naples founded by Frederick II.

1226 - Frederick II summons Imperial Diet of Cremona.

1229 - Frederick II, accompanied by Saracen guards and Sicilian and German knights, goes on Sixth Crusade as King of Jerusalem. Signs peace with Muslims without war.

1230 - Upon his return from Jerusalem Frederick suppresses Templar preceptories in Sicily.

1231 - Constitutions of Melfi become legal code for Kingdom of Sicily under Frederick II.

1233 - Cathars of France persecuted as heretics by first Inquisition.

1240 - Ciullo of Alcamo composes poetry in Sicilian language. First of a series of revolts by Sicilian Arabs, including some Christian converts, but Frederick retains trusted Saracen guards and court officers.

1241 - Mongol-Tatar army of Batu Khan arrives in central Europe after having sacked Kiev. Leads to foundation of "Golden Horde."

1244 - Fall of Jerusalem to Muslim forces.

CHRONOLOGY

1248 - Crusade to Egypt by Louis IX of France.

1250 - Death of Frederick II.

1254 - Death of Conrad IV Hohenstaufen.

1258 - Baghdad falls to Mongols.

Angevin Period

1266 - Charles of Anjou (brother of Louis IX of France) becomes king of Naples and Sicily following defeat of Manfred Hohenstaufen, natural son of Frederick II, at Battle of Benevento.

1268 - Young Conradin, a (legitimate) grandson of Frederick II and last Swabian claimant, is executed in 1268 following defeat at Battle of Tagliacozzo. Hohenstaufen Imperial line now extinct. Angevin period begins. It is thought that by now all of Sicily's remaining Muslims have converted to Catholicism. The multicultural golden age is ending.

1270 - Following Eighth (or "Tunisian") Crusade, funeral of Louis IX of France at Monreale, where his heart is preserved; canonized in 1297.

1273 - Rudolf of Hapsburg becomes king in Germany; his dynasty will succeed Hohenstaufens as Holy Roman Emperors.

Aragonese Period

1282 - Vespers revolt expels Angevin French and makes Peter III of Aragon King of Sicily. Neapolitan invasion of Constantinople is aborted as military resources must be diverted to Sicily.

1285 - Deaths of Charles I of Anjou and Peter III of Aragon, succeeded by their sons.

1302 - Peace of Caltabellotta treaty signed between Aragonese and Angevins. By now, Sicily is essentially monocultural and mostly Roman Catholic. Over the next few generations general literacy diminishes.

1306 - Beginning of a "Little Ice Age" in Europe.

1307 - Templars suppressed by King Philip IV "the Fair" of France but the estates of this order had already been confiscated in Sicily by Frederick II, ending its presence on the island.

1309-1377 - Avignon Papacy; Papal court in France. Western Schism follows from 1378 until 1417.

1315-1317 - Bad harvests due to wet, cool Spring and Summer lead to food shortages and Great Famine.

1321 - Dante Alighieri's *Inferno* (part of his *Divine Comedy*) mentions several Popes, Frederick II and Frederick's chancellor Pietro della Vigna (1190-1249).

1337 - Hundred Years' War begins between England and France; English invade France in 1346. (This was actually a series of conflicts rather than a single war.)

1347 - Genoan ships arriving at Messina from eastern Mediterranean bring bubonic plague ("Black Death") to Europe, killing some 20 million Europeans.

1353 - Giovanni Boccaccio's *Decameron* mentions Palermo's Cuba palace and King William II of Sicily.

1361 - A second wave of bubonic plague in Europe.

1377 - Chaos following death of King Frederick "the Simple" until arrival of his dynastic successor King Martin continues until 1392. Chiaramonte, Alagona, Peralta and Ventimiglia families (the "Four Vicars") usurp royal authority, sparking a feudal "civil war." Andrew Chiaramonte is eventually beheaded.

1380 - Tatars defeated at Kulikovo by Russians commanded by Dimitri Donskoy (who completed construction of the Kremlin in 1367).

1397 - Sweden, Denmark and Norway united by Treaty of Kalmar until 1523.

Castilian Period

1412 - House of Aragon succeeded by Trastámara dynasty of Castile based on Compromise of Ceuta.

CHRONOLOGY

1415 - Battle of Agincourt results in English victory.

1416 - Alfonso V "the Magnanimous" crowned King of Aragon, Sicily, later (1442) Naples, establishing diplomatic relations with burgeoning Ethiopian Empire and becoming important patron of the Renaissance.

1434 - University of Catania founded.

1447 - Johannes Gutenberg invents printing press using movable type; prints Bible in 1455. (Rudimentary printing plates were developed earlier in China but this publication marks beginning of mass publication.)

1453 - End of Hundred Years' War. Constantinople falls to Ottomans. Conclusion of Middle Ages usually dated to this year, but sometimes to 1492 or 1500. Renaissance has begun. Sicilian-born painter Antonello da Messina is part of this new movement.

1466 - Francesco Laurana, Renaissance sculptor, establishes workshop in Palermo.

1474 - Massacre of over 300 Jews at Modica who refused to pray in a Catholic church.

Spanish Period

1478 - Spanish Inquisition begins; in Sicily it lasts until 1782.

1492 - Edict against Jews (the "Alhambra Decree") forces widespread conversions and some emigrations in 1493. Albanian refugees arrive following Turkish invasions of Balkans. Spanish rule continues in Sicily until 1700s. Columbus lands in America, initiating European colonization.

1497 - Tribunal of the Inquisition ("Holy Office") formally instituted in Palermo to try "heretics."

1516 - Holy Roman Emperor Charles V, King of Spain and ruler of much of western Europe, becomes King of Sicily.

1526 - Outbreak of plague.

1530 - To protect Sicily from pirates and Turks, Charles V cedes Malta to Knights of Saint John ("Knights of Malta") as fief for annual feudal rent of a Maltese falcon.

1548 - Jesuits found their first *studium*, the future University of Messina.

1571 - European Christian fleet gathered at Messina defeats Turks at Lepanto.

1575 - Plague outbreak in Palermo.

1592 - Famine in western Sicily.

1606 - Wheat shortage.

1618 - Thirty Years' War begins. Sicily is involved as part of Spanish Empire.

1624 - Plague ends at Palermo after bones of Saint Rosalie are discovered, but her historicity is questioned by later historians.

1638 - Head tax imposed in Sicily to defray Spanish military expenses of Thirty Years' War.

1647 - Food riots in Palermo due to poor harvest and inefficient agricultural policy of landholders and government. A similar riot follows in Naples.

1651 - *Donativo* levied.

1669 - Major eruption of Mount Etna destroys several towns and reaches the Ionian coast at Catania.

1674 - Localized revolt in Messina by the city's oligarchs.

1681 - *Donativo* levied.

1693 - An exceptionally destructive earthquake strikes eastern Sicily, particularly Catania, Noto, Ragusa. Districts are rebuilt in new Sicilian Baroque architecture.

Savoyard and Austrian Rule

1713 - With Treaty of Utrecht Sicily comes under Savoy rule.

1714 - *Donativo* levied by King Vittorio Amedeo.

1718 - British fleet defeats Spanish at Battle of Cape Passaro. Spanish fleet defeats Austrians at Battle of Milazzo during War of the Quadruple Alliance.

1719 - Spanish troops defeat Austrians at Battle of Francavilla. Some 5,000 were killed or wounded in one of the largest land battles fought in Sicily since antiquity. Austrians then besiege Messina, which surrenders.

1720 - Sicily falls under Hapsburg rule as a condition of the Treaty of the Hague. (Savoys lose Sicily but become Kings of Sardinia.)

The Two Sicilies

1734 - Charles of Spain becomes King of Naples and Sicily (and Duke of Parma) following invasion, crowned in Palermo in 1735.

1743 - An epidemic strikes Messina.

1748 - *Donativo* levied by King Charles.

1754 - Italy's first university chair/department in economics established at Naples.

1759 - Charles becomes Carlos III of Spain. Forever separates Spanish Crown from those of Naples and Sicily, ceding Italian dominions to his son, Ferdinando I.

1764 - Famine strikes Sicily following bad wheat harvest.

1767 - Jesuits expelled from kingdoms of Naples and Sicily.

1776 - United States declares independence from Great Britain; France and Spain support Americans.

1778 - San Leucio (near Caserta) becomes first public housing complex/estate in Italy.

1779 - Precursor of University of Palermo founded as *Regia Accademia degli Studi San Ferdinando*.

1782 - Spanish Inquisition abolished in Sicily.

1783 - Peace of Paris treaties signed by Britain, France, Spain and United States end American Revolutionary War.

1788 - First public school for the deaf in Italy established in Naples (school founded in Rome in 1784 was private).

1789 - French Revolution begins.

1795 - First public botanical gardens in Italy open in Palermo (others were private or scholastic). Revolt in Palermo suppressed.

1796 - King of Naples and Sicily recognizes the United States of America; full diplomatic relations established in 1832.

1798 - Malta, part of the Kingdom of Sicily, occupied by Napoleonic fleet which expels Knights of Saint John. Following Britain's victory over the French, Malta and Gozo become British protectorate in 1800 and are never returned to Sicilian Crown.

1799 - Parthenopean Republic declared in Naples. Ferdinando I resides in Palermo.

1801 - Dwarf planet Ceres discovered based on work at astronomical observatory atop Palermo's Norman Palace.

1802 - Ferdinando I returns to Naples during Peace of Amiens.

1803 - Napoleonic Wars begin, end in 1815.

1804 - Jesuits restored in Kingdom of Naples.

1806 - British troops are based in Sicily as bulwark against possible Napoleonic invasion. King Ferdinand I again resident in Palermo.

1810 - Ferdinando II born in Palermo.

CHRONOLOGY

1812 - Under British influence, feudalism is abolished by new Constitution.

1814-1815 - Congress of Vienna.

1814 - General restoration of Jesuits in Europe (rehabilitated in southern Italy 1804).

1815 - Joachim Murat executed in Calabria following attempted incursion.

1816 - Kingdom of the Two Sicilies is established following Ferdinando's return to Naples; Sicilian constitution is suppressed when Neapolitan and Sicilian Crowns are formally unified.

1818 - The *Ferdinando I* becomes the first steamship in the Mediterranean.

1820 - Civil marriages and vital statistics records instituted in Sicily.

1821 - Rothschild Bank opens in Naples (closes in 1863 following unification).

1825 - Ferdinando I dies, Francesco I becomes king.

1830 - Francesco I dies, Ferdinando II crowned.

1832 - First glass recycling program introduced in Two Sicilies. First steel suspension bridge in Italy constructed over Gagliano River.

1836 - Maria Cristina of Savoy, queen consort, dies; beatified in 2014.

1839 - First railroad in Italy built from Naples to Portici. First gas-fuelled public lighting system introduced in Two Sicilies.

1841 - First seismic observatory in the world established at Mount Vesuvius.

1846 - First commercial electric telegraphs introduced in Europe.

1846-1848 - Bad grain harvests in Sicily and across Europe; Potato Famine worsens in Ireland.

1847 - Revolts in Messina. *Giglio delle Onde* becomes first steamship with screw propulsion in the Mediterranean.

1848 - Revolts begin in Palermo and spread across Europe. New constitution is enacted but soon abolished.

1852 - Two Sicilies sets up first functioning electric telegraph in Italy.

1856 - Britain and France recall their ambassadors from Naples. Congress of Paris formally ends Crimean War.

1859 - Ferdinando II dies, Francesco II becomes King of the Two Sicilies.

1860 - Northern Italian troops led by Giuseppe Garibaldi (1807-1882) embark in Sicily. At Bronte, Nino Bixio's troops become the first military contingent identified with the united Italy to massacre civilians. Sicily is annexed to the Kingdom of Italy.

Kingdom of Italy

1861 - King Francesco II of the Two Sicilies surrenders Gaeta north of Naples, exiled. Vittorio Emanuele II of Savoy, King of Sardinia, becomes King of Italy.

1862 - Fenestrelle, a "secret" Alpine prison for political detainees (mostly Two-Sicilies loyalists), becomes Italy's first concentration camp.

1866 - Revolt against Piedmontese occupation and annexation in Palermo, protests suppressed by Piedmontese troops.

1869 - Ecclesiastical property confiscated in Sicily, leading to closure of most monastic schools and (in the absence of state schools to substitute these) decrease in general literacy.

1877 - Mandatory public education instituted but few public (state) schools established south of Rome before 1900.

1882 - First major sulfur mines (rather than open pits) excavated in Sicily, resulting in exploitation of child labor.

1887 - Francesco Crispi (1818-1901), a bigamist, becomes Italy's first Sicilian prime minister (1887-1891 and 1893-1896).

CHRONOLOGY

1894 - *Fasci Siciliani,* a rural labor movement founded in Sicily, suppressed by force and summary trials. Death of King Francesco II of the Two Sicilies.

1896 - Italians suffer major defeat by Ethiopians at Battle of Adwa; some 7,000 Italian troops killed and 3,000 taken prisoner. Italy earns disdain of world's great military powers (Russia openly supports Ethiopia politically). Crispi government falls following resulting protests in Rome; Italy, followed by France and the United Kingdom, recognizes Ethiopia in 1897.

1898 - Bava-Beccaris Massacre in Milan.

1900 - King Umberto I of Italy assassinated at Monza.

1908 - Earthquake and tsunami destroy most of Messina, killing as many as 100,000 in Sicily and Calabria.

1911 - National census data reports that some 58 percent of Sicilians are illiterate. Italy occupies Libya (formerly an Ottoman territory), and many Sicilians migrate to the new Italian colony despite civil unrest. Rhodes is also occupied.

1915 - Italy enters the First World War.

1920 - Italy formally annexes occupied South Tyrol by terms of treaty ending First World War.

1922 - Fascist government installed; becomes dictatorship by 1924. Rijeka and territories in Istrian peninsula, now Slovenia and Croatia, occupied (illegally) by Italy, annexed formally in 1924. Fascists institute program to populate this region and South Tyrol (see above) with Italian-speaking settlers; by 1940 Italian is the principal spoken language of Bozen (Bolzano) and remains so today.

1924 - Giacomo Matteotti, member of parliament and outspoken opponent of Fascism, kidnapped and murdered by Fascist secret police; murderers granted amnesty by King Vittorio Emanuele III.

1925 - Death of Maria Sophia, last Queen of the Two Sicilies.

1925-1929 - Cesare Mori (1871-1942), the "Iron Prefect," nearly eradicates the Mafia, but in 1943 the Americans will vacate convictions of those posing as anti-Fascists, appointing several as mayors of small towns.

1929 - Lateran Treaties establish diplomatic relations between Italy and Vatican, ending state of war that lasted almost 60 years. Ecclesiastical marriages celebrated in Sicily since 1861 are thereby retroactively recognized by the Italian state, where Catholicism is confirmed as state religion.

1930 - *Enciclopedia Italiana* cites Antonio Meucci as inventor of the telephone.

1934 - Death of Alfonso, Count of Caserta, exiled half-brother and heir of King Francesco II of the Two Sicilies.

1936 - Italy invades Ethiopia and initiates genocide by poison gas and other means; is condemned by League of Nations. Sicilians and other Italians settle in "Italian West Africa" as part of rural colonization program. Under terms of Paris Peace Treaty of 1947, Italy will lose colonies and pay Ethiopia US $25 million in reparations, principally "in kind" (construction projects).

1937 - Physicist Emilio Segré discovers first "artificial" element, Technetium (Tc), at University of Palermo. Italy resigns from League of Nations.

1938 - Racial laws against Jews in Italy restrict civil rights, holding of public positions (including professorships), marriages with Gentiles. Emilio Segré, who is Jewish, leaves Italy; working with other scientists at the University of California at Berkeley (where he is later appointed professor), he discovers Astatine and Plutonium-239, and receives Nobel Prize in 1959.

1939 - Italy invades and occupies Albania; by terms of Paris Peace Treaty of 1947 Italy will pay Albania US $5 million in reparations.

1940 - Italy declares war on France and Great Britain. Italy invades Greece but its offensive is repulsed by counterattacks in Greece and Albania (the first Allied land victory of the Second World War). Under Paris Peace Treaty of 1947, Italy will pay Greece US $105 million in reparations.

1941 - Italians defeated by British and Ethiopian forces in Ethiopia; Italy declares war on the United States. Germany sends troops into Greece to bolster Italians.

1942-1943 - Allied forces defeat Axis troops in Libya and Tunisia; Italy's ephemeral colonial empire is thus completely dismembered. Italian and German troops are defeated at Stalingrad; under Paris Peace Treaty of 1947, Italy will pay Russia (Soviet Union) US $100 million in reparations.

1943 - Allied carpet bombing of Palermo begins in February; some 98 civilians are killed on first day while historic Magione church sustains extensive damage. In July, Allies occupy Sicily following largest amphibious invasion ever attempted (soon superseded by D-day landings in Normandy); Italian forces under Alfredo Guzzoni flee across Strait of Messina. In response to crushing defeat and loss of Sicily, King Vittorio Emanuele III removes Benito Mussolini from power. In September, Italy changes alliance and the king abandons Rome for Brindisi.

1944-1946 - Reclaiming the Istria region annexed to Italy in 1924, Slovenian and Croatian partisans expel or kill numerous Italians, relocated there under Fascist policy, in "Foibe" incidents. Allies and United Nations regard such reprisals, ubiquitous during the war, as reaction to earlier Axis actions (see Italian partisans below), but with Paris Peace Treaty (see below), Allied troops occupy free territory of Trieste in 1947.

1945 - War ends in Italy in late April, when Benito Mussolini is killed by Italian partisans armed by Americans. Allies acknowledge this resistance movement as cooperative but undisciplined; partisans sometimes undertook reprisals on unarmed civilians and had agreed to consign Fascist hierarchs to Allies.

Italian Republic

1946 - In May, Sicily granted political semi-autonomy by King Umberto II on American orders. In June, Italian women vote for the first time in the popular referendum establishing the Italian Republic. King Umberto II and his young son are exiled while formerly-exiled Bourbon descendants (children and grandchildren of late Alfonso, Count of Caserta) are permitted free entry into Italy.

1947 - Italy becomes first nation to acknowledge committing *crimes against humanity* (with reference to genocide in Ethiopia); generic war crimes also acknowledged and Italy begins payment of reparations to Ethiopia, Greece, other countries (total of US $360 million). Paris Peace Treaty (10 February) formally restores Rijeka and territories in Istrian peninsula (in Slovenia and Croatia) to Yugoslavia; Italy legally divested of *all* colonial possessions (Somalia, Libya, Rhodes). Allied troops leave Italy except for Trieste. Portella della Ginestra massacre results in deaths of 11 protesters near Piana degli Albanesi.

1948 - Italy begins receiving funds from the Marshall Plan even as it pays reparations to Russia (Soviet Union) and other nations; American aid to Italy totals $1.2 billion by 1952. Constitution of the Italian Republic chartered; semi-autonomy guaranteed to Sicily, Aosta, South Tyrol.

1949 - Land reforms fragment large agricultural estates (latifondi) in Sicily and permit distribution of property. Italian immigration to the United States resumes.

1950 - Salvatore Giuliano, bandit and outspoken proponent of Sicilian independence movement, is killed.

1952 - Danilo Dolci (1924-1997) establishes social movement at Partinico to combat economic inequality and organized crime.

1953 - Petroleum discovered off Sicily's southeastern coasts.

1954 - Allied Military Government cedes control of Trieste to Italy and Yugoslavia.

1955 - Italy permitted entry into United Nations; last Italian prisoners of war repatriated from Soviet Union.

1957 - Treaty of Rome establishes framework for European Union. Sicilian Mafia "Cupola" meeting in Palermo and American Mafia "Commission" meeting in Apalachin (New York).

1958 - *The Leopard* by Giuseppe Tomasi di Lampedusa (1896-1957) is published; in translation it is the first Sicilian work to become an international bestseller. The novel impugns "official" views of the *Risorgimento*.

CHRONOLOGY

1959 - United States naval air base established at Sigonella near Catania, NATO base later constructed next to this site.

1962 - Film *Divorce Italian Style,* with its story set in Sicily, is released abroad, bringing censorious attention to Italy's lack of divorce statutes.

1964 - Cardinal Ernesto Ruffini (1888-1967), Archbishop of Palermo, refutes existence of the Mafia and implies that social worker Danilo Dolci and author Giuseppe Tomasi di Lampedusa (see above) have "defamed" Sicily.

1968 - Towns in Belice Valley destroyed by major earthquake receive little emergency relief; many reconstruction funds are misappropriated.

1970 - Italian parliament legalizes divorce; law is confirmed by referendum in 1974. (In 2012 Italy will abolish legal distinction between children born to wed and unwed parents; in that year 25 percent of births in Italy nationally are to unwed couples, around 20 percent in Sicily.)

1978 - Italy legalizes abortion. (In 2014, several legal restrictions on the use of reproductive technologies in fertility treatment, such as gamete donation and in vitro fertilization, will be lifted in Italy.)

1981 - Italy bans theatrical release of *The Lion of the Desert,* a motion picture (starring Anthony Quinn, Oliver Reed, Rod Steiger, Irene Papas, John Gielgud, numerous Italians) depicting civilian massacres in Italian-occupied Libya; national censorship ends when film is finally broadcast on Italian satellite television on 11 June 2009.

1982 - Mafia assassinates Prefect of Palermo; organized crime is recognized in law as a felony.

1983 - Death of Umberto II, exiled King of Italy.

1984 - With update of Vatican concordat of 1929 (Lateran Treaties), Roman Catholicism ceases to be the official religion of Italy but Catholic Church continues to be recognized as a "state within a state." Francesco II of the Two Sicilies interred in Naples.

1987 - Mafiosi sentenced in "Maxiprocesso," first major trial of Sicilian organized crime figures in Italy under new laws, coinciding with "Pizza Connection" trial in the United States.

1992 - Judges Falcone and Borsellino assassinated by the Mafia.

1993 - Giuseppe Puglisi, a Catholic priest, murdered by the Mafia in Palermo's Brancaccio district. Beatified in 2013.

1996 - Italian legislation makes rape a violent felony comparable to assault. (Stalking will be outlawed in 2009.)

1997 - Italy fully implements last remaining conditions making it part of the Schengen Area.

2000 - In view of impending introduction of the euro, Italy mints the last *lira,* the currency introduced nationwide with unification.

APPENDIX 1

Kings of Sicily

Here the ordinal numeration is based on reigns as Kings of *Sicily*, so Emperor Frederick II is listed as *King Frederick I of Sicily*, while Emperor Charles V is *King Charles II of Sicily*. Names are given in English. To better elucidate dynastic connections, four genealogical charts follow this list, including one showing the Neapolitan monarchs, who at times were also Sicilian sovereigns. The kingdoms of Naples and Sicily were formally integrated with each other, as the same Crown, from 1130 until 1282 and then from 1816 to 1861.

House of Hauteville (Norman) 1130-1194
1071-1101 Roger I, Great Count of Sicily (son of Tancred of Hauteville)
1101-1105 Simon, Great Count of Sicily (son of Roger I, died in childhood)
1105-1154 Roger II, King of Sicily (younger brother of Simon) crowned 1130
1154-1166 William I "the Bad" (son of Roger II)
1166-1189 William II "the Good" (son of William I)
1189-1194 Tancred I (natural son of Roger, Duke of Apulia)

House of Hohenstaufen (Swabian) 1194-1266
1194-1197 Henry I (Emperor Henry VI)
1197-1198 Constance (daughter of Roger II), Regent
1197-1250 Frederick I (Emperor Frederick II)
1250-1254 Conrad I (son of Frederick)

THE KINGDOM OF SICILY

1254-1268 Conrad II "Conradin" (son of Conrad)
1258-1266 Manfred (natural son of Frederick II)

House of Anjou (French) 1266-1282
1266-1282 Charles I of Naples (son of Louis VII of France)

House of Aragon (of Barcelona) 1282-1410
1282-1285 Peter I (Peter III of Aragon, son of James I)
1285-1296 James (son of Peter I)
1296-1337 Frederick II (younger brother of James)
1337-1342 Peter II (son of Frederick II)
1342-1355 Louis (son of Peter II)
1355-1377 Frederick III "the Simple" (younger brother of Louis)
1377-1401 Mary (daughter of Frederick III)
1395-1409 Martin I "the Younger" (son of Martin of Aragon, below) wed Mary
1409-1410 Martin II "the Elder" (father of Martin I, above, son of Peter IV of Aragon)

House of Trastámara (of Castile) 1412-1516
1412-1416 Ferdinand I, son of John I of Castile
1416-1458 Alfonso "the Magnanimous" (son of Ferdinand)
1458-1468 John (younger brother of Alfonso)
1468-1516 Ferdinand II "the Catholic," King of Spain, son of John II of Aragon

House of Hapsburg (Spain) 1516-1700
1516-1556 Charles II (Emperor Charles V), King of Spain, son of Philip I of Castile
1556-1598 Philip I (son of Emperor Charles V, above), Philip II of Spain
1598-1621 Philip II (son of Philip I, above), Philip III of Spain
1621-1665 Philip III (son of Philip II, above), Philip IV of Spain
1665-1700 Charles III (son of Philip III, above), Charles II of Spain

House of Bourbon (Spain) 1700-1713
1700-1713 Philip IV (son of Louis, Dauphin of France), Philip V of Spain

House of Savoy (Piedmont) 1713-1720
1713-1720 Victor Amadeus, Victor Amadeus II of Savoy

KINGS OF SICILY

House of Hapsburg (Austria) 1720-1734
1720-1734 Charles IV, son of Emperor Leopold I

House of Bourbon (Two Sicilies) 1734-1861
1734-1759 Charles V (later Charles III of Spain), son of Philip V of Spain
1759-1825 Ferdinand III (from 1816 Ferdinand I), son of Charles
1825-1830 Francis I of the Two Sicilies, son of Ferdinand, above
1830-1859 Ferdinand II of the Two Sicilies, son of Francis, above
1859-1861 Francis II of the Two Sicilies, son of Ferdinand II.

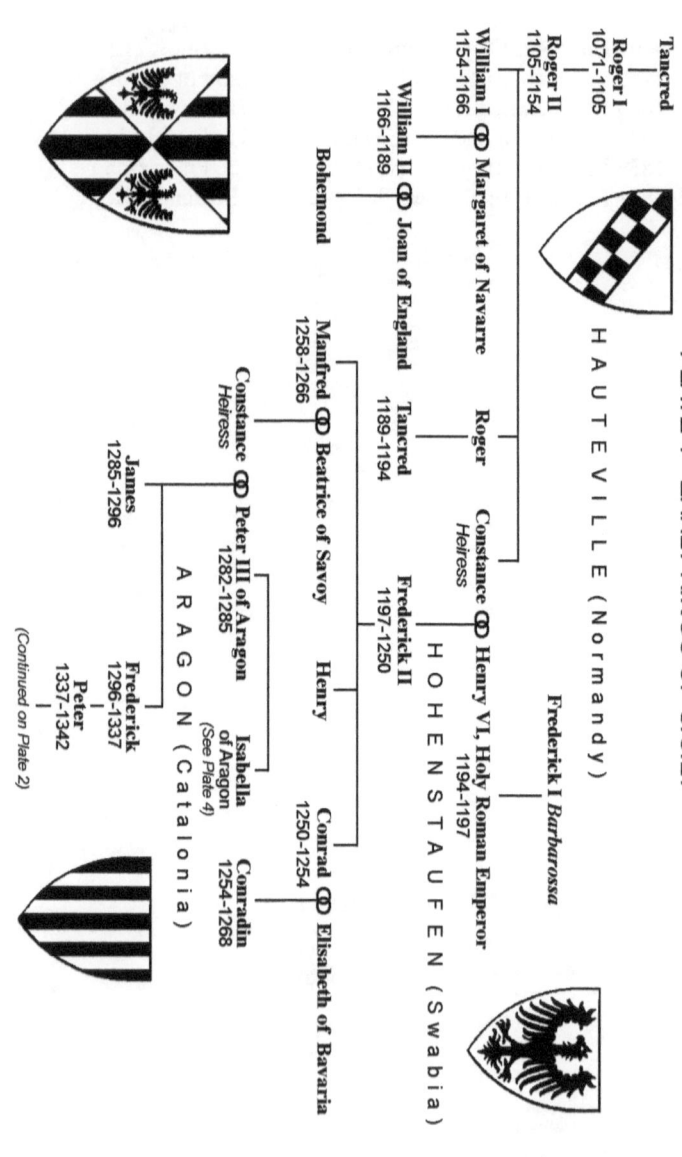

KINGS OF SICILY

PLATE 2 ARAGON, TRASTAMARA, HAPSBURG

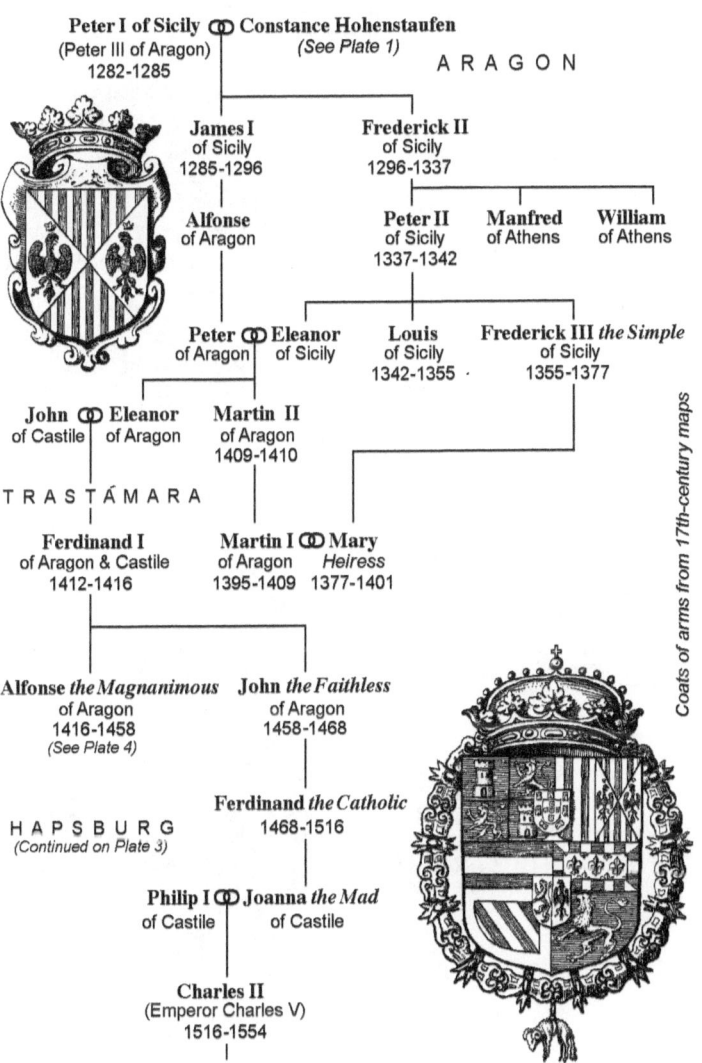

Peter I of Sicily ⊕ **Constance Hohenstaufen**
(Peter III of Aragon)   *(See Plate 1)*
1282-1285

A R A G O N

- **James I** of Sicily, 1285-1296
  - **Alfonse** of Aragon
  - **Peter** ⊕ **Eleanor**
    of Aragon | of Sicily
    - **John** ⊕ **Eleanor**
      of Castile | of Aragon
    - **Martin II** of Aragon, 1409-1410

- **Frederick II** of Sicily, 1296-1337
  - **Peter II** of Sicily, 1337-1342
  - **Manfred** of Athens
  - **William** of Athens
  - **Louis** of Sicily, 1342-1355
  - **Frederick III** *the Simple* of Sicily, 1355-1377

TRASTÁMARA

- **Ferdinand I** of Aragon & Castile, 1412-1416
- **Martin I** ⊕ **Mary**
  of Aragon   *Heiress*
  1395-1409   1377-1401

- **Alfonse** *the Magnanimous* of Aragon, 1416-1458 *(See Plate 4)*
- **John** *the Faithless* of Aragon, 1458-1468

HAPSBURG
(Continued on Plate 3)

- **Ferdinand** *the Catholic*, 1468-1516
- **Philip I** ⊕ **Joanna** *the Mad*
  of Castile | of Castile
- **Charles II**
  (Emperor Charles V)
  1516-1554

Coats of arms from 17th-century maps

THE KINGDOM OF SICILY

PLATE 3 HAPSBURG AND BOURBON

HAPSBURG
(Continued from Plate 2)

Charles II
(Emperor Charles V)
1516-1556

Philip I
King of Sicily & Spain
(Philip II of Spain)
1556-1598

Philip II
(Philip III of Spain)
1598-1621

Philip III ⚭ Elizabeth
(Philip IV of Spain)   of France
1621-1665

Louis XIV ⚭ Maria Theresa   Charles II
of France   of Spain
                               1665-1700

Louis
The Great Dauphin

BOURBON

Philip IV
(Philip V of Spain)
1700-1713

Carlo V
(Charles III of Spain)
1734-1759

Charles IV   Ferdinando I
King of Spain   of the Two Sicilies
                1759-1825

Francesco I
1825-1830

Ferdinando II
1830-1859

Francesco II
1859-1861

Coat of arms from royal decrees issued after 1816

336

PLATE 4 KINGS & QUEENS OF NAPLES

ANJOU

Louis VIII of France
├── Louis IX of France
│   └── Philip III ⚭ Isabella of Aragon *(See Plate 1)*
│   ├── Philip IV of France
│   └── Charles of Valois ⚭ Margaret
│   └── Philip VI of France
│   └── John II of France
│   ├── Charles V of France
│   │   └── Louis I of Orléans
│   │   └── Charles of Orléans
│   │   └── Louis XII of France 1501-1504
│   └── Louis I of Anjou *Heir Designate of Joanna I*
│   └── Louis II 1389-1399
│   └── René I 1435-1442
│   └── John II of Anjou *Pretender*
└── Charles I Naples 1266-1285, Sicily 1266-1282
    └── Charles II 1285-1309
        ├── Robert *the Wise* 1309-1343
        │   └── Charles of Calabria
        │   └── Joanna I 1343-1382
        ├── Philip of Taranto
        │   └── Philip of Taranto
        │   └── Louis of Taranto ⚭ Joanna II 1414-1435
        └── John of Durazzo
            └── Louis of Durazzo
                └── Charles III 1382-1386
                    └── Ladislas 1386-1389, 1399-1414

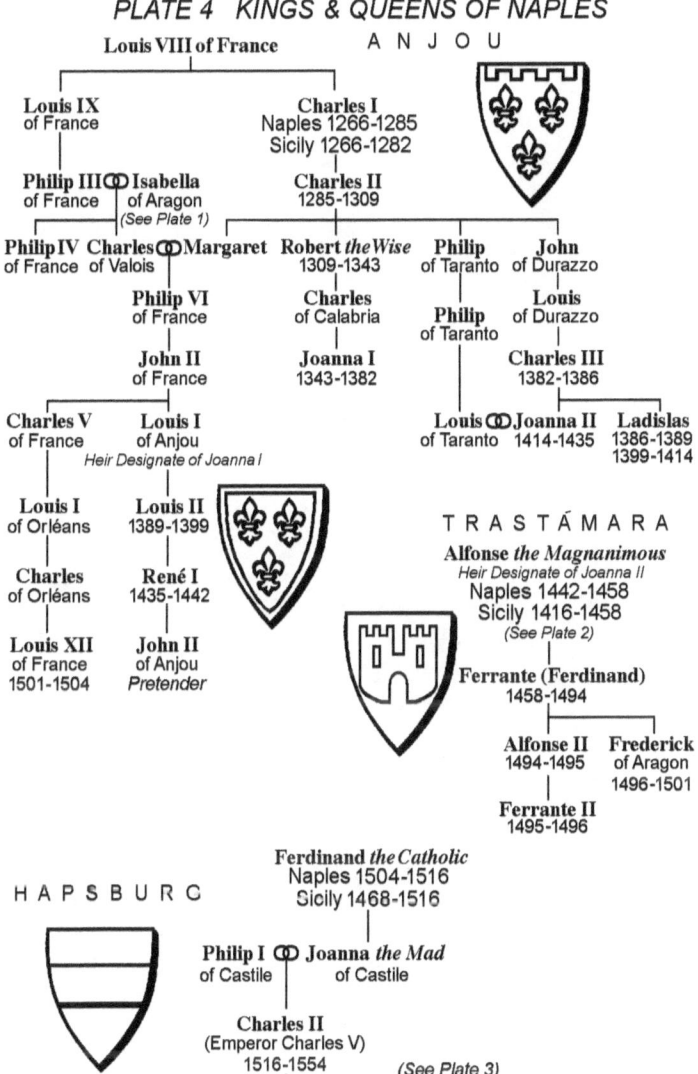

TRASTÁMARA

Alfonse *the Magnanimous*
Heir Designate of Joanna II
Naples 1442-1458
Sicily 1416-1458
(See Plate 2)
└── Ferrante (Ferdinand) 1458-1494
    ├── Alfonse II 1494-1495
    │   └── Ferrante II 1495-1496
    └── Frederick of Aragon 1496-1501

Ferdinand *the Catholic*
Naples 1504-1516
Sicily 1468-1516
└── Philip I of Castile ⚭ Joanna *the Mad* of Castile
    └── Charles II (Emperor Charles V) 1516-1554 *(See Plate 3)*

HAPSBURG

APPENDIX 2

Knightly Orders

Among the feudal institutions described in Chapter 3 is enfeoffed knighthood, an integral part of the manorial system introduced by the Normans. These landed knights, whose loyalty was, ultimately, to the sovereign, formed the kingdom's corps of elite fighting men, augmented by a regular army. By the end of the twelfth century there emerged various *orders,* or companies, of "crusading" knights whose first loyalty was to an elected leader, their *grand master.*

The role of the various orders of knighthood described here was, at best, incidental to Sicilian history, but such institutions were an outgrowth of the colorful medieval world of kingdoms and crusades. Like heraldry, their emergence coincided with that of the Kingdom of Sicily. No history of the *Regnum* would be complete without mentioning these orders, which were intimately linked to the monarchy, the nobility and the Church.

Indeed, those orders which, owing to historical happenstance, still exist in our times might be said to be the last living vestiges of Sicily's kingdom.

Medieval Orders of Chivalry

First we shall meet the knightly orders present in Sicily by 1200, specifically the *Knights Hospitaller* (later the Knights of Malta), the *Knights Templar* and the *Teutonic Knights*. These *military-religious* orders served specific roles, in Sicily and elsewhere. They might protect religious pilgrims or care for the sick. Of course, such knights were often called upon to engage in actual combat. Their ranks were drawn from the landed nobility. Many were the younger sons of barons who, excluded by the laws of primogeniture from inheriting familial estates, joined the orders to achieve a sense of purpose while serving their Maker. A fourth order, the *Knights of Saint Lazarus* (now the *Order of Saints Maurice and Lazarus* of the House of Savoy), cared for lepers; they briefly operated a hospice outside Palermo, Saint John of the Lepers.

By 1600, Sicilian noblemen were being decorated with various orders, especially those connected to Spain, such as the Order of Santiago. Although the earliest knights of these *monastic-military* orders (Santiago as well as Alcantara, Calatrava and Montesa) had participated in the Spanish *Reconquista* and various battles against the Moors, their role was not exclusively military after 1500.

Each dynasty brought its orders to Sicily for the duration of its rule. Vittorio Amedeo of Savoy bestowed the Order of Saints Maurice and Lazarus upon several Sicilians during his brief reign early in the eighteenth century.

In centuries past, some subjects of the King of Sicily were knighted by the Holy See, specifically in the Golden Militia, known today as the Order of the Golden Spur.

Several *dynastic orders* of chivalry were instituted by the House of Bourbon in the Kingdom of Naples. Naturally, these were bestowed in the Kingdom of the Two Sicilies, but in exile King Francesco II continued to award them. In law, this practice is based on the arcane principle of *fons honorum,* or "fount of honor," by which an exiled monarch and his heirs retain the right to bestow honors (knighthoods) and, in some cases, to create or recognize titles of nobility. Neither the last King of the Two Sicilies nor the last King of Italy lost these rights when they were deposed and exiled (in 1861 and 1946 respectively), as neither ever abdicated.

The dynastic orders of the Two Sicilies shall also be considered here; some are recognized by the Italian government, and two have a continuing canonical status in the Roman Catholic Church. The history of the House of the Two Sicilies after the death of its last king, in late 1894, lies beyond the scope of this work; here it may suffice to say that the dynasts of the House of the Two Sicilies descend from Alfonso, Count of Caserta, the younger half-brother of King Francesco II.

Knights of Malta

The Order of Saint John of the Hospital of Jerusalem was founded in the Holy Land around 1048, if not some years earlier, as a hospice and monastic community to care for the sick, by the Blessed Gerard, who was probably from southern Italy. According to longstanding tradition, the hospice was initially funded by Amalfitan merchants. In 1113, the Order received Papal approval. By this time it was an order of knights whose principal objective was the defense of pilgrims. It soon became a military as well as religious order which participated in many crusader activities and military campaigns. Gerard died in 1120, succeeded by a series of elected grand masters beginning with Raymond du Puy.

There were a few Siculo Norman knights of Saint John, or "Hospitallers," in Messina as early as the reign of King Roger II, but the Order's greatest influence in Sicily, in the form of commanderies and preceptories similar to those of the Teutonic Knights and Templars, was most felt at the beginning of the reign of Frederick II. It was he who later assigned Sicily's Templar commanderies to the Hospitallers following what he perceived as an affront by the arrogant Templars during his "Sixth Crusade" to the Holy Land in 1228-1229.

Though a number of Sicilian feudal knights of the Swabian era participated in the Crusades, apart from Frederick's single, peaceful Sixth Crusade they usually did so independently of their sovereign, leaving to join the military-religious orders. In general, although his policies changed based on circumstances, the freethinking Frederick chose to accommodate his Muslim subjects rather than offend them through such activities as crusading.

After the fall of Jerusalem the knights established their seat at Cyprus and, in 1310, at Rhodes, where they remained until a bloody defeat at Muslim hands in 1523.

In 1530 the Holy Roman Emperor Charles V, in his capacity as King of Sicily, ceded to the displaced knights the islands of Malta and Gozo once held by the Chiaramonte family which built Fort Sant'Angelo. The knights' Maltese dominion was a fief of the King of Sicily, its Grand Master a vassal. Thus an annual feudal rent was paid, though this was largely symbolic in practice. It included, for example, a Maltese falcon. The island would remain a feudal dependency of the Kingdom of Sicily as long as the knights governed it.

In granting Malta to the knights, Charles hoped they would provide a bulwark against incursions by the Ottoman Turks. This they did, but not without engaging in some piracy along the African coasts. Caravaggio spent some time in Malta, where the Order commissioned several paintings. The eccentric artist was imprisoned there in 1608 and eventually escaped to Sicily.

For several centuries a handful of military outposts along the southern coasts of Sicily were manned by the knights of Malta to defend the island from marauding pirates. By 1700 the inland commanderies were few and the coastal fortifications had been abandoned. The role of the knights in Sicily was never as important as in some other kingdoms, and scant vestiges of it remain except for a few buildings around Ragusa and Noto. In London, conversely, their legacy endures in place names such as Saint John's Wood and Saint John's Gate, though Henry VIII suppressed the Hospitallers in England.

Two prominent participants in the American Revolutionary War, the French admirals Francois de Grasse and Pierre André de Suffren de Saint-Tropez, received their naval training in the Order of Malta. At least twenty prominent French knights of Malta fought for the American cause.

A donkey acquired from the grand master de Rohan-Polduc by the Marquis de Lafayette was given to George Washington in 1786. Christening it *The Knight of Malta,* the general kept it on his estate in Virginia. (The Prologue mentions a similar gift made to Washington from King Charles III of Spain.)

Unfortunately, French amity toward the Order of Malta was not to last. On their way to Egypt, Napoleon's forces expelled the knights from their islands in 1798, in the process liberating a great number of slaves. The displaced knights were given hospitality in Sicily. Following the defeat of the French, Malta and Gozo passed to British control despite protests from the King of Sicily. The grand magistry was transferred to Messina and Catania and finally, in 1834, to its present location in Rome, where it enjoys extraterritorial sovereignty.

After the Order's expulsion from Malta, its decoration (the "Maltese Cross") grew popular as a "reward" for titled aristocrats, from whose ranks the serving (military) knights had been recruited for many centuries. By then its importance in Sicily had long diminished.

Yet the Order's survival owes more to the Sicilian kings than to any other monarchs save the Popes, not only from 1530 until 1798 but into the nineteenth century.

The Order of Malta has never forgotten its ties to the bygone Kingdom of Sicily. In a sign of friendship rooted in another age, it still maintains a cordial rapport with the non-regnant House of Bourbon of the Two Sicilies. By longstanding tradition, the Prince Grand Master of the Sovereign Military Order of Malta accepts the insignia of the dynasty's Order of Saint Januarius or the Constantinian Order. (The last two Grand Masters, both Englishmen, accepted both orders.)

Although the United States did not institute diplomatic relations with the Order of Malta by establishing an embassy in Valletta, there was occasional communication with the knights. In 1794 the Order of Malta proposed to protect American shipping in the Mediterranean in exchange for a piece of sovereign territory in the United States. This tempting offer, which might have altered the course of the Order's history in view of its eventual expulsion from Malta a few years later, was tactfully refused by the American ambassador in Paris, the future President James Monroe.

Knights Templar

Much legend and supposition surrounds the history of the Knights Templar, and even certain documents recently discovered in the Vatican archives about the end of the Order of the Temple shed little new light on the established facts. The Templars' Sicilian presence came to an end long before the Order disappeared across the rest of Europe in the early years of the fourteenth century.

The Order was founded in Palestine around 1118 by Hugh de Payens, a French crusading knight, to protect pilgrims in the Holy Land. A great number of these pilgrims had begun to arrive following the First Crusade in 1099. King Baldwin II of Jerusalem gave the knights, who took vows of poverty, some land on the Temple Mount, from which they took their name.

Like the Hospitallers, they often participated in battles against the Muslims, most famously against Saladin at Montgisard in 1177. Not only did the Templars establish a number of castles and commanderies in Palestine, they soon had many such communities across Europe. The wealth of the Templars, like that of the Hospitallers, rivalled that of many sovereigns, a fact that generated a certain degree of envy throughout Europe. This, of course, was not the case of the rulers of the prosperous Kingdom of Sicily.

As an aid to pilgrims and other travellers, the Templar network of preceptories and commanderies facilitated the novel means of letters of credit to transfer money. Essentially, a sealed document (a "cheque") issued by one commandery could be exchanged for actual funds (coinage) by another. In this way checking, as it came to be known and used in modern times, was introduced across Europe by the Templars, though paper currency was already in use in China. It is believed that the Templars' *cheque* was inspired by the *saqq* used by Arab traders, and it is highly probable that the *saqq* was utilized in Sicily during the Fatimid period.

Such instruments obviated the need for wealthier travellers to carry large amounts of gold or silver which could very easily be robbed by armed bandits.

Two of the larger Templar foundations in Sicily were Saint Nicholas of the Temple (San Nicolò del Tempio) in Bulgherano near Scordia before 1151 and the Saint Mary Carmine Church (Chiesa del Carmine) in Piazza Armerina. There were other commanderies at Caltagirone, Trapani, Siracusa, Butera and Lentini. The most important, at Messina, served as a major stopover for crusaders and pilgrims *en route* to the Holy Land by sea. The commanderies at Marsala and Trapani also served the Order in this regard, but Messina's was its major administrative center in Sicily.

The Hohenstaufens, as Holy Roman Emperors, were no more kindly disposed toward the Templars than other monarchs, and much preferred the Teutonic Knights, who for the most part were drawn from German Europe and sometimes lent military support to Imperial campaigns. By 1200, the Teutonic Order had particularly important commanderies based in Sicily in Palermo (the Magione) and Messina (Saint Mary of the Germans). The Hohenstaufens had inherited the Templars and Hospitallers of Sicily from their Hauteville predecessors, and there was no immediate effort to remove either order.

By right of his second wife, Isabella (Yolanda) of Brienne, Frederick II was King of Jerusalem. As we have seen, he arrived in Palestine leading the Sixth Crusade in 1229. Ostensibly, this was a military campaign to rein in the Muslims. In fact, Frederick reached an agreement with them while having himself crowned.

For this reason and others, the Templars did not support Frederick in the Holy Land. The king did not forget their treason. Upon his return to Sicily, he confiscated all their properties there and assigned these to the rival Hospitallers, though he left most of the Templar commanderies in peninsular Italy untouched. A few of the Sicilian holdings were still in the possession of the Hospitallers when they were expelled from Malta in 1798.

The Templars' removal from Sicily presaged their dissolution in 1312, when they were far wealthier than the Hospitallers despite holding only half as much land.

Given their colorful history, the Knights Templar are hardly forgotten. Their story has given rise to conspiracy theories and a large *corpus* of pseudohistory and historical fiction.

Teutonic Knights

The Order of Saint Mary of Jerusalem was founded in 1190 during the Third Crusade, on the model of the Hospitallers, to care for crusaders from central Europe taken ill. Pope Celestine III recognized the Order in 1192.

Henry VI and his suite of German barons and retainers were accepted only grudgingly by the Sicilian nobility. Out of the need for loyal military support, Henry installed several commanderies of the recently-founded Teutonic Order in Sicily, appropriating for them (from the Cistercians) Palermo's splendid Magione church and cloister, and constructing for them the Church of Saint Mary of the Germans in Messina, of which only a few walls and arches remain.

By 1198 the Teutonic Knights were a powerful military force in Palestine. Unlike the Templars, they warmly welcomed Frederick II during his visit in 1229.

The Teutonic Order left Palestine in 1291. Like the Templars and Hospitallers, they eventually garnered for themselves extensive holdings in Europe, establishing their grand magistry in Prussia in 1309. But their zealous military exploits in Poland and the Baltic lands — the infamous "Baltic Crusades" — rarely earned the knights any sympathy from the common folk. A major defeat by Polish and Lithuanian forces in 1410 spelled the end of the Teutonic Order's military and economic power. The Reformation's winds of change dealt it another strong blow.

The Teutonic Knights left Sicily in 1492 on Papal orders rooted in a request by the King of Spain.

The symbolism of the German decoration which became known as the *Iron Cross* was inspired by the Teutonic Knights' black cross on a white field. The Teutonic Order exists today as a quasi-chivalric, confraternal institution of the Catholic Church.

More information on these orders in medieval Sicily will be found in Lynn Townsend White's *Latin Monasticism in Norman Sicily* (1938) pages 234-240.

Dynastic Orders in the Two Sicilies

A number of dynastic and national orders of knighthood were bestowed by the Bourbon sovereigns from 1734 until 1861. Here these are presented according to their dates of foundation.

Only two of these orders were specifically Roman Catholic in character.

The others were bestowed irrespective of the recipient's religious profession. None were intended as "Italian" or "ethnic" institutions, although most of their knights came from what is now Italy.

There are numerous works dedicated to the study of these orders; those published before the fall of the Two Sicilies are the most reliable because they are based on the juridical realities that existed before 1860 rather than subsequent speculation or hypothesis hatched by would-be "experts" in later times. The definitive contemporary reference on the knightly orders of the Kingdom of the Two Sicilies during this period is *Saggio Storico degli Ordini Cavallereschi nel Regno delle Due Sicilie* (1832) by Raffaele Ruo, a Neapolitan jurist who was Notary of the Constantinian Order of Saint George.

The Constantinian Order of Saint George

This is the Neapolitan order having the longest history, and today it is a charitable institution that functions in much the same way as the Order of Malta. Its origins are military but it became dynastic while retaining its military-religious character, and in that respect its history is not unlike that of the Order of Saints Maurice and Lazarus of the House of Savoy. The Constantinian Order of Saint George was brought to Naples in 1734 by Charles de Bourbon, who inherited it from his mother's family, the Farnese.

Saint George, about whom there is much legend, is a patron of Greece, Georgia, England, Catalonia, Aragon and — unbeknownst to many — Sicily. He is also the patron saint of knights, horses and soldiers.

Among a number of military families struggling for control of the Balkans following the fall of Constantinople to the Turks in 1453 were the Angelus Comnenus, who claimed, with little justification, to be the legitimate pretenders to the Byzantine throne. In this they were supported by the opportunistic Venetians, who feared losing their strategic and lucrative territories around Albania to the invading Turks. By 1576, the Constantinian Order, founded in defense of the Christian faith, had obtained Papal approval and a special niche in canon law. Most of its knights were now Roman Catholic rather than Greek Orthodox. In imitation of the homonymous Papal "Golden Militia" mentioned above, it was sometimes referred to as the "Constantinian Golden Militia."

At the end of the seventeenth century, the last Angelus Comnenus heir ceded the hereditary grand magistry of the Constantinian Order to the sovereign Duke of Parma. Some three decades later, in 1731, Antonio Farnese, the last of his dynasty to rule Parma, lacking male heirs, was suc-

KNIGHTLY ORDERS

ceeded by a niece, Elisabeth (Isabella), who was by then married to King Philip V of Spain.

When her son, Charles, claimed his birthright in Parma before marching on Naples, the Constantinian Order was part of his patrimony. In Sicily, it was given the Magione, the church once held by the Teutonic Knights, where the Order's emblem can still be seen.

During the Bourbon era, there were a few Constantinian knights from countries beyond Neapolitan borders. One example among many is Anthony Plunkett, an Irishman invested in 1789.

An idiosyncrasy in its history is that this was not always regarded as a dynastic order *per se,* nor even as the order of a specific kingdom. Initially, it was, in essence, a military-religious order in the gift and protection of a specific dynasty. Its vicissitudes took it down the peninsula from Venice to Parma to Naples. Even after confiscating its numerous estates, the Kingdom of Italy continued to recognize the Order's survival, and hence its dynastic nature, a fact confirmed by a decision of the district court of Naples in 1921.

In that era the Constantinian Order was still active, having sponsored the operation of hospital trains during the First World War.

As Cardinal Secretary of State, Eugenio Pacelli, the future Pope Pius XII, became a Constantinian bailiff in 1929, the year the Vatican signed the Lateran Treaties with Italy. In exile in Portugal, King Umberto II accepted the Constantinian Collar in 1959; decades earlier, as heir apparent to the Italian Throne, he had worked to inter Francesco II in Italy.

On 23 April 1812, Francesco, Duke of Calabria (the future Francesco I), acting on behalf of his father, Ferdinando I, invested several Sicilian noblemen as knights of the Constantinian Order during a ceremony redolent of the Middle Ages in the Magione in Palermo. What follow are notes by Raffaele Ruo on such investitures held into the middle of the nineteenth century:

On the designated day, the Prelate and the King Grand Master or Delegate arrive at the church ceremony with any locally-resident knights in attendance. In the absence of at least two (uniformed) Constantinian knights to act as sponsors in the city where the investiture is convened, two knights of other Catholic military orders are invited to stand as sponsors.

Wearing the cape of the Order, the Prelate and Delegate enter and together genuflect before the Blessed Sacrament. The Delegate then takes a seat in the Sanctuary near the Pulpit. Vested accordingly, the Prelate prepares for the celebration of the Mass, seating himself at the place normally reserved for the Bishop.

Four pages enter, each carrying a platen (or basin) bearing the insignia of the Order, namely the mantle, the cross decoration, the gilt spurs and the sword with scabbard and belt. The postulant follows, flanked by the two knights sponsor. At the altar, this cortege bows to the Prelate and the Delegate. The pages place the insignia on a table in the Sanctuary, as the sponsors and postulant genuflect before the cross at the altar. The sponsors then take their places at the side.

The postulant remains before the altar, kneeling on a cushion, holding in his right hand a lit candle, while the Prelate celebrates the Order of the Mass of the Holy Spirit. During the Gospel reading, all of the knights draw their swords to demonstrate that they are prepared to defend the Faith. Following the Gospel, they sheathe their swords. During the Eucharist, the first member of the congregation to receive communion is the postulant.

Following the Mass, the sponsors escort the postulant to kneel before the Prelate and Delegate. To the Delegate one of the sponsors presents the diploma signed by the Grand Master, and this is read aloud. The postulant rises and the other sponsor turns to him explaining that nobody may be admitted to the Sacred Order who, with his voice and in his heart, has not first professed the Holy, Catholic and Apostolic Faith. The postulant then kneels before the Prelate and hears recited the words of profession from the Bull of Pius IV of 13 November 1564, following which he kisses the ring of the Prelate and the Gospel.

The blessing of the insignia follows, with the sprinkling of Holy Water over the mantle, cross, sword and spurs, presented in turn by the pages. The sponsors first display the mantle, unfolding it for the Prelate to recite a brief prayer before its embroidered cross. The postulant is then mantled by the two sponsors. The cross and collar (or ribbon) are presented by another page, blessed and kissed by the Prelate, and then placed around the postulant's neck with the assistance of the sponsors.

The third page approaches carrying the platen with the sword, scabbard and belt. One of the sponsors grasps and unsheathes the sword while the Prelate blesses it. The other sponsor then hands the sword to the Delegate who, together with the postulant, grasps it. Following some prayers, the Delegate returns the sword to the sponsor, who sheathes it. The sponsors then gird the postulant with the sword belt.

The armed postulant then draws the sword. Facing the congregation, he waves it three times through the air, starting with the point upward, bringing it downward to symbolically menace the enemies of Christianity. He raises it once more before sheathing it. Facing the altar, he then kneels on one knee before the Delegate.

The Delegate draws and raises his own sword high enough for the entire congregation to see. He then lowers the weapon to lightly tap each shoulder of the kneeling postulant, who henceforth from that moment is a Constantinian Knight. As he does this, the Delegate recites some phrases, dubbing the postulant in the name of God, the King of the Two Sicilies and Saint George the Martyr. The Prelate approaches and lightly taps the knight's left cheek in the Kiss of Peace. The knight is then invited to rise.

Finally, the fourth page presents the Delegate with the platen bearing the gilt spurs. The Delegate presents these for the Prelate's blessing, and then hands the spur-bearing platen to a sponsor. Each sponsor affixes a spur to a foot of the knight, while the Prelate reads a psalm.

As the Recessional, the Prelate cants the Hymn of Saint Ambrose. The knight and cortege process out of the Church.

If this ceremony is held in a private chapel, the Prelate is to be vested appropriately, while the Grand Master or Delegate would wear civilian attire.

The Order of Saint Januarius

In times past, every dynasty or kingdom had its premier order of chivalry whose knights wore a "collar" formed of links resembling those of a chain. Such an order had a limited number of knights, each of whom swore fealty to the king, who was the order's grand master. The first orders of this kind were England's Order of the Garter founded in 1348, the Savoys' Order of the Annunciation founded in 1362, and the Order of the Golden Fleece founded in 1430 (eventually bestowed in both Austria and Spain). Unlike the military-religious orders described above, whose original knights were men-at-arms skilled in combat techniques, these *collar* or *court* orders were a means of affiliating a faithful subject, usually a nobleman, with the monarch without the requirement of military service.

The order might be a reward for loyal service. While the order itself was not necessarily religious in nature, its ceremonial reflected the religion of its sovereign grand master.

Such an order was founded by King Charles of Naples and Sicily (later Carlos III of Spain) in 1738. This is the Order of Saint Januarius, which received Papal approval from Benedict XIV in 1741. Its original statutes reflected the times, for example forbidding knights to participate in duels.

Martyred in 305, Saint Januarius (San Gennaro) is the patron saint of Naples. His solidified blood, kept in two vials in the cathedral that bears his name, liquefies on his annual feast day, 19 September. (The author once witnessed this occurrence in the cathedral's sanctuary as a guest of the Archbishop of Naples; the substance, which contains blood as well as other compounds, did indeed liquefy when the portable reliquary containing it was slowly rotated by the late Cardinal Giordano.)

Charles also founded the Order of Saint Charles (see below).

The Order of Saint Charles

Founded in 1738 to recognize military service rendered during the recent conquest of Naples and Sicily, this was one of Europe's first orders of merit, obviously named for the monarch's patron saint, to whom he dedicated the opera house of Naples. Its cross was based on that of the Constantinian Order, the arms of which coincidentally resembling the Bourbons' fleur de lis. The Order became inactive when King Charles of Naples and Sicily left Italy in 1759. The insignia of the order of the same name instituted by him as King of Spain in 1771 is of a different design.

The Order of Merit of Saint Ferdinand

This Order was founded in 1800 to recognize individuals who had rendered exceptional service to the Crown. This included Neapolitans and Sicilians, as well as some British officers who were based in Sicily when the royal family resided in Palermo while Naples was occupied by republicans.

Despite its dedication to a Catholic saint, the Order never had a religious character. It has always been awarded irrespective of the conferee's faith.

It was part of a general trend in orders of knighthood bestowed for merit.

The Order of Saint George of the Reunion

Founded in 1819, this Order was intended to replace an order bestowed upon citizens of the Kingdom of Naples by the French during the Napoleonic occupation. The "reunion" refers to the peninsular region being reunited with the island of Sicily as the Two Sicilies.

The Order of Francis I

Francesco I of the Two Sicilies instituted this order of merit in 1829 to recognize achievement in the arts, letters and sciences. The decoration, typical of that era, is a white Maltese-style cross bearing four golden fleurs de lis between its limbs; in the center medallion is Francesco's royal monogram "F.I." The cross pends from a large golden coronet. The ribbon of the Order is deep red with a blue edge.

As head of his dynasty, Prince Alfonso, Count of Caserta, brother and heir of King Francesco II, bestowed the Order in exile into the twentieth century (one of his letters patent from 1906 is shown). Alfonso died in 1934.

This was the last order of knighthood founded in the Kingdom of the Two Sicilies, and as it reflects the esteem in which scientific, industrial and artistic progress were held, its decree of foundation follows.

Order of Francis I
Decree of Foundation

Francesco I, by the Grace of God King of the Kingdom of the Two Sicilies, of Jerusalem, etc., Duke of Parma, Piacenza, Castro, etc., Hereditary Grand Prince of Tuscany, etc.

It being one of our chief interests to promote by all the means at our disposal the zeal of our subjects in the exercise of various civil offices assigned to them by us, and ever desiring to foster advancements in the sciences and the fine arts, as well as in the various aspects of industry, agriculture and commerce upon which the continued prosperity of the kingdom depends; Considering that awards of honor and merit are the most powerful recognition of such virtuous and praiseworthy activities; Having heard our Council of State in Ordinary; We have resolved to sanction, and by these presents do approve the following law.

1. We hereby establish in our Kingdom of the Two Sicilies an order of knighthood, expressly intended to recognize civil merit, which shall bear the name of the *Royal Order of Francis I*.

2. Insofar as this distinguished order of knighthood shall be accorded the dignity of our illustrious and esteemed Crown, we declare ourself and our Royal Person the Sovereign Head and Grand Master of the aforementioned Order, and shall display its decoration and ribbon upon our Royal Person, as well as suspended from the royal coat of arms; and we desire that the Grand Magistry of the said Order shall always be vested in our Royal Crown.

3. The said Order shall have five grades, namely Knight Grand Cross,

Knight Commander, Knight, Conferee of the Medal in Gold, and Conferee of the Medal in Silver.

4. Exclusively those our subjects who have rendered to the Crown and to the state the most outstanding and loyal service in the exercise of the highest offices in the political, diplomatic, or judicial spheres, or in any branch of administrative or ecclesiastical service, may be decorated with the Grand Cross.

5. Those who have rendered extraordinary service in the exercise of important offices in the political, diplomatic, or judicial spheres, or in any branch of administrative or ecclesiastical service, may be decorated with the rank of Knight Commander.

6. Those who have rendered faithful service in the political, diplomatic or judicial spheres, or in any branch of administrative or ecclesiastical service, as well as those distinguished in scientific fields, writing and publishing, fine arts, or as the authors of great works, may be decorated with the rank of Knight.

7. The Gold Medal may be conferred upon those who have excelled in the abovementioned fields, having rendered important service at an elementary level.

8. The Gold Medal may likewise be conferred upon those who have displayed exceptional merit in the fine arts, and those who have introduced new industrial methods, or have introduced extraordinary procedures in the mechanical arts, or have notably improved the fields of agriculture or animal livestock development, or have promoted industry and commerce.

9. At all events, we reserve to ourselves the right to bestow the rank of Knight in the extraordinary instance of one of our subjects having executed a distinguished public project, or reflecting discoveries in one of the aforementioned fields of study.

10. The Silver Medal may be conferred upon those who, though not meeting all the requirements expressed in the aforementioned articles 7 and 8, have rendered worthy projects in the fields described.

11. Those in the military who have rendered distinguished civil service as described in the preceding articles 4, 5, 6, 7, 8, 9 and 10 may also be decorated in various grades of the Order.

12. The dispositions of the present law do not abrogate or diminish the effect of other sovereign resolutions established to reward merits in the fine arts or manufacturing; on the contrary, those so rewarded may be considered for the Gold or Silver Medal of this Order.

13. The rank of Knight Commander or Knight, as well as the Medal in Gold or Silver, may be bestowed upon worthy individuals according to the level of their service, in recognition of rare and virtuous merits demonstrated toward the Throne and the State.

14. Those Knights who continue to render distinguished service of such importance as to merit further consideration may be rewarded by us with bestowal of the rank of Knight Commander or Knight Grand Cross. On the same basis, those who have been decorated with the Gold Medal may be rewarded with the rank of Knight, and those decorated with the Silver Medal may be rewarded with the Gold Medal.

15. Our Ministerial Secretaries of State, regardless of their department, and our Lieutenant General in Sicily, shall advise us, through our Ministerial Secretary of State for the Royal Household, of the names, qualities and merits of those our subjects who have rendered services which should be recognized by decoration with a grade of the Order, including that of Knight Grand Cross; we shall reserve to ourself the ultimate decision to recognize merits such as are described by the present law.

16. The Knights Grand Cross shall have the privilege of entry into the Throne Room, and may attend Court dinners and royal receptions. They may display the cross of the Order in their places of business and in their coat of arms.

17. The Knights Commander shall have the privilege of attending Court dinners and royal receptions.

18. The Knights may attend royal receptions.

19. We reserve to ourself, according to the circumstances, and according to the nature and importance of services rendered by the individual decorated with the Order, to assign a pension as we see fit. Such pensions shall be paid from the Royal Purse until such time as we decide it opportune to establish a fund for the Order.

20. The insignia of the Order shall be a cross enamelled white between four gold fleurs de lis, bearing a center medallion upon which appears our cipher F.I., surmounted by the royal crown, encircled by an oak wreath enamelled green, this encircled by a blue band bearing the legend *De Rege optime merito* in gold letters, the medallion bearing on the reverse the inscription *Franciscus Ius instituit MDCCCXXIX*, encircled by an oak wreath enamelled green.

21. The decoration of Knight Grand Cross is the cross described herein, surmounted by a gold crown, suspended from the neck by a wide watered (moire) ribbon of deep red bearing at each edge a narrow blue stripe. The insignia of Knight Grand Cross also includes a badge to be worn attached to the left breast of the jacket. The said badge shall consist of the same cross as the neck decoration but of silver rather than white enamel, displaying between its arms four fleurs de lis, bearing at its center a medallion upon which appears our cipher F.I., surmounted by the royal crown, encircled by an oak wreath enamelled green, this encircled by a blue band bearing the legend *De Rege optime merito* in gold letters.

22. The decoration of Knight Commander is similar to that described in Article 20, except that it is slightly smaller, surmounted by a gold crown, suspended from the neck by a ribbon slightly narrower than that of the neck decoration of Knight Grand Cross.

23. The decoration of a Knight is similar to that of Knight Commander but slightly smaller, surmounted by a gold crown, suspended from the lapel buttonhole of the jacket by a ribbon slightly narrower than that of the neck decoration of Knight Commander.

24. The Gold and Silver Medals shall bear on the obverse our likeness in profile encircled by an oak wreath, this encircled by the legend *Franciscus I. Reg. utr. Sic. Hier Rex;* bearing on the reverse three fleurs de lis, one in chief and two in base, encircled by an oak wreath encircled by the legend *De Rege optime merito MDCCCXXIX*. The Medal is suspended from the lapel buttonhole by a ribbon slightly narrower than that of the decoration of Knight.

25. The precise measurements of the decorations and ribbons are indicated in a design which accompanies the original document of this decree.

26. The conferral of the aforementioned honors and awards shall be made by effect of royal rescript by our Ministerial Secretary of State for the Royal Household.

27. Our being desirous that no form of endeavour that could benefit the public good in some way be ignored, even if its merits have not been made known to the public, and wishing that such worthy activities which influence society, however indirectly, be recognized by this Order, we have determined that the Medal of Civil Merit instituted 17 December 1827 shall no longer be bestowed for services rendered expressly to the benefit of the King and the State, recognition of such services being addressed instead by the present law.

28. To that end we authorize the competent administrators to make known those deserving recognition with the awards mentioned in Article 27, submitting the relevant proposals and documentation to the office of the Ministerial Secretary of State for the Royal Household or, in Sicily, to the office of the Lieutenant General, who will forward these to the former. The names of those thus honored, as well as the services for which Our Royal Person has determined that they be recognized, shall be published in the official gazette of this Kingdom.

29. The affairs of the Order shall be managed by a Deputation composed of a President (who shall be a Knight Grand Cross), two Knights Commander and two Knights, one of whom shall serve as secretary and archivist. We shall nominate the members of the Deputation on the recommendations of our Ministerial Secretary of State for the Royal Household. Specific regulations shall establish the duties and internal functions of the Deputation.

30. As this Deputation shall depend upon the aforementioned Secretary of the Royal Household, it shall answer directly and exclusively to him.

31. In bestowing the Order, we shall rely upon the advice of the Deputation, whose responsibility it shall be to examine and consider the merits of the worthy services mentioned in Article 27.

32. The expenses of the Delegation, and of certain decorations which it shall please us to bestow, shall be drawn from the funds existing for our royal orders of knighthood under the Royal Secretariat and the Ministerial Secretary of State for the Royal Household. We desire and command that this our law signed by Us and ratified by our Councillor Minister of State and Ministerial Secretary of State of Grace and Justice, given under our great seal, registered and deposited with the Ministry and Royal Secretariat of State of the Presidency of the Council of Ministers, be published in our royal dominions by the competent authorities, who shall ensure accuracy of publication and timeliness in dissemination. Our Councillor Minister of State and President of the Council of Ministers is particularly charged with the duty of its publication.

Given at Naples this 28th day of September 1829

Soi-disant Pretenders and Faux Nobles

As a sober postscript, it should be noted that there are socially ambitious individuals, in Italy and elsewhere, who claim to be the "pretenders" to unborne crowns or the lawful heirs of Sicilian kings, and in the public mind — even among journalists writing for major newspapers — this sometimes creates confusion about historical facts. Some of these claimants award decorations which outwardly resemble orders of chivalry.

In this connection, it should be noted that Sicily's principal medieval dynasties (namely Hauteville, Hohenstaufen, Aragon, Trastámara) are long-extinct in their legitimate male lines, as are the imperial Byzantine dynasties, while living dynasts of the non-regnant houses of the Two Sicilies (Bourbon), Hapsburg-Austria, Hapsburg-Tuscany, Bourbon-Parma and Italy

(Savoy) are well-known and not convincingly impersonated.

Here the standard references consulted by researchers are the original (1988) edition of *Heraldry of the Royal Families of Europe* by Jiri Louda and Michael Maclagan and Volume I of the 1977 edition of *Burke's Royal Families of the World* by Hugh Montgomery-Massingberd.

In the same bailiwick are persons who claim hereditary titles of nobility (duke, marquis, count, viscount, baron) or blazons of arms to which they have no historical (genealogical) right.

Legally, this is moot because in 1948 the Italian Republic abrogated state recognition of citizens' titles of nobility, which are no longer recognized legally even by the Vatican. In the words of Nancy Mitford: "An aristocracy in a republic is like a chicken whose head has been cut off; it may run about in a lively way, but in fact it is dead."

Apart from original manorial investiture records in the state archive in Palermo, the published research references most highly recommended are *Nobiliario di Sicilia* (2 volumes, 1912) by Antonino Mango di Casalgerardo and *Storia dei Feudi e dei Titoli Nobiliari di Sicilia* (10 volumes, 1927) by Francesco San Martino de Spucches. There exists no *complete* published list of noble families of the Kingdom of Sicily, and many nobles failed to matriculate their titles in the new state after 1861, so in searching various books for information "absence of evidence is not evidence of absence."

Most of the nobiliary directories published after 1946 purporting to list "all recognized Italian noble families" are notoriously unreliable, a rare exception being the bulky 2011-2014 (Anno XXXII) edition of the *Annuario della Nobiltà Italiana,* which was edited by a competent team of genealogists. The first edition of this series was published in 1878 by the renowned heraldist Giovanni Battista Crollalanza, whose *Dizionario Storico-Blasonico* (1886) is Italy's most complete list of heraldic blazons (or armory).

A framework for sound epistemology leading to accurate research in these areas is presented in the author's *Sicilian Genealogy and Heraldry* (2013).

STATVTI E CAPITOLI
DELLA
MILITIA AVREATA, ANGELICA,
COSTANTINIANA, DI S. GIORGIO.

*DI NVOVO RIFORMATI, ET APPROBATI
dall'Illustrißimo, & Eccellentißimo Signore,
il Sig.* HIERONIMO ANGELO

Principe di Tesfaglia, Duca, & Conte di Driuasto, &c.
Sourano, Patrone, & Gran Signore dell' Ordine.

CON LICENZA DE' SVPERIORI.

IN VENETIA,
APPRESSO MICHEL BONELLI.

M D LXXIII.

Early printing of Constantinian Order statutes

THE KINGDOM OF SICILY

St Januarius *Francis I*

St Ferdinand

St Charles *Constantinian Order*

KNIGHTLY ORDERS

Noi Alfonso Borbone

Conte di Caserta

per successione nei legittimi diritti del Nostro Augusto Fratello
il Re Francesco II delle Due Sicilie

Gran Maestro del Real Ordine di Francesco I.

Volendo dare un attestato della Nostra benevolenza al Signor Alberto Renner Segretario di Sua Altezza Reale il Principe Giovanni Giorgio Duca di Sassonia nella fausta ricorrenza del matrimonio della Nostra amatissima Figlia Maria Immacolata con Sua Altezza Reale il Principe Giovanni Giorgio Duca di Sassonia, abbiamo determinato di nominarlo, come per la presente lo nominiamo Cavaliere di 2da Classe del Nostro Real Ordine di Francesco I.

In fede di che abbiamo sottoscritto di Nostra Mano il presente Diploma munito del Sigillo delle Nostre Armi.

Dato in Cannes il dì 25 Ottobre 1906.

Alfonso
G. M.

Bestowal of the Order of Francis I in 1906

APPENDIX 3

Sicilian Peerage

This list gives the names of Sicilian peers recognized in 1848. The Sicilian Parliament is described elsewhere in this volume. Representing the most affluent *stratum* of the nobility, the peers arguably constituted the wealthiest and most influential class in Sicily during the nineteenth century. Here they are listed by title, principal seat (territorial designation) and surname.

Prince of Aci Sant'Antonio - Reggio
Duke of Acquaviva Platani - Oliveri
Marquis of Alimena - Fatta del Bosco
Baron of Aliminusa - Milone
Prince of Aragona - Burgio
Marquis of Bagni - Daniele
Baron of Baucina - Calderone
Prince of Belmonte - Monroy
Baron of Belvedere - Bonanno
Prince of Biscari - Paternò Castello
Duke of Bivona - Alvarez de Toledo
Duke of Bronte - Nelson
Prince of Butera - Lanza Branciforte
Prince of Calvaruso - Trigona
Baron of Campobello - Sammartino
Prince of Campofiorito - Lanza Branciforte
Prince of Campofranco - Lucchesi Palli
Prince of Camporeale - Beccadelli di Bologna
Marquis of Camporotondo - Deodato
Marquis of Capizzi - Paternò Castello
Duke of Carcaci - Paternò Castello

Prince of Carini - La Grua
Baron of Casalnuovo - Di Maria
Prince of Cassaro - Statella
Baron of Castania - Galletti
Prince of Castelbuono - Ventimiglia
Prince of Castelforte - Gravina
Duke of Castelluzzo - Agraz
Baron of Castelnormando - Lucchesi Palli
Prince of Castelnuovo - Valguarnera
Prince of Castelvetrano - Pignatelli Aragona Cortez
Prince of Castiglione - Rospigliosi Gioeni
Duke of Castrofilippo - Contarini
Baron of Catenanuova - Reggio
Prince of Cerami - Rosso
Duke of Cesarò - Colonna
Prince of Comitini - Gravina
Baron of Ferla - Tarallo
Prince of Ficarazzi - Giardina
Baron of Ficarra - Musto
Prince of Furnari - Notarbartolo
Prince of Galati - De Spucches
Baron of Gallidoro - Vigo
Baron of Giardinello - Valguarnera
Marquis of Giarratana - Settimo
Baron of Godrano - d'Ondes
Duke of Gualtieri - Averna
Baron of Kaggi - De Spucches
Prince of Leonforte - Lanza Branciforte
Baron of Longi - Loffredo
Marquis of Lucca - Mastrogiovanni Tasca
Prince of Maletto - Monroy
Prince of Malvagna - Migliaccio
Marquis of Manchi di Bilici - Paternò
Marquis of Marineo - Pasqualino
Baron of Martini - Sabatini
Prince of Mezzojuso - Corvino
Prince of Militello - Lanza Filingeri
Duke of Misterbianco - Trigona
Count of Modica - Stuart
Prince of Mola - Mannamo

Prince of Monforte - Moncada
Marquis of Mongiuffi and Kaggi - Loffredo
Duke of Montagnareale - Vianisi
Marquis of Montemaggiore - Licata
Prince of Montevago - Gravina
Marquis of Motta d'Affermo - Castelli
Marquis of Murata Cerda - Santo Stefano
Count of Naso - Ioppolo
Marquis of Ogliastro - Parisi
Prince of Paceco - Sanseverino
Baron of Pachino - Starrabba
Prince of Palagonia - Turrisi Grifeo
Prince of Palazzolo - Ruffo di Calabria
Duke of Palma - Tommasi
Prince of Pantelleria - Grifeo
Prince of Partanna - Turrisi Grifeo
Prince of Paternò - Moncada
Baron of Pettineo - Paternò
Duke of Piraino - Denti
Baron of Prizzi - Calefati
Prince of Raffadali - Tortorici
Prince of Rammacca - Gravina
Duke of Reitano - Colonna
Prince of Resuttana - Di Napoli
Baron of Riesi - Pignatelli
Baron della Rocca - Cataliotti Valdina
Prince of Roccafiorita - Bonanno
Marquis of Roccalumera - Stagno
Prince of Rosolini - Platamone
Prince of Sant'Antonio - Vannucci
Baron of San Carlo - Filingeri
Marquis of San Cataldo - Galletti
Baron of San Cono - Trigona
Marquis of Santa Croce - Celestre
Marquis of San Ferdinando - Rostagni
Baron of San Pietro - Clarenza
Baron of Santo Stefano di Briga - De Spucches
Baron of Santo Stefano di Camastra - Trigona
Prince of San Teodoro - De Gregorio
Marquis of Sambuca - Beccadelli di Bologna

Prince of Scaletta - Ruffo
Prince of Sciara - Notarbartolo
Prince of Scordia - Lanza Branciforte
Duke of Serradifalco - Lo Faso
Duke of Sorrentino - Landolina
Marquis of Sortino - Specchi Gaetani
Prince of Spadafora - Spadafora
Duke of Sperlinga - Oneto
Marquis of Tortorici - Del Castillo
Prince of Trabia - Lanza Branciforte
Baron of Tripi - Merlo
Baron of Tusa - La Torre
Prince of Valguarnera - Alliata
Baron of Vallelunga - Papé
Duke of Vatticani - Termine
Baron of Villadoro - D'Onofrio
Prince of Villafranca - Alliata
Marquis of Villlalba - Palmeri
Duke of Villarosa - Notarbartolo
Baron of Villasmundo - Asmundo Paternò
Baron of Villaurea - Di Michele
Baron of Vita - Sicomo

APPENDIX 4

Genetic Legacy

The genetic record revealed by DNA haplotyping confirms what historians have always known about the diversity of Sicily's historic populations. The geographic origins of these peoples are indicated in one of this book's maps. Sicily's population, like its culture, has been essentially endogamous since around 1300.

Phylogeography is the most important development of the last twenty years in the field of historical research, particularly where it involves the migrations of ancient and medieval peoples. Every region of the world benefits differently from our knowledge of the genetic record. In the case of Sicily, it has validated recorded history rather than challenged it.

It used to be that genetic studies addressed subjects such as specific physical traits, identifying, for example, those in the population having blue eyes (around fifteen percent of Sicilians) or red hair (five percent), or the segment of the population carrying the gene for thalassemia (compliments of the Phoenicians and Greeks) or multiple sclerosis (the Normans).

Favism (hemolysis from G6PD deficiency) has been identified genetically. Genetic factors may partially account for the rarity of alcoholism among Sicilians.

What follows is only a very general approximation reflecting data from a constantly evolving field of study. Here there is no gospel. There exists no single "Sicilian haplotype" or haplogroup, no "Sicilian DNA" *per se*.

By percentage of the population, Sicily's Y (patrilineal) haplogroups are approximately: J (35), R (25), I (15), K (10), H (10), Others (5).

These proportions vary somewhat by locality. Allele frequencies usually change over time owing to factors like "genetic drift," so today's percentages may not precisely reflect what existed in 1300 or 1500. They are a footprint rather than a photograph. Therefore, one is cautioned against simply assuming, based on present statistics, that the "typical" Sicilian is 35 percent Greek, 20 percent Norman, 15 percent Berber, and so forth.

Useful as this information is, attempts to ascertain specific patrilineal Sicilian "ethnic" origins based on it should be undertaken with a certain degree of caution because haplogroups do not correspond precisely to medieval or modern notions of nationality or ethnicity. At best, they are approximate. For example, J2 is identified with Greeks but also with some Germans, while R1b is identified with Normans but also with some Spaniards. The isolation of sub-clades within a major haplogroup helps to identify smaller populations in more specific geographic areas at more specific dates.

Speaking very broadly, the most frequent Y haplogroups of the world's most conquered island may be correlated generally, but not exclusively, to the following populations:

- J1 - Arabs, Berbers, Carthaginians, Jews,
- J2 (M172) - Greeks, Romans, Jews, Spaniards,
- R1b (M173) - Germans, Goths, Normans, Lombards, Aragonese, Spaniards,
- I1 & I2b - Vikings and Normans,
- I & I2a - Elymians,
- G - Arabs and Elymians,
- N - Vikings and Normans,
- E1b1b - Arabs, Berbers, others,
- K - Arabs, Greeks, Berbers, Carthaginians,
- H - Arabs,
- T - Phoenicians, Carthaginians.

What we are actually identifying is common descent over many generations from a remote male ancestor. For example, everybody in the J2 haplogroup has the same patrilineal ancestor in the northern part of the Fertile Crescent around 6,000 BC (BCE).

Female lines are not to be overlooked. Matrilineal haplogroups trace mitochondrial DNA (mtDNA) through one's mother's mother and so forth. Bryan Sykes identified a number of European ancestresses he named the "Seven Daughters of Eve." He has since added greatly to this number with haplogroups on other continents. The haplogroups H (Helena), J (Jasmine), K (Katrine), T (Tara), U5 (Ursula), V (Velda) and X (Xenia) all reflect lineages found in Sicily.

Population genetics dispels simplistic theories about race, societal development and ancient migrations, complementing theories about the Neolithic Revolution based on discovery of sites such as Göbekli Tepe. The most viable hypothesis advanced regarding Haplogroup J2 and the earliest Sicilians is that it correlates with the first neolithic farmers, as opposed to simple hunter-gatherers, making their way from western Asia across the Mediterranean.

Genealogists are reminded that Sicilians are descended, through one line or another, from ancestors in *all* of these haplogroups, and it should be remembered that the haplotyping described here isolates only *two* ancestral lines (through the father's father and the mother's mother), omitting all the others. For example, one has eight great grandparents, with Y and mtDNA haplotyping relating to (or identifying) only two of them.

Nevertheless, genetics has some interesting genealogical applications apart from proving close kinship; an aristocratic family's claim to medieval Norman ancestry in the male line, built upon several centuries of boastful lore (a common occurrence among the presumptuous Sicilian nobility), can be cast into the realm of doubt by a simple DNA test.

There are numerous studies. Typical of these is a report published in the September 2008 issue of the *European Journal of Human Genetics,* namely "Differential Greek and northern African migrations to Sicily are supported by genetic evidence from the Y chromosome" 17(1):91-9. The paper's authors observe: "The general heterogeneous composition of haplogroups in our Sicilian data is similar to the patterns observed in other major islands of the Mediterranean, reflecting the complex histories of settlements in Sicily."

More generally, see *The Journey of Man: A Genetic Odyssey* (2004) by Spencer Wells, Explorer-in-Residence of the National Geographic Society and a former student of geneticist Luigi Luca Cavalli Sforza, himself the author of *Genes, Peoples and Languages* (2000). Another good entry is Stephen Oppenheimer's *Out of Eden: The Peopling of the World* (2004). Online, such resources as genetic genealogy databases are also informative.

APPENDIX 5

Milestones 1735-1860

The territory of the former Two Sicilies *circa* 1862 had a population of some seven million, with 3,216 students enrolled in its public universities, almost half the Italian national total (excluding the city of Rome) of 7,957. Piedmont-Sardinia, with a population of 4.2 million, had far fewer university students *per capita*.

An interesting list of "firsts" was presented in Michele Vocino's *Primati del Regno di Napoli* (1950).

Herewith, posthumous plaudits to a forgotten country in the form of a list of noteworthy achievements in the Kingdom of the Two Sicilies relative to the other pre-unitary Italian states.

- First pension system in Italy (2 percent deduction from salaries),
- Most printing presses of any Italian city (Naples with 113),
- Lowest commercial and personal taxes in Italy,
- Largest international commercial bank in Italy (de Rothschild in Naples),
- Largest naval yards based on number of employees (1900 in Castellammare di Stabia),
- Largest iron and steel engineering-manufacturing plant in Italy (at Pietrarsa),
- Largest iron casting foundry in Italy (Ferdinandea in Calabria),
- Oldest continuously-active opera house in Europe, the San Carlo in Naples (1737, rebuilt in 1816),
- Largest porcelain factory in Italy (Capodimonte, 1743),

- Largest royal residence in Italy (Caserta, 1752),
- First university chair/department in economics (Antonio Genovesi, Naples, 1754),
- First *public* botanical gardens in Italy (opened in Palermo in 1795); others were private or scholastic,
- Dwarf planet Ceres first observed (Giuseppe Piazzi, Palermo, 1801),
- First modern paved carriageway in Italy (Piana-Palermo, 1810),
- First steamship in the Mediterranean, the Ferdinando I (1818),
- First glass recycling program (1832),
- First steel suspension bridge in Italy (Gagliano River in 1832, components from Mongiana Works),
- First gas-fuelled public lighting system (1839),
- First railroad in Italy (Naples-Portici, 1839),
- First seismic observatory in the world (Vesuvius 1841),
- First steamboat with screw propulsion in the Mediterranean (the Giglio delle Onde 1847),
- First functioning electric telegraph in Italy (1852),
- Ranked 3rd country in the world for industrial development (1st in Italy) by Paris International Exhibition (1856),
- First adhesive postage stamps in Italy (1857),
- First submarine telegraph in Europe,
- First military steamship in Italy (the Ercole),
- First maritime code in Italy,
- First public housing complex/estate in Italy, 1778 (San Leucio near Caserta),
- Highest per capita number of physicians in Italy (1850-1860),
- First *public* school for the deaf in Italy (Naples, 1788); school founded in Rome in 1784 was private,
- Lowest infant mortality rate in Italy (1850-1860).

APPENDIX 6

Constitution of 1812

The Sicilian Constitution promulgated in 1812 enumerated a number of ideas succinctly summarized here. These reflected legal principles known in Great Britain and in the United States, as well as local customs. Here is a concise summary from the preamble and the sections covering personal rights and freedom of the press.

Preamble

The state religion is Roman Catholicism, and a Sovereign who professes any other faith is *ipso facto* deposed.

Legislative power is vested exclusively in Parliament, with laws effected upon royal approval. Laws may be proposed only by Parliament, not by the executive.

The Sovereign may approve or veto, but not alter, the bills submitted for his approval. Executive power is vested exclusively in the Crown.

Juridical authority is distinct and independent of executive and legislative power. There shall be a judiciary composed of justices and magistrates, subject to review by the two chambers.

The person of the Sovereign is sacred and inviolable.

Royal ministers shall be subject to the review and approval of Parliament, and may be tried by Parliament for crimes, including abuse of office in the exercise of their duties.

Parliament shall be composed of two chambers, namely the House of Commons and the House of Lords (Chamber of Peers).

As peers, eligible titled nobles will have one vote each. The High Notary of the Kingdom shall publish the roll of noble and ecclesiastical peers. The Sovereign shall enjoy the exclusive prerogative of calling or dissolving Parliament, but he shall be obligated to convoke a session at least once per year, even if by proxy.

No Sicilian citizen (the word *subject* is not used) may be arrested, exiled or in any way deprived of his rights except according to the new legal code.

Peers will enjoy privileges similar to those in England (to be established by statute).

Feudalism is abolished. All manors presently existing shall become allodial, hereditary according to succession by male primogeniture, but titles of nobility are not to be attached to the land. (To wit, purchase of a former barony does not make its buyer a baron.) Feudal rights of taxation and jurisdiction are abolished. Feudal investiture is abolished. Formerly feudal lords may retain their nobiliary titles *ad personam*.

All laws must pass through both chambers of Parliament as their only venue, but citizens may propose bills through the appropriate channels.

Personal Liberties

Under *Libertà, Dritti e Doveri del Cittadino*, freedom of speech is established. Any citizen may express any political opinion, without fear of harassment by the authorities. Sedition is outlawed.

Every citizen has the right to defend himself legally against any person, including magistrates.

No citizen may hold more than two paid positions in the public sector.

Nobody can be charged with an offense that was not part of the legal code at the time the offence was allegedly committed. That is to say, retroactive prosecution is proscribed.

Hunting is permitted on private property for deer, boar and other game in compliance with the relevant code. Specific hunting seasons are established, and trespassing on private property prohibited.

No person, community or ecclesiastical organization may claim financial compensation for losses incurred as a result of the abolition of feudalism, but specific cases may be addressed by the law courts. The state may not confiscate property without due legal process. A new financial code will address these matters in detail.

The rights of Sicilian citizens in Sicily are governed exclusively by the laws of the Kingdom of Sicily.

The Constitution shall be published, to be disseminated in localities, universities and schools.

By 1830, no citizen will be permitted to vote who cannot read.

No citizen may refuse to testify in a court of law unless (in a criminal trial) he is related to the accused.

No citizen may serve another national government without royal assent, and at all events may not take up arms against the Kingdom of Sicily.

Freedom of the Press

Under *Libertà della Stampa,* every citizen may print and publish his ideas without need of permission or censorship.

However, published criticism of the Catholic Church, its dogmas and interpretations of Biblical scripture, is subject to censorship and prosecution.

The Sovereign and the royal family may not be criticized explicitly in the press.

Statements that incite readers to commit crimes or disobey orders executed by judges are illegal.

Libel is illegal. It is illegal to publish defamatory personal (private) information regarding spouses and families. The publication of affronts to public decency is illegal.

Journalistic material must be signed by the author before two witnesses prior to its publication. The year and place of publication must be indicated. Religious material must have episcopal approval prior to publication.

APPENDIX 7

Nobiliary Laws 1743-1861

The nobility was an integral part of the monarchy. Here are a few laws often cited regarding the status of the nobility of southern Italy during the Bourbon period. Though not complete, this lists the most significant nobiliary legislation of the Bourbon era.

Decree (dispatch) 16 October 1743: Declaration of nobiliary status for prominent citizens of several cities, particularly Pozzuoli and Bitonto, based on families having lived in a noble manner for at least three generations.

Dispatch 19 January 1751: Governors of certain cities may transmit nobility to their heirs only with royal assent.

Pragmatic 25 January 1756: Identification of several classes of nobility based on long-established norms not satisfactorily codified during the preceding two centuries. Specifically identified are the feudal nobility, nobility by office (judges, generals, et al.), and the civic nobility (patriciate) of royal cities. These distinctions served to differentiate the status of military cadets.

Pragmatic of 6 October 1759: Establishes line of succession in the House of the Two Sicilies.

Dispatch 19 February 1757: Declares that royal assent is needed for appointments to local nobility in cities where there is a *mastra nobile*.

Dispatch 20 June 1763: Clarifies that petitions for recognition of hereditary nobility must be submitted in a specific genealogical format and to a specific office in Naples.

Dispatch 2 December 1770: Declares that hereditary nobility may obtain from feudal tenure or a personal title created by the Crown, or from certain ecclesiastical and civil offices.

Dispatch 23 April 1774: Descendants of certain *giurati nobili* (noble jurats) of Siracusa are ennobled.

Decree 24 December 1774: Identification of various professions which might engender nobility.

Dispatch 25 April 1778: Establishes that the legitimate descendants of nobles whose titles were created outside the Kingdom may have such titles recognized with royal assent.

Decree 27 November 1780: Confirms status of nobility to families residing in cities or towns which are now feudal (under a count or baron) but in the past were regarded as royal (demesnial or "free").

Decree 7 May 1795: Guarantees to certain high officials and their children the same privileges as nobles by birth.

Dispatch 27 October 1798: Establishes that certain high-ranking aldermen (jurats) traditionally regarded as nobles may be recognized legally as nobles only with royal assent.

Decree 20 December 1800: Prohibits nobles contracting marriages which are unworthy or indecent, without defining these terms explicitly.

Law 10 August 1812: In keeping with the recent constitution, feudal titles become personal, no longer attached to feudal land tenure.

Proclamation of 20 May 1815: Consent to recognition of both ancient and modern nobility in the Kingdom of the Two Sicilies (previously the kingdoms of Naples and Sicily) now being constituted; this places descendants of the titular (personal) nobility at parity with those of the previously-feudal nobility.

Dispatch 24 September 1827: Clarifies titular inheritance by male primogeniture and thenceforth to younger sons, brothers, nephews of the deceased, necessitating royal assent for transmission through any other line.

Rescript 4 March 1828: Confirms the longstanding practice of the husband of a lady titled in her own right to make use of his wife's title during the marriage and as a widower.

Decree 9 September 1832: Establishes the *Royal Commission for Titles of Nobility* in view of the abolition of feudalism and the increasing usurpation of nobiliary titles and appellations.

Ministerial Decree 7 December 1839: Confirms the effect of previous decrees abolishing feudalism regarding the personal, hereditary nature of nobiliary titles apart from land tenure.

Dispatch 6 March 1841: Before a title of nobility may devolve to a cadet, all senior heirs must cede their rights to him formally. This applies, for example, to the fifty year-old son of a ninety year-old man who has inherited a title from a recently-deceased elder brother. A rescript of 5 August 1843 specifies that the cadets referred to must be adults to be able to renounce their hereditary rights.

Rescript 4 March 1843: Any citizen of the Kingdom must obtain royal permission to accept a foreign title of nobility.

Rescript 2 December 1843: Addressing a circular issued (in error) by the Royal Commission for Titles of Nobility on 28 September in a specific case (a marquisate created in 1829), clarifies that titles so created devolve through male descendants in the direct, agnatic line, not through female collaterals.

Rescript 20 May 1851: Recognizes ancestral nobility of families of the civic nobility in cities (such as Salerno) where the patriciates of historic jurisdictional districts have been closed to new admissions since 1800.

Rescript 22 September 1852: Sicilian titles of ancient creation pass to direct descendants rather than to collaterals.

Rescript 29 July 1853: Clarifies that, in cases of female succession in the absence of male heirs, devolution is always based on seniority of age, and that the titles devolve to the legitimate heiresses who would have succeeded under the feudal system.

Rescript 10 September 1855: Establishes clearly that adoptive children may not succeed to the ranks of nobility of their adoptive parents.

Rescript 11 October 1855: Establishes that in-laws and other kin through marriage (affines) may not succeed to titles of nobility as if they were heirs by blood.

Rescript 13 February 1856: Clarifies that the law abolishing feudalism in the Kingdom of Naples (during the Napoleonic occupation) did not apply to the Kingdom of Sicily.

Rescript 15 October 1857: Establishes that serving as Justice of the Great Court (a supreme court) does not ennoble *ipso facto*.

Rescript 19 December 1857: Establishes that only the officers of the Royal Secretariat of State and their descendants are to be ennobled *ipso facto*.

Nobiliary Creations January 1861: Patents of nobility issued at Gaeta were to take effect upon the return of King Francesco II to Naples; this never occurred.

APPENDIX 8

Pragmatic of 1759

All but ignored by historians, this document merits at least passing attention for several reasons. Most obviously, in acceding to the wishes of the European leaders who hoped to avoid confronting the potentially destabilizing concentration of power in a single monarch, it separated the kingdoms of Naples and Sicily from rule by the King of Spain. While the preamble mentions the sovereign's *de jure* dominions (such as Jerusalem) as well as those he actually ruled, it is interesting that the phrase *the Two Sicilies* is used to describe the kingdoms of Naples and Sicily jointly even though they were not yet united officially or juridically, and the document effectively reiterates the sovereignty of both states, referring to these near its end as *the Kingdoms of the Sicilies*. It sets forth female succession in the absence of male heirs while offering insight into the approach taken to diagnose mental disabilities in royal families. Establishing laws of succession, this is, in effect, the foundation charter of the House of Bourbon of the Two Sicilies as a dynasty separate from the House of Bourbon of Spain. From Madrid, Charles offered guidance to young Ferdinando long after 1759, but it would emerge that father and son had little in common with regard to their ideas about government and foreign policy; for example, Ferdinando was a staunch ally of Britain while Charles was an early supporter of the United States. In domestic policy, Charles was far more enlightened than Ferdinando. For its era, this singular document is eloquent in its simplicity of language, clarity of expression, and transparent intent. The firstborn son excluded from the succession is not mentioned by name in the text; he was Filippo (1747-1777). The accompanying pedigree indicates kinship referred to in the pragmatic sanction, showing the legitimate line of descent into the twentieth century; if the Kingdom of the Two Sicilies had survived, Ferdinando Pio would have succeeded Alfonso (1841-1934), reigning until 1960. (Acting on Ferdinando's behalf, his daughter, Urraca, donated the papers of King Francesco II to the Archive of State of Naples following the Second World War.)

WE, Charles III, by the Grace of God King of Castile, Leon, Aragon, the Two Sicilies, Jerusalem, Navarre, Granada, Toledo, Valencia, Galicia, Majorca, Seville, Sardinia, Cordova, Corsica, Murcia, Jaén, Algarve, Alzira, Gibraltar, the Canary Islands, the East and West Indies, the Islands and Continent of the Atlantic Ocean, Archduke of Austria, Duke of Burgundy, Brabant, Milan, Parma, Piacenza and Castro, Hereditary Grand Prince of Tuscany, Count of Hapsburg, Flanders, Tyrol and Barcelona, Lord of Biscay and Molina, et cetera.

Among the grave burdens that the monarchy of the Spanish lands and the Indies, following the death of my beloved brother King Ferdinand VI, have visited upon me, is that of the clear mental incapacity of my firstborn son. Furthermore, the spirit of the treaties of the present century demonstrates the wishes of Europe, to the extent these can be granted justly, to divide the Spanish powers from those in Italy.

Seeing, therefore, the opportunity to appoint a legitimate successor in my Italian states as I depart for Spain, and seeking to choose him from among the many sons that God has given me, it is necessary to decide which of my sons is to be considered my secondborn legally for the purpose of succeeding to rule the Italian states and having no union with Spain or the Indies. This act for the tranquility of Europe, which I wish to guarantee to ensure that nobody is alarmed by my indecision in retaining in my person these Spanish and Italian powers together, requires that I now renounce my sovereign authority in Italy.

An important body composed of me and my Councillors of State, of a Castilian cabinet minister present here in Naples, of the Chamber of Santa Chiara, of the Lieutenant of the Cabinet of Naples, and the entire Council of Sicily, assisted by six physicians appointed by me, has determined that, insofar as examinations and observations have been made, the unfortunate prince is unable to reason, converse, or exercise rational judgement, and that his abilities have existed as such since infancy; not only is he presently incapable of morality or reasoning, but there appears to be not the slightest likelihood that he ever will be. Expressing a unanimous decision, this body of experts therefore concludes that he be excluded from consideration, and we shall therefore act as nature, duty and paternal affection dictate.

Therefore, finding myself in this fateful moment for Divine Will, I cede the legal right and capacity of secondborn to the Infante don Ferdinando, though my thirdborn son by nature. Because of his tender age, I have had to consider his tutelage. For my Italian states, as a king and as a father, I have undertaken to provide for this son, that he shall become an Italian sovereign while I am in Spain.

Firstly, I constitute the Infante don Ferdinando, by nature my thirdborn son, to receive from me the Italian states, undertaking, even if it be unnecessary, to emancipate him by the present act, which I wish to establish as most solemn. With the force of a legitimate act and indeed a law, he shall henceforth be free not only of my parental authority, but from my sovereign royal authority.

Secondly, I establish a Council of Regency for the duration of the minority of my thirdborn son, which must be sovereign of my states and holder of my Italian assets, acting to administer sovereignty and dominion during his youth and minority according to methods prescribed by me in an order of this day issued by my hand under my signature and seal, witnessed by my Councillor and Secretary of State of the Department of State and the Royal Household, which order shall be integrated into this act, having the same force of law.

Thirdly, I decide, and constitute in immutable and perpetual law of my Italian states and holdings, that the age of majority of those who succeed as sovereigns and rulers and enjoy freedom of administration be the sixteenth year fully computed (seventeenth birthday).

Fourthly, desiring likewise to establish in constant and perpetual law the succession of the Infante don Ferdinando, further enumerating the preceding sections, I establish that the line of succession be ordered according to male primogeniture from male to male.

In the absence of sons in that line of descent, succession devolves to the next male heir in the cadet line with respect to the last regnant dynast, be it a patrilineal uncle, brother or more distant kin, so long as it be the eldest male in the aforementioned line or its direct, patrilineal branch with regard to the Infante don Ferdinando or the last regnant king.

In the case of the absence of male heirs in the line of descent from Infante don Ferdinando, the line of succession shall be transmitted in turn to my other sons, namely Gabriele, Antonio and Francesco Saverio, and henceforth through their sons, in order of seniority of birth.

In the event of extinction of all heirs male descended from me, a female of the blood royal may succeed if she be my daughter or the eldest daughter of a prince in the senior line of descent, nearest in descent from the most recent king or the last, most recently-deceased prince. To wit, the right of succession is traced by primogeniture along the nearest agnate line of descent according to the order set forth above.

In the absence of female as well as male heirs, the succession shall devolve to my brother, the Infante don Filippo, and thence forth to his sons and male successors *ad infinitum*. In the absence of Filippo and his male issue, the succession shall devolve to my brother the Infante don Luigi and thence forth to his sons and male successors *ad infinitum*. In the absence of male posterity in these lines, daughters may succeed according to the prescription mentioned above.

Be it well understood that the order of the line of succession prescribed herein shall never result in the union of the Spanish Monarchy with the sovereignty of the Italian dominions.

In this way, either males or females descended from me as described above shall succeed to the Italian sovereignty, so long as they are not already declared Kings of Spain or Princes of Austria; otherwise they must declare themselves when there are other males to succeed to the Italian states and holdings based on this norm. In the absence of all heirs, the King of Spain, as soon as God graces him with a secondborn son, or with a grandson or great-grandson, shall transfer to this heir the Italian states, territories and holdings.

Having established the succession of my posterity to the Italian states and holdings, I humbly commend to God the Infante don Ferdinando, bestowing upon him my paternal blessing and inculcating in him the Roman Catholic religion, and the sense of justice, forbearance, vigilance and love of country which have aided me in faithfully and obediently serving my royal house.

I cede, transfer and give to the same Infante don Ferdinando, my thirdborn son by nature, the Kingdoms of the Sicilies and my other Italian states, holdings, territories, rights, titles and interests, and I cede to him the fullness of their traditions, so that none of these shall remain in my possession.

He, however, from the moment that I depart this capital, may with the Council of State and Regency administer all that I will have transferred, ceded and given to him. I hope that this my law of emancipation, constitution of age of majority, designation of tutelage and care of the child and minor (adolescent) king, succession to the said Italian states and holdings, transfer and endowment, will abound him with a love for the people, in tranquility with my royal family, finally contributing to the peace of Europe.

The present order shall be signed by me and by my son the Infante don Ferdinando, bearing my seal, witnessed by the aforesaid Councillor and Secretary of State, also acting as Regents and Tutors of the aforementioned Infante don Ferdinando.

Given at Naples this 6th day of October, 1759

Signed: Carlo, Ferdinando

NOI CARLO III.

Per la grazia di Dio Re di Castiglia, Leone, Aragona, delle due Sicilie, Gerusalemme, Navarra, Granata, Toledo, Valenza, Galizia, Majorca, Siviglia, Sardegna, Cordova, Corsica, Murcia, Jaen, Algarves, Algezira, Gibilterra, delle Isole Canarie, delle Indie Orientali ed Occidentali, delle Isole e Continente del Mare Oceano; Arciduca d'Austria; Duca di Borgogna, Brabante, Milano, Parma, Piacenza, e Castro; Gran Principe Ereditario di Toscana; Conte di Absburg, Fiandra, Tirolo, e Barcellona; Signore di Biscaglia, e Molina, &c. &c.

FRA le gravi cure, che la Monarchia delle Spagne, e delle Indie, dopo la morte dell'amatissimo mio Fratello il Re Cattolico Ferdinando VI. Mi ha recato, è stata quella, che è venuta dalla notoria imbecillità della mente del mio Real Primogenito. Lo Spirito de' Trattati di questo Secolo mostra, che si desideri dall'Europa, quando si possa eseguire senza opporsi alla Giustizia, la divisione della Potenza Spagnuola dall' Italiana. Vedendomi perciò nella convenienza di provveder di legittimo Successore i miei Stati
A   Italiani

Preamble of the Pragmatic of 1759

THE KINGDOM OF SICILY

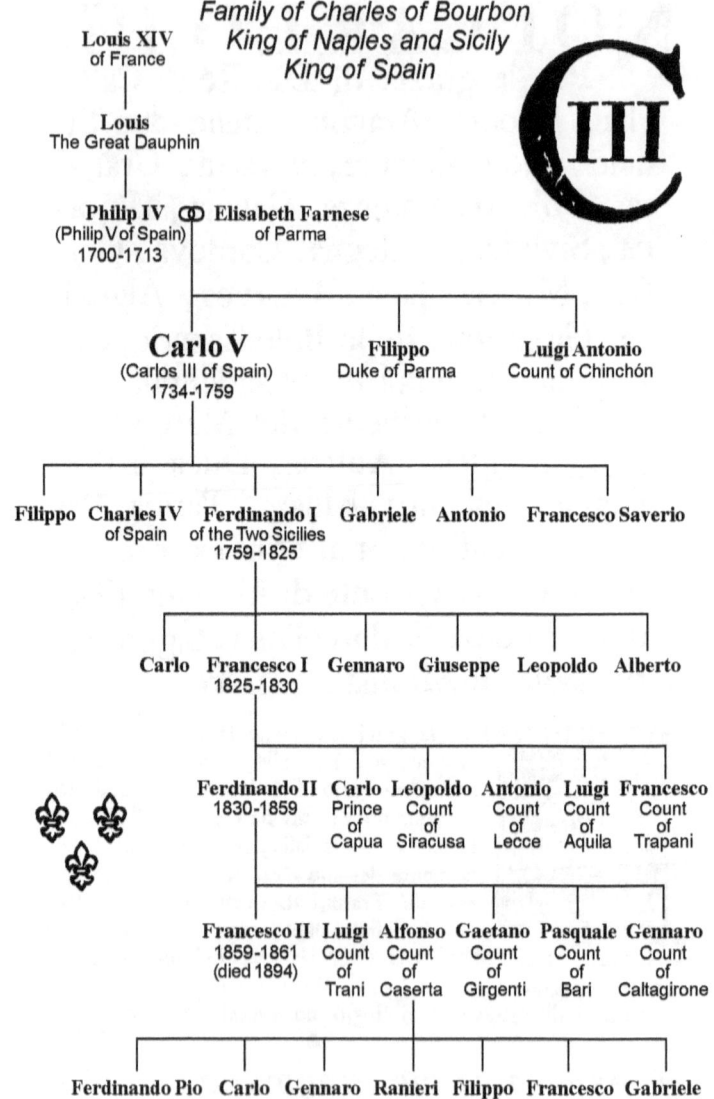

SOURCES, NOTES, BIBLIOGRAPHY

"As this history is intended for the general reader — if he still exists outside the writer's imagination — such distracting paraphernalia as footnotes have been dispensed with as much as possible. The cult of the footnote, involving, at its apogee, a page crammed with encyclopaedic detail in small type to a solitary line of text, is no doubt a proof of diligence, but it may also be a tedious form of exhibitionism."

— Sir Harold Acton, *The Bourbons of Naples*

Concurring with Sir Harold's opinion, your author elected to use end notes rather than footnotes.

Both original sources and published references are listed by chapter. The notes following these initial paragraphs are based on uniform numbering rather than a separate series for each chapter. Not every fact in the text was drawn directly from the works cited, which in some instances are listed chiefly for the reader interested in learning more about a specific topic.

Complete documentation supporting every statement made in this book would necessitate a list running to hundreds of pages. However, most of the books listed here contain fairly detailed bibliographies.

Medieval sources aside, an effort has been made to indicate only the most reliable, most accurate works. The listing of any chronicle, monograph or academic paper does not, by any stretch of the imagination, constitute an endorsement of its contents *in toto*. The reader should bear in mind that works noted in an earlier chapter may also contain information pertinent to a subsequent one, and vice versa, and these are not usually listed twice.

Some translations of medieval texts included in this volume are the author's; he first consulted some of these before 1990 in the original Latin, but some are now available in English or Italian translation. The translation of the Pragmatic of 1759 is the author's.

Prologue

No deification is intended. Nothing presented here is meant to imply that George Washington or Charles III, however enlightened they may have been for the times in which they lived, were flawless individuals. Their treatment of persons in their households speaks volumes.

Involving personal relationships and legal issues, both situations were somewhat more complex than what is concisely described here. Washington's behavior is perhaps the more disturbing of the two.

Charles III marginalized, and virtually exiled, his younger brother, Luis Antonio de Bourbon, Count of Chinchón, best known to posterity for becoming history's youngest cardinal at eight years of age. As an adult, Luis Antonio renounced his religious vocation. In 1776 he married morganatically, something which probably would have excluded him from the succession set forth in the Pragmatic of 1759 (see Appendix 8).

George Washington's zealous attempts to capture the escaped slave Oney "Ona" Judge do not speak well of the first President of the United States and his wife, Martha, for whom she was a personal servant. Miss Judge died in New Hampshire in 1848, free but still, strictly speaking, a fugitive. Her story is a grim footnote to the history of slavery in the United States, where this institution was abolished belatedly in 1863, with the law emancipating the slaves applied in some parts of the country only two years later at the end of the bloody American Civil War.

Chapter 1

Several Greek sources record early Sicilian history. Some are recognized as more reliable than others, and some seem to conflict with others. Among the chief sources are the *Histories* of Timaeus and the *Bibliotheca Historica* of Diodorus Siculus, complemented by the work of Thucydides. Plutarch is a "secondary" source but the only surviving one for certain events. Such as they have survived, the writings of Philistus, Athanas and Ephorus (which were sometimes incorporated into the works of later writers) are worthy of consideration. The work of Herodotus is relevant to Sicily as regards the Greco-Persian Wars. Roman histories are many, though few focus on Sicily exclusively.

The work of poets such as Theocritus are of value for general descriptions of Sicily, and Pindar wrote about the island. The *Natural History* of Pliny the Elder is useful for its descriptions of the island's flora and fauna. Strabo's *Geographica* was the best Mediterranean guide of its age. All of these works are available in transcription and translation.

Mythology is also helpful in this area. A good compendium of Greek mythology is *The Greek Myths* (1955) by Robert Graves, but some readers may find Edith Hamilton's *Mythology* (1940) more engaging.

Written histories are, of course, augmented by the archeological record

SOURCES, NOTES, BIBLIOGRAPHY

and (more recently) by genetic data.

Thapsos is a fine example of Mycenaean culture, which here seems to have amalgamated somewhat with the native Sicanian civilization. The discovery at Segesta, the Elymians' *Egesta,* of a form of script similar to that used in Anatolia suggests a connection with Asia Minor. At Motya, the Phoenician *stelae* bear motifs resembling what one finds in Egypt. Jewelry and other artefacts are also significant.

The classic work on the Goths is the *Getica* of Jordanes. Some modern historians question the Swedish and Danish origins attributed to this civilization. Works on the Ostrogoths and Vandals are more numerous, and more profound, than they were thirty years ago. Fine examples are *People and Identity in Ostrogothic Italy, 489-554* (1997) by Patrick Amory and *The Vandals* (2010) by Andrew Merrills and Richard Miles. (For original sources, see Procopius of Caesarea in the notes for Chapter 2.)

1. Various structures in Europe are older than the Maltese temples, but most of these cairns or mounds of simple construction served as burial sites, while the megalithic edifices in the Maltese islands were places of worship erected around massive trilithons. Malta's Hal Saflieni Hypogeum, carved around 3300 BC (BCE), is recognized by UNESCO as the only known prehistoric underground temple in the world. It is an impressive site the author recommends visiting. Malta is also interesting for its language, a modern Siculo Arabic (see notes for Chapter 2).

Chapter 2

A primary contemporary source for the reign of Justinian in Constantinople and the Byzantine victories over the Ostrogoths and Vandals is the account of Procopius of Caesarea. Two fine introductions to Byzantine history and culture are *Byzantine Civilisation* (1933, 1969) by Steven Runciman, who wrote several books on this topic, and John Julius Norwich's three-volume series *Byzantium* published beginning in 1989.

Some of the more reliable descriptions of the Fatimid world come to us from Mohammed al Maqdisi, who was born in Jerusalem around 945.

The best overview of the Muslims and Arabs in Sicily published thus far is *A History of Islamic Sicily* (1975), by Aziz Ahmad, issued by Edinburgh University Press as part of its Islamic Surveys series. Its author was Professor of Islamic Studies at the University of Toronto. Michele Amari's *Storia dei Musulmani di Sicilia* (1854), taken as gospel by some Sicilians, should be read very critically because many of its "facts" are uncorroborated by original sources; Amari may be the first modern writer to refer to Roger II as a "baptized sultan." A historical benchmark unfortunately overshadowed by Amari's work is Alfonso Airoldi's *Codice Diplomatico di Sicilia sotto il Governo degli Arabi* published by the *Stamperia Reale* (the royal press) in 1790; this survey was formerly the definitive reference consulted by Sicilian Arabists, along with works by Salvadore Morso, a competent professor of Arabic whose monographs appeared long before Amari's books.

The Arabs (1976), by Peter Mansfield, is a fine introduction to the history, culture and society of the Arab world. *Siculo Arabic* (1996), by Dionisius Agius, is a study of the language spoken by Sicily's Arabs, of which a modern form is Maltese.

Alexander Metcalfe's *Muslims and Christians in Norman Sicily: Arabic Speakers and the End of Islam* (2011) is an insightful study into a specific period, with clues to the Arabic influence on the Sicilian language; Italian linguistic historians have also considered this subject at length. By the same author is the more general work *The Muslims of Medieval Italy* (2009), which covers the status of the Muslims until 1300.

For a contemporary Arab description of Sicily, see the note on ibn Hawqal (below). Barbara Kreutz's *Before the Normans: Southern Italy in the Ninth and Tenth Centuries* (1996) addresses this period, with a focus on peninsular Italy.

For insights into the status of the Jews during this period, see Gil, Moshe, "The Jews in Sicily under Muslim Rule in the Light of Geniza Documents" in *Italia Judaica 1* (1983), pages 87-134.

The Eastern Schism: A Study of the Papacy and the Eastern Churches during the XIth and XIIth Centuries (1955), by Steven Runciman, approaches its subject with a fair degree of balance. A pragmatic theological treatment of the underlying issues is to be found in John Meyendorff's *Orthodoxy and Catholicity* (1966).

The chief original (contemporary) source describing the Norman conquest, mentioning the prior rapport with George Maniakes, during this era, is Godfrey Malaterra's *De Rebus Gestis Rogerii Calabriae et Siciliae Comitis et Roberti Guiscardi Ducis Fratris Eius*. Another essential source is *Gesta Roberti Wiscardi* by William of Apulia. Amatus of Montecassino's eloquent *L'Ystoire de li Normant* exists as a (later) French translation.

2. The best contemporary source for the descriptive geography of Sicily during this era is Mohammed ibn Hawqal, who visited in 972. Scholars have attempted to map the Arab city of Bal'harm based on ibn Hawqal and other sources, a daunting task because most of the landmarks standing in 1071 no longer exist. An early modern description is Salvadore Morso's *Descrizione di Palermo Antico* (1827); as a competent professor of Arabic,

Morso deserves much of the praise subsequently heaped upon the imaginative Michele Amari. For the Fatimid period, a good effort is Ferdinando Maurici's *Palermo Araba: Una sintesi dell'evoluzione urbanistica 831-1072* (2015). For the Norman period, see Henri Bresc's *Palermo al Tempo dei Normanni* (2012). The monographs by Rosario La Duca, a Palermitan historian, contain some useful information in this area, along with a great deal of conjecture. The locations of some sites, based directly on ibn Hawqal's descriptions, are beyond cavil; for example, the Santagat Gate stood near Sant'Agata alla Guilla, a Byzantine-era church along the Punic walls and Papireto River, *guilla* being a corruption of the Arabic *wadi,* river bank.

3. Harald Sigurdsson reigned as King Harald III of Norway from 1046 to 1066, the year he was killed at the Battle of Stamford Bridge by King Harold II "Godwinson" of England, who in turn was defeated at the Battle of Hastings by William the Conqueror.

Chapter 3

Several books are generally instructive on the subject of feudalism and medieval life without romanticizing it. Key among these are works which deal in some way with Norman feudalism in England, Sicily or Normandy. A very good introduction to daily life is Morris Bishop's book *The Middle Ages* (1968), while Carl Stephenson's *Mediaeval Feudalism* (1942) also mentions Sicily. Maurice Keen's *Chivalry* (1984) lays to rest many myths and misconceptions. The revised (2000) edition of Richard Barber's classic work, *The Knight and Chivalry,* is informative, though hardly the last word. A fine background study is *The Birth of Nobility: Constructing the Aristocracy in England and France 900-1300* (2005) by David Crouch.

A good treatise on the institution in Sicily, though perhaps influenced by historical clichés, is *Il Feudalismo in Sicilia* (1847) by Diego Orlando. A more recent analysis is Mario Caravale's "La Feudalità nella Sicilia Normanna" in *Atti del Congresso Internazionale di Studi sulla Sicilia Normanna, Palermo 4-8 dicembre 1972* (1974), pages 21-50.

An insightful economic study was penned by the erudite David Abulafia, namely *The Two Italies: Economic Relations Between the Norman Kingdom of Sicily and the Northern Communes* (1977).

Idrisi's geography of Sicily during the twelfth century identifies localities, their populations and agriculture. A detailed map of Sicily based on Idrisi's observations accompanies Luigi Santagati's *La Sicilia di al-Idrisi ne Il Libro di Ruggero* (2010). See also *Carte Comparèe de la Sicile* (1859) by Michele

Amari. The part of the *Catalogus Baronus* that survives refers to manors in peninsular Italy rather than Sicily.

Manors are indicated in many locality maps drawn between 1820 and 1850, found in the series *Direzione Centrale Statistiche* retained at the Palermo Archive of State. For information on genealogy, heraldry and the nobility generally, see the author's *Sicilian Genealogy and Heraldry* (2013), a research guide.

A general survey of the coinage minted in Palermo from the Phoenician era until 1836, accompanied by numerous photographs, is Francesco Sapio Vitrano's "La Zecca di Palermo dai Primi Insediamenti Fenici al 1836" in *Archivio Storico Siciliano,* Series 3, Volume 20 (Palermo 1970), pages 107-202. A good description of the coinage and measures of the late twelfth century is found in Lucia Travaini's "La Monetazione del Regno di Sicilia al Tempo di Tancredi" in *Tancredi, Conte di Lecce Re di Sicilia* (2004), pages 193-206. See also *Le Monete Siciliane dai Bizantini a Carlo I d'Angio 582-1282* and *Le Monete Siciliane dagli Aragonesi ai Borboni 1282-1836* (1959) by Rodolfo Spahr.

Mention was made of early parliaments and the (unsupported) Sicilianist claim to historical precedence. As regards England's parliament, *A History of the House of Lords* (1988) by Frank Pakenham, Earl of Longford, is one of the most readable overviews.

A good architectural examination of Sicilian manorial castles (such as those of Caccamo and Mussomeli) is Rodolfo Santoro's "Architettura Castellana della Feudalità Siciliana" in *Archivio Storico Siciliano,* Series 4, Volume 7 (Palermo 1981), pages 59-113.

For the role of the Roman Catholic Church, and especially its monastic and knightly orders, an early study of value that has withstood the test of time is *Latin Monasticism in Norman Sicily* (1938) by Lynn Townsend White, with its lengthy bibliography. This also considers the Greek Orthodox Church. In that regard, an interesting document is to be found in "Foundation of a Monastery in Byzantine Calabria 1053/54" a translation by Adele Cilento and David Routt, in *Medieval Italy: Texts in Translation* (2009), pages 506-507.

Note that some (Protestant) authors writing in English insist on the imprecise term *Basilian* in referring to the Orthodox Church after 1054, while many (Catholic) Italians use the equally vague adjective *bizantino* (Byzantine) rather liberally. The author contends that both words are potentially misleading, preferring *Byzantine* in reference to the culture generally rather than the Greek Orthodox Church specifically.

4. The knightly orders attracted the younger sons of feudatories from around Europe. See the appendix. Also Desmond Seward's *The Monks of War: The Military Religious Orders* (1996).

5. See Mendola, Louis, "English and Italian Legacy of the Norman Knight Figures of Monreale" in *The Coat of Arms,* journal of The Heraldry Society, London, edited by John P. Brooke-Little, Norroy and Ulster King of Arms; NS Volume X, Number 166, Summer 1994 (ISSN 0010-003X), pages 245-254. This is extracted in Chapter 18 of the author's *Sicilian Genealogy and Heraldry* (2013).

6. The last Sicilian peers are listed in an appendix.

7. A chapter of *Sicilian Genealogy and Heraldry* (see above) is dedicated to onomatology.

Chapter 4

Some original sources, such as those of Godfrey Malaterra, William of Apulia and Amatus of Montecassino, are mentioned at Chapter 2 (above). Alexander Telese (Alessandro Telesino) wrote the *History of King Roger of Sicily*. Additional contemporary chronicles are the *Liber ad Honorem Augusti* of Peter of Eboli, the *Chronicon Beneventanum* of Falco of Benevento, the *Chronicon sive Annales* of Romuald Guarna of Salerno (the frontispiece of an early imprint is included near the end of this book's map section), and the *Chronica Regni Siciliae* of Richard of San Germano, as well as Arab sources like ibn al-Athir and ibn Khaldun. The chronicles of Goffredo of Viterbo are pertinent to studies of Frederick Barbarossa.

Some of these have been translated into modern languages from the original Latin. The *Liber de Regno Siciliae* or *Historia Hvgonis Falcandi Sicvli de Rebus Gestis in Siciliae Regno* attributed to the man known as "Falcandus" was first published in Paris in 1550 by Martin Gervais de Tournay; his transcription was made from a manuscript, now presumed lost, which was then in the possession of Matthew Longuejoue, Bishop of Soissons. The four surviving manuscripts, being copies, may vary slightly from the original chronicle written by the hand of "Falcandus" or one of his scribes. In Italian we find Vito Lo Curto's excellent *Il Regno di Sicilia* (Ciolfi, Cassino 2007); in English there is a superlative translation and analysis by Graham Loud and Thomas Wiedemann, *The History of the Tyrants of Sicily by 'Hugo Falcandus' 1154-1169* (Manchester University Press 1998).

The theological writings of Gerhoh of Reichersberg shed light on the Normans' rapport with the Papacy. A history was published in 1897 as *Monumenta Germaniae Historica.*

Evelyn Jamison (1877-1972), perhaps the greatest medievalist of her time to focus on Norman Sicily, cogently argued, in her *Admiral Eugenius of Sicily: His Life and Work and Authorship of the Epistola ad Petrum and the Historia Hugonis Falcandi Siculi* (London 1957), that "Falcandus" was probably Eugenius of Palermo (c. 1130-1202). Jamison authored numerous articles of immense value; her transcription and translation of the *Catalogus Baronum* was published in 1972.

Ferdinand Chalandon's *Historie de la Domination Normande en Italie et en Sicile* (1907) was the first major "generalist" work. In English, John Julius Norwich followed in this tradition with two books, *The Normans in the South* (1967) and *The Kingdom in the Sun* (1970).

Fine studies since 1990 are *The Norman Kingdom of Sicily* by Donald Matthew (1992) and *Roger II von Sizilien* by Hubert Houben (1997). Graham Loud's *Roger II and the Creation of the Kingdom of Sicily* (2012) is an analysis and translation of some key sources into English, like Alexander of Telese and Falco of Benevento.

A number of academic articles are of value. See, for example, Jeremy Johns' "The Norman Kings of Sicily and the Fatimid Caliphate," *Anglo-Norman Studies XV* (1995), pages 133-159, and the series of fine essays by various scholars in *The Society of Norman Italy* (Brill 2002). See also Benedetto Vetere's "Tancredi di Lecce nella Storiografia Medievale" in *Tancredi, Conte di Lecce Re di Sicilia* (2004), pages 1-32. Reported in the same collection (pages 33-44), Cosimo Fonseca offers some observations on the modern historiography in "Tancredi di Lecce nella Storiografia Moderna." (These papers were presented at an academic symposium held in Lecce in 1998.)

See also the varied studies reported in *Atti del Congresso Internazionale di Studi sulla Sicilia Normanna, Palermo 4-8 dicembre 1972* (1974). Additional "Italian" commentary (for what it's worth) will be found in Volume 1 of Rosario Gregorio's' *Considerazioni sopra la storia di Sicilia dai tempi normanni sino ai presenti* (1972).

Not to be overlooked are Ronald Broadhurst's eloquent translation of *The Travels of Ibn Jubayr* (1952), Alexander Metcalfe's *Muslims and Christians in Norman Sicily: Arabic Speakers and the End of Islam* (2011), and Jeremy Johns' *Arabic Administration in Norman Sicily: The Royal Diwan* (2002).

Benjamin of Tudela's *Itinerary*, or "The Voyages of Benjamin," was first published in English translation in 1840 (the frontispiece of an early Latin printing appears near the end of this book's map section). Richard Barber's *Henry Plantagenet* (1964) is a good biography. See also Jacqueline Alio's *Margaret: Queen of Sicily* (2015).

8. The translation of the *Alexiad* recommended is E.R.A. Sewter's annotated work, *The Alexiad of Anna Comnena*, published by Penguin in 1969.

SOURCES, NOTES, BIBLIOGRAPHY

The *Alexiad* was first translated for publication in English by Elizabeth Dawes in 1928.

9. The *Assizes* are preserved in two surviving manuscripts, both transcribed decades after Roger's reign. *Codex Vaticanus Latinus 8782* has forty-four statutes (clauses), or "assizes," and a preface. A later manuscript, *Codice Cassinese 468,* is abbreviated in form but includes seven additional statutes. That the contemporary chronicler Falco of Benevento mentions Roger's controversial introduction, at Ariano, of the ducat but not the new legal code suggests to some scholars that the *Assizes* were issued somewhat later and elsewhere. (See also note 18 below.) However, the juridical infrastructure mentioned in the *Assizes* was in place throughout the kingdom within a few years of the code's presumed (and generally accepted) date of promulgation. An early modern analysis is to be found in Hans Niese's *Die Gesetzgebung der Normannischen Dynastie im Regnum Siciliae* (1910). An insightful essay on the legal significance of the *Assizes* is "The Birth of the Ius Commune: King Roger II's Legislation," by Kenneth Pennington, in *Rivista Internazionale del Diritto Comune,* Number 17 (2006).

10. See Makdisi, John, "The Islamic Origins of the Common Law," *North Carolina Law Review* (June 1999). Among the English institutions thought to have been influenced by Islamic law are the Inns of Court and perpetual endowment. As early as 1955, Henry Cattan noted the striking similarity between the perpetual endowment of a trust and the Muslim principle of *waqf*. A very succinct overview is presented in Chapter 25 of *The Peoples of Sicily*.

11. The original manuscript, *Tabulario della Cattedrale di Palermo,* pergamena numero 22, consulted by the author.

Chapter 5

The best modern biography of Frederick II is David Abulafia's *Frederick II: A Medieval Emperor* (1988). *Friedrich der Zweite,* an earlier (1927) biography by Ernst Kantorowicz, is useful for basic facts and dates but sometimes lacking in balance as it was part of a nationalistic zeitgeist born in Germany in the wake of the First World War.

A good background introduction to this period in the history of central Europe is *Germany in the High Middle Ages c. 1050-1200* (1986) by Horst Fuhrmann.

THE KINGDOM OF SICILY

The *Chronica* of Salimbene degli Adami is one of the most important sources for the reign of Frederick II. However, it seems to have been written beginning around 1282, so it might not be contemporary. As a Franciscan, Salimbene may have entertained a somewhat biased view of the monarch who suppressed his order in Sicily.

The *Letters* of Pietro della Vigna, Frederick's sometime chancellor, have much to offer.

Richard of San Germano is another important source (see the notes for the previous chapter). For various details see the *Acta Imperii Inedita Seculi XIII et XIV* (published in 1880), edited by Eduard Winkelmann. The *Registro della Cancelleria 1239-1240* was published as an appendix of the Constitutions of Melfi printed by Gaetano Carcani in 1786.

The Liber Augustalis or Constitutions of Melfi (1971) by James Powell is an excellent translation and analysis of the Constitutions of Melfi.

Brief commentary on the legal rights of women guaranteed by the *Constitutions* is presented, from the Italian (and male) point of view, in Mazzarese Fardella, Enrico, "La Condizione Giuridica della Donna nel Liber Augustalis" in *Archivio Storico Siciliano,* Series 4, Volume 21-22 (Palermo 1997), pages 31-44.

Frederick's *De Arte Venandi cum Avibus* is preserved in manuscript. The first English translation was published in the United States in 1943 as *The Art of Falconry.* This was translated by Casey Wood and Marjorie Fyfe. A fine Italian translation by Anna Trombetti Budriesi was published in 1999 as *L'Arte di Cacciare con gli Uccelli.* This is accompanied by a Latin transcription.

For the history of the Jews in the years from 1061 to 1250, an insightful outline is Raphael Strauss's *Die Juden im Königreich Sizilien unter Normannen und Staufen,* published in Italian as *Gli Ebrei di Sicilia dai Normanni a Federico II* (1992). For later periods see the notes for Chapter 7.

An informative book about the Papacy during the early years of Swabian rule is *Innocent III: Leader of Europe 1198-1216* (1994) by Jane Sayers. See also James Powell's *Innocent III: Vicar of Christ or Lord of the World?* (1963).

Two "historical travelogues" should be mentioned as readers may find them interesting for social context. Richard Cassady wrote *The Emperor and the Saint: Frederick II of Hohenstaufen, Francis of Assisi, and Journeys to Medieval Places* (2011). In the same mold is Mary Taylor Simeti's *Travels with a Medieval Queen* (2001) about Constance of Hauteville.

The definitive history of the Magione Basilica, conventual church of the Teutonic Order for many centuries, is *La Magione di Palermo negli Otto Secoli della Sua Storia* (1975) by Rocco Russo.

SOURCES, NOTES, BIBLIOGRAPHY

A number of fine works deal with the Sicilian language. Some are more reliable than others. One of the better ones is Salvatore Giarrizzo's *Dizionario Etimologico Siciliano* (1989). An obvious shortcoming of many recent publications is their focus on *modern* Sicilian rather than the medieval tongue.

12. One of the best surveys published thus far is *The Kingdom of Sicily 1100-1250: A Literary History* (2005) by Karla Mallette.

13. The title *King of the Romans,* from the contemporary phrase *Romanorum Rex,* is deceptive insofar as it refers to rulers of what is now Germany; in German it is often the more descriptive *Römisch-deutscher König,* and hence an alternate English term is *King of the Germans.* During the period in question, it was an elective title for the one German king who did not answer to any other, used before his coronation as Holy Roman Emperor by the Pope. Normally, the Pope would not crown a claimant who had not already been elected King of the Romans by the Germans themselves. Frederick was acclaimed (actually reconfirmed) as King of the Romans in 1220.

14. The pretext was support of young Prince Alexius (later Alexius IV), son of the recently-deposed Byzantine Emperor Isaac II, in an internecine feud of Constantinople's Angelus dynasty. The reigning Emperor, Alexius III, was a brother of Isaac II (and so uncle of Prince Alexius). He had overthrown and imprisoned Isaac, but Prince Alexius managed to escape to the German court of Philip, the brother Henry VI. (Philip was married to Prince Alexius' sister Irene Angelina.) Crusaders initially intending to reach Jerusalem via Egypt were taken by Venetian ships to Constantinople for what was proposed as a "side trip" to restore Isaac II and his son to power before continuing southward to Palestine. Instead, they perpetrated all manner of atrocities at Constantinople, with rather few knights making their way to Palestine. Pope Innocent III was appalled at news of the slaughter, effectively a ruthless "crusade" against fellow Christians, although he later sent an army against the Cathars in the bloody Albigensian Crusade. Nevertheless, the so-called "Latin Empire of Constantinople" established in the wake of this genocidal conquest survived in some form until Byzantine Greek forces reclaimed the city in 1261. Eight centuries after the Fourth Crusade, Pope John Paul II apologized to the Patriarch of Constantinople for this crime against humanity.

15. Following Constance's *de facto* renunciation of Legatine authority, the next monarch to assert such rights, or at least the next one to do so openly

and formally (as a legal declaration), was Ferdinand the Catholic late in the fifteenth century. King Philip II of Spain instituted the juridical office of *Judex Monarchiae Siciliae* in 1597. In 1715, Pope Clement XI revoked the privileges of the so-called *Monarchia Sicula,* but this did not end the academic (or juridical) debate.

16. Oft-quoted in our times is an oxymoron popularized by Michele Amari describing Roger II as a "baptized sultan." The same has often been said of Frederick.

17. Much like English, the Sicilian of 1300 was very different from the modern language spoken five centuries later. There was very little serious study of Sicilian prior to the nineteenth century, and Modern Sicilian was long disparaged as a "dialect" of Italian spoken by the illiterate masses but rarely ever written; it lacks a standard orthography and a true future tense, and there are several dialects of it (Palermitan, Catanian, etc.). Although his translations and dictionaries contain much of value, the folklorist Giuseppe Pitrè (1841-1916) entertained some whimsical notions about the Sicilian language.

18. That the *Assizes of Capua* were deemed necessary might lead a skeptic to question the effect of the earlier *Assizes of Ariano* (believed to have been issued around 1140), or indeed to wonder whether the latter were ever officially formulated or widely disseminated. Thus far, a manuscript copy of the *Assizes of Ariano* dated to circa 1140, if it survives, has yet to be discovered. However, in his researches in the Vatican Archives (where he had access to a number of uncatalogued, unindexed manuscripts), the author found an apparent reference to the *Assizes* that may be dated tentatively to circa 1146, referring to issuance of the *Assizes* in 1141 (sic). See also note 9 above.

19. Italians have debated the phenomenon of "civic culture" for centuries, but especially since unification. Regional differences are somewhat less pronounced than they used to be, and they have been colored since 1860 by national developments affecting Italy as a whole. While the author begs to differ with some of its conclusions, this topic is addressed in Robert Putnam's *Making Democracy Work: Civic Traditions in Modern Italy* (1993).

20. Here a superlative treatment, with an eye to the human element, is *Four Queens: The Provençal Sisters Who Ruled Europe* (2007) by Nancy Goldstone.

21. There was kinship through several lines, the following being the most significant here. They were second cousins to Manfred through their mother, Elizabeth, sometimes "Beatrice," daughter of Philip Hohenstaufen (the younger brother of Henry VI) and Irene Angelina (daughter of the Byzantine Emperor Isaac II and widow of King Roger III of Sicily). In this lineage the common ancestor was Frederick Barbarossa (viv. 1123-1190). They were third cousins to Charles of Anjou through his mother, Bianca (Blanche) of Castile, the common ancestor in this lineage being Alfonso VII of Castile (viv. 1105-1157). After the defeat at Tagliacozzo, Frederick continued to fight against the Angevins in Sicily; he surrendered in 1269 and escaped to Tunisia, which he later defended against the invading knights of the Eighth Crusade (or "Tunisian Crusade") led by Charles' brother, Louis IX of France. Henry was less fortunate; following the Battle of Tagliacozzo, he was imprisoned until 1291.

Chapter 6

Chief contemporary sources are Salimbene's *Chronica* (see Chapter 5), written by a Franciscan, and *Cronica di lu Rebellamentu di Sichilia contra Re Carlu* (The Rebellion of Sicily against King Charles), written anonymously in Sicilian around 1290. Some historians attribute authorship of the latter to Atanasius of Iaci, a monk who lived near Catania during the War of the Vespers.

The most objective modern account, distinguished for its international perspective, is *The Sicilian Vespers: A History of the Mediterranean World in the Later Thirteenth Century* (1958) by Steven Runciman. Michele Amari's *La Guerra del Vespro Siciliano* (1843), though perhaps useful in some respects, should be read only with a very critical eye.

King Charles I of Naples remains a contentious figure. A departure from the usual demonization of him is to be found in Jean Dunbabin's *Charles I of Anjou: Power, Kingship and State-Making in Thirteenth-Century Europe* (1998).

The author's observation about the ready capitulation of certain fortresses (viz. Caltanissetta Castle) during the Vespers is based on his consultation of *De Rebus Regni Siciliae*, register entries 1528 and 1529, being decrees of King Peter issued at Solano in March 1283. The original manuscript is kept at the Archivo de la Corona de Aragón in Barcelona. The castellan at "Pietrarossa" Castle, a fortress located outside the village of Caltanissetta, surrendered quite readily to a small company of knights, whose leaders were pardoned by King Peter. Little of the structure remained following an earthquake in the sixteenth century, but in 1282 it was quite large.

22. The Mafia is briefly considered later. Until around 1800, organized crime, such as it was, consisted principally of banditry and the corruption of the estate agents, the infamous *gabellotti,* who controlled the larger *latifondi* on behalf of absentee landlords who preferred to live in the major cities. Despite some fanciful theories, and generic use of the word *mafia* before that time, there is little evidence of this form of criminality flourishing before circa 1770, but extortion was commonplace by 1900. Although the Mafia was never very centralized, meetings of its leaders, the "Cupola" in Palermo and the "Commission" in Apalachin (New York), in 1957, lent it a greater hierarchal structure and made it a truly international enterprise, its growth facilitated by the failure of juridical authorities in either country to recognize it as a reality until the 1970s, when it was selling heroin. (Early public revelations came from Leopoldo Franchetti in Italy in 1876, and Joseph Valachi in the United States in 1963.) Finally, in 1987, some *mafiosi* were sentenced in the "Maxiprocesso," the first major trial of Sicilian organized crime figures in Italy under new laws, coinciding with the "Pizza Connection" trial in the United States. The "Mafia family" is an American import; in Sicily, at least until around 1980, the Mafia was based more on localized cells, the *cosche* or clans of specific towns or urban districts, than on strictly hereditary lines. *Mafiosi* used to be secretive; now their names and mugshots are routinely published in the *Giornale di Sicilia*. (See also note 55.)

23. In view of the subsequent destruction of all the remains of Louis IX except for a solitary finger at Saint-Denis, the traditional resting place of French kings, his heart (and viscera) at Monreale is the most substantial bodily relic that survives. Louis was canonized in 1297.

24. See the books by Runciman and Meyendorff at the notes for Chapter 2 above; also the expositions in Chapter 8 of *The Kingdom in the Sun* by John Julius Norwich and Chapter 11 in *The Peoples of Sicily*. Essentially, the Schism of 1054 was the result of several major theological differences that came to the fore in the wake of centuries of misunderstanding. By most accounts, this began with the Iconoclast Controversy in 726. By the eleventh century, the true meaning of the *filioque* passage in the Creed, thought to reflect differing concepts of the Holy Trinity, was hotly debated. The question of Papal primacy was another issue; by tradition the Pentarchy viewed the Patriarch of the West (Rome) merely as the "first among equals," *primus inter pares,* not as a figure of universal authority over the other four patriarchs. As the remaining patriarchs of the Pentarchy (Constantinople,

Alexandria, Antioch, Jerusalem) recognized no theological pronouncements or dogmas emanating from Rome after 1054, the chasm only widened over time. Even though few Orthodox Christians ever accepted its conditions, the Council of Lyon (1272-1274) was the last serious attempt to heal the rift (Thomas Aquinas died *en route* to it).

25. As a result of these dynastic unions, the Crown of Hungary eventually came into possession of the Neapolitan House of Anjou.

26. He would live to become Charles II of Naples. His English nickname is a literal translation of the Italian *zoppo*, for the orthopedic condition that forced him to limp. This may partially account for his father's disdain for this "imperfect" son in an age when princes were expected to master such arts as sword fighting while mounted in the saddle but also standing. Historians have been far kinder to Charles II than to his father.

Chapter 7

Fine accounts and analyses will be found in *An Island for Itself: Economic Development and Social Change in Late Medieval Sicily* (2003) by Stephan Epstein. See also *The Decline and Fall of Medieval Sicily: Politics, Religion and Economy in the Reign of Frederick III, 1296-1337* (1995) by Clifford Backman.

Despite its publication during the Fascist era, a good Italian account of the reign of this monarch is Antonino De Stefano's *Federico III d'Aragona Re di Sicilia 1296-1337* (1937). The classic work is Francesco Testa's *De Vita et Rebus Gestis Federici II* (sic), published in Palermo in 1775. (Note the chronic confusion in the king's ordinal; in Sicily this younger son of Peter of Aragon, of Vespers fame, is usually referred to as "King Frederick II of Sicily.")

Vanished Kingdoms (2012), by Norman Davies, has an interesting chapter on the Aragonese Empire.

A fine transcription of the Peace of Caltabellotta, with annotations by Antonino Franchi and Benedetto Rocco, first published in the journal *Quaderni di Ho Theologos* in March 1985, was republished in monograph form as *La Pace di Caltabellotta* in 1987.

For a description of the brief reign of King Peter II of Sicily, see Corrado Mirto's "Petrus Secundus dei Gratia Rex Siciliae, 1337-1342" in *Archivio Storico Siciliano,* Series 4, Volume 2 (Palermo 1976), pages 53-126. Also by Corrado Mirto is a monograph covering the history of the *Regnum* to the middle of the fourteenth century, *Il Regno dell'Isola di Sicilia e delle Isole Adiacenti dalla Sua Nascita alla Peste del 1347-1348* (1986). His opinionated analysis regarding the Aragonese and the War of the Vespers may strike some readers as less than objective.

Some correspondence between Frederick III of Sicily and Joanna I of Naples was transcribed from Vatican codices by Antonino Mango and published in 1915 as *Relazioni tra Federico III di Sicilia e Giovanna I di Napoli*.

For some observations on feudal administration of the vast County of Modica under the Chiaramonte family, see Enzo Sipione's "La Contea di Modica sotto i Chiaramonte 1296-1392" in *Archivio Storico Siciliano*, Series 4, Volume 6 (Palermo 1980), pages 112-130.

A good overview of feudalism during this period is Antonino Marrone's monograph *Repertorio della Feudalità Siciliana 1282-1390* (2006). The *Ruolo di Bartolomeo Muscia* (1692) lists feudatories circa 1300 and circa 1400. *Teatro Genologico* (1647), by Filadelfo Mugnos, is most reliable for details after 1400.

An insightful study which might serve as a general indication of what administration was like in Sicilian towns during the Aragonese period is Lucia Sorrenti's "Le Istituzioni Comunali di Troina nell' Età Aragonese" in *Archivio Storico Siciliano*, Series 4, Volume 4 (Palermo 1978), pages 111-167.

Concerning the bitterness between Catalans and Latins, a rather romanticized account of the Luna-Perollo feud is *Il Famoso Caso di Sciacca* (1726) by Francesco Savasta.

A good study of the architectural style sometimes referred to in Sicily as "Chiaramontian Gothic," with special reference to Palermo's Steri, is *Lo Steri di Palermo e le sue Pitture* (2003) by Ettore Gabrici and Ezio Levi. See also Ferdinando Bologna's *Il Soffitto della Sala Magna allo Steri di Palermo* (1975, 2002).

Here we have concentrated on monographs, but there have been many specialist articles ("papers") published over the decades. Typical of these is David Abulafia's "Economic Activity of the Sicilian Jews around 1300" presented at the *Italia Judaica* conference held in Palermo in 1992. See also Scandaliato and Gerardi's "Gli Ebrei in Sicilia nel Medioevo: Cultura e Lingua," in *Archivio Storico Siciliano*, Series 4, Volume 21-22 (Palermo 1997), pages 114-133.

The concubines of Martin the Younger, including the mother of Frederick, Count of Luna, the illegitimate son who almost become king, are discussed in Alberto Boscolo's "Su 'la Bella Sanluri' Ultima Amante di Martino il Giovane Re di Sicilia" in *Miscellanea in Onore di Roberto Cessi*, Volume 1 (1958), pages 357-364. Boscolo makes reference to a medieval manuscript, but information about Tarsia Rizzari had already been published in *Somma della Storia di Sicilia* (1850) by the distinguished Niccolò Palmieri, where she is identified as a native of Catania. The aristocratic Rizzaris held various positions as judges and officials in Catania and Caltagirone.

Some fine work has been published about the Jews of Sicily and their expulsion/conversion in 1493. A good general work is *Between Scylla and Charybdis: The Jews in Sicily* (2011) by Shlomo Simonsohn, the foremost expert on Sicily's Jews. Complementary to this is *The Former Jews of this Kingdom: Sicilian Converts After the Expulsion 1492-1516* (2003) by Nadia Zeldes. Note that Professor Simonsohn's extensive research is reported in a highly detailed multi-volume opus, *The Jews in Sicily*.

The chief synagogue and mikveh of Palermo seem to have educed more debate than those of Siracusa; here a fine study is that of Nicolò Bucaria and David Cassuto, "La Sinagoga e i Miqweh di Palermo alla Luce dei Documenti e delle Scoperte Archeologiche," in *Archivio Storico Siciliano*, Series 4, Volume 31 (Palermo 2005), pages 171-209.

The section on Caterina de Monteverdi is republished from Jacqueline Alio's *Women of Sicily* (noted elsewhere). Most of this information is drawn from two works by the erudite Nadia Zeldes, namely *The Former Jews of this Kingdom* (mentioned above) and Chapter 6 in Volume 1 of *The Conversos and Moriscos in Late Medieval Spain and Beyond* (2009). The trial transcript, apparently lost, was extracted in Alberto Rizzo Marino's *Gli Ebrei di Mazara* (reprinted in 1971). Most of the transcripts of the Sicilian trials for "Judaizing" were destroyed following the abolition of the Inquisition in Sicily in 1782, and this appears to be the only detailed record of a trial held specifically for this crime to have survived. In that respect, it is a unique extant account of such an experience.

For the state of medicine during this period, see "Medicine in Southern Italy, Twelfth-Fourteenth Centuries: Six Texts," translated by Monica Green, in *Medieval Italy: Texts in Translation* (2009), pages 311-327.

27. The shore was then much nearer Palazzo Steri than it is today. Some years ago, a headless body identified as Chiaramonte's was discovered in a grave in the family chapel next to the Steri.

28. This is probably what marked the beginning of Catania's challenge to Messina for prominence in eastern Sicily. To this day, the Catanians boast of having the island's first university. The University of Messina was founded in 1548, and the University of Palermo was established in 1779 as the *Regia Accademia degli Studi San Ferdinando*.

29. See "Jewish Nobles in Late Medieval Sicily" in Mendola, Louis, *Sicilian Genealogy and Heraldry* (2013), pages 275-278.

Chapter 8

De Rebus Siculis (1560), by Tommaso Fazello, is the standard history consulted by modern writers for events during this period. *Sicanicarum Rerum Compendium* (1562), by the erudite Francesco Maurolico, has a slightly contrasting viewpoint, that of Messina versus Fazello's Palermitan perspective, reflecting the spirited rivalry between the two cities. See also *Storia Generale della Sicilia* (1831) by Francesco Ferrara and *Storia del Regno di Sicilia* (1844) by Giovanni Di Blasi.

Other significant works are *Storia delle Finanze del Regno di Napoli* (1839) and *Storia Economica-Civile di Sicilia* (1841) by Lodovico Bianchini, republished in an omnibus edition in 1960.

For the *donativi*, resulting in the *riveli* (tax declarations) paid by various communities in 1651, 1681, 1714 and 1748, see *La Finanza Locale in Sicilia nel '600 e '700* (1994) by Alfredo Li Vecchi, which presents tables and a concise analysis.

Another useful work is the series *Storia Civile e Politica del Regno di Napoli* (1796) by Pietro Giannone and Carlo Pecchia.

In English, an interesting study is *The Government of Sicily under Philip II of Spain: A Study in the Practice of Empire* (1951) by Helmut Koenigsberger, who published various papers in this area.

For modern population trends, a good overview is *Dinamiche Demografiche nella Sicilia Moderna 1505-1806* (2002) by Domenico Ligresti.

For details of the visit of Charles V in Sicily see Salvatore Agati's *Carlo V e la Sicilia* (2009).

Some commentary about Charles III and historiographical views of him is found in "Il Regno di Carlo III di Borbone nel Dibattito Storiografico" by Francesco Brancato, in *Archivio Storico Siciliano,* Series 4, Volume 17 (Palermo 1991), pages 135-155. See also Charles Petrie's *King Charles III of Spain: An Enlightened Despot* (1971).

A superb general analysis, especially with regard to the economy after 1500, will be found in *A History of Sicily* (1968) by Professor Denis Mack Smith, published in two volumes. Although one might disagree with some of his conclusions, the scholarship is sound, and this work (far superior to anything on the subject emanating from Italy during the same period) is much recommended over the condensed edition published with the contributions of other authors in 1987.

Antonino Venuti's landmark *De Agricultura Opusculum* (1516) was the first modern agricultural treatise published in Sicily. For the technical aspects of agriculture during the reign of Charles III see Filippo Nicosia's

SOURCES, NOTES, BIBLIOGRAPHY

Il Podere Fruttifero e Dilettevole (1735).

Anything written by Italians about the pre-1860 history of Italy (and indeed most of Europe) that was published from 1860 to around 1950 should be read very critically due to Savoyard, unificationist and then Fascist influences in the academic establishment; indeed, tenured professors educated during the Fascist era were still to be found teaching at Italian universities in the 1980s. Italian historians' perspectives, tainted by political bias, were highly questionable regarding everything from the War of the Spanish Succession to the Russian Revolution. (For more recent revisionism, see the notes for Chapter 10 below.)

Often cited by Italians, the lengthiest history of the Savoy dynasty, Francesco Cognasso's *I Savoia* (1971), should be ingested, if at all, only with a few tablespoons of salt, as its author was an outspoken advocate of the Fascist regime who repudiated modern historiographical methods accepted in more democratic environments (viz. Great Britain and the United States).

30. All Joanna's children were crowned. Her son, Ferdinand, eventually succeeded Charles as Holy Roman Emperor. Eleanor became Queen of France, Isabella became Queen of Denmark, Mary became Queen of Hungary, and Catherine became Queen of Portugal. Joanna's younger sister, Catherine of Aragon, wed King Henry VIII of England, by whom she bore a daughter, later Queen Mary I of England, who earned the sobriquet "Bloody Mary" for her zealous persecution (and executions) of Protestants.

31. Maqueda was praised by contemporary historians as well as later scholars. See Rosa Guccione Scaglione's "Sul Viceregno di Bernardino de Cardines, Duca di Maqueda, 1598-1601" in *Archivio Storico Siciliano,* Series 4, Volume 4 (Palermo 1978), pages 289-318.

32. Outbreaks of bubonic plague were fairly frequent. A detailed study is "Due Episodi di Peste in Sicilia, 1526 e 1624" by Calogero Valenti, in *Archivio Storico Siciliano,* Series 4, Volume 10 (Palermo 1984), pages 5-88. Studies undertaken since 2000 have placed the historicity of Saint Rosalie in some doubt. Genetic testing has revealed the bones attributed to her to be those of a male. By tradition, it was claimed that Rosalie lived in the Norman era, yet no contemporary medieval record mentions her.

33. See De Gregorio, Domenico, *Cammarata: Notizie sul Territorio e la Sua Storia* (1986), pages 260-261.

34. It would have been imprudent, and quite unnecessary, to compile a list of "members" in such a group. The reader is cautioned against interpreting literature about the *Beati Paoli* (such as the book by Luigi Natoli) as anything more than historical fiction. The very phrase *Beati Paoli* is anachronistic, coined much later to identify this tiny movement, along with colorful descriptions of its members wearing black hooded robes (faintly evocative of ninja attire) as part of a sect.

35. While Louis XIV, whose precise motives are the subject of scholarly debate, has often been identified as the culprit in the events leading to this war, Europe's patchwork of states both large and small created myriad political complexities that could threaten the balance of power. Alliances changed frequently, and many nations besides France were greedy for territory. Louis probably feared his nation being geographically "encircled" by Hapsburg monarchies in the future. A fine overview is *The War of Succession in Spain, 1700-1715* (1969) by Henry Kamen. For details and background, a useful reference is *The Treaties of the War of the Spanish Succession: An Historical and Critical Dictionary* (1995) by Linda Frey. More generally, see *The Wars of Louis XIV 1667-1714* (1999) by John Lynn. The war had global consequences; its North American theatre was referred to by British colonists in the future United States as "Queen Anne's War."

36. British possession of Gibraltar is still a point of contention between Great Britain and Spain three centuries later. Spanish monarchs attempted to regain the territory by siege in 1727 during the brief Anglo-Spanish War and again in 1779.

37. "King of Sardinia" thus became the principal title of the Savoy monarchs, who continued to rule Piedmont and Savoy. The dynasty was often referred to as the "Royal House of Sardinia," which of course it was. At its foundation in 1297, the Kingdom of Sardinia and Corsica was ruled from Aragon.

Chapter 9

The Bourbons of Naples (1956) and *The Last Bourbons of Naples* (1961) by Harold Acton are the definitive works for that dynasty's history from circa 1700 until 1861. The most detailed biography of King Francesco II is *L'Ultimo Re di Napoli* (1982) by Pier Giusto Jaeger. Arrigo Petacco's *La Regina del*

Sud (1992) concentrates on Queen Maria Sophia; the lengthiest study of her presently available in English is Chapter 12 of Jacqueline Alio's *Women of Sicily* (2014). The "Archivio Borbone" at the Naples Archive of State is an important source of information for researchers (see notes for Chapter 10).

The official record of events until the time of its publication is *Cronaca Civile e Militare delle Due Sicilie sotto la Dinastia Borbonica dall'Anno 1734 in Poi* (1857) by Luigi del Pozzo.

A good contemporary guide to architecture in and around Naples is *Nuova Guida di Napoli* (1826) by Giovanni Battista de Ferrari and Mariano Vasi.

A fine reference for the topography and agriculture of Sicily immediately before unification is Vito Amico's *Dizionario Topografico della Sicilia* (1859). For culinary history generally, see *Sicilian Food and Wine* (2015) by Francesca Lombardo.

Recent studies by a number of scholars are presented in *The Risorgimento Revisited: Nationalism and Culture in Nineteenth-Century Italy* (2012), edited by Silvana Patriarca and Lucy Riall.

The various facts presented in this chapter are quite widely known if rarely published (Acton and others have noted a few of these), though that is changing due to the impetus of the internet and the growing number of Italian scholars whose work is challenging the bromides of the unification movement. One of the first Sicilian authors to do so was Giuseppe Tomasi di Lampedusa, whose novel, *The Leopard* (1958), offers some interesting commentary on the unification war and the events surrounding it.

Under the Volcano: Revolution in a Sicilian Town (2013), namely Bronte, and *Garibaldi: Invention of a Hero* (2008), both by Lucy Riall, deal with the invasion of 1860 and its aftermath.

One of the first works to openly challenge the Italians' hagiographies of their unificationist heroes was Denis Mack Smith's *Cavour and Garibaldi 1860: A Study in Political Conflict* (1954, 1985). See also his *Mazzini* (1994).

One may debate legal principles in light of their enforcement versus their literal codification. Many of Italy's best jurists were Neapolitans, and a useful contemporary treatise on criminal law in the Two Sicilies will be found in Pietro Ulloa's *Amministrazione della Giustizia Penale nel Regno di Napoli* (1835), which compares the laws of this nation to those of others.

For the rapport with the United States of America, see Howard Marraro's *Diplomatic Relations between the United States and the Kingdom of the Two Sicilies* (2 volumes, 1951-1952).

A detailed contemporary description of the sulfur mining industry late in the nineteenth century was provided by Philip Carroll, the United States Consul in Palermo, in "Sulphur Mines in Sicily" a consular report of 1888 published in *Scientific American Supplement* in 1891. His candor in this and other matters earned Carroll expulsion by the Italian authorities in 1890 because the Italian government sought to conceal from foreign observers the work conditions (and the widespread exploitation of child labor) in Sicilian sulfur mines. Obviously, the Italian government could not censor what was published abroad.

38. Events in the Kingdom of Naples were predicated on those across Europe and the Mediterranean. Specific foreign policy was conditioned by the actions of the great powers in a setting where smaller nations like the Italian states were little more than pawns. (In Naples, however, another factor was Queen Maria Carolina's adverse influence on Ferdinando's actions.) The successive unification movements in Italy and Germany were, in part, a response of smaller states to the hegemony of larger nations in conflicts like the Napoleonic Wars. For an excellent overview, see *Napoleon's Wars: An International History 1803-1815* (2009) by Charles Esdaile.

39. This led to the leaders of the subsequent unification movement frequently being characterized by the Papacy as freemasons, whether they were or not. Some, such as Giuseppe Garibaldi, were indeed freemasons, while others simply adopted quasi-masonic practices. Even so, to describe the majority of them in this way would be overzealous. In this regard, it is worth noting that freemasonry itself took varying forms based on its own "rites" and local practices, and that it was legal for a few years during the reign of Charles de Bourbon in the eighteenth century despite Papal proscriptions. In its essence, freemasonry was not specifically monarchist or republican, nor was it intrinsically revolutionary.

40. As surely as the *fuitina* (elopement) has disappeared, the long shadows cast by many social practices of this era are still omnipresent in Italy, where the infamous *raccomandazione* (preferment), nepotism, clientelism (with its bribes and political favors) and sexism (sexual harassment and gender inequality) are a normal part of life. Hence the Italian adage that *siamo ancora nel Medioevo,* "we're still in the Middle Ages." News of these phenomena sometimes makes its way into the international press. As regards nepotism, *The Economist* (in "Higher Education in Italy: A Case for Change," 15 November 2008, page 32) states that "this week news emerged of a university rector who, the day before he retired on October 31st, signed a decree to make his son a lecturer," going on to explain that, "At Palermo University, as many as 230 teachers are reported to be related to other teachers." The

Italian neologism for *nepotism* in one place on a grand scale is *parentopoli*. Even the most superficial perusal of Italian newspapers and websites will confirm that these social diseases infect Turin, Milan and Bologna as well as Naples, Palermo and Rome; it comes as no surprise that not a single Italian university is ranked in the world's top hundred according to reports issued by European, British and American agencies or reporters. Recent analyses by Transparency International place Italy among the most corrupt nations of the European Union and western Europe. For reports and statistics on issues related to gender, see "Sicily's Women Today" in Jacqueline Alio's *Women of Sicily: Saints, Queens and Rebels* (pages 193-200). While one is reluctant to characterize twenty-first century Italy as a misogynistic gerontocracy little changed since the days of its monarchies, some statistics are startling; only around fifty percent of Italian women are employed in the workforce, with the figure hovering around thirty-five percent in Sicily. Outsiders are sometimes slow to recognize the extent and gravity of these problems in Italian society; an example of political corruption of the "bread and circuses" variety was the literal purchase of votes in Palermo for five euros each, reported by Salvo Palazzolo as a national story in "In Sicilia trenta voti pagati 150 euro" in *La Repubblica* (28 May 2015, page 11). In 2015, the politically-appointed director of Palermo's chamber of commerce (a public agency that administers business licensing and other services) pleaded guilty to corruption; he had demanded a payoff of a hundred thousand euros to grant an exclusive concession to a pastry maker for shop space at the Palermo airport, and was exposed when the victim wore a "wire" during their meeting while police were listening at the other end.

41. Caricatures of this kind were a prominent feature in propaganda after 1860 as the new regime sought to denigrate the previous one. A leading scholar has keenly observed that in school history books Ferdinando II was "disparaged as the wicked 'King Bomba' for his bombardment of the civilian population of Messina in 1847, whereas the subsequent Piedmontese bombardment of Genoa, Ancona and Gaeta was either applauded or ignored." See Mack Smith, Denis, "Documentary Falsification and Italian Biography," in *History and Biography: Essays in Honour of Derek Beales* (Cambridge 1996), page 181. While every blemish of the Two Sicilies was highlighted, Savoyard blights like the infamous "Piedmont Easter Massacre" of 1655 were conveniently expurgated from the Italian history imparted to school children. (See also the section "Supplementary Sources" following the notes for Chapter 10.)

42. There is no doubt that the revolutions were, in the end, essentially political, but some scholars are inclined to point out that the root cause was simply economic even if, in certain cases, this was merely a pretext. The bad harvests, and the resulting food scarcity, combined with an industrial slump, were key factors across central and western Europe. See "Economic Crises and the European Revolutions of 1848" by Helge Berger and Mark Spoerer in *Journal of Economic History*, Volume 62, Number 2 (2001).

43. Even if the role of Sardinia-Piedmont were, *arguendo*, excluded, the international aspect of things to come after 1859 was downplayed by Italianist historians writing between 1861 and 1946, who would have us believe that the unification movement and the ensuing war were exclusively domestic (Italian) efforts achieved without foreign diplomatic or military support. The "official" (government) views of two more recent events are equally incomplete, or "selective." The Americans and British are rarely mentioned in the Liberation Day (25 April) festivities marking the end of the Second World War in Italy in 1945, with some extremist politicians actually ascribing the victories in Turin and Milan almost exclusively to the Italian partisans rather than to the American Fifth Army. The roles of King Umberto II and the Allies who forced his hand are seldom mentioned in connection with Sicilian Autonomy Day (15 May), which commemorates Sicily's regional autonomy being granted in 1946 by the Kingdom of Italy and not, as many erroneously presume, by the Italian Republic, which did not yet exist. (These phenomena are a simple matter of observation for anybody who lives in Italy, but they are addressed in some books mentioned in the notes for the following chapter.)

44. Some historians place the beginning of the *Risorgimento* movement in the eighteenth century. The beginning of the political unification movement is often dated to the Congress of Vienna. In common parlance the proper nouns *Unificazione* and *Risorgimento* are often used interchangeably in Italy, where the more patriotic-sounding *Unità d'Italia* is also heard.

45. The achievement of Catholic "emancipation" in Britain in 1829 lent an air of legitimacy to British criticisms of the Two Sicilies, yet Britain still had an established church, while its Ireland policy left much to be desired, realities which made certain British criticisms of other states seem overzealous. Although far fewer criticisms emanated from the United States, these might be seen to reflect still greater hypocrisy coming from a place where slavery still existed. At all events, most of the critics themselves were viewed as progressives in their own countries.

46. The comparative wealth of the pre-unitary Italian states circa 1859 was calculated by Italian economists and bankers who were by no means advocates of regional autonomy. Based on deposits in millions of gold lire — indicative as a proportional measure even without converting its exchange value into today's currencies — this was: Two Sicilies (Naples and Sicily) 443.2, Papal State 90.6, Grand Duchy of Tuscany 84.2, Kingdom of Sardinia (including Liguria) 27.1, Venetia (under Austria) 12.8, Lombardy (under Austria) 8.1, Duchy of Parma 1.2, Duchy of Modena .4. Published in Francesco Saverio Nitti's *Scienze delle Finanze* in 1903, these statistics were subsequently confirmed by other economists following the fall of the Kingdom of Italy, for example by Anteo d'Angio in *La Situazione Finanziaria Italiana dal 1796 al 1870* in 1973 and by Nicola Zitara in *L'Unita d'Italia: Nascita di Una Colonia* in 1971.

47. Italian unification was indeed important, but mostly to a population numbering just shy of twenty million in an area significantly smaller than California. The expanding United States already had a population of thirty million during the same period, while the population of the vast Russian Empire was around seventy million (more than Italy today). Italy's unification is studied very little outside of Italy because, unlike the *Magna Carta*, the American Revolution or even the works of Karl Marx, it reflected no novel political principles that ever had an impact outside one country. Giuseppe Mazzini, the lone exponent of the movement whose ideas ever gained (or merited) much currency outside Italy, was marginalized, appreciated by his own people more after his death than during his life.

48. Accompanied by several companions, Francesco Crispi, a native Sicilian fluent in the Sicilian language and the Albanian dialect spoken in Sicily, arrived *incognito* on the island before Garibaldi to drum up support among the population. It is thought that he bribed several Sicilian generals in western Sicily, something that would not seem out of character for a man inclined to opportunism and even duplicity (see the next chapter). Naturally, documentary proof of bribery is elusive, but if actions speak louder than words several Sicilian generals' ready capitulation to inferior forces is, at the very least, worthy of suspicion. It is obvious enough that the new government would not conserve traces of activities such as bribery, but these early actions established the precedent of censored documents "disappearing," a phenomenon to which the erudite Denis Mack Smith sagely dedicates the greater part of his Introduction in *Italy and Its Monarchy* (see the notes for the following chapter), and an essay, "Documentary Falsification

and Italian Biography," in *History and Biography: Essays in Honour of Derek Beales* (Cambridge 1996), pages 173-187. (See also note 41 above.) Foreign policy was equally deceptive (see note 52). The practice of preventing access to important records was continued by the Italian Republic, especially with regard to war crimes (see note 54 regarding Alcide De Gasperi and requests from Ethiopia). In the resounding words of the American statesman Daniel Patrick Moynihan: "Everyone is entitled to his own opinion, but not his own facts."

Chapter 10

This chapter is not intended as a detailed study of the Kingdom of Italy, the Fascist regime or the Second World War. In English, two sober histories of this period are *Italy and Its Monarchy* (1989) by Denis Mack Smith and *The Fall of the House of Savoy* (1972) by Robert Katz. *The Pursuit of Italy: A History of a Land, Its Regions, and Their Peoples* (2011) by David Gilmour is an objective view of Italy's regionalism based on centuries of history. John Dickie's *Darkest Italy: The Nation and Stereotypes of the Mezzogiorno, 1860-1900* (1999) is a fine exposition.

For an insightful study into the situation in Sicily leading to the uprisings of 1866, see Lucy Riall's *Sicily and the Unification of Italy: Liberal Policy and Local Power 1859-1866* (1998).

An interesting look at Sicily's social and legal situation just fifteen years after unification is Leopoldo Franchetti's *La Sicilia nel 1876: Le Condizioni Politiche e Amministrative* (1876), in which he considers the island's mores, widespread criminality (the Mafia) and generally poor administration; while the views of Franchetti, a Tuscan, were clearly biased, they were a refreshing improvement over those of contemporary Sicilian commentators like the folklorist Giuseppe Pitrè, who glorified the figure of the *mafioso*.

For insights into the status of the urban poor beginning around 1868, see "Assistenza e Beneficenza a Palermo dopo l'Unità ed il Progetto 'La Casa dei Poveri' di Giacomo Cusmano" by Maria Teresa Falzone, in *Archivio Storico Siciliano*, Series 4, Volume 10 (Palermo 1984), pages 154-177.

In Italy a number of recent books confront unificationist revisionism (and denialism) and the socio-economic failures of unification itself. One translated into English is Pino Aprile's *Terroni: All that has been done to ensure that the Italians of the South became southerners* (2011). Giordano Bruno Guerri's *Il Sangue del Sud: Antistoria del Risorgimento e del Brigantaggio* (2010) and Gianni Oliva's *Un Regno Che è Stato Grande: La Storia Negata dei Borboni di Napoli e Sicilia* (2011) consider the revisionism that infected Italy after 1860. *Memorie del Sud* (1999), edited by Andrea Orlandi, presents a number of revelatory details regarding the peninsular half of the Two Sicilies and the war of 1860-1861. Published in 2005, Eric Salerno's *Genocidio in Libia* is a rare example of Italian "corrective revisionism" regarding Italy's colonial misadventures.

For the Second World War, the best general histories are Carlo D'Este's *Bitter Victory: The Battle for Sicily, 1943* (1988) and Rick Atkinson's more recent entry, *The Day of Battle: The War in Sicily and Italy, 1943-1944* (2007). There are also more specialized studies and memoirs. A noteworthy analysis from the German perspective is *The Battle of Sicily: How the Allies Lost Their Chance for Total Victory* (2007), by Samuel Mitcham and Freidrich von Stauffenberg. Also of value are *Assault on Sicily: Monty and Patton at War* (2007) by Ken Ford and *Drop Zone Sicily* by William Breuer (1997).

A look at espionage is provided in *Operation Mincemeat* (2010) by Ben Macintyre. Here one of the players was Ian Fleming, who later achieved fame for his James Bond novels.

In the text, reference was made to *Crusade in Europe* (1948), a memoir by General Dwight D. Eisenhower.

A History of Fascism, 1914-1945 (1995), by Stanley Payne, is a fine overview. Philip Cannistraro's *Historical Dictionary of Fascist Italy* (1982) is a good reference.

Following the war, myriad former Fascist officers made their way into public life, as far as the Quirinal. A distinguished exception was Sandro Pertini, who had been a leading partisan (and who the author had the privilege of meeting in 1982).

Though generally ignored by Italian school history curricula (hence the widespread ignorance or "denial" of the facts among many Italians in Italy), the numerous war crimes perpetrated by the Royal Italian Army have been extensively documented by scholars and journalists, as well as Allied military intelligence and various international agencies. To cite, *pro forma,* just a few articles: "Italy's Bloody Secret" by Rory Carroll in *The Guardian,* London, 25 June 2001; "Italy: Airbrushing History of Nazi Puppets" by Alfio Bernabei in *Searchlight* magazine (UK), January 2002; "Britain and the 'Hand-over' of Italian War Criminals to Yugoslavia 1945-48" by Effie Pedaliu in *Journal of Contemporary History* (UK, US), October 2004, Volume 39, Number 4, pages 503-529.

Much information, such as accounts of the Palermo Bread Massacre, can be garnered from contemporary newspaper reports, court transcripts and eyewitness descriptions. A candid commentary on the presentation of history by Italian officialdom following the war is Gianni Oliva's monograph *L'Alibi della Resistenza* (2003).

A *corpus* of archival material survived the exile of the Neapolitan and Italian dynasties in 1861 and 1946. The "Archivio Borbone," which includes most of the papers of King Francesco II that were conserved, was deposited with the Naples Archive of State by Princess Urraca in 1951; the dates of these documents of the royal household range from 1713 to 1890. For reasons too complicated to outline here, certain documents were retained by the royal family. The greater part of the "personal" archives of King Vittorio Emanuele III and his son King Umberto II have been destroyed, but a few records of the royal household were preserved by Colonel Francesco Scoppola (a confidant of Umberto II) and others.

For a scientific paradigm applicable to Italy's (and Italians') pseudohistory and historical denial regarding the unification war, Fascism, crimes against humanity and other developments, see *Denying History: Who Says the Holocaust Never Happened and Why Do They Say It?* (2009 edition) by Michael Shermer and Alex Grobman. That book's authors consider matters such as proof standards which are relevant to the Italian model.

Caveat lector: Some bizarre ideas have been hatched in post-war Italy, many of them colored by nationalism or extremist politics, and some involve unjustified revisionism or simple historical denial of one kind or another (leading to pseudohistory). For example, commentary about Operation Husky sometimes emphasizes the few isolated incidents of Americans shooting unarmed Italians as if these occurrences reflected official policy or trends rather than rare, and terrible, breaches of discipline (as the Allies had hundreds of thousands of troops on the ground a few infractions were statistically inevitable). Another camp claims that the Americans owe their victory — resulting from endless aerial bombardments preceding what was then the largest amphibious military invasion in history — largely to gangsters like Lucky Luciano and Vito Genovese, working with the rustic Mafia of Calogero Vizzini. Such views are unsurprising in a place where university students are taught that William Shakespeare was a Sicilian from Messina. To paraphrase Abraham Lincoln, "you can fool some of the Sicilians all of the time, and all of the Sicilians some of the time, but you cannot fool all of the Sicilians all of the time." Sicily's best historians, those few whose work is cited in the preceding pages, are serious independent scholars working outside the academic and political spheres. The less serious ones, the propagandists, should heed the wise message of an old Sicilian proverb: "Flies can't fly into a closed mouth."

49. Acton, Harold. *The Last Bourbons of Naples.* Methuen, London, 1961; page 523. The passage quoted is Acton's translation.

50. As regards the historical memory of this incident, a particularly telling report eluded international press coverage. On 14 August 2011, on behalf of the President of the Italian Republic, the national official responsible for the celebrations marking the unification's sesquicentennial officially apologized to the mayors, councils and residents of Pontelandolfo and Casalduni, which suffered at the hands of Piedmontese troops on 14 August 1861 during a reprisal for allegedly having supported "brigands." To thunderous applause, he declared: "Io vi chiedo scusa, a nome della Repubblica Italiana." ("I apologize to you on behalf of the Italian Republic.") See the *Corriere della Sera,* 14 August 2011, page 41, "Pontelandolfo, scuse per un massacro: il ricordo dei civili uccisi come rappresaglia contro i briganti 150 anni fa."

51. Scholars dispute whether this revolt was initially anti-Savoy or pro-Bourbon. It probably began as the former, quickly evolving into the latter. The early involvement of local aristocrats and bureaucrats strongly suggests a political scope. Based on a theory that it was simply an anti-government insurrection and — like most such riots — freed prisoners from the Ucciardone jail, a more eccentric faction of historical writers has even suggested, in a far more colorful (if unsupported) theory, that it was instigated by the Mafia!

52. In the infamous Article 17 of the Treaty of Wichale negotiated with Ethiopia in 1889, the Italian translation disseminated by Italy stipulated that henceforth Ethiopia's foreign affairs were to be conducted exclusively by the Italian government while the Amharic text stated nothing of the kind. Based on this deception, Italy sought to claim Ethiopia as its protectorate, an assertion challenged by Russia and France (both nations contested Italy's intentions and the translation's veracity) as well as Ethiopia itself. For details see Chapter 6 in Marcus, Harold, *A History of Ethiopia* (1994).

53. The telephone in use in Italy in 1930 when the Fascists took up the cause of Antonio Meucci (1808-1889) was based on the patented design of Alexander Graham Bell (1847-1922), a fact conveniently ignored in Italian nationalist propaganda of that era. For a balanced essay regarding Meucci's work, see John Klooster's *Icons of Invention: The Makers of the Modern World from Gutenberg to Gates* (2009), Volume 1, pages 207-208, 210-217. See also Howard Rockman's *Intellectual Property Law for Engineers and Scientists* (2004), pages 107-109. For information on his device drawn from contemporary court records, see "The Telephone Claimed by Meucci: Affidavits,

specification etc." in *Scientific American Supplement* (22 November 1884), Number 464, page 7407, and "Meucci's Claims to the Telephone" in *Scientific American Supplement* (19 December 1885), Number 520. (In *Scientific American* and elsewhere, most of the diagrams illustrating ideas claimed by Meucci were drawn and published *after* the details of Bell's patented design were publicly revealed.) A treatise on the invention of the telephone would be a lengthy one; in passing, it should be noted that Elisha Gray and Johann Philipp Reis conceived what some have described as functional "telephone prototypes," and that there was a ruling against Meucci in New York on 19 July 1887 in *American Bell Telephone Company versus Globe Telephone Company, Antonio Meucci et al.* (31 Fed 728, SDNY), while Bell never lost any of the hundreds of cases challenging his patent, facts outlined by Rockman, *op. cit.* The crux of the matter is that Meucci's *teletrofono* was not patented and no *prima facie* evidence was presented to support the thesis that it was even capable of achieving true voice transmission; Meucci's device was, at best, a "precursor" of the telephone. A second fallacy, corollary to the first one (that Meucci invented a working telephone before Bell), occurs when young Italians are led to believe that the entire world credits the invention to Meucci. Beyond telephony, there remain many vestiges of nationalist bias in Italy's academic, legal and commercial spheres; blunt censorship reflecting it continued until quite recently (see note 58), diminishing with the increasing use of the internet after 2000.

54. The reparation figures (in US dollars) are: $25 million to Ethiopia (principally "in kind" via construction projects), $105 million to Greece, $100 million to the Soviet Union, $5 million to Albania, $125 million to Yugoslavia (not entirely remitted). American aid to Italy (the Marshall Plan) was $1.2 billion by 1952. In addition to reparations, the Russians demanded that numerous war criminals be tried; the Americans and British demurred because such trials, coming at the dawn of the Cold War, would open the door to the election of a parliamentary majority supportive of the Left favored by Stalin. Alcide De Gasperi, prime minister from 1945 to 1953 and a leader of the Christian Democrats, explicitly ordered archivists to refuse requests from Ethiopia for the relevant records on activities connected with Italian crimes against humanity (for similar practices described by Denis Mack Smith see note 48). Only two Italians ever stood trial for war crimes committed between 1935 and 1945. Vestigial bitterness remains; as recently as the early years of the present century, Italy's motion in the United Nations to have the *Foibe* killings of Italian civilians in Istria (an occupied territory Italy lost after the war) by Yugoslav partisans from 1943

SOURCES, NOTES, BIBLIOGRAPHY

to 1945 recognized as war crimes was vehemently vetoed by Croatia and Slovenia, receiving no endorsement whatsoever from any permanent member of the Security Council. Since 2005, when Italian politicians, reacting to the refusal of the United Nations to approve Italy's motion, began to commemorate the killings in public observances and openly criticize Croatia, there have been several diplomatic rows with the Croatian government. (In fact, the mutual hatred complicated diplomacy for decades following the war; the Allied Military Government ceded control of Trieste to Italy and Yugoslavia only in 1954, the territorial division being formalized with the Treaty of Osimo in 1975.)

55. The Licata episode is mentioned by Rick Atkinson, *op. cit.* That the Americans enlisted the cooperation of *mafiosi* like Calogero Vizzini during the Allied occupation following Operation Husky, and even placed a few in positions of minor authority, has given rise to some popular myths. Sicilian-born Charles "Lucky" Luciano helped the American government to obtain the cooperation of longshore (port) workers in New York following the fire that destroyed the SS Normandie (an ocean liner being retrofitted for troop transport) in February 1942; Nazi sabotage was suspected in the destruction of a vessel believed to be faster than any German submarine. Luciano was not involved directly in Operation Husky, although he provided some intelligence. American mobster Vito Genovese, who knew Vizzini and Luciano, served as a military translator. Charles Poletti, the former governor of New York who became the United States Army's chief administrator for public affairs in Sicily, had no known connection with these men, and as he was fluent in Italian he would not need a translator. The idea that the American military would be incapable of fighting its way from Gela to Palermo without Mafia help is patently absurd. There is little doubt, however, that Vizzini, Luciano and Genovese advanced their criminal careers through their activities in Italy during and immediately after the war. By 1960, the Sicilian Mafia was imitating American gangsterism. The phrase *cosa nostra* ("our thing") is an Americanism. (See note 22 regarding Mafia origins and organization.)

56. Lieutenant Commander James C. Risk, present as an observer in the Quirinal in May and June 1946, recounted this episode to the author in 1992. It is published here for the first time. No Italian commentator or historian, not even the right-wing journalist Indro Montanelli (1909-2001), has ever written about this incident, which was absolutely unknown to Italians for almost seventy years. The Americans were reluctant to investigate

this kind of infraction (reportedly widespread) because to do so might prompt the complete annulment of the referendum, thereby necessitating another balloting in an atmosphere of equal acrimony. The citizenry was already bitterly divided in the war's aftermath; the occupiers wanted to finish the job and go home, and anyway the Americans favored a republic.

57. With the end of Italy's monarchy, the only territory ruled by a dynasty having unabashedly Italian roots was serene Monaco, the tiny Francophone principality of the House of Grimaldi. This Genoan mercantile family had a medieval presence in Palermo, where their chapel is preserved in the basilica dedicated to Saint Francis of Assisi.

58. The pervasive censorship regarding Fascism and the lost war was not confined to school history texts. In 1981 the government, at that time controlled by the Christian Democrats, refused to license the theatrical release of *The Lion of the Desert,* a motion picture (starring Anthony Quinn, Oliver Reed, Rod Steiger, Irene Papas, John Gielgud and numerous Italians) depicting civilian massacres in Italian-occupied Libya. The film was finally broadcast by Italian satellite television on 11 June 2009. For a contemporary review see "Lion of the Desert: Bedouin vs Mussolini" by Vincent Canby in *The New York Times* (17 April 1981).

59. Emigration for economic reasons is not a thing of the past. Today a great number of Italians still leave their country in search of employment opportunities abroad, and cities like London and Toronto have extremely large populations of Italian immigrants. Presently (2015) nearly 200,000 Italians emigrate each year, although the official figure reflects around half that number because the phenomenon is underreported (many young Italians enter EU countries as tourists or students but choose to stay). See "Young Italians abandon la dolce vita to move to Britain" by Nick Squires (in *The Telegraph,* 8 October 2014), which states that, "the registered population of Italians living in London is 220,000, but officials believe the true figure to be closer to half a million. Italians make up the fourth largest European community in the capital, after Poles, Irish and French." According to most estimates, as many as ten thousand Italians migrate to Australia each year, but some return to Italy after a year or two.

60. The *mondine* are depicted in the 1949 film *Riso Amaro,* released in Anglophone countries as "Bitter Rice." Much legislation has been dilatory. Rape became felony assault in 1996, stalking became a crime only in 2009,

the legal distinction between children born to wed and unwed parents was abolished in 2012, and legal restrictions on the use of reproductive technologies in fertility treatment (gamete donation, in vitro fertilization, etc.) were lifted in 2014. Statistics on women and employment are reported at note 40.

Epilogue

Events prior to 1946 are a matter of historical record. The living descendants of the kings of the Two Sicilies and Italy are private citizens. As regards persons living today, it is not the author's intent to pit the Savoys and the Neapolitan Bourbons against each other personally in a kind of continuing feud, something some monarchists and royalty fanatics have attempted to do over the years.

61. The Italian Republic formally recognizes the orders of chivalry bestowed by the House of the Two Sicilies, with special reference to the Constantinian Order of Saint George (see Appendix 2). Following the death of Alfonso, Count of Caserta, the exile was somewhat complicated in practice. Princess Urraca (1913-1999) once explained to the author that her father, Ferdinando Pio (Alfonso's son and head of the dynasty from 1934 to 1960) could enter Italy before 1946 for a brief visit on condition that plainclothes police officers accompanied him wherever he went. Here your author cannot resist recounting an anecdote. At a reception of the Order of Malta in Rome, when an Italian noblewoman lamented the "reduced economic circumstances" of the "poor Savoys" (King Umberto was then living in exile in Portugal but he was hardly impoverished), feisty Urraca rejoined, "Well, the Savoys ended up with more money than *they* left us!"

Supplementary Sources

Rushing in where angels fear to tread, the author has included in chapters 9 and 10 a few details gleaned from oral accounts that transcend the extant documentary record. Involving the kind of social or "micro" history mentioned in the Introduction, these accounts detail incidents which, by their very nature, are not likely to have been recorded when they occurred. However, they concern specific events or circumstances that are relevant to more general history, either by supporting known facts or by providing context.

The author's approach is not altogether exceptional, as historians and journalists often conduct interviews to supplement their investigations.

Serving as an American naval officer during the Allied occupation, James Risk (see note 56) once spent an afternoon with King Vittorio Emanuele III. He endorsed the supposition that the penultimate Italian monarch was anything but ignorant, and probably cognizant of what the Fascists were doing over the course of two decades. Jim Risk was less impressed by Lucky Luciano, who he met after the war. His opinion about Joseph Stalin, who he met in Russia in 1949 during a brief diplomatic stint, was slightly more favorable.

Achille di Lorenzo, the Neapolitan colleague of Umberto Nobile who served as General Mark Clark's special liaison assistant during the Italian Campaign, provided useful information about the liberation of his country as the Americans made their way up the peninsula.

As a young priest, Jacques Martin spent time in the Vatican during the war years; his reminiscences were informative.

Among military personnel consulted over the years, two American veterans stand out for their keen knowledge of Sicilian society just before the fall of the Kingdom of Italy. Richard Tambe was a soldier present in Sicily during Operation Husky and then in France following the Normandy invasion. Anthony Di Carlo, a multilingual army officer who worked in American military intelligence in France and Germany, had spent a few years in Italian schools during the Fascist era. Both men were highly conversant with the history of Sicily from the Vespers to the Second World War.

Nuggets of information sometimes emanated from less exalted quarters. Published histories mention the fact of medical supplies, including the antimalarial chloroquine, being introduced in Sicily by the Americans, but it was interesting to hear the account of an old man in the Sicanian Mountains of how people died in the malarial marshes until the Americans arrived.

Equally interesting was the commentary of Eleonora Sara, who worked in the censorship division of the Palermo post office in the years immediately before 1940.

There were some interesting coincidences. James Risk was present at the ball at Palazzo Gangi during the Allied occupation of Palermo, but Stefania Mantegna, the author's cousin, also spoke of it.

Apropos family lore, an example concerning the fall of the Kingdom of the Two Sicilies dwells just beyond the threshold of living memory. This is worth outlining.

When the author was around thirteen, he approached Maria Grazia Vizzini (his grandmother), who was born in 1901, with some "facts" he had read about Garibaldi and the unification. The response — from a taciturn woman not given to expressing forceful political opinions — was a set of contrary facts and an acerbic comment to the effect that history was written by the victors; she then recited to her misinformed (read ignorant) grandson Aesop's fable "The Man, the Lion and the Statue." What followed was a blunt (and necessary) "reality check," and an object lesson in the way we should study history — questioning comfortable clichés while recognizing that no written record is complete. History professors talk about this, the Vizzini family lived it.

The Vizzinis were exceptionally well-educated for their times; Maria was fluent in Italian, English and French, and she married a man descended from mayors, judges, jurats, feudal landholders and the occasional saint.

Maria's grandfather, Vincenzo Vizzini, was a royal courier whose travels took him around Sicily and Calabria. Armed with revolvers, the couriers held officer rank, and Vincenzo saw the events of 1860 unfold; he began his career around 1850 serving the Bourbons and then, following the establishment of the new state in 1861, ended it in the service of the Savoys. Vincenzo witnessed the unification movement and its war in Sicily.

Vincenzo's son, Niccolò, was born in 1866 and lived to be ninety-seven. This was Maria's father. He was a living link to her from a man who saw Sicily's last dynastic transition.

Maria explained that the late Niccolò was educated in Sicily by teachers who presented *two* versions of unification history. In those days, the "official" history in the texts approved by the incipient state was studied only perfunctorily. More time was dedicated to the *actual* history, the verbal one drawn from recent memory of events. As Maria explained, the typical Dominican priest teaching the course would close the history book and say to students something like, "Now, boys, I'm going to tell you what *really* happened in 1860."

Significantly, this seems to have been a fairly widespread practice in Sicily's Catholic schools until around 1880, certainly outside the major cities, beyond the censorship of the civil authorities. Granted that its presentation may have reflected the clergy's antipathy toward the anticlerical government that confiscated ecclesiastical property, it dealt with factual events.

As such activity was punishable in law, or at least strongly discouraged by it (a situation similar to the teaching of English under Fascism), a hypothetical, contemporary written record would likely be a police report or court document. That is the nature of existing evidence that certain former Jews, *anusim,* were still adhering to specific Jewish religious practices after 1493 (viz. Caterina Monteverdi in Chapter 7), although in some such families specific undocumented practices (such as Kosher culinary traditions) survived long afterward.

That the Dominicans were teaching corrective history in 1880 is nearly as important as the content of what they were teaching. Clearly, they didn't accept the official accounts of events unequivocally, in a state of unbridled awe. They knew better.

Into the twentieth century, family lore of the kind described here survived in a democratic environment *outside* Italy, whereas in Fascist Italy it would likely have been suppressed, or at least trivialized, by society in general. (For Italy's more recent response to the flawed historiography of certain incidents connected to the unification war, see note 50.)

In Italy, a few aristocratic families preserved collective memories of the events of 1860. *The Leopard,* a historical novel by Giuseppe Tomasi di Lampedusa, reflected this kind of tradition; it was published a century after the events it describes. A contemporary comparison would be the preservation of oral history in families involved in the American Civil War, the War Between the States, fought from 1861 to 1865. Indeed, *The Leopard* has been compared to *Gone With the Wind.*

Even if its details were to be dismissed as "hearsay," the Vizzini example implies, at the very least, that some Sicilians were unpersuaded by the nationalist historiography that held sway after 1860, and that their skepticism was passed down to subsequent generations.

Italy is not the only nation to wrestle with its recent past. The author was present at the belated funeral of Hailé Selassié in Addis Abeba in 2000, a quarter-century following the death of the emperor whose army (with Allied help) defeated the Italians in Ethiopia in 1941, and who lived to be assassinated by his own people. Those of us attending were united in our desire to commemorate the man and to celebrate Ethiopia's history; among us were journalists, diplomats, Rastafarians, and a few elderly war veterans wearing lion skins and bearing spears.

Let us heed Voltaire's unequivocal words: "Only in a free country can history be written well."

INDEX

Personages are listed by surname, given name or dynasty according to how they are best known in common parlance (e.g. Boccaccio, Dante, Hauteville). Ordinal numeration of kings is based on general usage and not necessarily on their reigns as Kings of Sicily. (For concordance see Appendix 1.) The reader should note the Arabic transliteration and American spelling. Most Italian sovereigns after 1700 are identified in Italian, so *Francesco* for Francis, *Vittorio Emanuele* for Victor Emmanuel. For the most part, the following entries refer to the main text and appendices but not the notes, where many more topics are mentioned.

Acton, Lord (John), 248
Adams, John, 259
Adelaide del Vasto, 109-111
Adrian IV, Pope, 124-125
Adrianople (Edirne), battle of, 71
Africa. See Egypt, Libya, Tunisia, etc.
Agatha, Saint, 70, 232, 267
Agatho, Saint, 75-76
Aghlabids, 76-78
Agriculture. See olives, grain, etc.
Agrigento, 62-64, 78
Aiello, Matthew, 125-132 passim.
Akragas. See Agrigento.
Alagona family, 186-188

Alaric, 71
Albania, Albanians, 192, 195, 235, 298, 346
Alcamo, Ciullo of, 146, 185
Alcoholism, 365
Alfonse the Magnanimous, 190, 332
Alfonso III of Aragon, 181-182
Alfonso de Bourbon (Count of Caserta), 289, 296
Algebra, 79
Almonds, 267
Alpetragius (al-Bitrugi), 148
Aluntium (San Marco), 106, 110, 209

Amalric, King of Jerusalem, 131

Amari, Michele, 25, 31, 387-390 passim, 396, 397

Amirs. See Emirs.

Amphitheatres and theatres, ancient, 9, 64, 69

Anagni, Treaty of, 182

Anatolia, 60, 62, 367, 387

Andria, Roger of, 135

Angevins (see also Charles I, Charles II), 147, 166, 171-180, 332

Anjou, House of. See Angevins.

Antonello da Messina, 193

Anusim. See Jews.

Anweiler, Markward of, 143, 145

Apostolic Legateship. See Papal Legateship.

Apulia (Puglia), 74, 113, 125, 149, 152, 155, 163, 169, 245

Aquileia, Diet of, 159

Aquinas, Thomas, 153, 171, 174, 399

Arabic language, 63, 76, 80, 88, 108, 111, 122, 130, 147, 148

Arabic numerals. See Hindi-Arabic numerals.

Arabs (See also Aghlabids, Fatimids, Kalbids, Moors), 28, 30, 77-82, 105, 109

Aragon and Aragonese, 149, 176, 180-190

Aragonese kings, See Peter III of Aragon, et al.

Arancina (rice ball), 118, 148

Archimedes, 64, 67

Architecture, 13, 64, 67, 81, 116, 141, 192, 208, 223

Archivio Storico Siciliano (academic journal), 29

Ardinghelli, Maria Angela, 238

Arethusa, 59

Arianism, 71

Ariano. See Assizes of Ariano.

Aristocracy. See nobility.

Art. See mosaics, etc.

Artichokes, 63

Asia. See China, India, Palestine, etc.

Assizes of Ariano, 28, 32, 90, 115-116, 393, 396

Assizes of Capua, 151, 156

Astronomy, 22, 147, 148, 237, 252

Athens, 189

Attila. See Huns.

Augsburg, Peace of, 208, 217

Augustine of Hippo, 71

Augustus. See Caesar Augustus.

Augustus III of Poland, 233

Austria, 137, 156, 206, 218, 230, 232, 236, 247, 259, 271, 295

Auto-da-fé (atto di fede), 195

Ayyubids, 131, 134, 137, 153-154

Baghdad, 79, 80, 133

Baldwin I of Jerusalem, 111

Bal'harm. See Palermo.

Balsamo, Paolo, 249

Banditry, 208, 216, 222, 224, 244, 344

Banks, 253

Barbapicciola, Giuseppa, 238
Barbary pirates, 207, 211, 342
Barcelona, 148, 183, 188
Bari, 74, 113-114, 125, 139
Baron (title), 85-96, 356
Baronage. See feudalism, nobility, peerage.
Barons (class). See feudalism, nobility, peerage.
Baroque architecture, 223, 225, 231, 234
Basilian clergy. See Orthodox Church.
Batu Khan, 161-163
Bava-Beccaris Massacre, 294
Beati Paoli, 224, 260, 404
Beccadelli, Antonio, 194
Becket, Thomas, 128, 131
Belisarius, 73
Bell, Alexander Graham, 297, 413
Bellini, Vincenzo, 266
Benaveth (ibn Abbad), 152
Benedictines, 76, 96, 108, 185
Benevento, Battle of, 168
Bentinck, William, 254-255
Berbers, 76-78
Bernavert (Bin al Wardi), 107
Bible, 68, 193
Bixio, Nino, 284
Black Death. See bubonic plague.
Boccaccio, Giovanni, 318
Bohemond of Hauteville, 110
Bonaparte, Joseph, 254
Bonaparte, Napoleon, 250-252
Bonellus, Matthew, 126-127

Boniface VIII, Pope, 182-183
Brancati, Vitaliano, 297
Branciforte family, 208, 219
Brienne, John of, 152, 155
Brienne, Yolanda (Isabella) of, 152, 164, 344
Britain. See England.
Bronte, 285, 289
Brown, Thomas Qaid, 120
Bubonic plague, 74, 187, 206, 212, 218
Byzantine Greeks. See Byzantines.
Byzantines, 70-84 passim, 96, 103, 109, 121-125, 174-180
Byzantium. See Constantinople.
Cabot (Caboto), Sebastian, 212
Caccamo, 89, 97, 126
Caesar Augustus, 68
Cagliostro (Giuseppe Balsamo), 243-244
Cairo, 10, 79
Calabria, 74, 80, 110-112, 122, 136, 169, 226, 259, 285
Calatafimi, 80, 178, 283
Caltabellotta, Peace of, 183-184, 232
Caltagirone, 194
Caltanissetta, 177, 298
Canals. See kanats.
Cannizzaro, Stanislao, 267
Capodimonte, 234-235
Caponata, 148
Caracciolo, Domenico, 248-249
Caravaggio (Michelangelo Merisi), 221, 342

Carbonari, 260-262, 274
Carini, Baroness of. See Lanza, Laura.
Carlo III of Spain (Carlo V of Sicily), 55, 233-246
Carlo Alberto Savoy of Sardinia, 264, 272, 274, 292
Carlo Felice Savoy of Sardinia, 254, 261
Carroll, Philip, 293, 405-406
Carthage, 62, 64, 65, 67, 73
Carthaginians. See Punics.
Caserta, 56, 234, 239, 248, 303
Castilian dynasty (Trastámara). See Alfonse the Magnanimous, Ferdinand the Catholic, et al.
Castles, 28, 89, 97, 110, 130, 155, 178, 187, 222, 300
Castrogiovanni. See Enna.
Catalogus Baronum, 87, 390, 392
Catalan Gothic, 192, 208
Catalans (Catalonians). See Aragonese.
Catania, 62, 82, 130, 136, 189, 222, 231, 266
Catania, University of, 192, 227
Cathars, 160, 166, 395
Catherine of Aragon, 207
Catholic Church (see also Papacy), 93-97, 116, 124, 166, 185, 195, 208-209, 238, 291
Cato the Elder, 67
Cavalli Sforza, Luigi, 367
Cavour, Camillo Benso di, 273, 275, 278, 282-283

Cefalà Diana, 81
Cefalù, 62, 90, 116, 179
Celestine III, Pope, 135, 138, 345
Censorship, 223, 228, 276, 291, 296, 305, 329, 414, 418
Ceramic art. See majolica.
Ceres (planet), 252
Charlemagne, 93
Charles I of Naples, 95, 147, 169, 171-179, 332
Charles II of Naples, 171, 179
Charles III of Spain. See Carlo III.
Charles V Hapsburg (of Spain), 205-207, 210-211, 217
Charles VI of Austria, 226-230 passim.
Checking (paper payments), 343-344
Cheeses, 148, 267
Chess, 78, 100
Chiaramonte family, 187-189
China, 78-79, 97, 209
Chivalry. See knighthood.
Chocolate, 213
Cholera, 265
Christ. See Jesus.
Churchill, Winston, 9, 286, 304
Cicero, 12, 68
Citron, 118
Citrus fruit, 78, 85, 97, 117, 118
Ciullo of Alcamo, 146, 185
Clark, Mark, 418
Clement IV, Pope, 167
Climate of Sicily (and climate change), 106, 184, 247

INDEX

Coinage, 99-100, 113, 152
Collecta (tax), 98, 161, 186, 191
Columbus, Christopher, 195
Common law, 124
Comnena, Anna, 311
Comnenus dynasty. See Manuel Comnenus, et al.
Congress of Vienna, 258, 264, 271
Conrad I of Sicily, 154, 164-165, 331
Conrad II (Conradin), 165-169 passim, 332
Constance of Aragon, 148-149, 152
Constance of Hauteville, 94, 132-135, 145, 331
Constance of Hohenstaufen, 166, 175, 179
Constans II, Eastern Emperor, 75
Constantine the Great, 70
Constantinian Order, 296, 343
Constantinople, 10, 70, 72, 74-76 passim, 79, 81, 121, 133, 141, 165, 174, 175, 193
Constitution of 1812, 255-256, 259, 371-373
Constitution of 1848, 272
Constitution of Bologna (1796), 257
Constitution of Piedmont (1848). See Statuto Albertino.
Constitutions of Melfi, 91, 144, 156-159
Conversos (anusim). See Jews.
Cordoba, 132
Coronation (rite), 94, 112
Cosenza, 268
Cotton, 78, 125, 213
Cottone, Gaetano, 252
Count (title), 90, 108, 256
Counter Reformation, 206, 209
Crispi, Francesco, 284, 293, 294
Crusades. See First Crusade, Second Crusade, etc.
Cuba Palace, 117, 318
Cuccagna, 220
Cuisine, 63, 97, 118, 148, 267
Cyprus, 134, 154, 341
Dante Alighieri, 146, 183, 185, 186
Dar al-hikma (house of wisdom), 153
Decameron. See Boccaccio.
Deer, 61, 85, 98, 372
Denialism, historical (revisionism). See historiography.
De Roberto, Federico, 293
Dialect. See Sicilian language.
Dialogue. See Ciullo of Alcamo.
Diaspora. See Jews.
Di Blasi, Francesco, 249
Di Blasi, Giovanni, 22
Diodorus Siculus, 24, 64, 386
Divine Comedy. See Dante.
Divorce, laws on, 11, 157, 159
Diwan, 108, 120
DNA. See genetics.
Dominicans, 174, 185, 246, 292
Donativo (tax), 98, 191, 194, 196, 227, 228, 237, 254
Doric architecture, 59, 64

Doxopatrios, Nilos, 116
Droughts, 220, 269
Ducat, 100, 116
Ducetius, 62-63
Duke (title), 216, 256
Durres (Durazzo), 133
Earthquakes, 130, 222, 223, 249
Eastern Roman Empire. See Byzantines.
Economy, 119, 123, 186-189, 196, 213, 227, 242, 243, 249, 263
Edmund of England, 165-167
Edrisi. See Idrisi.
Education, 28-29, 76, 79, 185, 192, 199, 209, 288, 291-292, 301
Edward I of England, 95, 179, 182
Egesta. See Segesta.
Egypt, 62, 79, 151, 153, 163, 250, 342, 395
Egyptians, ancient, 62, 387
Eighth Crusade. See Tunisian Crusade.
Eisenhower, Dwight, 24, 301
Eleanor of Aquitaine, 137, 138
Elections. See referendum.
Electoral fraud. See referendum.
Elopements. See fuitina.
Elvira of Castile, 111-113
Elymians, 62, 65, 366, 387
Emigration, 26, 95, 293, 299, 305
Emirates. See Emirs.
Emirs, 77, 79-82, 94, 103, 107, 108, 109, 111
Enciclopedia Italiana, 297
England (also United Kingdom), 55, 94, 105, 113, 117, 124, 128, 132, 136, 149, 150, 161, 206, 207, 213, 229, 248, 251, 273, 281, 299
Enlightenment, 57, 224, 237, 248
Enna (Kasr'Janni), 59, 82, 89, 107, 109, 177
Epistemology, historical. See historiography.
Erice (Eryx), 62, 65, 89, 90, 152
Ethiopia, 294, 297, 319, 328
Etrog. See Citron.
Etna, Mount, 59, 60, 130, 222, 292
Etruscans, 62, 65
Euclid, 75
Eunus, 68
Euphemius, 77
Evreux, Judith of, 105-106, 109, 125
Excommunication, 97, 143, 165, 169, 181, 207, 228
Extortion, 244, 398
Falcandus, Hugh, 22, 24, 130, 391-392
Falconry, 142, 162, 163
Famines (see also droughts), 184, 213, 243, 249, 269
Farms (see also latifondi), 85, 90, 96, 97, 100-101, 187, 221, 222, 267, 293, 295, 367
Fasci Siciliani, 293
Fascism, 25, 296-303 passim, 411
Fatimids, 78-89, 97, 99, 108, 116, 118, 131, 192
Fauna, 61, 85, 98, 117, 372, 386
Favara Palace, 82, 118,

Favism, 365
Fazello, Tommaso, 22, 402
Femicide. See honor killings.
Fenestrelle (prison), 290, 299
Ferdinand I of Castile, 190, 332
Ferdinand the Catholic, 195, 332
Ferdinandea (Graham Island), 263
Ferdinando I of the Two Sicilies, 246-253 passim, 259, 261, 333, 379
Ferdinando II of the Two Sicilies, 262-272 passim, 280-281, 333
Feudalism, 74-75, 83-87, 89, 90, 91, 92, 96, 108, 121, 129, 255, 256, 259, 339, 372
Fibonacci (Leonardo Pisano Bigollo), 148
Ficuzza, 253
Filadelfi (movement), 262, 265
First Crusade, 97, 109, 110
First World War, 295
Fiume. See Istria.
Fleming, Ian, 411
Florio, Vincenzo, 267
Food. See Cuisine.
Forests (and deforestation), 61, 68, 84, 106, 185, 210, 220, 236, 245
Four Vicars, 188
Fourth Crusade, 141, 174, 395
France, 55, 114, 136, 137, 161, 173, 175, 218, 222, 225, 229, 232, 249, 250, 258
Francesco I of the Two Sicilies, 254-255, 261-262
Francesco II of the Two Sicilies, 280-281, 285, 293, 307, 340, 350-351
Francis of Assisi, 146, 161, 166, 185
Franciscans, 161, 164, 185
Frederick I (Barbarossa), 124-131 passim, 135, 159
Frederick II (Emperor), 11, 94, 97-98, 100, 139-146 passim, 149-156, 163-164
Frederick II of Sicily, 183-184, 332
Frederick III the Simple, 187-188, 332, 399-400
Freemasonry, 260, 275, 284, 406
French Revolution, 249-252 passim, 260, 262
Fuitina (elopement), 257, 406
Fulda Massacre, 161
ibn al-Furat, Asad, 77
Gabellotti (gabelloti), 221, 222, 244, 245, 256, 398
Gaeta, 285, 289
Gagini, Antonello, 194
Gaiseric. See Genseric.
Garibaldi, Giuseppe, 277, 282-285 passim, 406, 409
Gela, 62, 415
Gelon of Syracuse, 64
Genealogies (pedigrees), royal, 334-337, 384
Genealogy, Sicilian, 365-367, 401
Genetics (DNA), 365-367
Genoa, Genoans, 98, 125, 150, 169, 174, 180, 192, 217, 243, 277
Genoard, 117-118, 145

Genovese, Vito, 412, 415
Genovesi, Antonio, 237, 370
Genseric (Gaiseric), 72
Gentile, Giovanni, 297
Geography of Sicily, 60-61, 117, 119, 133, 210, 388, 389
George of Antioch, 114, 121, 123
Germans (and Germany), 31, 69, 70-2, 75, 113, 129, 139-170 passim, 206, 258-259
Ghibellines, 140, 149, 167, 169, 171, 174, 175
Gibraltar, 227, 231, 380, 404
Giovane Italia (Young Italy), 262-263, 275
Girgenti. See Agrigento.
Gladstone, William, 272
Göbekli Tepe, 60, 367
Goethe, Johann von, 238, 244
Golden Horde, 161-162
Gothic architecture, 192, 208, 400
Goths, 71-74, 387
Gozo. See Malta.
Grain (wheat), 61, 68, 101, 109, 125, 192, 193, 210, 213, 215, 220, 231, 243, 244, 245, 253, 267, 269
Grand Alliance, 225
Grapes (viticulture), 63, 247
Great Britain. See England.
Great Famine (1315), 184
Great Schism (1054), 95, 103, 125, 174-175, 388
Greeks, ancient, 56-69 passim, 70
Greeks, Byzantine. See Byzantines.
Greek Orthodoxy. See Orthodox Church.
Gregory IX, Pope, 154, 161
Gregory XVI, Pope, 264
Guelphs, 140, 149, 167, 169, 171
Guilds (maestranze), 98, 222, 227
Guiscard. See Hauteville, Robert Guiscard.
Guzzoni, Alfredo, 301
Habsburg. See Hapsburg dynasty.
Hadrian, Emperor, 69
Hafsids, 194
Halkah district (Palermo), 40, 109
Halycos River, 65
ibn Hamdis, 107
Hamilcar. See Hannibal, Punic Wars.
ibn Hammud, 107
Hannibal, 67
Haplogroups. See genetics.
Hapsburg dynasty. See Charles V, et al.
Harald Hardrada Sigurdsson, 81, 389
Harems, 126, 127, 162
Hastings, Battle of, 95, 104, 389
Hauteville dynasty. See Roger II, William I, Constance, Tancred, et al.
Hauteville, Robert Guiscard, 104-105, 133
Hauteville, William Iron Arm, 81
Ibn al Hawas, 82
ibn Hawqal, Abdullah, Emir, 82
ibn Hawqal, Mohammed, 133
Head tax, 219

INDEX

Henry II of England, 124, 128, 132, 392
Henry VIII of England, 207, 342, 403
Henry VI Hohenstaufen, Emperor, 132, 135-141, 143
Heraldry (coats of arms), 22, 28, 92, 113, 391
Hindi-Arabic numerals, 79, 99, 124, 148
Historiography, 23, 25, 27, 31, 69, 183, 291, 410, 411, 412, 420
History, oral, 417-420
Hohenstaufen dynasty. See Henry VI, Frederick II, et al.
Holy Alliance, 260
Holy Land. See Palestine.
Holy Office. See Inquisition.
Holy Roman Empire, 80, 113, 121, 124, 135, 138, 140, 150, 151, 161, 167, 184, 205-206, 209, 210, 217, 218, 231, 253
Honor killings (femicide), 211
Honorius IV, Pope, 182
Hospitallers (Knights of Malta), 54, 89, 134, 155, 196, 207, 211, 251, 341-343
House of wisdom. See dar al-hikma.
Humbert. See Umberto.
Hundred Years War, 193
Huns, 71
Husky, Operation, 16, 300-301, 412, 415, 418
Hyblaean Mountains, 36, 60, 63
Hymera (Imera), 64
Ice Age, Little, 184
Iconography, 131, 147, 203, 398
Idrisi (Edrisi), 80, 97, 119, 127, 133
India, 78, 79
Industrial Revolution, 243, 247, 268
Industry, 192, 231, 234, 243, 247, 248, 258, 261, 266, 268, 270, 275, 286, 305, 370
Inferno. See Dante.
Ingrassia, Giovanni, 212, 218
Innocent III, Pope, 143, 148, 151
Innocent IV, Pope, 162, 165
Inquisition (Spanish) and Holy Office, 56, 194-196, 200, 201, 204, 208-209, 224, 231, 245-246, 248
Interdicts, 124, 155, 182, 184
Investiture, feudal, 92, 372
Investiture, knightly, 91, 347-349
Irrigation. See Kanats.
Isaac II Angelus Comnenus, 133, 141, 395, 397
Islam. See Muslims.
Istanbul. See Constantinople.
Istria, 296, 305
Italian Republic, 60, 159, 304-305
Italian unification. See Risorgimento.
Italy (after 1860), 287-309
James of Aragon (King of Sicily), 181-183, 332
Januarius (Gennaro), Saint, 349-350
Jefferson, Thomas, 248, 250, 259
Jerusalem, Kingdom of, 111, 121, 131, 134, 152-155

Jesi, 139

Jesuits, 56, 209, 245-246, 253, 259

Jesus Christ, 68, 86, 95

Jesus, Society of. See Jesuits.

Jews, 28, 68, 69, 70, 78, 80-81, 195, 108, 115, 130, 133, 152, 156-157, 161, 185, 188, 194, 198-204

Joan (Joanna) of England, 132, 135-137

Joanna II of Naples, 191

Joanna the Mad of Castile, 205

John of England, 150, 165

John the Faithless, 194

bin Jubayr, 80, 130, 132, 133

Judaism. See Jews.

Judeo Arabic, 108

Judith of Evreux, 105-106, 109

Julius Caesar, 68

Justinian, 73, 75, 114-115

Juvarra, Filippo, 225

Kairouan (Qayrawan), 76, 77, 109

al-Kalbi, Hassan, 79

Kalbids, 79-82 passim, 94, 108

al Kamil, Malik (sultan), 153, 154, 163

Kanats, 40, 41, 78, 82, 117

Kasr district (Palermo), 40

Kasr'Janni. See Enna.

Kastriota. See Scanderbeg.

Khalesa district (Palermo), 40, 108

Khalbids. See Kalbids.

Knighthood, feudal, 83-85, 87, 90-92, 108, 113, 115

Knightly orders, 89, 134, 141, 149, 155, 196, 339-359

Komenos dynasty. See Comnenus, Comnena.

Koran, 76, 192

Lanza, Laura, 211

Lateran Treaties, 296, 347

Latifondi (estates), 196, 216, 221-222, 245, 256, 294

Latin in liturgy, 96, 122

Laurana, Francesco, 193

Law and legal codes (see also Maliki Law, Assizes of Ariano, Constitutions of Melfi, Constitution of 1812), 78, 93, 94, 108, 114-116, 124, 131, 157, 158, 191, 197, 199, 228, 235, 255-260, 298

Legitimate birth, 96, 115, 329, 417

Lemons. See Citrus fruit.

Lentini, Giacomo of, 146

Leopard, The (novel), 328, 420

Lepanto, Battle of, 211

Libya, 121, 211, 295, 299, 327, 329

Lipari Case (1711), 228

Literacy, 11, 28, 76, 185, 288, 291, 293, 301

Literature of Sicily, 107, 146, 185, 224, 297, 420

Lombard League, 159-161

Lombards, 74-75, 81, 90, 103, 114, 121, 159, 160, 171

London, 236, 416

Longobardi, Nicolò, 209

Longobards. See Lombards.

Louis IX of France (saint), 13, 161, 166, 173, 229

Louis XIV of France, 225, 229, 404

INDEX

Louis the Grand Dauphin, 225
Louis of Sicily, 186-187
Lucera, 152, 168, 169, 171
Luciano, Charles, 412, 415
Lucy, Saint, 70, 163, 213
Luna family, 190
Luther, Martin, 218
Lutherans. See Protestants.
Macinato (tax), 210
Madiyah (Tunisia). See Mahdia.
Madonian Mountains, 36, 60, 61, 245
Madrid, 225, 239, 379
Maestranze. See guilds.
Mafia, 172, 222, 245, 296, 398, 415
Magellan, Ferdinand, 211-212
Maghrebim. See Jews.
Magione church, 141, 208, 344, 345, 347
Magna Carta, 150, 157, 165
Magna Graecia (Megara Hellas), 65
Mahdia, 109, 111, 113
Maio of Bari, 124-127 passim.
Majolica (ceramic), 267
Majorana, Ettore, 298
Malaria, 113, 165, 179, 210, 302, 418
Malaterra, Godfrey, 388
Maliki Law, 78, 114, 124
Malta (and Gozo), 9, 60, 61, 89, 187, 207, 211, 250-253, 284, 299
Malta, Knights of. See Hospitallers.
Maltese language, 111, 388
Mamertines, 66
Mancuso, Elvira, 298

Manfred Hohenstaufen, 164-169 passim, 175
Maniakes, George, 81, 82, 103
Manorialism. See Feudalism.
Mantegna, Stefania, 303
Manuel I Comnenus, 121, 125, 133
al Maqdisi, Mohammed, 387
Maqueda, Bernardino de (viceroy), 215, 403
Marconi, Guglielmo, 297
Margaret of Navarre, 122, 130
Margaritus of Brindisi, 134
Maria Amalia, Queen, 233, 234, 238
Maria Carolina, Queen, 246, 249, 250, 254, 258, 406
Maria Cristina Bourbon (Queen of Sardinia), 254
Maria Cristina Savoy (Queen of the Two Sicilies), 264, 265, 280, 307, 308
Marquis (title), 90, 191, 216-217, 356
Marriage practices, 111, 115, 157, 159, 211, 257, 297
Marsala, 78, 283, 313, 344
Marsala wine, 248, 267
Martel, Charles, 77
Martin IV, Pope, 178, 179
Martin I the Younger, 189, 332, 400
Martin II the Elder, 189, 190, 332
Martorana church, 116, 123, 124, 131, 132
Marvuglia, Giuseppe Venanzio, 253
Marx, Karl, 278
Mary (Mother of God), 70, 203

431

Mary (Maria) of Aragon, 187-189, 332
Masons. See Freemasonry.
Matteotti, Giacomo, 296
Maurolico, Francesco, 22, 402
Mazara, 77, 82, 152, 198
Mazzini, Giuseppe, 262, 268, 274, 275, 278, 282
Medici, Gian Gastone, 223
Medicine, 98, 115, 157, 188, 212, 370
Melfi, Constitutions of. See Constitutions of Melfi.
Messina, 22, 61, 62, 99 104, 130, 136, 141, 152, 176, 187, 209, 222, 249, 269, 285, 295
Messina, Antonello da, 193, 194
Messina, Maria, 298
Messina, University of, 209, 401
Meucci, Antonio, 277, 297, 413-414
Michael II, Byzantine Emperor, 77
Michael VIII Palaeologus, 174, 175
Migration. See emigration.
Mikvehs, 13, 200-201
Milan, Edict of, 70
Milan Massacre. See Bava-Beccaris Massacre.
Milazzo, 178, 230
Mileto, 110
Mincemeat, Operation, 299
Minoans, 10, 61
Mints, 193
Modica, 90, 187, 194, 213
Modica Massacre, 194
Mohammed, Prophet, 75, 119
Monasticism, Catholic. See religious orders.
Monasticism, Orthodox, 96, 116
Monreale Abbey, 13, 81, 89, 173, 207
Monte San Giuliano. See Erice.
Monteverdi, Caterina, 198-204
Montgomery, Bernard, 301
Moors (in Spain), 79, 148, 215, 340
Morabit, 152
Mori, Cesare, 296
Mosaics, 69, 74, 75, 95, 116, 131
Mosques, 30, 81, 82, 107, 152, 192
Mount Etna. See Etna.
Mozia (Motya), 62, 387
Muhammad, Prophet. See Mohammed.
Mühlberg, Battle of, 208
Mulberries (see also silk making), 78, 97
Multiculturalism, 10, 60, 107, 184
Multiple sclerosis, 365
Murat, Joachim, 254, 259
Muslims (and Islam), 75-82 passim, 94, 96, 98, 108, 121, 127, 130-135, 152, 169, 171, 185
Mussolini, Benito, 296
al Mustansir, Sultan, 169, 173
Mycenaeans, 61
Mythology, ancient, 9, 59, 63, 64, 70
Naples, 57, 152, 170, 172, 173, 179, 183, 191, 212, 232-288 passim.
Naples, University of, 152-153
Napoleonic Wars, 250-254, 258, 342

INDEX

Naxos (in Sicily), 62
Nazi regime, 298, 303
Nebrodian Fir, 98, 106
Nebrodian Mountains, 36, 60, 90, 96
Neofiti (conversos). See Jews.
Neolithic Revolution, 367
Nepotism, 206, 244
Nicea, Council of, 70
Nicholas II, Pope, 103-104
Nicholas III, Pope, 175
Nicholas IV, Pope, 182
Nicodemus, Bishop, 104
Nobility (see also Feudalism), 84-92, 101, 124, 156, 181, 196, 223, 256, 375-378
Norman Palace (Palermo), 9, 81, 110, 113, 117, 254
Normans, 81, 90, 103-138
Norman-Arab architecture, 13, 81, 116-117
Norsemen (Vikings), 81, 366
Noto, 82, 107, 223
Novelli, Pietro, 221
Novelli, Rosalia, 221
Odoacer, 72
Offamilias, Walter, 30, 129, 131
Oleasters. See olives.
Oleoculture. See olives.
Olives, olive oil, 46 (map), 63, 65, 85, 196
Oncia. See onza.
Onza (coin), 100
Oranges. See Citrus fruit.
Orders of chivalry. See knightly orders.

Organized crime. See Mafia.
Orthodox Church, 94, 96, 104, 116, 132
Ortygia. See Syracuse.
Ostrogoths. See Goths.
Ottoman Empire, 192-195 passim, 206, 207, 211, 218, 229, 243, 295, 341, 346
Paestum, 238
Palatine Chapel. See Norman Palace.
Palazzotto, Girolamo, 231
Palermo, 9, 22, 62, 65, 77, 79, 80, 94, 107-108, 117, 126-127, 132, 145, 152, 169, 176, 196, 205, 218, 235, 249, 253, 269-270, 283-284, 290
Palermo Bread Massacre, 303
Palermo, University of, 249, 298
Palestine (Holy Land), 111, 121, 129, 131, 134, 137, 152-155, 343, 344, 345, 395
Palmer, Richard, 124, 127, 129
Panormita. See Beccadelli, Antonio.
Panormus. See Palermo.
Pantocrator, Christ. See Iconography.
Papacy, 83, 97, 103, 104, 113, 114, 120, 122, 124, 128, 138, 143, 149, 154, 155, 161, 162, 166, 174, 175, 191, 209, 235, 296, 347
Papal (Apostolic) Legateship, 109, 111, 128, 145, 228, 231
Paper, invention and use of, 79, 99, 158

Paris, Congress of (1856), 273
Paris, Matthew, 163
Paris Peace Treaty (1947), 304
Parliament, 92, 189, 194, 210, 216, 233, 235, 252, 254, 255, 260, 361, 371-372
Parthenopaean Republic, 251
Pasta. See Spaghetti.
Patton, George, 300, 301
Paul of Tarsus (saint), 69
Pax Romana, 68
Peasantry. See popolino.
Peerage, Sicilian, 92, 256, 361-364
Peloponnesian War, 13, 29, 65
Peloritan Mountains, 36, 61
Peralta family, 186, 187
Perche, Stephen, 129
Perollo family, 190
Persephone, 59
Persia, Persians, 64, 79
Peter II of Sicily, 184, 186
Peter III of Aragon (Peter I of Sicily), 166, 175, 176, 178, 179
Peter IV of Aragon, 187-190
Philip III of France, 173, 179
Philip IV of France, 182, 318
Philip II of Spain, 210, 215
Philip III of Spain, 215, 226
Philip IV of Spain, 218
Philip V of Spain, 226, 227, 229, 232, 233
Phoenicians. See Punics.
Phylogeography. See genetics.
Piazza Armerina, 69, 89, 344
Piazzi, Giuseppe, 252, 256, 370

Piedmont (see also Sardinia, Kingdom of), 167, 227, 232, 264, 272, 274, 282, 305
Piedmont Easter Massacre, 292, 407
Piracy, 111, 152, 194, 198, 207, 211, 213, 342
Pirandello, Luigi, 297
Pisa, Pisans, 98, 150
Pistachios, 63, 118
Pitrè, Giuseppe, 396
Pius IX, Pope, 272, 276, 280
Plague. See bubonic plague.
Plantagenet. See Henry II, Joan of England, et al.
Platani. See Halycos.
Plato, 59, 66
Plebiscite. See referendum.
Pliny the Elder, 386
Podestà, Fascist, 296
Poetry. See Sicilian School.
Poland, 218, 233, 235, 271, 345
Polish Succession, War of, 232
Polo, Marco, 97
Pompeii, 235, 238
Popes. See Papacy (or specific Pontiffs by name).
Popolino (underclass), 220, 266
Population genetics. See genetics.
Population of Sicily, 130, 198, 288
Porcelain, 235, 369
Porcelet, William of, 178
Portici, 234, 266
Poverty, 216, 220, 223, 266, 287, 293, 295, 301

INDEX

Pragmatic of 1759, 241, 379-383
Prince (noble title), 231, 256
Procida, John of, 175, 178, 179, 180
Proletariat. See popolino.
Prostitution, 115, 152, 157, 201, 302
Protestants, 166, 206, 207, 208, 209, 215, 217-218, 227, 276, 292
Proto Sicanians. See Sicanians.
Ptolemy, 119
Puglia. See Apulia.
Punic Wars, 66-67
Punics, 9, 62, 64-67 passim, 365-366
Pyrrhus, 65-66
Qadits of Sicily, 82
Qayrawan. See Kairouan.
Quasimodo, Salvatore, 297
Quran. See Koran.
Railroads (railways), 264, 266, 270
Rape, laws on, 11, 115, 157, 159
Ravenna, 70, 72, 74, 163
Raymond VI of Toulouse, 137
Rebiba, Scipione, 209
Referendum of 1860, 287-288
Referendum of 1946, 303-304
Reformation, Protestant. See Protestants.
Regnum (defined), 10-11, 112
Religion. See Muslims, Jews, etc.
Religious orders. See Benedictines, Dominicans, Franciscans, Jesuits.
Renaissance, 193
Revisionism, historical. See historiography.

Revolt of 1866, 272, 290
Revolts of 1848, 269-272
Rex filius (title), 94
Rice, cultivation of, 78
Richard Lionheart, 136-137
Riots of 1647, 219-220
Risorgimento, 273-274, 262, 272, 273-283 passim, 304
Riveli (donativi tax rolls), 26, 196, 277
Rivers. See Geography.
Robert of Hauteville. See Hauteville, Robert Guiscard.
Robert the Wise of Naples, 184
Roger I, 97, 104-112
Roger II, 86, 112-123
Roger III (Rex Filius), 137, 138, 141
Roman Empire. See Romans.
Romanesque Gothic, 141, 164
Romans, 61, 66-71
Rome, 70, 72, 124, 135, 151, 169, 236, 251, 272, 302
Rometta, 79
Roosevelt, Franklin, 304
Rosalie, Saint, 218, 267, 276
Rothschild Bank (Naples), 260, 290, 369
Ruffo, Fabrizio, 251
Runciman, Steven, 31
Russia, 243, 260, 268, 278, 298, 299
Saint Rémy, John of, 178
Saints. See Agatha, Louis, Lucy, et al.
Saladin (Salah ad-Din Yusuf ibn Ayyub), 131, 134, 137, 153

Salamis, Battle of, 64
Salemi, 267, 283
Salerno, 112, 125, 136, 153, 262
as-Samsam, Hasan, 82
Saracens. See Arabs.
Sardinia, Kingdom of (see also Piedmont), 229, 254
Savoy dynasty (see also Vittorio Amedeo II, Vittorio Emanuele II, Umberto I, et al.), 30, 226-228 passim, 254, 264, 265, 279
Scanderbeg (George Kastriota), 192
Scarlatti, Alessandro, 225
Schism (1054). See Great Schism.
Schools, 79, 152-153, 185, 291, 292
Sciacca, 78, 168, 190
Scibene Palace, 118
Sclafani family, 187
Scot, Michael, 147, 186
Second Crusade (1145-1149), 121
Second World War, 299-303
Segesta (Egesta), 59, 62, 64, 68
Segrè, Emilio, 298, 299
Selinus (Selinunte), 62, 63
Sephardim. See Jews.
Serfdom (in Sicily), 87-90, 100, 101, 108, 115, 121, 158
Serpotta, Giacomo, 225
Shakespeare, William, 190, 221
Shia Islam, 78
Shiites. See Shia Islam.
Sicanian Mountains, 36
Sicanians, 10, 61, 62
Siceliots. See Greeks.

Sicilian language, 108, 146-147, 185, 197, 234
Sicilian School, 146
Sicilian Vespers War, 146-147, 176-180
Sicily. See specific topic.
Sicily, ancient, 59-70
Siculo Arabic, 111
Sigurdsson, Harald. See Harald Hardrada.
Sikels (Sikelians), 10, 62
Silk making, 78, 97, 213, 248
al-Siqilli, Jawhar, 79
Siqilliyyat (of ibn Hamdis), 107
Siracusa. See Syracuse.
Sixth Crusade (1228), 153-155
Slavery, 68-69, 100-101, 158, 208, 211, 217, 235, 252, 292
Society of Jesus. See Jesuits.
Sonnet, 146
Souks (suks), 77, 81, 145
Spaghetti, 97, 119
Spanish rule (post-1492), 195-226
Sperlinga, 177
Stalin, Joseph, 304
Statuto Albertino, 25, 272, 292
Steri Palace, 187, 189, 196, 208
Street markets. See souks.
Stupor Mundi. See Frederick II.
Suffrage, women's, 288, 304, 305
Sugar cane, 78, 97, 210, 221, 231
Suleyman the Magnificent, 206
Sulfur, 247, 266, 273, 286, 293
Sulphur. See sulfur.
Sunni Islam, 78, 133

INDEX

Swabians. See Germans, Hohenstaufens.
Synagogues, 72, 80, 107, 199, 204
Syracuse (Siracusa), 31, 62-66 passim, 68, 69, 70, 72, 75, 77, 107, 130
Tacitus, 69
Tagliacozzo, Battle of, 169
Tancred Hauteville, 126, 131, 135-138 passim, 141
Tanucci, Bernardo, 242, 246, 247
Taormina, 62, 64, 81, 130, 177
Taranto, 126
Tarì (coin), 99, 100, 147
Tarxien (Malta), 61
Tavola (bank), 210
Taxes. See collecta, donativo, head tax, macinato, etc.
Telegraph, 270-271, 370
Templar, Knights, 155, 343-344
Temples, ancient, 9, 59, 61, 62, 64, 70
Teutonic Knights, 141, 149, 153, 196, 345
Thalassemia, 365
Theatres (ancient). See Amphitheatres and theatres.
Theocracy in Sicily, 84
Theocritus, 64
Theodoric the Great, 72
Theotokos. See Mary.
Third Crusade (1189), 136, 137
Thirty Years' War, 217-219
Thucydides, 13, 64
Tomasi di Lampedusa, Giuseppe, 420

Totila, 74
Toumanoff, Cyril, 23, 290
Trapani, 78, 82, 189, 199, 207
Trastámara dynasty. See Alfonse the Magnanimous, Ferdinand I, Ferdinand the Catholic.
Trent, Council of, 206
Trinacria (symbol), 63
Trinacria, King of, 183
Tripoli (in Lebanon), 134
Tripoli (in Libya), 121
Triskelion. See trinacria.
Troina, 97, 105-106, 300
Tudela, Benjamin of, 130
Tunisia, 72, 76-79 passim, 109, 111, 123, 194, 207, 211, 299
Tunisian Crusade (1270), 173, 174
Turin, 227, 260, 264, 272, 276, 286
Turkey. See Anatolia, Constantinople, Ottoman Empire.
Turks. See Ottoman Empire.
Tuscan language, 146, 197, 234
Two Sicilies, 63, 180, 238, 241-286, 345
Umberto I of Italy, 294
Umberto II of Italy, 302-304 passim, 347
Underclass. See popolino.
Unification, Italian. See Risorgimento.
United Kingdom. See England.
United States of America, 55, 242, 248, 250, 268, 293, 294, 300-302, 305
Universities. See Catania, Messina,

Naples, Palermo.
Urban II, Pope, 83, 97
Urban IV, Pope, 165-166
Vaccarini, Giovanni, 231
Vandals, 71-72, 76
Van Dyck, Antoon, 221
Varangian Guard, 81
Vassalage. See feudalism.
Vatican. See Papacy.
Vatican City. See Rome.
Venice, Venetians, 74, 100, 121, 123, 159, 212, 346, 347
Ventimiglia family, 188, 191
Verdi, Giuseppe, 266
Verga, Giovanni, 266
Vesalius, Andreas, 212
Vespers War. See Sicilian Vespers War.
Vicars. See Four Vicars.
Viceroys, 92, 95, 190, 191, 208, 215, 220, 227, 228, 229, 233
Viceroys, The (novel), 293
Vico, Giambattista, 237, 238
Vidimura of Catania, 188
Vienna, Congress of. See Congress of Vienna.
Vienna, Peace of (1738), 233
Vienna, Treaty of (1731), 232
Vikings. See Norsemen.
Visigoths. See Goths.
Viticulture. See grapes.
Vittorio Amedeo II of Savoy, 226-229
Vittorio Emanuele II of Italy, 274, 282 285
Vittorio Emanuele III of Italy, 286, 294, 296, 302
Volcanic eruptions, 222, 263
Voltaire (François Arouet) quoted, 55, 151, 297, 420
Vote. See referendum, suffrage, etc.
Waldensians, 227, 292
Walter of the Mill. See Offamilias.
Washington, Booker T, 295
Washington, George, 57, 250
Westphalia, Peace of, 1648, 219
Wheat. See Grain.
William I of Sicily, 113, 122, 123-127
William II of Sicily, 128-134
Wines, 65, 247, 248, 267
Women's rights, 115, 157, 159, 304, 305
Woodhouse, John, 247-248
World War I. See First World War.
World War II. See Second World War.
Xerxes, 64
Young Italy. See Giovane Italia.
Zirids, 109, 111, 123
Zis. See Palermo.
Zisa Palace, 117
Ziyadat Allah, 77

www.ingramcontent.com/pod-product-compliance
Lightning Source LLC
Chambersburg PA
CBHW031401290426
44110CB00011B/224